# The Blitzkrieg Story

# The BLITZKRIEG Story

CHARLES MESSENGER

Charles Scribner's Sons
NEW YORK

# Contents

# Maps

# Preface

This book sets out, as its title suggests, to describe the evolution of blitzkrieg as a technique of war. The literal translation of the term — 'lightning war' — indicates quick victory, something for which men have striven throughout history. The sense in which I have used it, however, is that coined in the late thirties which implies quick victory through the harnessing together air power and mechanised ground forces to defeat the enemy by means of *dislocation* rather than the direct wholesale *destruction* of his armed forces.

Although victory by dislocation has always been possible, the advantages of speed, range and mobility bestowed upon the attacker by advent of the internal combustion engine significantly broadened the prospects of its achievement. It not only gave greater potential for surprise, and shock action, it also enabled war to be waged in an entirely new dimension — in the air. During the World War 1 the internal combustion engine was still relatively in its infancy. At the same time, technological developments in other fields during the previous century had made defence significantly more powerful than attack, as was borne out by the frustrations of trench warfare. Yet, by November 1918 efforts to break the shackles of static warfare had enabled the foundations of the blitzkrieg concept to be laid.

The popular view of the development of the doctrine between the wars is that the British evolved the theory and that this was eagerly grasped by the Germans, once Hitler came to power. Like most popular theories this is an over-simplification. Others besides the British thought on similar lines during the 1920s, and it was not merely military conservatism which precluded the technique's adoption in countries other than Germany in the early part of the World War 2. Likewise, the concept was not immediately seized upon by the Nazis in 1933 as Germany's salvation. Again, the arguments for and against the efficacy of this concept ranged not just over narrow military pastures but broke into the fields of politics, economics and social attitude as well. In order to display to best effect these arguments, and the differing approaches, I have covered the years 1919-39, blitzkreig's gestation period, by using five case studies, represented by Britain, USA, Germany, France and the USSR. In each country, circumstances and attitudes were different thus, I hope, enabling the reader to have a clearer understanding of the differing states of preparedness of the belligerents in 1939. In addition, I have interwoven another thread into this part of the tapestry by adopting a type of biographical approach towards those individuals who were most closely connected with the theory and practice of blitzkrieg.

I have limited my treatment of World War 2 to those campaigns and parts of campaigns which illustrate most directly the use and misuse of the blitzkrieg technique. I accept that I have not described all examples of its use, but I have aimed at avoiding the danger of obscuring the lessons behind an all-embracing narrative of the war. Likewise, when dealing with the Israelis, who have been the only true practitioners of the technique since 1945, I have concentrated my attention on Sinai.

Several people have given me help to a greater or lesser extent during the time I have spent on this book. To attempt to name all would take up too much space and lay me open to ommissions through human error. I shall therefore confine myself to a few who have made significant contributions. To Brian Bond of the War Studies Department, King's College, London, I am very grateful for valuable advice and criticism, particularly concerning the influence of Liddell Hart, of which he has made a deep study. Peter Vigor of the Soviet Studies Research Centre at RMA Sandhurst very kindly read and commented on those sections dealing with Soviet military doctrine. Photographic acknowledgements appear elsewhere, as do those to publishers, but I would like to single out Major General Nigel Duncan of the Royal Armoured Corps Tank Museum, and James Lucas of the Imperial War Museum for particular thanks. Major Ian Fowler gave valuable assistance in reproducing photographic material, and my father, who as a technical staff officer had close connections with tanks for twenty years, gave me useful information in the course of several discussions. My deep gratitude is also due to Major and Mrs Mike Gaffney; the former acted as a 'guinea pig' reading over the manuscript as the latter, tackling my own inexpert typing and illegible writing with commendable *sangfroid*, typed it. Finally, as are all part-time authors with families, I am deeply indebted to my wife, children and dog for so patiently putting up with my frequent lack of involvement in house maintenance, garden and family entertainment over the period of my confinement.

*Camberley, Surrey 1976*                                    Charles Messenger

# 1
# Origins

The origins of blitzkreig lay in the static deadlock prevalent on the Western Front during the years 1915-17. Both sides went to war in August 1914 convinced that the fighting would last only weeks. The Germans believed that the Schlieffen Plan would enable them to knock out France as easily as they had done in 1870, leaving them time enough to turn on Russia, before her unwieldy mobilisation machine had run its full course. The Allies shared the same optimism. The French Plan XVII envisaged an attack on the German centre, which once broken would enable the Western Allies to reach Berlin in six weeks. The Russians too were confident of being able to overrun the vulnerable East Prussia salient and march on Berlin from the east. Both sides foresaw a war fought in Napoleonic terms, in which the key to success was to concentrate at the decisive point (the German *Schwerpunkt*) and use superiority in numbers to achieve victory.

But the war was not over by Christmas 1914. It was to drag on in theatres spread all over the globe for over four exhausting years. The pundits of 1914 were proved wrong, but the reasons for this were not readily apparent to them. It was easy to point to inept generalship — Von Moltke's transfer of troops to the Eastern Front at the critical moment and his inability to control his army commanders, which brought about the demise of the Schlieffen Plan. The Battle of the Frontiers, which resulted in 300 000 French casualties in the first few days of the war. The inefficiency of the Russian High Command, which led to the disaster of Tannenburg. But this was hardly scratching at the surface. The real cause lay much deeper.

The Wars of the 18th and early 19th Centuries were fought with muskets, with an effective range of 100 yards at best, and smooth bore cannon, which could not fire effectively over 1 000 yards. Consequently, provided the attacker could mass superior enough numbers, the odds were that he would succeed, given sufficient determination. During the middle part of the 19th Century technological developments caused a gradual change in the situation. The introduction of rifling in both cannon and small arms increased weapon ranges, enabling the defender to start engaging the attacker earlier, and thus inflicting greater casualties on him. Breechloading took over from muzzle-loading, producing a faster rate of fire, and the ability to load as well as fire behind cover. Finally, the advent of the machine gun and magazine rifle also put more weight on the side of the defensive. The latter stages of the American Civil War, the Russo-Turkish War of 1877-8, the Boer War of 1899-1902 and the Russo-Japanese War of

1904-5 all pointed the way to the increasing power of the defensive. Yet the lessons of these wars were for the most part ignored. The long shadow of Napoleon still covered the theoretical European battlefield. The only way to victory was the attack, and in the years before 1914 each of the major European powers came up with varying ideas as to how the attack could best succeed.

The French, smarting from their defeat at the hands of Prussia in 1870, believed, inspired by the writings of one of the casualties of that war, Ardant Du Picq, that the driving force behind the French soldier was his unquenchable spirit, his élan. This was at its best in the attack. Consequently the French attacked in August 1914 using much the same formations and colour of uniform as their forebears had one hundred years before. The Germans concluded that superiority in firepower, especially artillery, was the secret. Their studies of the Russo-Japanese War convinced them that this could be best achieved by having a preponderance in medium and heavy artillery. The British too, with the indignity of their reverses at the hands of the Boers during the early part of that war still fresh in their minds, threw off traditional ideas of parade ground tactics, but concentrated on improving the marksmanship of the individual infantry-man, rather than increasing firepower as a whole. The Russians, with their vast manpower resources but only limited industrial base, hoped that sheer superiority in numbers would win the day for them. All the combatants hoped and planned for a quick victory, but it was not to be. Its place was taken by the agonising frustrations of trench warfare.

By Christmas 1914 the land war was taking place across two long scars in the European countryside. One ran for some 475 miles from Switzerland to the North Sea, while the other ran from the Baltic down to the Carpathian Mountains, with a small subsidiary running across the north western part of Serbia. As far as the warring nations were concerned, this state of affairs was only temporary, and they were to continue to believe this for the next three years. The very vastness of the Eastern Front produced relatively more spectacular results than in the West, but long-term achievements in the shape of overall victory by the Central Powers against Russia were not brought about so much by success in the field, as by the canker of discontent within Russia itself. It was this that brought Russia to the peace table of Brest-Litovsk in early 1918. Throughout the war the main centre of attention was to lie in the West, and it was in this theatre that trench warfare was most predominant.

Throughout the years 1915-17 it was increasingly believed that the deadlock on the Western Front could only be broken by having sufficient superiority of artillery firepower at the decisive point. During 1915, while the Germans under the direction of von Falkenhayn concentrated on defence in the West and attack in the East, the British and French strove to prove this point. At first they were hampered by a shortage of munitions, both having only prepared for a short war. The Germans quickly learnt to dig deeper in order to protect themselves better against the ever increasing weight of the Allied artillery barrages. At the commencement of the barrage

10

they would retire to their dugouts and emerge once the barrage had ceased, the signal that the attackers were on their way across No Man's Land. They had plenty of time to set up their weapons. The shelltorn ground, coupled with the amount of equipment that the British and French infantrymen were expected to carry, reduced the rate of advance to a crawl. The German machine guns were thus provided with plenty of targets. Those who succeeded in breaking into the German trenches seldom survived for long, because of the German ability to counter-attack quickly and the difficulty of reinforcing success on account of the inefficiency of communications. Whereas gains were measured in hundreds of yards, the loss in casualties was in thousands.

The year 1916 brought no respite. The twin mincing machines of Verdun and The Somme cost the French, British and Germans together some 1 700 000 casualties for little in material gain. It seemed that attrition was the only answer to the problem. The longer the massacre went on the more likely it was that one side or the other would crack through sheer exhaustion. None of the high commanders had dreamt that the war would become like this, consequently none was mentally equipped to find immediate solutions to the deadlock. Perhaps the most apt description of their dilemma is given in C. S. Forester's penetrating novel *The General*:

'In some ways it was like the debate of a group of savages as to how to extract a screw from a piece of wood. Accustomed only to nails, they had made one effort to pull out the screw by main force, and now it had failed they were devising methods of applying more force still, of obtaining more efficient pincers, of using levers and fulcrums so that more men could bring their strength to bear. They could hardly be blamed for not guessing that by rotating the screw it would come out after the exertion of far less effort; it would be a notion so different from anything they had ever encountered that they would laugh at the man who suggested it.' [1]

Yet possible methods of 'rotation' were introduced in the years 1915-16. The first was a strategic solution to the problem in the Franco-British expedition to the Dardanelles in early 1915. This was the brainchild of Winston Churchill, then First Lord of the Admiralty. He reasoned that because the forces on the Western Front were so evenly matched a quick victory was unlikely. Turkey had joined the Central Powers camp in October 1914. By invading the Dardanelles, Turkish pressure would be taken off the Russians and the capture of Constantinople might lead to Turkish surrender and pose a threat to Germany and Austro-Hungary, which both could ill afford to ignore. In the event, the expedition, although it gained toeholds on each side of the Straits, failed, becoming nothing more than an extension of the stagnant conditions of the Western Front. If the generalship during the initial stages had been better, more success might have resulted. However, it is very questionable as to whether it would have had the far-reaching results hoped for by Churchill, in view of the fact that the Western Front would have had to be stripped of troops, leaving the Germans with a dangerous superiority. Also, the long lines of communication would have made it difficult to maintain a large force.

The other two approaches were technological in nature. On April 22nd, 1915 the German Fourth Army, under the Duke of Wurttemburg, overwhelmed the French 45th Algerian Division, which was holding the northern shoulder of the Ypres Salient. They did it by an artillery bombardment of xylyl bromide gas shells, which caught the unprotected Algerians completely unawares, leading to the hurried evacuation of their positions. By nightfall a five mile gap had appeared in the lines and the Allied situation was only saved by the Germans taking time to consolidate their immediate gains rather than pushing on immediately. During the next five weeks a bloody battle was fought, the Germans trying to reach Ypres and the Allies trying to stop them. In the event, the Germans, although they succeeded in reducing the size of the Salient, did not gain their objective. Makeshift methods of anti-gas protection had been quickly introduced on the Allied side, and this enabled them to combat subsequent gas attacks during this battle. The use of gas failed because the element of surprise had been compromised by using it in too small a quantity.* By the autumn of the same year the Allies were also using gas and both sides were learning to live with this weapon, which would continue to be used until the end of the war.

The other new weapon introduced at this time was the tank. The use of motor vehicles for war purposes had already been envisaged before war broke out in 1914. All the major European nations had produced armed motor cars during the decade before 1914, but none had really thought deeply about possible uses for them in a European war and consequently their numbers were small. It was only when war actually broke out that their value for reconnaissance and raids was realised. Very quickly they became armoured, but once trench warfare set in their use became severely restricted. But, as early as October 1914 imaginative minds in Britain had started to consider the possibility of using some form of tracked vehicle to overcome the obstacles created by the newly created trenches.

The invention of the tank can be attributed to no single man or agency. On one side the Admiralty, who had been involved in armoured car operations carried out by the Royal Naval Air Service in support of their aircraft in Flanders during the first three months of the War, became increasingly interested in the idea, spurred on by Winston Churchill, the First Lord of the Admiralty. On the other, there was a group headed by Colonel Swinton, the official war correspondent in France, and Colonel Hankey, Secretary to the Committee for Imperial Defence. Both parties

---

* It was not the first time that the Germans had tried out this new weapon. A type of irritant had been used against the French near Neuve Chapelle in October 1941, but it was so inefficient that its use here was not discovered until after the war, Xylyl Bromide had been tried out against the Russians at Lodz in January 1915, but the extreme cold caused it to freeze instead of vaporizing.

were quite clear that what was wanted was a machine capable of crossing trenches and destroying wire entanglements, which would have its own integral firepower and be protected from enemy fire. In February 1915 a Landships Committee was formed, and the first prototype tank, 'Little Willie', was produced in June of that year. It is interesting to note that the French, quite independently of the British, were also thinking along similar lines. Here again, two separate agencies were initially at work. The armaments firm of Schneider, led by an engineer called Brillié, spent the early part of 1915 exploring the possibilities of a tracked armoured car. There was also a parliamentary deputy, J. L. Breton, who since November 1914 had been interested in improved techniques for cutting wire, a very necessary part of the preparation of any attack on trenches. He evolved the idea of a mechanical wire-cutter mounted on an agricultural tractor, and was put in touch with Brillié. Military representation on this project was provided by an artillery officer, Colonel Estienne, who during the latter part of 1915 had evolved an idea for an armoured tracked fighting vehicle to aid the advance of the infantry.

The first to introduce tanks onto the battlefield were the British. Little Willie's successor, which was of a rhomboidal* as opposed to the box-like shape of Little Willie, seemed to fit the original specification and an initial order for 40 was placed in the autumn of 1915. The first tactical doctrine for their employment was embodied in a memorandum written by Swinton in February 1916. He believed that:

'. . . the Tanks will confer the power to force successive comparatively unbattered defensive lines, but . . . the more speedy and uninterrupted their advance the greater the chance of their surviving sufficiently long to do this. It is possible therefore, that an effort to break through the enemy's defensive zone in one day may now be contemplated as a feasible proposition.' [2]

He felt that artillery should concentrate on counter-battery work, since the enemy's guns constituted the main threat to the tanks. Tanks were able to deal with wire, machine-guns and earthworks on their own, but he suggested that aircraft could help by dropping bombs on enemy gun detachments. The latter was taken up by Hankey, who approached General Henderson, the Director of Military Aeronautics, but the idea did not come to anything. However it was perhaps the first positive glimmer of what in years to come was to evolve into the blitzkreig technique. The conclusion to Swinton's paper was to provide a bone of contention between the tank enthusiasts and the more conservative military elements for many years, and not just in the British Army. The conclusion read: 'It seems that, as the tanks are an auxiliary to the infantry, they must be counted as infantry and in operation be under the same command. [2] Haig, by now commanding the British Expeditionary Force (BEF) in France, had been impressed by

* The lower part of its profile was shaped like the effective part of a very large wheel.

this paper and wanted some tanks to be available at the start of his Somme offensive in July. However, in spite of promises that 75 would be ready for him by August, only 60 with barely trained crews, were despatched by the end of that month. Swinton, in his memorandum, had emphasised that they should not be used until a sufficient number was available. In the event, the temptation to try out this new weapon on the battlefield as soon as possible was too great. The lesson of the German's limited use of gas at Ypres in 1915 had not been learnt. Only 49 tanks went into action on September 15th, 1916 at Flers on the Somme. Many suffered mechanical failures before coming into action, but those that did succeed in breaking into the German lines acquitted themselves well. The Germans were taken completely by surprise, and the Chief of Staff of the German Third Army Group was moved to write: 'The enemy . . . have employed new engines of war, as cruel as effective. No doubt they will adopt on an extensive scale these monstrous engines, and it is urgent to take whatever methods are possible to counteract them.' [3]

They were used once more, ten days later, before the close of 1916, but by that stage few were mechanically fit. The tank had shown itself as a means for breaking the deadlock of trench warfare, but many more would be needed before their contribution would become significant. In the meantime that valuable asset of any new weapon, surprise, had been lost.

As a result of this first use of tanks the French had to revise their ideas on the employment of their own tanks. Estienne had, like Swinton, originally envisaged tanks being used in a surprise mass assault on the German lines, their attack being followed up by the infantry. But, because the British had caused the element of surprise to be lost, the doctrine had to be changed. During the winter months their role became more diluted until they found themselves as merely complementary to the artillery, taking on targets which the preparatory bombardment had failed to destroy. It is signficant that the name by which the first French tank units were called was *Artillerie d'Assaut*. Because of production problems the French tanks did not see action until April 1917, during Nivelle's disastrous offensive at Chemin des Dames. In this, and in subsequent actions, the French tanks, Schneider and then later St Chamond heavy tanks, were not a success. It was not so much in the way that they were employed, but more that they were mechanically unreliable and had a poor obstacle-crossing capability in comparison with the British tanks. As a result Estienne suggested that the British should continue to concentrate on heavy tanks, while the French produced light tanks. Indeed, in the previous year he had already set in motion a design through the motor firm of Renault.

Meanwhile, the British tank force spent the Winter 1916-17 expanding and training for the next year's campaign season. In November 1916 one of the tank staff officers wrote a paper entitled 'A Tank Army', whose message would provide another bone of contention in the future. Captain Martel, whose name will appear elsewhere in this book, started his paper by saying:

'No present-day army could fight against an army of say 2 000 tanks, and

14

it therefore follows that all large continental armies will have to make use of tank armies in the future. Except in very wooded or mountainous countries a tank army will probably in the future take the place of the present unprotected soldier. In any case the tanks will be of such great importance that future great wars are almost sure to start with a duel between the tank armies of the respective sides.' [4]

He likened these tank armies to fleets fighting on land, and believed that the prime role of the tank would be to knock out other tanks. He foresaw the tank as a weapon in itself, and did not consider infantry and artillery at all. But, as Liddell Hart himself said '. . . it strongly influenced the train of thought in tank-minded circles towards the visualisation of future warfare in a naval frame. [4]. Martel showed this paper to a newly arrived officer at the Tank Headquarters in France, Major J. F. C. Fuller. The latter thought it unrealistic in that he was certain that tanks would always be an adjunct of the infantry. Within a few months he would have a radical change of mind.

Like its French counterpart, the fortunes of the British Tank Corps reached a low ebb during the first part of 1917. Although the tanks themselves were becoming more mechanically reliable, they failed to make the hoped for impression during the Spring and Summer of 1917 because of the way in which they were used. Dispersed in penny packets to support infantry attacks over ground too churned up by artillery fire to enable them to move properly, they began to get a bad name for themselves. Added to this was the German realisation that tanks were vulnerable to shellfire. It was at this stage that Fuller now set himself on the path that would gain him the reputation as the foremost protagonist of the tank in the world.

The Third Battle of Ypres, which became synonymous with 'Flanders Mud', opened on the July 31st, 1917, and by the third day of the battle Fuller felt that it was stillborn as far as the Tank Corps were concerned. The commander of the Tank Corps, General Elles, turned down his initial suggestion for the halting of the current offensive in favour of a joint Franco-British attack on St Quentin. Fuller then produced an alternative plan which entailed launching a series of 'Tank Raids'. He envisaged five or six raids to take place over the next six months, each raid using some 200 tanks with two infantry or cavalry divisions in support, together with aircraft, artillery and engineers. This force would penetrate the German lines, do as much damage as possible, and retire again within a matter of hours. The idea would be to cause a lowering in enemy morale. Perhaps after five or six of these raids the Germans would be sufficiently softened up to warrant a major offensive in the spring of 1918. For almost a month Fuller's plan vegetated at GHQ. Then Byng, commanding the Third British Army, took up the idea and suggested that the rolling chalk downlands to the east of the old Somme battlefield, which was held by his army, were ideally suited to such an action. But to Fuller's horror, Byng decided to take the plan one stage further. Instead of a mere raid he envisaged a full-scale attack.

The result of all this was the Battle of Cambrai, which opened with an attack by some 400 tanks, led in person by the commander of the Tank Corps, General Elles. Behind them followed six divisions of infantry. Besides being the largest number of tanks yet assembled for an attack, there were other novel features. The element of surprise, which had, because of the lengthy preparatory artillery bombardments, so often been missing in the past, once again took its place on the battlefield. All tank movements to assembly areas behind the start line took place under cover of darkness. An embargo was placed on all wireless and telephone links used by the infantry. Unfortunately the same was not done for artillery communications and the Germans did gain some inkling 24 hours before the attack that something was up, although they knew not quite what. Most important, Tank Corps Headquarters managed to persuade Byng to do away with a preparatory bombardment. The weather further helped in that dawn broke with the battlefield shrouded with fog.

Another innovation was the allocation of aircraft in the ground attack role to co-operate closely with the tanks. Mention has been made earlier of the RNAS operations in France and Belgium during the opening months of the war. In this instance the aircraft were used to locate likely targets such as bodies of German cavalry, which the armoured cars went in and destroyed. At this stage the primary role of the aircraft was reconnaissance in support of the ground forces, although there were attempts to use the aircraft as a bomber. The Germans had used their Zeppelin airships for this purpose from the very beginning and the Allies attempted to knock out the Zeppelin bases using aircraft armed with primitive bombs. The year 1915 had seen an extension to the use of air power. In order to carry out successful aerial reconnaissance and, at the same time prevent the enemy from doing the same, it was realised that it was essential to have air supremacy. Hence aircraft were introduced for the specific purpose of shooting down enemy aircraft. At the same time, besides spotting for artillery, aircraft were used to take on ground targets beyond artillery range. During the Battle of the Somme aircraft were used to attack ground targets in the vicinity of the front line, but this was only a minor task, which was not allowed to detract from the primary roles of reconnaissance and the counter-air battle. Not until Cambrai were squadrons specifically detailed for 'ground strafing'.

The first day of the Battle of Cambrai was almost overwhelmingly successful. A hole was punched through the heavily fortified Hindenburg Line and an advance of up to five miles achieved on a seven mile front. Such an advance had taken four months to achieve on the Somme the year before. Significant too were the comparatively few casualties suffered by the infantry, who advanced protected by the tanks. As for the latter, a tank driver describes what it was like:

'There was a steady rise in the ground across No Man's Land, and as we crawled on in front of the infantry and demolished the knife-edged entanglements, the 'bus was spattered repeatedly with hysterical left and right sweeps of machine-gun fire. The whole panorama now was just like a set piece of thousands of fountains of fire spurting from the solid earth. There was, as yet, very little response from the enemy artillery and as we reached the German front line the machine-gun fire ceased too. Gradually there became a substantial increase in the enemy shelling, but it was very erratic. In zig-zagging (remember, a tank had to stop to change direction, so this manoeuvre was very ponderous) to avoid any concentration on our weak spots, I noticed the infantry . . . were now at grips with batches of German soldiery. We fired several machine-gun bursts in their direction; but it was unnecessary, as they were already throwing down their weapons and surrendering to the Tommies. We fought our way to the wire and then, after slowing down for a few seconds, I opened the throttle to the fullest extent and, without a hitch, plunged through the barbed wire. Our tracks flattened out a clear pathway through which the infantry followed.' [5]

Meanwhile in the air above, Lt Lee of 46 Squadron RFC, which was equipped with Sopwith Camels, was tasked with attacking German 5.9 inch artillery batteries to the south of Cambrai itself (some seven miles behind the German front line):

'We pass over the rear wave of the advance, reserve and supply tanks, field artillery, support troops and so on, then quickly catch up the first wave . . . I see the ragged line of grey diamond-shaped monsters, thirty to fifty yards apart, stretching into the mist on either flank, rolling unevenly forwards, their tracks churning round, their exhausts throwing out blue-grey smoke. I see, behind each tank, a trudging group of infantry, casually smoking, looking up at us . . . Then we have passed them, we're ahead of the advance and approaching the Boche. Smoke-shells burst ahead, a flash of red flame and masses of belching cloud, which we speed through — nauseous-smelling stuff that stings the eyes . . . Now we reach the rear of the Hindenburg defence system, two lots of trenches, with troops in field grey waiting in them, their forward view blocked by a pall of smoke. We issue out of the screen so low and fast that they have no time to fire and as we skim over their heads, I see them staring up at us in incredulous amazement.' [6]

Although the churchbells rang in England for the first time since the outbreak of war to celebrate this spectacular success, not all had gone well. Because every infantry commander wanted to have his share of tanks to support his troops onto their objectives, the tanks had to be spread across the whole front. This left few tanks available to form a reserve. Fuller had wanted the tanks to concentrate only on certain vital areas of ground, which would have enabled this to happen, but he was overruled. Consequently there were few tanks left to exploit these initial successes. Those that had been in action required mechanical attention, beside which their crews, after more than twelve hours' confinement in ambient temperatures of over 100°F, were in need of rest.

Fuller had laid down very rigid rules by which the tanks and infantry were to work together. It was essential that the infantry kept right up behind the tanks, and that they advanced in double file, using the tanks as cover. One division, the 51st Highland, chose to ignore this, keeping the infantry 100 yards behind the tanks in extended order by sections. Consequently they lost the protection of the tanks. In the 51st Highland Division's sector lay the Flesquières Ridge, a prominent feature garrisoned by three infantry battalions, two machine gun companies and several batteries of artillery. As the tanks came up towards this feature they were taken on by the German guns, which caused several casualties from the machine guns. Neither arm was in a position to help the other and by the end of the day the ridge was still in German hands. This led to the third shortfall. The original plan had called for the Cavalry Corps of four divisions to be passed through the gap made in the Hindenburg Line. These would capture Cambrai, seize crossings over the River Sensée, after which the Third Army would proceed to sweep north and west up the German line towards Valenciennes. By early afternoon on November 20th the time was ripe for the Cavalry to move forward to exploit the situation. Unfortunately, apart from one squadron of Canadian Cavalry (Fort Garry Horse), they stayed where they were and the chance was lost. The reason was that, having heard about the setbacks on the Flesquières Ridge, they did not believe that their moment had come. As a result of these shortcomings subsequent days saw the attacks grind slowly to a halt as the Germans, recovering from their initial shock, poured more and more reserves into the threatened area and counter-attacked with increasing severity. By November 30th they were in a position to launch a major counter-attack. In character it would be different to anything so far seen on the Western Front.

The origins of this new German type of assault lay far away on the Eastern Front. Since May 1915 the Germans had always had in mind an assault along the Baltic Coast in order to turn the right flank of the Russian Armies. During the big Austro-German offensive of the Summer of 1915 they had tried to do this but had found themselves up against a formidable obstacle in the River Dvina. The linchpin of the Russian defences was the city of Riga, lying at the mouth of the Dvina. Further attempts were not made until the late Summer of 1917 when, with the failure of the Kerensky offensive, the Germans believed that low Russian morale would enable them to crack this nut and perhaps carry the offensive on towards St Petersburg. The task was given to General von Hutier and his Eighth Army. Rather than try and attack Riga itself, von Hutier decided to bypass it and get across the river further south. To attack across a river under the eyes of the enemy is one of the more difficult operations of war. Von Hutier believed that the only way to success was to rely heavily on surprise. This meant that his preparatory bombardment must be short, yet at the same time it must be effective. It so happened that earlier in the summer the Germans had developed a new gas. This was diethyl sulphide, called Yperite by the Germans because it was at Ypres that it was first used. It smelt of mustard and soon came to be known by this name. Mustard gas is a persistent agent which produces casualties through blistering and vomiting. It has a significant advantage in that one part in four million parts of air is sufficient to cause casualties. Hence it can be easily combined with high explosive (HE) in an artillery shell. Consequently, when von Hutier attacked on the September 1st he only used five hours worth of preliminary bombardment, of which the first two were mainly gas. As with the British at Cambrai, he used lowflying aircraft in support and crossed the Dvina with the minimum of casualties. However, von Hutier himself was surprised by the ease with which he got across and his rather pessimistic timetable for subsequent phases enabled the Russians to recover before he was able to achieve a complete breakthrough, although he succeeded in capturing Riga itself.

Encouraged by the initial success of this new tactic, the Germans now looked elsewhere to try it out. It so happened that General Conrad von Hotzendorf, the Austrian Chief of Staff until February 1917, and now an army group commander on the Italian Front, had been agitating for a joint Austro-German attack on the Isonzo sector of the Italian Front since the beginning of the year. Earlier, the Germans had not been prepared to provide many troops to assist their ally against Italy, being too engrossed in the Western Front. On the Isonzo Front itself, the Austrians and Italians had between them lost an inordinate number of men in eleven major battles, beginning in June 1915. Both sides were exhausted by the late summer of 1917, but the Austrians believed that they could break through the Italian lines provided that German support was available. In September Hindenburg finally acceded to their wishes, and it was agreed to supplement the existing 23 Austrian divisions on this front with seven German and seven further Austrian divisions. On October 24th at 0200 hours the bombardment opened with a deluge of gas shells on the Italian Lines. It lasted only one more hour than the more limited operation at Riga, and was mixed with HE as before. The attack went in and by the end of the first day the Italian Second Army had been broken and the Austro-German advance was ten miles deep. The new tactics had been shown to work once again, but the Central Powers had started with two advantages. Firstly the Socialist press in Italy had exploited the exhaustion of the Italian troops beforehand, and many had become disillusioned with the war. Secondly, Cadorna, the Italian Commander, having realised that an offensive was about to be launched, thanks mainly to Austrian deserters, had made the mistake of putting all his reinforcements in the frontline, where they took the full shock of the initial bombardment. Suffice to say, by November 10th, when the offensive ran out of momentum, the Italians had been pushed back to the line of the River Piave, some 80 miles behind their original frontline.*

It was these new attack methods which the British were to face in the Cambrai counter-attack. After being initially surprised on the first day of

---

*During this offensive Erwin Rommel, then a young officer serving in a German Mountain division, won Germany's highest award for valour, the Pour Le Merite.

the battle, the Germans quickly set in hand preparations for a counter-attack. Some 20 divisions were assembled to the east of the town of Cambrai, and on November 30th the counter-attack was unleashed. Once again it was a question of a short sharp bombardment of gas mixed with HE. Again, the Germans advanced in small groups, leaving aside centres of strong resistance. Low flying aircraft and artillery provided close support. Surprise was achieved and for the first 48 hours of the attack the British were thrown into confusion. After this, thanks to determined counter-attacks on the part of the British, supported by the few remaining tanks, the counter-offensive died away. But, by December 7th the British had been thrown back some three miles from the line of their furthest gains.

Although the German effort was not as spectacular as at Caporetto it had shown that their new tactics could work on the Western Front. For the British too, the tank had regained its reputation and they believed that this could provide the basis for victory on the Western Front in 1918. The French also increased their orders for the Renault Light Tank, planning to assemble some 3 500 for a surprise attack in 1918. The Americans, who were starting to arrive in France in ever increasing numbers (they had declared war on the Central Powers in April 1917), also became enthusiastic. One junior officer, newly assigned to the American Tank Service, wrote to his wife on the November 26th, 1917 as follows:

'Since the English success the other day lots of people have suddenly discovered in the tanks they have always had faith and now express a desire to accept the command of them but fortunately I beat them to it by about four days . . .' [7]

Captain G. S. Patton, Jnr. was to become the famous American armoured leader of World War II.

In the meantime the reverses during the latter part of the Cambrai battle had caused concern in Britain and a public enquiry was set up. Yet, instead of identifying and analysing the new-style German tactics, it merely contented itself with trying to find scapegoats. This was to have dire consequences a few months later.

German strategy for 1918 was formulated at a conference held at Mons on November 11th, 1917. By this time Russia was virtually out of the war and Italy was very shaky after Caporetto. Yet Austro-Hungary, Bulgaria and Turkey, Germany's other allies, were becoming dangerously exhausted. There was also the spectre of the Allies receiving ever increasing reinforcements from America. In time this would mean that Allied superiority on the Western Front would become insupportable. Ludendorff, the German Chief of Staff, resolved that it was imperative to launch a major attack in the West before the Americans were in a position to influence the balance of forces. From this he deduced that he must make his effort before the end of March. He also decided to attack the British rather than the French because the former had less country in which to manoeuvre, and would be bound to secure their lines of communication by retreating northwards towards the Channel. Out of this planning conference were to evolve the five German drives of the spring and summer of 1918. Ludendorff was a believer in the necessity of developing a sound tactical doctrine before making any strategic plans. He now had a good tactical doctrine for the offensive and hence felt himself able to plan an offensive strategy in the West. Von Hutier, the victor of Riga, and his chief artilleryman Colonel Brüchmuller were transferred from the Eastern Front in order to train the attack divisions.

The practical experience of Riga and Caporetto had caused the Germans to refine their tactics and during the Winter 1917-1918, the attack divisions being now trained to conduct a four phase attack. Firstly the short artillery bombardment would concentrate on neutralising the British front and support lines. Then special units of *sturmtruppen*, who had been selected as the cream of the German infantry, would move forward under a creeping barrage. They would infiltrate the British lines and make directly for the British close support artillery positions, which they would knock out. Behind them would follow 'battle units' consisting of a mix of infantry, machine guns, mortars, field engineers and artillery observation officers. Their job would be to invest the strongpoints bypassed by the storm troops. Finally, conventional infantry would have the responsibility of clearing up remaining enemy resistance. As each echelon caught up with the one in front, the forward echelon would move on again. Artillery observation officers were employed well forward, with the authority to change fire plans at will. This meant that artillery fire could be adjusted on the progress of the spearhead of this attack, something which had not been possible in previous German or Allied attacks on the Western Front. The German troops were imbued with a new offensive spirit, which was well described by Ernst Junger, a young storm troop officer:

'The brazen spirit of the attack, the spirit of the Prussian infantry, swept through the massed troops assembled here in the opening spring on the soil of France to go through the ordeal of battle.

If the aim of the higher command had in view was not attained, it was certainly not the fault of the officers and the men. After forty-four months of hard fighting they threw themselves upon the enemy with all the enthusiasm of August 1914. No wonder it needed a world in arms to bring such a storm-flood to a standstill.' [8]

When the dawn of March 21st, 1918 broke the British were unprepared to meet such an onslaught. The reasons were twofold. Firstly they were very stretched, especially in the area of the River Somme where the Germans were to make their first attack. At the Allied Conference at Boulogne in September 1917 it had been agreed that the British should take over more of the French line. Cambrai and the need to rush troops to Italy after Caporetto had postponed this move, but by the end of January Haig had extended the British front some 25 miles southwards, just over the River Oise. At the same time, Lloyd George, the Prime Minister, fearful that Haig might embark on another bloodbath like the Third Battle of Ypres, placed an embargo on reinforcements from Britain. The result was that Haig was forced to reduce each division by three infantry battalions. Gough, commanding the Fifth British Army, found himself defending 42 miles of front in the very area in which the Germans were about to attack. To do this he had twelve of the new weakened infantry divisions and three cavalry divisions. The British defence doctrine was also not suitable for dealing with the new German attack tactics, in fact it played right into the hands of the Germans. A GHQ Instruction dated December 14th, 1917 laid down that there were to be three defensive lines. The first, or Forward Zone, would consist of a series of wired-in strongpoints. The object of these was to force the Germans to deploy large numbers of troops to capture them. Unfortunately the possibility of infiltration was not taken into account and the defenders of these strongpoints were merely condemned to death or capture. Two or three miles to the rear lay the Battle Zone and some four to eight miles behind this was located the Rear Zone. Two thirds of the defenders were committed to the first two lines of defence, both of which were in German artillery range from the start. This was in contrast to the Germans who had come to realise that it was essential to keep as many troops as possible outside artillery range, as had the French, and both insisted on at least two thirds of their forces being so deployed. The British had not learnt this lesson, just as they had not made the effort to draw the right deductions from the latter days of the Battle of Cambrai. Yet there were mitigating circumstances. Ever since early 1915, apart from the Second Battle of Ypres, they had adopted an offensive posture. They had not gone through a Battle of Verdun like the French or experienced prolonged defence like the Germans on the Somme in 1916 or at Ypres in 1917.

By March 21st the British, especially in the Fifth Army sector, where the Rear Zone had not yet been dug, had had too little time to complete their defences. Gough found himself faced by 33 divisions, belonging to von Hutier's Eighteenth Army and von der Marwitz's Second Army. To the North the 14 divisions of Byng's Third British Army, occupying 28 miles of front, faced the 14 divisions of von Below's Seventeenth Army. Once again fog, as it had done at Cambrai, came to the aid of the attacker. Five hours of bombardment by 6 000 guns and then the attackers went in. After two hours the fighting had reached the Battle Zone, and by dusk on a front stretching for 40 miles from Arras down to the River Oise the Germans had closed up to, and in some places beyond the Rear Zone. Small wonder, that by the end of the first day Gough's army had been thrown into confusion. During the next two days the Germans continued to push back Gough's troops. French reinforcements had been rushed up from the south, but these also found themselves caught up in the retreat. But, although von Hutier was driving all before him, his two fellow army commanders to the north were having a harder time against Byng and the momentum of their attacks was decreasing. It was on March 23rd that, in view of this situation, Ludendorff now made a fatal mistake. Instead of reinforcing von

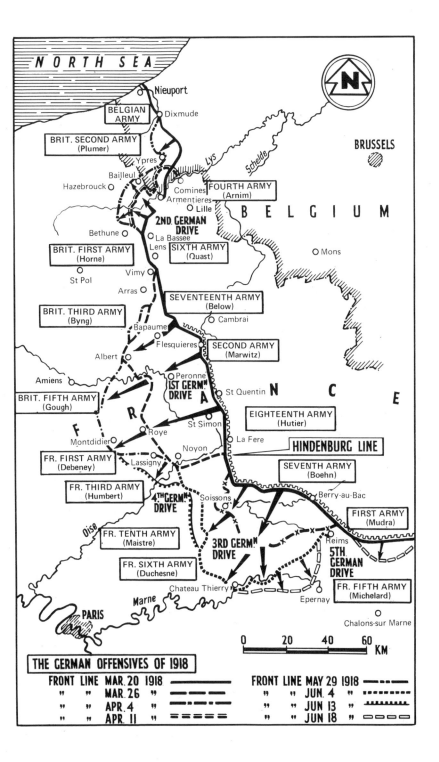

THE GERMAN OFFENSIVES OF 1918

Hutier's success he ordered the three armies to continue the attacks in divergent directions. Von Below was to turn north-west, von der Marwitz was to continue westwards while von Hutier was ordered to turn south-west in order to drive a wedge between Gough and the French to his south.

By now the Germans were fighting over the old Somme battlefields which slowed down their mobility. Because of their policy of merely replacing casualties in the forward units rather than rotating of complete units, the storm troops themselves were getting tired. They had also been indoctrinated into believing that the British were suffering from a shortage of supplies because of the U-boat campaign in the Atlantic. The sight of well stocked depots and canteens, which they had overrun, demonstrated that this was not so, and morale suffered. Meanwhile, more and more French divisions were being rushed up from the south, while in the north, Plumer, commanding the Second British Army in the Ypres Salient offered up no less than twelve of his fourteen divisions in return for battered Third and Fifth Army ones. More important, the Allies finally realised the need for an Allied commander-in-chief with executive powers in order to control and co-ordinate the Allied effort. The Doullens Conference of March 26th appointed Foch to this task. Thus, on March 28th Rudolf Binding, a German Staff officer, recorded:

'Today the advance of our infantry suddenly stopped near Albert. Nobody could understand why. Our airmen had reported no enemy between Albert and Amiens . . . Our way seemed entirely clear. I jumped into a car with orders to find out what was causing the stoppage in front. As soon as I got near the town I began to see curious results. Strange figures, which looked very little like soldiers and certainly showed no signs of advancing, were making their way back out of the town. There were men driving cows before them on a line; others who carried a hen under one arm and a box of notepaper under the other . . . Men dressed up in comic disguise. Men with top hats on their heads. Men staggering. Men who could hardly walk.' [9]

Exhaustion and the overwhelming temptation to fall off the line of march in order to pillage had finally put paid to the first German drive. On that same day Ludendorff gave orders for another offensive to be mounted to the north, in the area of the River Lys. This was to open on April 9th.

Although Ludendorff managed to scrape up 26 divisions for this operation, code-named 'Georgette', only 12 of these were attack divisions, compared with the 47 used for Operation Michael. On the other hand, the Armentières-La Bassée sector, against which Georgette was to be mounted, was also thinly held by the British. Of the six divisions in and around this sector four were recovering from the effects of Michael, and another, the 2nd Portuguese Division, was in such a low state of morale that it was about to be relieved. This left only one division, the 55th West Lancashire Territorial, which was fully up to strength. This held the southern part of the sector. During the days before the attack the German artillery was moved northwards to this sector under the direction of the indefatigable Brüchmuller. On April 7th and 8th both the area to the north and that to the south of the threatened sector were subjected to mustard gas attacks. Once again the attack opened with the now familiar five hour bombardment, and again fog was present to aid the German attack. When the attack itself went in the Portuguese broke immediately and apart from 55th Division in the south, the other divisions quickly fell back. By the evening of the 9th the Germans had succeeded in punching a hole six miles deep and ten miles wide in the British line.* During the next three days the Germans continued to push westwards still aided by their ally, fog. But, as with Michael, momentum started to die away. On the 12th the crisis came; for the first time fog was absent and the Royal Air Force was able to gain air superiority and inflict heavy damage on the attacking troops. By the end of the month the battle was over.

The noteworthy aspect of this second drive was that the British had learnt from their experiences in March. Defence was becoming more flexible and they were learning how to delay the German advance by the use of booby traps and delayed action mines.† The Germans were still suffering from the same disease as in March. Ludendorff himself complained of the German tendency to be distracted by captured supply dumps, especially those containing food. The discipline of the front line units was starting to wither. During the latter stages of the offensive a milestone was reached with the first recorded tank v tank action.

The Germans had been slow to adopt the tank. Their first, an A7V, a 30-ton tank, was not completed until December 1917, and only five of these were available for the March offensive. They did have some captured British tanks, mainly as a result of the latter days of Cambrai, and when they did use tanks they were generally successful. But, with the Allied blockade causing shortages of raw materials, they were never able to build more than a few themselves and hence the tank was not a fundamental ingredient of their offensive doctrine. Yet on the April 24th outside the village of Villers-Bretonneux British and German tanks came up against one another for the first time. The Germans had managed to collect together thirteen of their A7Vs to lead an attack by four storm divisions. Villers-Bretonneux itself was soon captured and the situation looked critical. At this point three British Mark IVs, two of them 'females' armed with machine guns only, arrived on the scene. Sighting the lead German tank, they engaged it. The two 'females' proved no match for the 57mm gun of the German and were soon forced to withdraw. The British male tank engaged the A7V from the flank with its 6pdr and forced it to overturn into a sandpit. Two other German tanks now arrived but were turned away by the intense fire from the Mark IV 'male'. The German attack faltered and seven British Whippets (light tanks armed with machine guns) attacked the German infantry and put them to fl¡ght, inflicting some

---

* This grave situation caused Haig to issue his famous 'Backs to the Wall' message.
† First used by the Germans during their withdrawal to the Hindenburg Line in March 1917.

400 casualties. It was a minor affair, but foretold the shape of things to come.

Ludendorff was now getting desperate. He had shot his bolt against the British and the Americans continued to pour men into France. He now believed that although the British had held they were exhausted and were being propped up by the French. Remove this prop and he could then afford to deal with the British piecemeal. Hence he directed that a third offensive now be mounted against the French in the Chemin des Dames area. On May 27th the Germans struck. Foch had laid down that the only way to defeat the Germans was to dispute every inch of ground; there would be no voluntary surrender of positions. The British, who had sent four tired divisions down to the Chemin des Dames area to rest, were aghast at this, as was Pétain, who had been made Chief of Staff at the end of April 1917 in order to deal with the mutinies that had broken out in the French Army as a result of the ineptitude shown by Nivelle in his attacks at Chemin des Dames. In his Directive No. 4 issued to the French Armies in December 1917 he had emphasised the importance of defence in depth. As a result of studying German pamphlets on the subject he became convinced that it was important to hold strong counter -attack forces well back. His concept was to draw the attackers on until they were beyond the range of their supporting artillery, and then to hit them in the flank with his reserves. This meant that ground would be voluntarily given up to the enemy, which was an anathema to many of the French commanders, who had been imbued since the start of the war that no piece of *La Belle Patrie* should ever be given up without a fight. Unfortunately Duchesne, commanding the French Sixth Army and its attached British divisions in the Chemin des Dames sector, and his immediate superior Franchet d'Esperey were both followers of Foch rather than Petain. The troops were packed into a strip of country only five miles deep with the River Aisne at their backs. Consequently when the Germans attacked on May 25th they were able to cut through the Sixth Army with ease and by the end of the day had advanced 12 miles, a record for the Western Front. By the 30th they were 30 miles deep into the territory held by the French, and only 60 miles from Paris. But, Pétain did not panic by throwing his reserves piecemeal into the fight, instead he continued to hold them well back. Once again, the Germans succumbed to the temptation to pillage, and when they came up against Pétain's reserves the steam had gone out of them and the offensive was brought to an end.

Ludendorff now found his troops occupying a very exposed salient and felt it necessary to widen it. His fourth drive was made between Montdidier and Noyon and launched on June 9th. By this time the French were most concerned about the possible threat to Paris, and Foch had issued an order on June 2nd telling Pétain 'to stop the enemy's advance to Paris at all costs,' and that 'the means consists of a foot-by-foot defence of the ground in this direction, pursued with the utmost energy.' [10] This again prevented Pétain from implementing his elastic defence, and once again von Hutier had initial striking successes. However this time Pétain was able to use his reserves in the counter-attack role and these went in on the 11th giving the Germans a bloody nose and stopping the offensive.

The German Army was now suffering a very serious deterioration in morale. Many felt that it was not capable of carrying on with offensive operations, but Ludendorff resolved to have one more attempt. His original plan was to contain the French with an attack on either side of the city of Rheims and then put his main effort against the British in Flanders. Gouraud, commanding to the east of Rheims, was a follower of Pétain, but the two army commanders to the south-west of the city were not. When the 52 German divisions were launched into the attack on the July 15th, Gouraud fell back leaving machine gun posts to hamper the Germans. As soon as they were beyond their supporting artillery he let loose his own artillery upon them and brought the attack to an immediate halt. On the other side of the town it was initially a different story. The defenders suffered the weight of the German artillery bombardment and allowed the Germans to cross the River Marne. For a time Rheims itself was in danger, but then the attackers found themselves thwarted by the solid line of Pétain's reserves. By midday on the 16th the attack was at a standstill, and two days later Pétain launched a furious counter-attack preceded by tanks, which drove the Germans right back. From now on the Germans were forced to adopt the defensive. Pétain had proved that the only way to counter these shock tactics was to adopt a fluid or mobile defence, and to launch counter-attacks at the moment when the attackers had been caught off balance, with their supporting artillery unable to help them.

Meanwhile, Colonel Fuller, still the principal staff officer at the British Tank Corps HQ, had taken the next step in developing his doctrine of tank warfare. Although the Whippet tank had done good work during the second German drive, its cross-country mobility was not good, and an improved model, the Medium C was designed in December 1917. It was not however to reach France until after the end of the war. In spite of this, Fuller and others at the Tank Corps HQ had, in April 1918, worked out a specification for a successor to the Medium C, the Medium D. This would have even better mobility and, more important, would have a speed of 20mph. On May 24th Fuller produced a paper entitled *'The Tactics of the Attack as affected by the Speed and Circuit of the Medium D Tank'*. It was to become known as 'Plan 1919', and was to be the foundation stone for the champions of mechanised warfare in the 1920's and 1930's, and indeed for blitzkreig. He propounded a completely new thesis, namely that the first objective in the attack should be the disorganisation of the enemy's command. Once this had been achieved his front could then be attacked. 'Tactical success in war is generally gained by pitting an organised force against a disorganised one.' This could best be achieved by launching an initial attack of Medium D's and aircraft, which would make straight for the enemy headquarters at Army level (he assumed that these would be located some 20 miles behind the frontline). The tanks would destroy the headquarters, while the aircraft bombed supply and road centres. He emphasised that care should be taken not to destroy signal communications since '. . . the confusion resulting from the dual attack carried out by the Medium D tanks and the aeroplanes should be circulated by the enemy. Bad news confuses, confusion stimulates panic.' The 'Breaking Force', consisting of heavy tanks, infantry and artillery would now penetrate the enemy's front, being followed by the 'Pursuing Force' of light tanks, lorry-borne infantry and cavalry, who would chase the disorganised force back for 150 miles, by which time Fuller felt that they would surrender. [11] Although this would require an Allied Tank Force of 5000 tanks, which caused some heartsearching, Foch accepted the plan in principle as the doctrine to be followed if the war was to continue into 1919. The war finished in November 1918, but elements of the plan were used during the last few months.

With the petering out of the final German drive in July 1918, it was the turn of the Allies to take to the attack. After a dress-rehearsal at Le Hamel on July 4th, the British attacked first in an effort to break through the heavily fortified German Hindenburg Line. The Battle of Amiens, which started on the August 8th did show that parts, at least, of Fuller's Plan 1919 were practicable. The initial assault succeeded in penetrating the German lines to a depth of eight miles on the first day. The plan was then for light tanks, cavalry and armoured cars to exploit the breakthrough. Unfortunately the tanks were tied down to working with the cavalry, and it soon became clear that this was nigh on impossible in that they went at different speeds. When not under fire the cavalry outstripped the tanks, but once fire was opened the cavalry, being very vulnerable on their horses, fell behind. Yet the odd action did go to show that Fuller was on the right lines. One Whippet, named 'Musical Box', set off on a lone expedition behind the German lines, shooting up camps, reserves and transport, until finally being put out of action after some ten hours. The one British armoured car battalion (17th Bn Tank Corps), whose Austin armoured cars were towed across the trenches by tanks, caused havoc behind the German lines and even shot up a German advanced Corps headquarters.

Once again though, as at Cambrai, mechanical failures, the exhaustion of the tank crews, besides battle casualties, meant that the number of tanks available for subsequent days decreased sharply. As the numbers available decreased, the casualties increased and the attack was stopped after the fourth day. Next the French, and then the Americans, attacked. In each case the story was the same. As the supply of tanks ran out so the attacks slowed down. By the time the end came in November very few tanks were still in a fit state to be operating with the forward troops. None of the subsequent attacks after August 8th saw the tanks doing any more than operating as support to the infantry. Both the Americans and the French kept them strictly tied to the infantry, and the British did not repeat the more revolutionary aspects of August 8th. The only innovation of note during the last few months of the war was a development in the concept of air support to the ground forces.

In May 1918 the French had formed the 1st Air Division, which consisted of 40 squadrons, for the purpose of supporting offensive operations. It made its debut at Soissons on August 18th, supporting an attack led by tanks. Later in August, General Mason M. Patrick, chief of the American Air Service, organised the US air squadrons on the Western Front in a similar way. Brigadier-General William Mitchell was appointed to command this force which was designated Air Service, First US Army. For the American attack at St Mihiel in September, Mitchell managed to borrow the 1st Air Division and, with his own force, had a total of some 1 500 aircraft with which to support the ground operations. While two thirds of the force were employed in interdiction tasks well beyond the front line, in order to hamper the German efforts to bring up reserves, as well as maintaining air superiority, the remainder were used in direct support of the attacking troops in the ground strafing role. The operation was most successful, but Mitchell did not have another chance to develop his ideas before the war ended, although he was contemplating the dropping of a complete division by parachute behind the German lines should the war have continued into 1919.

Thus, by the end of the war in November 1918 the essential ingredients of blitzkrieg were already present on the battlefield. The Germans had contributed the art of infiltration and shock action, although the latter at this stage was in the shape of artillery. The Allies had introduced the tank. Both appreciated the value of psychological dislocation, and each had used the aircraft in the ground support role to a greater or lesser extent. It now remained to be seen as to who would best interpret the experience gained from World War 1.

**Notes**

1  Forester, *The General* pp 141-2.
2  Swinton, *Eyewitness* pp 198-214.
3  Fuller, *Memoirs of an Unconventional Soldier* p 81.
4  Liddell Hart, *The Tanks* vol 1 pp 93-4.
5  Macksey, *To the Green Fields Beyond* p 13.
6  Gould Lee, *No Parachute* pp 162-3.
7  Blumenson, *The Patton Papers* p 445.
8  Junger, *Storm of Steel* p 242.
9  Binding, *A Fatalist at War* pp 209-210.
10  Liddell Hart, *Foch: Man of New Orleans* Vol 2 p 341.
11  Fuller, *Memoirs* op cit pp 322-336.

# 2
# The Twenties —
# Decade of the Theorists

The terms of the Treaty of Versailles, which formally ended the state of war which existed between the Allies and Germany, are significant not only in the efforts made to ensure that Germany could never again have the potential of an aggressor, but also with regard to the particular weapons of war which were deemed aggressive as opposed to defensive. Besides drastically limiting the size of the armed forces, artillery was restricted to 105mm and less, and this, together with machine guns and small arms, was strictly limited in quantity. On top of this, Article 171 banned the use, manufacture and storage of gas, and the manufacture and importation of tanks and armoured cars. In addition, Article 198 baldly stated that 'the armed forces of Germany must not include any military or naval air forces.' All existing aeronautical material had to be surrendered to the Allies. Thus Germany was left with none of the tools of blitzkrieg with which to experiment. Meanwhile the major powers on the Allied side commenced a speedy rundown of their huge war machines. They were naturally keen to devote the major part of their budgets to reconstruction. The threat had passed and they were now quick to adopt traditional foreign policies once again. Thus the USA, in spite of President Wilson's efforts to set up the League of Nations, soon became her old isolationist self when the Senate refused to ratify the Treaty of Versailles in March 1920, automatically rejecting American participation in the League. Britain too, turned her attention more to her Empire, leaving only France to worry about the dim possibility of a resurgent Germany. Across the other side of Europe, the former member of the Allied cause, Russia, was too involved in a civil war to concern herself too much with what went on outside her borders.

**Three Apostles of Air Power**
The first few years of peace saw dramatic advances in the field of the theory of air power. It is significant that in Italy, Britain and the United States the apostles of air power should have independently come to the same conclusions on the employment of air power in the future. First to strike was the Italian General Guilio Douhet, who in 1921 published a book entitled *The Command of the Air*. His theory originated with the use of strategic bombing by Italy against Austria across the Alps. He advocated the need for an air force independent of the army and navy. He defined 'command of the air' as being '. . . in a position to prevent the enemy from flying while retaining the ability to fly oneself.' [1] Having achieved this, he stated that

it would be possible to bomb an enemy into submission with little assistance from the other two services. He listed likely targets as industrial and commercial establishments, important buildings, communication centres and arteries, and civilian centres. He believed that an enemy state could be paralysed both physically and mentally by this type of attack; the army and navy being reduced to a role of mopping up. As he baldly stated in a second part to the book (added in 1926):

'. . . the Independent Air Force is shown to be the best way to assure victory, regardless of any other circumstances whatever, when it has been organised in a way suitable to winning the struggle for the command of the air and to exploiting the command with other forces.' [2]

His writings were not published outside Italy until the 1930s, and he remained unknown to other countries until then.

Meanwhile, Britain produced her own apostle, Trenchard. The Royal Air Force had been granted the status of a separate service in April 1918, when the RFC and RNAS were merged. Yet, while the bulk of the new service continued to support the Army and Navy, part was given an independent mission under the title of the Independent Air Force (IAF). The origins of this formation lay in the German bombing attacks on England during the early part of 1917. After a particularly heavy raid on London in July a committee had been set up under General Smuts to produce recommendations on defence against attacks from the air. The subsequent report, besides recommending the formation of the RAF as a separate entity, also took a look into the future:

'. . . The day may not be far off when aerial operations with their devastation of enemy lands and destruction of industries and populous centres on a vast scale may become the principal operations of war, to which the older forms of military and naval operations may become secondary and subordinate.' [3]

Public pressure forced the Government into retaliatory raids, and the 41st Wing RFC was formed in October 1917 for this very purpose. It was from this that the IAF grew. Throughout the last few months of the war this force carried out strategic, as opposed to tactical bombing operations in the shape of attacks on communications and industry inside Germany. It was titled 'Independent' to emphasise that, unlike the remainder of the RAF, it was entirely divorced from the operations of the ground forces.

Trenchard became Chief of the Air Staff in 1919. He believed that the RAF could only retain its separate identity if a role was found for it other than support for the other two services. His experience with the IAF naturally turned him towards the strategic bombing role. He claimed in his postwar despatch on the IAF that '. . . the moral effect of bombing stands undoubtedly to the material effect in a proportion of twenty to one.' [4] Hence he envisaged an air force made up mainly of bombers. Now, to the government of the day the bomber was regarded as an offensive weapon, and not the type of article that a peaceful democracy should be including in its armoury. But Trenchard argued that it was a deterrent to other nations considering war. At the same time, he declared that only the RAF could effectively stop an enemy air attack, but not by using ground defences or fighter interceptors. The only way to prevent such an attack was to go to the root of the problem.

'Instead of attacking a machine with 10 bombs we should go straight to the source of supply of those bombs and demolish it, and the same with the source of production of the machines. It was a quicker process than allowing the output to go on.' [5]

He was able to get his way, after an embittered struggle with the other two services, and in 1923 the decision was made to build up a Home Defence Force over five years of 35 bomber and 17 fighter squadrons. The fact that there were any fighter squadrons at all was only because Trenchard saw them as a sop to the politicians and civilians. By 1925 some 26 squadrons were ready, but only nine were bomber. The Government, in the light of the international atmosphere of disarmament, brought about by the Geneva Protocol of 1924 and the Locarno Treaties of 1925, decided to delay completion until 1935. Yet, in spite of this, Trenchard continued to champion the cause of the bomber, especially its moral effect, and continued to resist, as a major role for the RAF, air support for the Army and Royal Navy.

In the same way that Trenchard influenced RAF doctrine, so Mitchell, the same officer who had commanded the Air Service, First US Army in 1918, left his impression on American thought. The Dickman Board, a board of US Army officers which sat throughout 1919, to consider the lessons of the World War 1, saw the air arm as being auxiliary to the ground forces. Since they were drawing their conclusions from the operations on the Western Front it is not surprising that they should have thought this way. As far as the French were concerned, they had wished the American Air Service to concentrate on pursuit and observation. Although several production plans were drawn up few American aircraft were produced and the Americans had to use British and French aircraft, and those provided were mainly fighters and reconnaissance aircraft. Mitchell had employed tactical bombers, but these were operated by French and British crews. Only one American squadron actually took part in strategic bombing operations. This arrived at the front two days only before the end of the war, and was deactivated less than a month later. Hence US experience in this field was minimal. As a result of the recommendations of the Dickman Board the Air Service was made a distinct branch of the Army by the 1920 National Defence Act, which was to shape the American armed forces for the next twenty years.

'The air arm, as a result of the limited experience of World War I, had been moved from the status of a useful weapon in a subordinate position within one of the technical services (the Signal Corps) to a self-sufficient role in the combat line.' [6]

The problem was now to determine what this 'self-sufficient role' should be. General Mason M. Patrick, the non-flying Chief of the Air Service, AEF, was quite clear that the war had 'clearly demonstrated' that the function of observation for surface forces was 'the most important and far-reaching mission of aviation in war.' [7] Pershing in his final report put forward no ideas on air warfare, and certainly, as far as bombing was concerned, a statistical study done on British bombing operations prior to the formation of the Independent Air Force had concluded that it took 'two bombing squadrons to equal the work of one 155mm gun.' [8] Patrick's belief also tied in well with the US aircraft production programme finally inacted just before the end of the war, and hence the official role of the Air Service would be primarily air reconnaissance in support of the ground forces throughout the 1920's. There was official effort to acquire a balanced force, with a tactical and strategic capability,

'But it was too late; the damage had been done. . . . Having failed to analyse the experience of the war objectively and systematically, the Air Service saddled itself with an inadequate doctrine, which it had found hard to escape. Once that doctrine, no matter how faulty, had become part of the heritage of World War I, it proved difficult to alter.' [9]

This then was the atmosphere in which Mitchell was trying to propagate his doctrine of strategic air power. He was inspired by Trenchard, whom he had met in France, and felt that there was no reason why America should not follow Britain's example in establishing an independent air arm. Because of the geographical position of the United States, Mitchell had to argue his doctrine in a different way than his European counterparts. In the 1920's it was still believed that any attempted invasion of the continental United States was most likely to be from the sea. Hence the security of the American coastline was uppermost in the minds of the planners. Mitchell argued that to continue to allow this to be the responsibility of the US Navy was outdated. He believed that modern air power was very effective against ships, and set out to prove this with a series of practical demonstrations. In July 1921 he bombed the ex-German battleship *Ostfriesland*, the cruiser *Frankfurt* and a destroyer off the mouth of the Chesapeake, following this up in September by sending the old battleship *Alabama* to the bottom. The battleships *Virginia* and *New Jersey* suffered a like fate in 1923. The results, although impressive, did not have the effect that Mitchell hoped for, except to help convince the US Navy that it should retain its own air component. Mitchell, thwarted in his attempts to make an independent air arm the prime means of defence of the United States, now became even more outrageous in his attitude. He accused the War Department and the General Staff with criminal negligence over the loss of the airship

*Shenandoah* and in the eyes of the authorities he had gone too far. His court-martial followed and the court convicted him on charges of insubordination, suspending him from duty for two and a half years. He decided to resign from the service, which meant that he would have free rein to propagate his theories.

His first major work *Winged Defence* appeared shortly after his resignation. Mitchell was now looking at air power in more general terms, and much of what he wrote was similar to the doctrines of Douhet and Trenchard. Like them he believed in the air weapon for its effect on enemy morale, particularly as it was able to carry the war deep into the enemy's homeland.

'In future the mere threat of bombing a town by an air force will cause it to be evacuated, and all work in factories to be stopped. To gain a lasting victory in war, the hostile nation's power to make war must be destroyed . . . Aircraft operating in the heart of an enemy's country will accomplish this object in an incredibly short space of time.' [10]

Although he believed in the strategic potential of air power he did differ from Trenchard and Douhet in some respects. He did not subscribe to Douhet's ideas for an all-purpose aircraft. At the same time, he did not believe, like Trenchard that the bomber would always get through, and that the only sure form of defence was to attack the sources of production. 'It was proved in the European war that the only effective defence against aerial attacks is to whip the enemy's air force in air battles.' [11] He believed in the fighter and felt that it should be complementary to the strategic bomber. His own experiences in 1917-18 had convinced him that the role of close support to ground forces should not be forgotten, but he thought that this air support must be controlled by an independent air arm, and not by the Army. Like Liddell Hart he advocated that the traditional prime objective of the armed forces, the enemy's armed forces, was wrong and that the mere threat of air attack would be enough to throw an enemy into confusion.

'It is now realised that the hostile main army in the field is a false objective, and the real objectives are the vital centres . . . The result of warfare by air will be to bring about quick decisions. Superior air power will cause such havoc or the threat of such havoc in the opposing country that a long drawnout campaign will be impossible.' [12]

He, too, believed in the use of gas as an air delivered weapon. Its great advantage would be that:

'It is unnecessary that . . . cities be destroyed, in the sense that every house be levelled with the ground. It will be sufficient to have the civilian population driven out so that they cannot carry on their usual vocations. A few gas bombs will do that.' [13]

34

But like the other champions of air power Mitchell was convinced that the strategic bomber was a war winner. He had his disciples in the Air Service, and from the remoteness of Randolph Field in Texas they set about putting Mitchell's ideas into practice. In the meantime, perhaps Mitchell's 'kicking against the pricks' had not been entirely in vain. In 1926 Congress allowed the Air Service to be given the somewhat grander title of Army Air Corps, creating the post of Assistant Secretary of War for Air so that it would have some political representation, and laying down that the Air Corps should have a senior representative on the Army General Staff. The Lampert Committee, formed from the House of Representatives in 1925, had recommended an independent air force, but the Army and Navy lobbies proved too strong for this. In spite of all, the military component of the American air arm remained wedded to the idea that the primary role of aircraft was reconnaissance. During the decade of the Twenties the official aircraft acceptance figures were 812 pursuit, 228 bombers and no less than 2 593 observation aircraft.

Douhet, Mitchell and Trenchard had all been intimately involved in the development of this new dimension of warfare during 1914-18. All three saw the significance of the aircraft as its ability to overcome natural and artificial obstacles on land and sea and to carry the war to the enemy's homeland. They believed that by striking at the roots of the enemy's will to fight — government, industry, civil population — that they could achieve victory without suffering the carnage of the two older media of warfare. Indeed, it was victory by psychological dislocation as emphasised by Fuller in Plan 1919 and later by Liddell Hart in his theory of the indirect approach. The apostles of air power were forced into isolation, to a greater or lesser extent, during the Twenties because the atmosphere of peace and disarmament caused governments to shy away from such a seemingly offensive weapon as the bomber. Armies and navies, too, who had owned and nurtured the aircraft in its infancy as a supporting weapon to themselves, did their best to obstruct attempts to form air forces with a solely independent strategic role. For they thought that these moves would rob them of their own air support and, even worse, threaten to make them superfluous in future war. Thus throughout the decade air forces were to contribute little to the formulation of the blitzkrieg doctrine.

## Britain and Mechanisation

British defence policy in the 1920s was bound up by a rule drawn up by the War Cabinet led by Lloyd George in August 1919. It was initially an assumption that 'the British Empire will not be engaged in any great war during the next ten years, and that no Expeditionary Force is required for this purpose.' [14] It became known as the 'Ten Year Rule' and was to last until 1932, when the period was reduced to five years. Because it was assumed that 'no major war' meant primarily no war in Europe, priority of defence was directed towards the Empire, in particular towards guarding communication routes and providing against 'bush fire' conflicts which might arise in the Middle and Far East. In this setting there did not appear to be a role for mechanised forces. Small wonder then did those in high places, with one or two exceptions, have little enthusiasm for the tank and its proponents. In spite of this there were those who had been involved with tanks during World War I, and some later converts who would champion the cause of the tank during the decade of the 1920s. It was they who would evolve the blitzkrieg concept.

At the end of the war in 1918 the British Tank Corps was riding on the crest of the wave. Foch had accepted Fuller's Plan 1919 in principle and had called for the British to produce 3 500 tanks, as part of an Allied force of 10 000. Haig, too, in his final despatch, had praised the work of the Corps during the last few months of the War.

'Since the opening of our offensive on August 8, tanks have been employed on every battlefield, and the importance of the part played by them in breaking up the resistance of the German infantry can scarcely be exaggerated. The whole scheme of the attack of August 8 was dependent upon tanks, and ever since that date on numberless occasions the success of our infantry has been powerfully assisted or confirmed by their timely arrival.' [15]

It would seem that their place in the Army of the future was assured. But to the majority of professional soldiers, who had been serving before 1914, it was now a time to get back to 'real soldiering', to forget the stagnation of the Western Front, and to turn once again to the type of fighting, on which they had been nurtured. The change of defence priorities in favour of the Empire instead of Europe suited them. In this atmosphere the Tank Corps was going to have to fight just as strongly for survival as the Royal Air Force.

The problem was that the tank was a child of the trenches. Since trench warfare was unlikely to return there was little point in keeping the tank. 'The tank proper was a freak. The circumstances which called it into existence were exceptional and are not likely to occur again. If they do, they can be dealt with by other means.' [16] This was how one senior officer put it, although he did go on to discuss the importance of having mechanical transport, which was not bound by roads. The horse cavalry, who had not shone on the Western Front, could point to Allenby's successes with mounted troops in Palestine. They continued to regard themselves as the *arme blanche* and had several officers in high places who could ensure that they were not sacrificed on the altar of mechanisation. Typical of their arguments was:

'I do not for one moment decry the tank: it is going to be a very great feature in our Army of the future, but to commence replacing our cavalry and infantry by tanks would be to gamble with the Forces of the Crown in a way which the stodgy-minded Briton will never allow . . . ' [17]

Their arguments were mainly in this emotive vein, but appealed to those in positions of influence, who merely reduced their strength from 28 to 20 regiments. The Tank Corps, on the other hand, after bitter wrangling, was allowed to become a separate corps composed of four battalions only, compared to its strength of 25 at the end of the war.

Fuller, now working at the War Office, in a branch that dealt with training, was soon putting pen to paper. It was to be the start of a decade of copious writing, which would gain him faithful disciples, but at the same time make him many enemies. His opening broadside was his entry for the Gold Medal Essay competition of 1919. This was, and still is, one of the most prestigious of the Services writing competitions, and the subject was: *The application of recent developments in mechanics and other scientific knowledge to preparation and training for future war on land.* Using the motto of 'Racehorses don't pull up at the winning post', Fuller took the opportunity to expand on Plan 1919. After emphasising that the civil sciences and the army must work together, he went on to note that:

'The change in the art of war effected by the introduction of the petrol engine on the battlefield has been stupendous, for it has opened a new epoch in the history of war to which we can find no parallel in land fighting, the nearest approach being the replacement of sails by steam as the motive means in naval warfare.' [18]

He believed the mobility produced by the internal combustion engine to be the watchword of the modern army. The protection, mobility and firepower of the tank would mean that it could replace the infantry on foot, and the cavalry on horseback. He won the competition, but the only other entry, from an infantryman later to transfer to the Tank Corps, also preached the armoured cause, but went even further in advocating that the Army as a whole should be converted to tanks. Also, one of the two judges was Swinton, who had contributed so much to the early development of the tank.

The publication of Fuller's essay caused a furore. Although his suggestions for mechanisation had been mild (a prototype division of 12 infantry battalions, each to include a tank company, four horsedrawn artillery brigades, together with two mechanised ones, and a cavalry component of two horse cavalry regiments and a tank battalion), it was the suggestion that mechanisation would enable large reductions in manpower to be made, which outraged the military establishment. Significantly, the French had his paper translated, and wished to award him the distinction of *Officier d' Academie*, which the War Office refused to sanction. Much the same topic was set in 1922, when it was next the turn for a military, as opposed to naval or air, topic. This time the winner produced a more orthodox, and therefore acceptable, approach. He argued that tanks needed infantry with them to protect them from anti-tank guns. Besides ' . . . ground can only be occupied and consolidated by infantry, and that arm alone can protect tanks at rest.' He believed in the importance of air power, although he felt that strategic offensives against cities alone would leave the enemy's air forces unmolested enough to threaten the attacker's air bases. He saw the infantry, supported by aircraft and artillery preparing the way for a tank strike. This far his argument was sound, and his ideas on infantry/tank co-operation were what came to pass in the Second World War. Where he did go astray, although at the time it was accepted thinking, was to state that 'cavalry, by their ubiquity and individual initiative, can gain local information better than by any machine-borne groups of men . . . ' He acknowledged that cavalry were vulnerable to the fire of 'mechanical arms' and that they needed tanks to work with them. This conveniently forgot the lessons of tank/cavalry co-operation on the Western Front. He concluded this portion of his essay by stating: 'No commander will ever have as many tanks as he wants, and if the cavalry can be protected from the dangers of wire, tanks and bombing, there will still be work for them in battle.' [19] He did not expound on the modifications needed to be made to the cavalryman and his horse for this to happen. This paper is important in that it does represent the moderate view during the 1920's, which believed that there was a place for all arms, old and new, in the order of battle.

Meanwhile, Fuller's writing gathered momentum. In 1920 he published an account of the doings of the Tank Corps in the war. At the end he looked to the future, and reiterated that warfare would be based on 'mechanical' rather than 'muscular energy' and that this coupled with the protection and firepower of the tank would produce 'a new direction . . . that of the moving firing line; the knight in armour was once again reinstated, his horse now a petrol engine and his lance a machine gun.' He advocated that ' . . . weapons form 99 per cent of victory. Consequently the General Staff of every army should be composed of mechanical clairvoyants, seers of new conditions, new fields of war to exploit, and new tools in this exploitation.' Looking at other new weapons, he foresaw poison gas being used to obliterate all life on the frontiers, while aircraft attacked the centres of industry and government. [20]

Yet, in spite of Fuller's growing extremism, he was appointed as an instructor at the Staff College in 1922. This marked him for promotion into the higher ranks. Here he dedicated himself to getting the students to ponder on warfare of the future, as opposed to the past. He wanted to get his lectures published in book form, but was forbidden to do so by the then Chief of the Imperial General Staff (CIGS), Lord Cavan, whose policy was 'don't rock the boat'. Nevertheless Fuller had produced another book shortly before he went to Camberley. This was a much more wide-ranging work than his previous writings. Considering war as a whole he believed that tactics were of two types, 'grand', whose objective was to 'paralyse or disintegrate the enemy's command' as he had originally expounded in Plan 1919. This was achieved by surprise, envelopment, penetration and attrition. On the lower level there were the four acts of minor tactics, assembly, approach, attack and pursuit. He then examined how the new weapons of war fitted into this scheme. The problem was that: 'a novel weapon or means of warfare, like an unknown plague, fills the imagination of man with horror and intangible fear.' [21] He took gas as a prime example of this, and argued that gas could be an ideal weapon in that, besides ease of manufacture, secrecy and battlefield economy, it was humane in that incapacitants could be used rather than killing agents. Antidotes could be also developed and no permanent damage was done to property. In the same way the aeroplane, which might well replace armies and navies in the future, was also a humane weapon.

'If a future war can be won at the cost of two or three thousand of the enemy's men, women and children killed, in place of over 1 000 000 men and incidentally several thousands of women and children, as was the case in France during the recent war, surely an aerial attack is a more humane method than the existing traditional one?' [22]

Finally, Fuller returned to the war on land. He saw a requirement for two types of tank. The light tank, with a speed of 25mph, he paralleled to the battle cruiser or cavalry. When battle was joined these would attempt to turn the enemy's flanks, while medium tanks, heavily armoured and gunned, would destroy the enemy tank force and make a penetration. They would also be the artillery of the future. The infantry were to be relegated to being mere 'fortress troops', which signified that Fuller did agree that only infantry can occupy and hold ground successfully. He did, however, say that they could become an offensive weapon, provided they were motorised and armoured, i.e. they required armoured personnel carriers (APCs) as used by modern mechanised infantry. He concluded by stating that in order to improve military transport, artillery and infantry were to be mechanised in that order. This was not one of his better pieces of writing, although it is interesting how close he was to Douhet's way of thinking, even though he had not heard of Douhet at the time. There is evidence that Fuller himself was dissatisfied with this book, particularly with the line of argument, which was very muddled in places.

In practice, the Tank Corps was in desperate need of a tank of sufficient speed in order to try out new ideas on mobile warfare. A Medium D prototype had been tested in 1920 but, although its amphibious capabilities were impressive, it proved to be very unreliable. At the same time Colonel Johnson, its designer, had been called upon to design a light tank suitable for operations outside Europe. This underwent initial trials in September 1921, but again, in spite of showing some promise, proved very prone to mechanical breakdown. It was clear that, although Johnson showed imagination, his models required a lot more research in order to perfect them. Time costs money, and so in the meantime the War Office commissioned the firm of Vickers to produce a tank. It was of less ambitious design than Johnson's, but was more reliable. This became the Vickers Medium, which was to be the workhorse of the Tank Corps for the next fifteen years. It mounted a 47mm gun, but was very thinly armoured as well as having many other snags. It did, however, have a speed of 18mph, which was enough to start putting into practice some of the theories of mechanised warfare. As Liddell Hart said:

'The Vickers . . . became the practice instrument of a revolutionary development in tactics and strategy. It was the first fast tank that came into service, the first in any Army, and thus of prime value in stirring the imagination of soldiers by presenting a visible demonstration of armoured speed in action.' [23]

At the same time, the chassis of the Vickers medium was used to develop a self-propelled artillery piece, mounting an 18 pounder gun, thus partially satisfying Fuller's demands for mechanisation.

Fuller had been advocating since early 1919 for the formation of an experimental mechanised brigade, and the War Office had accepted his ideas in principle. A few halfhearted attempts were made, but little good came out of the trials. Meanwhile, as with the RAF, the Tank Corps (given the prefix 'Royal' in 1923 in recognition of its service on the Western Front) had to justify its existence by finding a role in defence of the Empire. For this purpose independent armoured car companies were formed, and by 1925 there were no less than eleven in existence and they had seen service in Germany, as part of the Occupation troops, Ireland, India and the Middle East. At the same time the ranks of the Corps were being swelled by officers from other arms, who saw in it a chance to be allowed to think to the future and to be given the necessary encouragement to do so, which was lacking in their own arms. Among these officers were Hobart, Lindsay and Broad, who would soon come to the forefront of the mechanisation crusade.

In 1926 Milne took over as CIGS. He chose Fuller to be his Military Assistant, and it seemed at last that the advocates of mechanisation had been vindicated. Even further confirmation in this belief had come when Sir Laming Worthington-Evans took over as Minister of War in 1925. He was on record as having stated as early as 1921 that 'the general view is that mechanical means of fighting must be developed to the fullest.' [24] One of Milne's first tasks, once he had assumed his appointment, was to question Fuller on his ideas for an experimental force, although his own views on the subject had been set out for him by General Campbell, the GOC Aldershot. While accepting that World War I had shown that the value of cavalry had greatly diminished, Milne and Campbell felt that the main problem lay in the fact that the infantry were too slow.

' . . . The most decisive battle of the whole war, that between the tanks of either side, will take place when the infantry is still far distant from the scene of action. Not to increase our tank force in order to keep infantry is, in my opinion a suicidal policy.' [25]

The result of this initial enthusiasm was that financial approval was given in March 1926 for a force to be organised, but it was to be a year before it materialised. Eventually a brigade size force was formed on Salisbury plain, consisting of a battalion of mixed armoured cars and machine-gun carriers, a tank battalion, and a mechanised machine-gun battalion with mechanised artillery and engineers. Fuller was selected to command this force, but resigned when he found that he was also expected to command a conventional infantry brigade and act as garrison commander at the same time, which he suspected would restrict his activities. A more conventionally minded infantryman took his place.

The trials carried out were important, not so much in giving impetus to the mechanisation of the Army, but more that out of them arose a divergence of ideas, even among the enthusiasts themselves, as to how mechanised forces should be employed. Milne, in a address to the senior officers of the force on September 8th, 1927, put forward the view that the 'armoured brigade' had been formed to 'revive the possibility of generalship' by means of increasing mobility on the battlefield. He believed that infantry and cavalry divisions would still exist in the future, but their transport would be mechanised and they would have mechanised units operating with them. There would, however, be armoured divisions, which would be kept separate for strategic purposes.

'A force of this description you can use as a swinging blow to come round the flank. It is an armoured force intended for long distance work. It may be necessary to employ it as an armoured force for close work, but essentially what I am aiming at is a mobile force that can go long distances and carry out big operations and turning movements . . . ' [26]

This lecture was given much publicity at the time, but did not represent the official War Office view. This was more clearly stated in the first British Army manual on the use of armour, *Tank and Armoured Car Training Volume II — War 1927 (Provisional)*.

This went halfway only in supporting Milne's concept. While accepting that 'the duty of tanks is to assist the other arms and at times to act independently of them', the manual did not see armoured forces being used strategically:

' . . . They represent a highly mobile, self-contained force of limited strength, particularly suited for undertaking tasks with a limited objective within the main plan, for the execution of which rapid and sustained movement is a primary consideration.'

Distant objectives were not possible because of the vulnerability of tanks to artillery fire, and the lack of adequate means of intercommunication between vehicles. The point was made, however, that armoured fighting vehicles (AFV's) were 'weapons of opportunity' and should not be tied down to 'close physical contact with cavalry or infantry.' But this was not the end to the watering down. Lt Col Charles Broad, a tank officer in charge of the War Office branch dealing with organisation for war, had drafted Milne's lecture. In November 1927 he spoke at the RUSI on the future organisation of an 'Armoured Force', Milne himself taking the chair. He added little further to what Milne had already said, yet at the end of the lecture Milne warned that he took no responsibility for Broad's remarks. He went on to say that 'we have to act cautiously, so as not to upset the traditions, the esprit de corps, and the feeling of the Army as a whole.' [27] The opposition this time was not so much from the cavalry, but from the infantry. The 1927 Mechanised Force had thrown the 3rd Division infantry into a dilemma. In the words of the Experimental Force commander, Collins 'whatever distances they covered on foot, the Mechanised Force could still apparently 'make rings round them' '. [28] This had led to a deterioration in morale and Burnett-Stuart, the 3rd Division commander, felt that something must be done about it. He therefore emphasised the shortcomings of the Force, especially as to its sensitivity to ground and the fact that only a small part of it had been armoured, thus making it vulnerable to small arms fire. At the annual Staff Conference, held at the Staff College in January 1928, Milne, although still sympathetic to the armour cause, stated that financial restrictions prevented any more than gradual progress, and that it would be many years before an armoured division would appear. This came as a shock to the progressive elements of the Army, who had hoped for Milne's continuing encouragement. In order to bolster the infantry, troop-carrying 6-wheelers were added to the Experimental Force for 1928, but nothing further was done to demonstrate the tactical or strategic potential of the Force. However, at a demonstration given to members of parliament the final assault of the tanks was supported by RAF aircraft in the ground-attack role.

The 1927 Manual had recognised the use of aircraft reconnaissance to support mechanised operations on the ground, and Army co-operation squadrons existed for this purpose. No other use of airpower was considered in conjunction with ground forces, because firstly, the RAF concentrating as they were on the Trenchard doctrine of bomber power, were not interested. Charles Broad illustrates the Air Ministry attitude:

'At about this time I accompanied a War Office party on a visit to an RAF practice camp . . . We asked 'if they could strafe ground targets'. This put them on their mettle, and we were allowed to suggest targets on which they put up a most convincing demonstration. A week or two later this was followed by a letter from the Air Ministry to the War Office, referring to this incident, requesting that Army officers should not encourage RAF officers to act contrary to Air Ministry policy.' [29]

The Army Council got their own back when they complained that the aircraft used in the 1928 manoeuvres of the Experimental Force made their low-flying attacks 'so excessively low . . . that the morale of the troops, especially the infantry was being shaken by those head-scraping and ear-splitting devices.' [30] This showed that the War Office also was not very enamoured by the idea of offensive ground support.

In 1927, appeared another book on the subject of mechanisation. This was Liddell Hart's *The Remaking of Modern Armies*. Liddell Hart had made a name for himself when just after the end of the War he had, as a young officer, rewritten the infantry training manual. Invalided out of the Army as a result of war wounds, he joined *The Daily Telegraph* soon becoming assistant military correspondent. He had first become interested in armoured warfare through the writings of Fuller, and in 1921, when he was invited to write an article for the *Encyclopeadia Britannica* on the theme of the infantry still being 'Queen of the Battlefield', he realised that he could not produce satisfactory arguments and stepped across to join Fuller in his crusade. His first major work on modern warfare had appeared in 1925 under the title *Paris, Or the Future of War*. He had, however, while rewriting the infantry training manual in 1920 already developed his idea of the 'Expanding Torrent'. In this he proposed that commanders at every level should ensure that their reserves were so placed as to support that part of their force which was having the most success in attack. He recognised that the German drives of 1918 had failed because this principle had not been maintained. *Paris* had criticised the strategical approach to World War I, that of the destruction of the enemy's armies, arguing instead for an aim of psychological dislocation. This could be achieved by a combination of two methods. Firstly, the enemy must feel threatened from more than one direction, thus throwing him into a dilemma as to how and where to position his forces. Secondly, his confusion must be aggravated by paralysing his communications and command centres. Fuller had expounded on this second method in *The Reformation of War* as a development of Plan 1919.

*The Remaking of Modern Armies* can be divided into two parts. In the first Liddell Hart looked at the implications of mechanisation. He saw that the effective role of the infantry was being fast eroded in the face of the theoretical potential of the tank. Like Fuller he believed that the place of the infantry on the battlefield could only be restored if it were mechanised. He criticised, however, the efforts being made to mechanise infantry transport without doing the same to the infantryman himself. As he said '. . . the sight of a string of fast cross-country motor vehicles crawling behind a 2-3mph column on foot is as painful anachronism as it is a pitiful waste of mobile vehicles.' [32] He argued instead for fully mechanised infantry taking much the same form as Fuller's 'land marines'. Artillery should be self-propelled in order to support adequately the tanks and mechanised infantry. This led him on to suggest that any expeditionary force of the future should be wholly mechanised. Tanks should not be regarded as an 'extra arm or mere aid to the infantry', but instead they

'. . . are the modern form of heavy cavalry, and their correct tactical use is clear — to be concentrated and used in as large masses as possible for decisive manoeuvre against the flanks and communications of the enemy, which have been fixed by the enemy — themselves mechanised — and artillery.' [33]

This was where Liddell Hart started to differ from Fuller. Fuller, as we have seen, saw infantry as mere followers up to the tanks, while Liddell Hart saw infantry operating as a force in their own right, threatening the enemy from a different direction. It was part of his theory of the 'Indirect Approach', which he had first raised in *Paris, Or the Future of War*. Fuller did not, unlike Liddell Hart, fully realise the increased flexibility which mechanised forces had, with regard to the effect on enemy morale. The second part of the book is taken up with this 'moral objective' as Liddell Hart called it. He criticised Clausewitz for believing that the destruction of the enemy's will came below that of the destruction of his military power and country as objectives in war.

'... His vital mistake was to place 'will' last in his list, instead of first and embracing all others, and to maintain that the destruction of the enemy's military power was essential to ensure the remaining objects.' [31]

Like Douhet, Trenchard and Fuller, he suggested that the air was perhaps the best means to destroy the enemy's will advocating simultaneous attacks on centres of civilian population.

In the same year another book was produced, which violently attacked Liddell Hart's and Fuller's ideas. V. W. Germains' *The Mechanisation of War* is instructive in that it does give reasoned and logical argument as opposed to the emotive arguments of many conservative officers. The foreword was written by no less a military expert than Sir Frederick Maurice, who launched a venomous attack on Fuller's thesis that war was a science and not an art. Germains argued that the tank had been no more than a 'useful if expensive' weapon on the Western Front. He made much of the fact that the most successful offensive, that of the Germans in March 1918, had been made with hardly any tanks. He believed that

'With armies in all countries PARED DOWN TO THE MINIMUM [sic] requirements of peace, it seems probable that a period of rapid manoeuvre fighting in the next war will be followed by a general stalemate, as in the last. Mobile columns of tanks and 'mechanised infantry' will neutralise one another; aircraft will bomb and counter-bomb, the result will be trench-war in which new weapons will mean new problems, such as at present no man can foresee.' [34]

He dismissed Liddell Hart's use of mechanised forces in the 'Indirect Approach':

'By skilful use of his railway-net and road net, and given vigilance against surprise, there can be no doubt but that a well-equipped defender can always anticipate attack by a relatively slow cross-country mechanical attack.' [35]

He thought that the mechanisation enthusiasts fell into the pitfall of assuming that the enemy would not be so placed. He also felt that there was

44

too much emphasis on speed, and not enough on 'fighting' and 'staying power'. To him the latter was most important as he did not believe that a future European war would be short. To Liddell Hart's suggestion that a future BEF should be mechanised he expressed doubts on financial grounds. Because the next war would be long it was necessary to support any BEF with a large 'national army'. No government could afford to mechanise such an army in peacetime, but for it to be effective it must be organised 'more or less upon present day lines.' The danger lay in money being spent on mechanising the BEF at the expense of the reserves. If this were the case then ' . . . mechanisation is a game not worth the candle. There will be no real punch behind our mechanisation.' [36]

The debate had now shifted from merely one on the employment of the tank. Mechanisation was being looked at for its wider implications on national defence as a whole. In 1929, as a result of the 1927 and 1928 trials, a new pamphlet was produced. *Mechanised and Armoured Formations 1929 (Provisional)* was more than an instruction on the tactical employment of tanks. It was an attempt to examine the employment of mechanised forces as a whole. Its foreword is interesting in that it produced an irrefutable argument for the mechanisation of the Army as a whole:

'During the past decade mechanisation has been rapidly on the increase in all walks of life. The army in its general form must be modelled on civil life and, consequently, must also mechanise gradually.' [36]

It is indicative that the proponents of a permanent United States Army mechanised force should have used the same argument at the same time.*
The 'Purple Primer', as it was called from the colour of its cover, was a brave attempt to give encouragement to progressive thought at a time when the military hierarchy were beginning, in the light of economic difficulties, to have second thoughts about giving too much encouragement to mechanisation. Liddell Hart criticised the 'Purple Primer' for not going far enough.

'I would have liked to see the new manual deal more fully with the strategic potentiality of armoured forces for a long-range thrust into the enemy's rear, to cut his communications and arteries of supply.' [37]

He also criticised the lack of consideration given to air/ground co-operation, the use of tanks at night and, more importantly the disregard of infantry being part of an armoured force. The absence of air support has already been explained in the words of Charles Broad, the author of the 'Purple Primer'. The problem of night operations was purely technical.

The question of inclusion of infantry in armoured formations was more controversial. On the one hand, the trials of 1927-8 had shown that infantry in its present form, even with motorised transport, could not keep up with

*See page 53.

the tanks. Yet the infantry themselves appeared unwilling to become 'tank marines' for fear that they might be swallowed up by the Royal Tank Corps. There was too the financial consideration, in that money did not exist to mechanise the Army as a whole. To use unarmoured lorries, which would have a sales potential on the civilian market was one thing, but to design and produce an armoured infantry carrier with no civilian sales prospects was an expensive exercise and unacceptable with the very limited defence funds available. Broad had to work within the guidelines of the General Staff, who had laid down that the tank had two roles, one being strategic, the timely attack on the flanks or rear of the enemy, and the other strictly tactical, the close support of cavalry or infantry. Hence he described two types of brigade, the armoured brigade, which included self-propelled artillery, and an infantry brigade, having machine gun carriers and a battalion of light tanks. He was taking care not be be accused of trying to form an 'all tank' army. Yet behind the scenes he suggested to Milne that an armoured corps should be formed from ten cavalry regiments, two infantry battalions and the four existing tank battalions. It was an attempt to ' . . . turn selected but representative parts of the Army into a *corps d'elite*, equipped with the most modern weapons and thinking progressively instead of dragging its feet, held back by progressive laggards'. [38] Needless to say, the suggestion was not taken up. The 'Purple Primer' did however contain much of both Fuller and Liddell Hart. Liddell Hart's 'moral objective' was emphasised:

'A hostile commander will be embarrassed by the fact that any point within 100 miles of an armoured formation is liable to attack by it.'

and:

'The moral and material effect of AFV's on other arms is great. They can, in fact, render immobile, by threat alone, such infantry formations as are unsuitably equipped.'

Like Fuller, the manual pointed out that tanks had good protection against air and gas attack, and highlighted the need for different types of tank for reconnaissance, infantry support and shock action.

One would have thought that the apostles of mechanisation had won their fight and that mechanisation would now proceed. Unfortunately this was not to be. Two months after the publication of the 'Purple Primer'* a Labour Government took office. Its pacifist idealism combined with the economic slump killed any progress in mechanisation for the time being. First to suffer was the Royal Tank Corps itself. Colonel Lindsay, in his position as Inspector of the RTC, highlighted it in a memorandum of May 1929:

---

*Significantly the Germans managed to obtain a copy of the 'Purple Primer', sold to them by a Captain Baillie Stuart, who was imprisoned in the Tower of London.

'We have not got one single tank of any description that is fit for war . . . Therefore the first thing we must do is to re-arm the Royal Tank Corps throughout, otherwise we may be caught a few years hence with our present tanks, and the whole idea wrecked through complete failure of our equipment. In addition we shall never progress in design unless we continue to issue to Service Battalions each year a certain number of tanks of the latest design.' [39]

The main problem was finance. During the 1920's there were only enough funds to design one new tank per year, and never enough models to allow soldiers to test them. Also the firm of Vickers had a monopoly in tank design, and what they produced was implicitly accepted by the War Office. Vickers had introduced a 16-ton tank in 1928 to replace the Medium, but the depression put a stop to this being introduced into service. During the early thirties tank production concentrated on light tanks, firstly because they were cheaper, and secondly because Carden, the chief tank designer at Vickers, was a believer in speed as opposed to firepower. Although this policy would suffice for the experiments in the handling of armoured formations, which would take place in the early part of the thirties, it would mean that Britain would enter the war in 1939 with few suitable tanks for inclusion in these formations.

## The United States

American military thought in the 1920's and 1930's was much influenced by the American policy of isolationism. The participation of the United States in World War I had led its President, Wilson, to hope that America would now be prepared to take her place as a world power and concern herself with the affairs of the world as a whole. It had been Wilson's Fourteen Points which had provided the basis for the Treaty of Versailles, and it had been Wilson himself who had laboured hard to set up the League of Nations as an instrument to prevent future conflict. Unfortunately in March 1920 the United States Senate refused to ratify the Treaty of Versailles since it did not wish any further commitment in Europe, thereby rejecting American participation in the League of Nations. Yet, in spite of this introverted behaviour, America was interested in preventing war in the future, but this had to be without commitment to Europe. Thus in July 1921 President Harding invited all former Allies to Washington for a disarmament conference, which resulted in the Washington Naval Treaty of 1922, restricting the size of navies and individual ships. Meanwhile, the vast majority of Americans were not interested in defence and merely wanted to continue the expansion of the American economy.

In November 1918 the American Tank Corps had, in existence or planned for, some fifteen tank brigades, each of a heavy battalion of British Mark VIII's and two light battalions of French Renaults. It had had its successes on the Western Front and there seemed no reason why it should not find itself established as a permanent arm in its own right. Brigadier-General Rockenbach, who had commanded the Tank Corps in France, became the commander of the Corps as a whole and set up his headquarters at Fort Meade, Maryland. He was clear what he himself wanted — two brigades of heavy tanks, one independent light battalion and a light battalion for each division. He accepted that Mark VIII's and Renaults would have to continue to be used for the time being, but laid down his specifications for a new tank:

> 'Not over 18ft long, not over 18tons in weight, 10HP per ton of weight. The ground pressure not over 9lbs, the same as that of a man, to be armed with a cannon of caliber of less than 6pdr, or over 3-in and 2 machine guns . . . with smoke device for offensive and defensive use. Speed to vary from one mile per hour up to twelve crossing country. Special attention to be devoted to improving of visibility.' [40]

Unfortunately Rockenbach never made it clear as to how he saw tanks being employed in the future. He was given plenty of opportunity, yet in a lecture entitled *The Tank Corps* given to the General Staff College in October 1919 he could only say vaguely that:

> '1. All that is claimed for the Tank Corps is that it is not fettered by English ideas in operation . . . nor by French low mechanical knowledge . . . nor by our own abnormal use of Tanks with the First American Army [in driblets and in close infantry support]. It has resisted entangling alliances and to date is not Infantry, Artillery, Motor Transport, Engineers or even Aviation, notwithstanding its great value to each of these services, causing deep thought as to which of them it should be.
> 2. Ludendorff's ignorance of Tanks caused the death of many German soldiers and the stampede of many more. [But] he is correct in stating that tanks should be used in masses or not at all . . . ' [41]

This attitude must have been discouraging to his subordinates. Patton, who was commanding the 304th Tank Brigade at this time, was quite clear that the Tank Corps must be kept as a separate arm:

> 'The tank is new and for the fulfillment of its destiny, it must remain independent. Not desiring or attempting to supplant infantry, cavalry, or artillery, it has no appetite to be absorbed by any of them . . . Absorbed . . . we become the stepchild of that arm and the incompetent assistant of either of the others . . . ' [42]

Yet, even he at this stage lacked the vision of Fuller, failing, although doubtless he must have heard of it, to foresee the potential of Plan 1919. He did, however, avidly read Fuller's *Tanks in The Great War* when it was published in 1920, but commented that Fuller had elaborated his ideas to:

> ' . . . doubtless a possible but at present impractical extent, because Nations of such sufficient wealth and resources to provide such mechanic

armies are by the very nature of their wealth those nations [which] are incapable of looking on war in a serious manner and are willing to devote to it only their minimum effort.' [43]

In the event, the Dickman Board, concluded that:

'Important as has been the effect of these mechanical developments and special services, their true value has been as auxiliaries to the Infantry. Nothing in this war has changed the fact that it is now, as always heretofore, the Infantry with rifle and bayonet that, in the final analysis must bear the brunt of the assault and carry it on to victory.' [44]

Because of Rockenbach's failure to produce any idea of an independent role for the tank the Dickman Board could go only on the employment of American tanks on the Western Front, which had been purely as infantry support. The result was that the National Defense Act of 1920 scrapped the Tank Corps and placed all tanks under the Infantry. Those operating tanks would bear the designation of 'Infantry (Tanks)'. It is interesting to note that the Chemical Warfare Service, formed because of the employment of gas on the Western Front, and the Air Service, which had been part of the Signal Corps, both retained their status as separate arms. It has been suggested (45) that the Tank Corps only failed to retain its separate identity because Rockenbach was not a graduate of West Point, whereas the head of the Chemical Warfare Service was. It is more likely that it was because of Rockenbach's inability to put forward any role for the tank other than infantry support.

Although the tanks had now been made part of the Infantry the General Staff would not commit themselves on the tactical requirements for them. It was only after pressure by the Ordnance Board, who were responsivle for design and development, did the General Staff finally confirm in April 1922 that: 'the primary mission of the tank is to facilitate the uninterrupted advance of the rifleman in the attack.' [46] In the same year the Chief of Infantry did mention that tanks might be used in a breakthrough, but added that 'speed, a large cruising radius and an adequate supply of ammunition are essential to such a mission.' [47] The Mark VIII's and Renaults of the time did not possess either of the first two qualities. As if to confirm this, the Field Service Regulations of 1923 disparagingly said that 'motor transportation finds limited tactical employment in the use of tanks and cross-country tractors.' The reaction of many of the wartime officers of the Tank Corps was to revert to their original branches of the service. Although officers like Eisenhower and Patton fully realised the potential of the tank they felt there was little hope in making headway in a small specialist part of a larger branch, especially as they had had to drop many grades from their wartime ranks. Both, now back in the infantry and cavalry respectively, continued to champion the cause of the tank for a time in the service journals of the day. But, according to Eisenhower: 'The doctrine was so revolutionary as compared with World War I practice, that we were threatened with court-martial.' [48] Hence both were forced to remain silent and show more loyalty to their parent branches.

Besides Rockenbach's failure to give the necessary lead to his officers, and their own disillusionment, there was another reason for the apparent stagnation in thought on mechanised warfare during the major part of the 1920's. Until the National Defense Act of 1920 came into being there had been in existence the Tank Board, which had been the major formulator of tank policy and the sounding-board for new ideas. On the disbandment of the Tank Corps, the Board lay in abeyance until late 1924 when it was reconstituted with four members. Its mission appeared encouraging: ' . . . to keep abreast of mechanical improvements, co-operate with the ordnance and other arms and branches of the service in matters of mutual interest to them and the Tank School, and to facilitate tank development.' [49] Unfortunately the members of the Board were only detailed part-time and were unable to devote enough energy to make it an effective mouthpiece. It was not until 1928 that three officers were made full-time members. In the meantime the tank organisation was fixed at two heavy tank regiments equipped with a mixture of Mark VIII's and Renaults, and some divisional light tank companies — a watered down version of Rockenbach's demands. The official infantry doctrine divided tanks into two types similar to the French concept of the *chars d'accompagnment*, which accompanied the infantry, and the *chars de manoeuvre ensemble*, which were more powerful tanks designed to operate on the line of effort of larger infantry formations in the breakthrough. For this concept the Renaults were employed in the former role and the Mark VIII's in the latter. There was flirtation with the idea of a medium tank to cover both roles, and prototypes were built in the early 1920's, but these were found to be far heavier than originally stipulated and too costly for the slender tank budget of the time. Hence the infantry became firmly committed to the light tank in the accompanying role and continued to envisage its use against the sole backcloth of the trench-bound deadlock of 1914-1918.

Yet, in spite of all these obstacles, the service journals of the time did contain much debate on the employment of tanks, and it is through these that we can get a very good idea as to the ideas that lay behind the development of the first American experimental mechanised force. At the start, some officers who were still prepared to speak out could point to the successes of the Allied tanks in 1918, especially the British penetration of the seemingly impregnable Hindenburg Line, as a basis on which to build a mechanised force. The typical infantry rebuff to this was that 'it was not the British tank that broke the Hindenburg Line, but the British bayonet in the hands of a soldier threatening the foe man to man.' [50] On no account were the tanks going to be given the chance to assume a *prima donna* role and thus threaten the infantry's rightful position as 'Queen of the Battlefield', as had happened in Britain.

Although Fuller's and Liddell Hart's ideas might appear heretical to the military establishment, their articles were published in these service journals. There were also detailed reports in these journals on the early British experiments with mechanised forces, which were attended by American officers. Thus the *Infantry Journal* of January 1926 carried a detailed report on the British manoeuvres of 1925, which saw the Vickers Medium being put through its paces. While noting that this tank would lose its mobility if employed with infantry, the report concluded that it should form the basis of a highly mobile force' . . . to be held in reserve and then moved rapidly forward to support threatened points or to overcome unexpected resistance; to take part in flanking movements as support for other mobile troops, and to operate with the advance and rear-guards.' The report is indicative of the thinking of the time. Although the writer was clear that this tank could not be tied to the apron strings of the infantry he was not prepared to follow his deductions through to the logical conclusion of allowing formations of this type of tank a more independent role. American officers still regarded the tank as very much an auxiliary weapon. Significantly a US cavalryman present at the same manoeuvres even went so far as to suggest that, while admitting that the tank was a vaulable aid to cavalry, ' . . . because of the development in the air' cavalry were becoming even more important. [51]

Yet it was from the unlikely source of the US Cavalry that the first homegrown considerations for a fully mechanised force appeared. Although the US Cavalry had seen very little actual combat on the Western Front, the Dickman Board concluded that the experience of 1917-18 had 'furnished but few reasons for change in our doctrine for the strategic employment of cavalry.' The roles of the US Cavalry at the time included the defeat of enemy cavalry, breaking up the enemy's communications, flank and rearguards, pursuit, harrassment and reconnaissance. The Board was, however, careful to add that it was 'improbable that the conditions of Northern France' would be reproduced in the United States. [52] Thus the cavalry were happy and able to turn the clock back to 1916 when they had shown their worth in Pershing's Mexican expedition. They could even afford to adopt a somewhat bumptious air:

'There is no doubt that some positions of the Germans on the Western Front, the taking of which cost us many casualties, could have been taken in a comparatively brief time and with comparatively small losses with a sudden launched cavalry attack supported by the fire of artillery and machine guns.' [53]

As one senior cavalryman was moved to write.

As with the British Cavalry, the American Cavalry's hero at this time was Allenby, who had employed large numbers of horsemen in his highly successful campaign against the Turks in Palestine. But, in an open letter to the *Cavalry Journal*, which was published in January 1922, he pointed out, although reassuring as to the future of the horse on the battlefield, that 'cavalry enterprise is aided, too, by mechanical means of transport — lorries, tanks, armoured cars — assuring supply, while fighting cars and swiftly moving tanks can work in co-operation with cavalry and horse artillery over any ground.' [54] He had used these techniques in Palestine with success, but the conditions in this theatre were very different to those on the Western Front. Allenby's letter did provide the necessary encouragement for the more progressively minded officers to air their views in print. In July of the same year the *Cavalry Journal* published an article by Major Bradford E. Cheynworth, Infantry (Tanks) which propagated the idea of investigating the possibilities of a 'cavalry' tank. He diplomatically commenced his thesis by saying that 'one need not saw back in fear that the tank will replace the horse. On the contrary it is likely to enhance the value of the horseman as it has strengthened the infantryman on foot.' [55] He then suggested that cavalry was only effective against hasty and disorganised defence, and he felt that tanks would be of great assistance if the cavalry came up against prepared infantry positions. In the same issue, Patton, in his final blow for some time on behalf of the tank, went further in arguing for the reformation of the Tank Corps as a separate branch [56]. This was, of course, out of the question since it was in direct contradiction to the law of the land.

These articles produced an outcry from the more conservative ranks of the cavalry. Although ready to concede that perhaps tanks could support cavalry as well as infantry, they were, like their British counterparts, panic-stricken by the thought that one day the petrol engine might replace the horse. Much of their argument rested on the fact that, in comparison with the horse, the tank could only operate successfully on certain types of terrain. The national policy of isolationism meant that it was unlikely that the US Army would find itself again involved in a European fracas. More likely would it be involved in the Pacific or the southern half of the American Continent, where terrain was, to a large extent more suited to the horse. Allied to this argument was that of the logistical problems more inherent in a tank than in a horse. As Patton later (1929) succinctly put it: 'An unfed motor stops; a starved horse takes days to die.' [57] However, in spite of this opposition, the decision was taken in 1927 to attach an air corps observation squadron, a tank unit and an armoured car unit to each cavalry division. A platoon of Renaults from the 2nd Tank Company took part in the 1st Cavalry Division manoeuvres of that year. Their slow speed meant that they were of little value on their own and so, in order to make use of them, they were carried in lorries (portéed) and offloaded when required to come into action. The conclusion from this experiment was that a tank with a road speed of 18mph and a cross-country speed of 12mph would be a ' . . . valuable adjunct to the cavalry.' [58]

The same year produced a more radical development. The Secretary for War, Dwight F. Davies, visited Britain, and while over there had the opportunity to witness part of the trials of the British 1927 Experimental Mechanised Force. So impressed was he that on his return to the States he directed that a similar force should be formed. This came into being at Fort Leonard Wood (Camp Meade), Maryland, in July 1928. The War Department instructions to the Commanding General, Third Corps, in whose area of responsibility Fort Leonard Wood lay, directed that the force

' . . . should not be considered as a divisional unit but rather, because of its special characteristics, as a force of special mission in the accompaniment of which troops of infantry or cavalry divisions will co-operate.' [59]

It was emphasised that the tank was the basis of this force and that ' . . . the Tactics of the force as a whole shall be predicated upon supporting and assisting the attack of the tank elements, and upon the quick consolidation and securing or exploiting the success in the tank attack.' For the first time the tank was being considered as a supported, as opposed to supporting, arm. The rub was that, while the members of the force were enjoined to ' . . . be imbued with the spirit of the utilisation of speed which modern equipment will afford', speed was what their hardly modern equipment most lacked. The two tank battalions involved were still equipped with Mark VIII's and Renaults, although four M1's, experimental 21 tonners with a top speed of 14mph, were attached to the force.

Because of its obsolete equipment the Force was not an immediate success. But the three month trial, after which the Force was disbanded, had sown the seed. It so happened that the officer in the G-3 Branch* of the War Department who had been given the task of covering the trial was a cavalryman, Major Adna B. Chaffee. He became very enthusiastic with the concept of a mechanised force and strongly advocated the introduction of such a force into service on a permanent basis. He was supported in this by the War Department Mechanised Development Board, who had also watched the experiment closely. In the same way as Broad in the 'Purple Primer', they argued that ' . . . in the commercial world the machine has largely replaced manpower; so in the Army must we, to the fullest practicable degree, use machines in place of manpower in order that our manpower can occupy and 'hold' without terrific losses incident to modern firepower.' [60] Summerall, the Chief of Staff, was converted, and one of his last acts before leaving office in October 1930 was to give the order: 'Assemble that mechanised force now, station it at Fort Eustis, Virginia. Make it permanent, not temporary.' [61]

In the meantime the infantry saw themselves getting left out of the drive towards mechanisation, and in 1929 the 34th Infantry conducted motorisation trials. In the next year General Fuqua, the Chief of Infantry, in an address to the Army War College, made it quite clear as to which arm was going to be dominant on the battlefield in the future:

' . . . Let me say to those who see the Infantry no longer our basic force on the battlefield of the future, that it is now our basic arm, that, the very weapons and methods — motorisation, chemical agencies, automatic and machine weapons, and armed armoured track vehicles — that some claim will replace infantry, will be used by infantry to perform missions of gaining and holding ground.' [62]

*Equivalent to the British Operations Branch.

In the same year he was able to report to the Military Affairs Committee of the House of Representatives that out of 1 000 Renaults and 100 Mark VIII's left to the Army in 1918, 947 and 94 respectively were still serviceable. This determination that the infantry should retain control of the tanks and the unwillingness of politicians to allow adequate funds to introduce more modern AFV's into service in view of the large stocks of obsolete models still serviceable would result in a stormy passage for Summerall's legacy.

**France**
France entered the decade of the 1920s conscious that her manpower had been bled white during the years 1914-18. In spite of this her army had survived, albeit having come close to disaster with the mutinies of 1917. It was an army which had been forced to throw away all pre-war doctrine in the opening months of the war. Instead of making its name with *élan* in attack, doggedness in defence, as symbolised by Verdun, had become its sterling quality. This was to influence French military thought throughout the years 1919-1939. Two other factors contributed to the paucity of thought in the French Army. Firstly, throughout the 1920s Pétain was President of the Army Council (supreme commander) and even when he retired in 1930 his influence continued to be felt as that of Trenchard would influence the RAF. Pétain had made his name in defence. Secondly, the heavy officer casualties of the War had thrown up many mediocre officers in positions of high command. These officers would have never succeeded in the Army of 1914. This encouraged '. . . a new type of professional soldier . . . pliant and conformist, unwilling to risk the future by meddling with new ideas.' [63]

Yet this is not to say that there was no attempt to draw different conclusions from 1914-1918. General Estienne, the founder of the French tank force, did speak out in favour of mechanisation throughout this period. He, like Fuller, saw in the tank the means of pushing the pendulum back towards the offensive. At the beginning of 1920, in a lecture to junior officers in Paris, he was advocating the formation of an armoured force whose eventual composition would be no less than 100 000 men, 4 000 tanks and 8 000 trucks with the capability of being able to advance 50 miles in a day or night. He had also seen the value of close air support as provided by the 1st Air Division in 1918. Unfortunately both Estienne and his compatriots in the Air Force were left out in the cold when it came to drawing up the military tactical concepts for the 1920s. The committee under Pétain responsible for this task did not include a single tank officer or aviator. When the findings of the Committee were published in October 1921 under the title of *Provisional Regulations for the Tactical Handling of Formations* it became clear that no effort had been made to extrapolate beyond 1918. Indeed, much had been based on Pétain's pamphlet the *bouquin rouge*, which had been issued to the French Army after the 1917 mutinies. This had emphasised the power of the defensive and had laid stress on the idea that attacks should be against limited objectives. Regrettably Pétain seemed to have forgotten the success achieved by his concept of mobile defence in the summer of 1918. However, in his favour were two factors which influenced his thinking. Firstly, no-one in France wanted her to suffer as she had done during the Great War. There was a widespread belief that this could only be done by fighting outside the French frontier. Secondly, much of France's industrial base was situated near the frontier, particularly in the north-east. This precluded the use of mobile defence within borders if France's industry was to be kept intact. Hence Pétain was drawn towards the idea of a solid defensive line along the French frontier. He did not foresee a counter-attack being launched until the enemy had worn himself out against this line. It would also take time for sufficient material to be assembled in order to guarantee the success of this counter stroke. He was convinced that victory in 1918 had come only as a result of the limited objective attack supported by the maximum possible fire. In the end the infantry would still be the 'Queen of the Battlefield' and everything else would be placed to support the infantryman onto his objective. Hence the tank, as in the American Army, was placed strictly under the infantry. Tanks ' . . . increase the offensive power of the infantry by facilitating its advance into combat', as the *Instructions* put it.

It was in these *Instructions* that the foundation of the Maginot Line lay. At first there was disagreement with Pétain's concept of the single unbroken line. A commission set up under Joffre to study the problem of frontier defences recommended a system of separate fortified areas at intervals between the North Sea and the Swiss border, between and around which a mobile and aggressive army could mount an offensive at the right time and in the most favourable circumstances. This was more in keeping with the idea of the mobile defence, but after a time Joffre resigned and his place was taken by General Guillaumat, a Pétain supporter. Thus the idea of the single line went ahead, although it was appreciated that for political reasons the line could only cover the Franco-German border. At the beginning of 1928 work started on two experimental sites, but it was not until André Maginot became Minister of War in November 1929 that work began in earnest.

Significantly an early supporter of the Maginot concept was a junior officer, one Charles de Gaulle, a protegé of Pétain. After two years fighting on the Western Front de Gaulle had been captured and spent the last two years of the war as a prisoner of war of the Germans. After a tour with the French Military Mission in Poland during the time of the Bolshevik invasion, he became a history instructor at the French military academy, St Cyr. Pétain had been his commanding officer prior to and at the beginning of the war. He attended the Army Staff College in 1922 and, although he made a name for himself as an original thinker and speaker, he was not the prophet of armour that he was to become in the 1930s. Two of his fellow students, Chauvin and Cailloux, were tank enthusiasts, who believed that the tank should be used in an independent strategic role, but de Gaulle does not seem to have been fired by them. He had had no practical experience of tanks himself, and regarded them merely as objects for further research and development. He had hoped to stay on as an instructor, but this was not to be and after a period on the staff he was assigned to the command of an infantry battalion. Throughout this time he and Pétain remained in close touch. During the decade of the twenties de Gaulle was more concerned with the abstract than tactical or strategic concepts. Subjects like high command, leadership and morale occupied him more than the practical mechanics of warfare, and, whether he was speaking or writing, he always held Pétain up as the shining example of how military affairs should be conducted. He did this to an extent that many regarded him as Pétain's mouthpiece.

Meanwhile, Estienne continued his struggles to get the tank recognised as a weapon in its own right. The French Army was left with a legacy of 3000 Renault Light Tanks at the end of the war. These were to provide the bulk of the French tank force throughout the period between the wars. Estienne drew up designs for a medium tank in 1921 and a prototype mounting a 75mm gun was produced some five years later. However, scarcity of money, most of which was devoted to the construction of the Maginot Line, and lack of official doctrine and interest, held up its coming into service as the Char B for another ten years. In the meantime steps were taken to introduce more motorisation into the Army. An experimental light infantry division was set up in the early 1920s consisting of nine battalions of motorised infantry supported by tractor drawn artillery. The number of armoured cars in the cavalry divisions rose from 18 to 36 in 1923 and by the end of the decade one of the three horse brigades had been motorised as a regiment of truck-borne *Dragons Portés*. To the dedicated tank man this was small solace. Colonel Lindsay summed up these attempts as providing a force which was ' . . . merely mounted infantry, merely something moved quickly by modern means to some point where it can fight in the old-fashioned manner.' [64]

The French, like the Americans, considered their air force as part of the army throughout the 1920s. Again, they believed that reconnaissance was the prime task. Although they used air power in North Africa and Syria during this period, little was done to provide offensive support to the ground forces, aircraft being used mainly for logistical tasks such as transport and casualty evacuation.

## Germany

The fortunes of the German Army in the 1920s were largely bound up in one man, General Hans von Seeckt. As head of the *Truppenamt*, or 'Troop Office' in the Ministry of War during the period 1919-1926, he was responsible for salvaging something from the damage wreaked by the terms of Versailles. He had been a staff officer for most of his career, and during World War I he had held varied such appointments. After spending the first year of the war as chief of staff to a corps on the Western Front he had then been transferred to the East, occupying successively the positions of chief of staff to Mackensen's 11th Army, chief of staff to the Austrian Archduke Carl and, finally, chief of staff to the Turkish Army in the field. Thus most of his experience had been away from the static conditions of the

Western Front. This undoubtedly influenced General von Seeckt's thinking.

The Versailles terms had put von Seeckt in an awkward position. He had hoped that the Allies would allow Germany to retain an army of at least 300 000 men. In fact, the French wanted a 200 000 man army, but as a short-term conscript army in order to prevent it becoming a refuge for the hard core of the Imperial German Army. The British argued that if the army was a conscript one it would mean that the entire German manhood could be trained for war, and proposed a long service army instead. In the event, the British got their way and the 100 000 man long service army came into being officially at the end of March 1920. Von Seeckt believed that Germany still faced a threat on two fronts, from Poland in the east and France in the west. His small army was incapable of dealing with both these two threats, and hence he had to think of some way round the problem. His solution was to accept the fact that the army, as it stood, was incapable of defending Germany, and that it should be regarded as a skeleton, which in time of trouble could have sufficient meat grafted onto it. Hence was born the idea of the *Fuhrerarmee*. Private soldiers were trained to act as NCOs, NCOs as officers and junior officers to fill the higher ranks. Each company, battery or squadron was given the traditions of a regiment from the old Imperial Army. This had the dual result of maintaining morale and preparing the way for rapid expansion. In effect the Reichswehr, as the army was called, became a cadre for a mass army.

As regards tactical doctrine, von Seeckt carried with him his experiences of the relatively more mobile warfare of the Eastern Front. He felt that mobility was the only way to offset his current lack of numbers. Although the terms of Versailles were stringent with respect to numbers of vehicles allowed in the Reichswehr, motorised infantry were exercising in the Harz Mountains as early as 1921 using requisitioned civilian lorries. Von Seeckt saw the Reichswehr as being specifically the core of a mobile shock force. The *Truppenamt* believed that the German army had been unable to win the war because they had failed to interfere with the French mobilisation, failed to prevent French re-deployment and failed to recognise the limitations of infantry on their feet and horsedrawn transport. The army had been unable to react quickly enough to produce a decisive blow. Thus many believed that mobility would be the dominant factor in the next war. Some did tend towards the French idea of the domination of firepower, but they were in a minority. Von Seeckt did not follow Douhet's hypothesis that air power was all prevailing, but he did appreciate the usefulness of an air force. In a future war the air battle would be the first phase. An air force would have the twin tasks of knocking out the opponent's air force and disrupting his mobilisation. The air battle would be followed up by professional armies, while defence forces would be mobilised to guard the homeland base.

'In a few words then, the whole future of warfare appears to me to lie in the employment of mobile armies, relatively small but of high quality and rendered distinctly more effective by the addition of aircraft, and in the simultaneous mobilisation of the whole defence force, be it to feed the attack or for home defence.' [65]

He saw the peacetime army acting as a 'cover' or shield to protect mobilisation in much the same way that the French had begun to look on the Maginot Line. He believed that emphasis in training must lie in technical aspects and mobility and felt that a small army did have advantages in that it was less expensive to equip with new weapons than a large one.

Von Seeckt showed an interest in mechanisation, especially in tanks. Certainly by the mid 1920s the professional military magazine *Militar Wochenblatt* carried a monthly supplement *Der Kampfwagen* ('The Tank') which contained articles on the employment and equipment of tanks, and posed tactical problems concerning their handling. It so happened that on the staff of the *Truppenamt*, in the Inspectorate of Transport Troops worked a young officer, Captain Heinz Guderian. By the mid 1920s he had become a tank enthusiast, reading everything he could on the subject, particularly the books of Liddell Hart and Fuller. He had also witnessed the French use of tanks and aircraft at Soissons in August 1918, which had left a deep impression on him. By 1928 he had become an acknowledged expert and was instructing on tank tactics. In this same year experimental exercises were carried out using dummy tanks, civilian cars with canvas or sheet metal frames. By the end of the 1920s he had clarified his thoughts:

'In this year, 1929, I became convinced that tanks working on their own or in conjunction with infantry could never achieve decisive importance. My historical studies, the exercises carried out in England and our own experiments with mock-ups had persuaded me that tanks would never be able to produce their full effect until the other weapons on whose support they must inevitably rely were brought up to their standard of speed and cross-country performance. In such a formation of all arms, the tanks must play the primary role, the other weapons being subordinated to the requirements of the armour. It would be wrong to include tanks in infantry divisions: what was needed were armoured divisions which would include all the supporting arms needed to allow the tanks to fight with full effect.' [66]

So the idea of the panzer division was born, and in the summer of 1929 use was made of an imaginary such division on exercise. This was long after von Seeckt's demise from office. He himself, although grasping the fundamental element of the blitzkrieg concept, never saw in the tank the potential that Guderian did. For instance, perhaps coloured by the fact that Versailles had laid down that the Reichswehr should consist of seven infantry and three horse cavalry divisions, he believed that there was still a role for cavalry on the battlefield of the future. He thought that it would be a very long time before mechanisation as opposed to motorisation was advanced enough to influence the battle and hence, like so many others, was not prepared to look deeply enough into the crystal ball. 'He certainly played

58

with it, turned it over in his hands once or twice and looked at it closely; but he laid it down, although still with an open mind.' [67]

Yet, although von Seeckt may not have seen the tank as the ideal ingredient for his war of the future, he undoubtedly laid the foundations for the German Blitzkrieg machine. Perhaps his most significant contribution to this was the setting up of the secret agreement with Russia, whereby German officers were able to gain 'hands on' experience of modern equipment denied to them by Versailles. By the beginning of 1920 von Seeckt became convinced that Germany and Russia, the two outcasts of Europe could help one another. Indeed, both had a common loathing for the newly independent state of Poland. There is much evidence that the new Bolshevik state, still in the grips of civil war felt the same way as von Seeckt, particularly with a view of enlisting help in restoring the Russian armaments industry, which war had reduced to tatters. By the end of 1922 agreement had been reached. [68] The Weimar Republic would set up factories in the Soviet Union and supervise the manufacture of aircraft, submarines, guns and ammunition. In return the Russians agreed to allow the Germans to set up training grounds at Lipetsk for flying, a poison gas school and factory at Samara, and later a tank training centre in Kazan. These were set up from 1924 onwards, and German officers were smuggled into Russia in order to train there. It was in the realm of flying that the greatest value was gained. Von Seeckt, although no Douhet or Trenchard, did believe that the air force should be a separate independent service, and had established a small air section under a Captain Wilburg in the *Reichswehrministerium*. In addition some 180 experienced pilots had been distributed throughout the Reichswehr in order to spread knowledge on air matters. Article 201 of the Versailles Treaty had specifically forbidden the manufacture of aircraft, but this was relaxed in 1922 when the Allies agreed that Germany might manufacture civil aircraft of limited performance in terms of speed, range, ceiling and payload. Von Seeckt decided that he could build the basis of an air force through civil aviation and by the time he had finished in office all German civil aviation was concentrated under Lufthansa, whose head, Erhard Milch, was appointed by von Seeckt and would become one of the prime architects of the Luftwaffe of the 1930s. It also provided the necessary boost to the aviation industry. The firms of Messerschmidt, Junkers, Dornier and Heinkel became well established and were also able to design, build and test combat aircraft in Russia. Lipetsk itself was set up in 1925, and between then and 1933 some 120 officers, including Student, Kesselring, Stumpff and Sperrle, who were to become household names within a few years, underwent fighter training alone. In addition, tactical flying exercises were carried out in conjunction with Red Army ground forces, albeit under primitive conditions. At the same time von Seeckt formed the German Flying Sport Association, which, under the camouflage of gliding, gave initial flying training to pilots and produced air-mindedness in the German people as a whole. All of this was done under the eyes of the Allied Control Commission, which was there to enforce the Versailles Treaty. When it withdrew in 1928 it became easier to manufacture clandestine armaments on German soil, and in that same year the building of tanks started at Gasonwerk. The result of all this can be summed up in a memorandum written by Krupp, head of the famous armament firm of that name, during World War 2: 'Of the guns which were being made in 1939-1941, the most important were already developed in 1933.' [69] The same could be said for aircraft, but less so for tanks.

## Soviet Union

When the Red Army held its first May Day Parade in 1920 it presented a sorry spectacle. Ill-discipline was apparent among the soldiers, and the only modern equipments on display were a few foreign tanks, some armoured cars and three foreign aircraft. Although the Red Army was triumphant in the Russian civil war, it had suffered at the hands of the Poles, especially in front of Warsaw in August 1920, which put paid to the idea of exporting communism westwards by force. Significantly the Russian commander at Warsaw was Mikail Tuchachevski, a man of noble descent, who was to become the Red Army's von Seeckt. As a young officer in the Russian Imperial Guard, he had been taken prisoner by the Germans in 1915, and for a time had been in the same prison camp as Charles de Gaulle, although no evidence exists that they ever met. On repatriation in 1918 he joined the Red Army and rapidly rose through the ranks, until May 1920 found him commanding the Western Front, when war against Poland broke out. Outnumbering the Poles by almost two to one, the Red Army was initially successful, but at the eleventh hour, when almost everyone in the West believed Poland to be finished, Pilsudski, the Polish commander, suddenly counter-attacked in front of Warsaw and threw the Red Army back beyond the Polish frontier. Tuchachevski had failed because his supplies could not keep up with his rate of advance and coordination between him and Yegarov's South Western Front broke down. Henceforth he believed that the Red Army must be as disciplined and as well-equipped with modern weapons as any western army.

The decade of the twenties was taken up by arguments as to what shape the Red Army should take. Not until 1929 would Field Service Regulations be issued, and up to that time the Army would have to rely on the old 1914 Imperial Field Regulations for tactical doctrine. Initially, on the one hand, stood the school of ex-Imperial Army officers under General Svechin, who had thrown their lot with the Reds in the civil war, and had been welcomed for their professional advice. They believed that the Red Army should be a properly organised regular army, and that too much should not be read into the lessons of the civil war. Frunze, Tuchachevski and other successful leaders of the civil war also believed in a regular army, but for different reasons. They saw it as a means for expanding communism into other lands, but taking note of the civil war, believed that a highly mobile regular army was essential. Finally, there were the theorists led by Trotsky, who accepted the need for a regular army to act as a 'cover', but also placed emphasis on a large territorial force. They pointed out that the Red Army of the civil war had been a militia and wanted it to remain so. However, the idea that the

Red Army should be a small professional one ran contrary to the Marxist ideal which relied on drawing strength from the masses of the people. Hence by 1924 a compromise had been reached whereby a regular army of 29 infantry divisions and a territorial army of 42 infantry divisions would be formed. Frunze, who by now had superseded Trotsky as the War Commissar, was also a believer in what he called 'revolutionary mobility'. The civil war, because of the vast area over which it was fought, lack of troops and mechanical transport, had put horse cavalry in the limelight. This was the only arm which could cover distance in a reasonable space of time, and hence great reliance had been placed on it. It became, in Frunze's eyes, the arm of 'revolutionary mobility', and to this end the regular Red Army would have 12 such divisions, while the territorial army would only have four.

At the same time another argument raised its head. This was the posture which the Red Army should adopt. Should it train for a defensive or offensive war? The Ex-Imperial School under Svechin believed that the attitude should be defensive, arguing that in any case the Red Army, as proved in Poland, would not be ready to take to the offensive for many years to come. In this they were supported by Trotsky while he was still in office. The Frunze school disagreed saying, as he himself maintained:

'The tactics of the Red Army were and will be impregnated with activity in the spirit of bold and energetically conducted offensive operations. This flows from the class nature of the workers' and peasants' army and at the same time coincides with the requirement of military art.' [70]

Once again Frunze got his way and, although Svechin's school continued to teach defensive tactics until 1931, their view became increasingly unacceptable until they were finally branded as 'bourgeois theoreticians'.

Thus by 1924 the Red Army was committed to the offensive, and was relying on a mobility, which at that time it did not have. Although, Frunze himself was committed to horse cavalry, as Trotsky had been, the Russians did not blind themselves entirely as to the potential of mechanised forces. Fuller's *Tanks in the Great War* was published in Russia in 1923, and also in that year the War Industry Main Directorate (GUVP) undertook a study of tank design and related Red Army requirements. The first designs were influenced by the heavy tanks of World War I, but the first homegrown tank was a light tank, the T18 (a version of the French Renault), produced in 1927. Frunze died in November 1925 and was succeeded by Voroshilov. He realised that the Red Army could not improve its mobility unless it concentrated on motorisation, but at the time he took office Soviet industry was still not in a position to support this. Hence the decision was made by Stalin to harness the first Five Year Plan, which started in 1928, to the needs of the Army. As the Soviet magazine *Economic Review* put it:

'In drawing up our five-year plan we must pay great attention to those branches of our economic system in general and of our war industries in particular which will play the main role in consolidating the defensive powers of our country and ensure economic stability in time of war. Industrialisation also means development of our war industries.' [71]

In the meantime an attempt was made in 1926 to persuade the Wiemar Republic to increase its financial stake in the Soviet war industry, but after this overture had been exposed in both the Reichstag and the British Press the German Government felt forced to turn it down.

The Red Army was now firmly tied to the fortunes of the First Five Year Plan. But, with this decision made, it was now possible to produce a tactical concept. This appeared in the Field Service Regulations of 1929. It shows much of the influence of Frunze and Tuchaveski, latter having been Chief of Staff of the Red Army since 1926. The regulations stated that the most decisive form of manoeuvre was offensive action leading to encirclement. This relied heavily on cavalry and armour. If it was not possible to execute a turning movement because the enemy had extensive flanks a breakthrough would have to be used relying on artillery support and co-operation between all arms. The prime role of the tank was still to be infantry support, but higher formations would hold independent groups of tanks to be used primarily to take out enemy artillery. Finally aviation was to be used on a mass scale in support of the ground forces. Much of this doctrine reflected current German thinking and illustrates the close co-operation between the two armies and air forces at this time. During the years 1926-7 alone some 27 Russian officers had visited Germany for attachments and to attend exercises, while 39 Reichswehr officers had returned the compliment. In the late summer of 1928 General von Blomberg (later to become Chief of Staff of the Wehrmacht) visited Russia. In his report he stated:

'... The command staff finds itself with respect to us [the Reichswehr] in the conscious status of pupils. The knowledge of German military literature and of German writing is frequently astonishing. To have studied the German principles in practice counts as a personal distinction, and an assignment to the Reichswehr as something which is specially sought after.' [72]

Unfortunately, although the Russians appeared to understand the principles, they did not seem to have the flexibility of mind to apply them, and this was to create difficulties for them during the next few years. But, in spite of this, by the end of the twenties the Russians had already in existence an experimental mechanised formation remarkably similar to those of Britain and the USA.

The Red Air Force (VVS) also showed the influence of Germany. From the end of the civil war onwards great importance had been attached to it. It is significant that it did not suffer the same rundown as the Red Army during the years 1921-3 and that also there was a very high proportion of members of the communist party in its ranks. Like von Seeckt with Lufthansa, the Russians set up a state civil airline, Aeroflot, which did much to further design and experience. They also had their parallel to the German Flying Sport Association, *Osaavkim*. They firmly believed that the prime role of the air force was to support the army. In the early twenties this was mainly through reconnaissance, but later was to change to fighter ground-attack.

The decade ended with the first chance to try these new ideas out in practice. The Soviet Government had an agreement with the Chinese over operating rights on the Chinese Eastern Railway in Marchuria. However, Chang Kai Shek objected to this and brought his influence to bear on the provincial Manchurian army to oppose the Russian interest. Consequently, in 1929, the Soviet government set up the Trans-Baikal Group of the Detached Far Eastern Army under S.S. Vostretsov to oppose the Manchurian army, who numbered some 10 000 men, in the area 500 miles north west of Harbin on the Chinese Eastern Railway. The Trans-Baikal Group, consisting of some 9 000 men with a few T18 tanks and aircraft, was ordered to carry out an encirclement of the Japanese forces, thus using the classic manoeuvre of the 1929 Regulations. On November 17th, 1929 the Russians attacked, and it became quickly apparent that there were defects in training. The supporting artillery lost contact with the infantry making the main attack, and the tanks, who were supposed to be supporting the infantry, became separated from them, attempting to break through the anti-tank defences on their own without success. The infantry, meanwhile, became pinned down by machine gun fire. In effect, the Russians found themselves learning the same lesson that the British had in front of the Flesquières Ridge on the first day of the Battle of Cambrai. Yet, in spite of these upsets, the Russians were reasonably successful in their encirclement, although the Chinese were eventually able to break out. Significantly, little attempt was made to pursue them, apart from a few aircraft harrassing the fleeing Chinese with machine gun fire.

**Other Countries**

Other countries also became enamoured, to a greater or lesser extent, with the idea of mechanised warfare. The Poles had had a tank regiment, equipped with Renault light tanks, operating under the French on the Western Front during the closing stages of the War. This regiment had fought as detached companies during the Russo-Polish War, but the slow speed of the Renault limited its effectiveness in the fluid conditions which prevailed. However the Poles did have some spectacular successes using armoured cars, especially in strategic raids. After the end of the war the Poles became influenced by French doctrine, tying their tanks to infantry support and using armoured cars with the cavalry in the reconnaissance role. The Japanese took up the tank in 1925, again tying it to infantry support. Italy, interestingly enough, had been the first country to use armoured vehicles in war when she employed motorised infantry, carried in Fiat trucks, at the Battle of Zanzur in 1912 during her campaign against the Turks in what is now Libya. She had used armoured cars to a limited extent during the Great War, but only formed her first tank unit in

December 1918. In 1926 tanks became a specialised arm, but as with so many countries they were dedicated to infantry support.

Thus, by the end of the 1920s the major powers had accepted that the tank now had an assured place on the battlefield. The majority continued to see it in its traditional role of infantry support. However the influence of the British 'evangelist' school led by Fuller and Liddell Hart had made a deep impression on the more progressive thinkers in other countries. Their thesis that the tank would restore mobility to the battlefield was becoming accepted in Germany, where the lessons of 1918 had been thoroughly digested. It suited the Red Army, which was looking for a revolutionary (in more senses than one) concept of warfare. Shock action in the shape of the AFV acting in concert with the aeroplane also appealed as a means of preventing the static conditions of the Western Front from recurring. Yet there was strong opposition from those who believed that the tank should remain tied to the apron strings of the infantry, from those who believed that the aircraft could 'go it alone', from those who thought a mechanised army too expensive and, finally, from those who believed that the blitzkrieg concept was aggressive and not in keeping with the belief that World War I had been 'the war to end wars.'

**Notes**

1   Douhet, *The Command of the Air* p 26.
2   Ibid, p 84.
3   Cole, *Royal Air Force 1918* p 9.
4   Divine, *The Broken Wing* p 162.
5   Webster & Frankland, *The Strategic Bombing Offensive Against Germany 1939-45* vol 1 p 55.
6   Holley, *Ideas and Weapons* p 149.
7   Air Service Information Circular No 2, *Final Report of the Chief of Air Service, AEF* p49.
8   General Staff Statistics Branch Report No 110, *Statistical Analysis of Air Bombardment* p 23.
9   Holley, op cit pp 173-4.
10  Mitchell, *Winged Defense* pp 126-7.
11  Ibid, p 199.
12  Mitchell, *Skyways* pp 255-6.
13  Ibid, p 262.
14  Minutes of War Cabinet Meeting 15 Aug 19. (Public Record Office).
15  Liddell Hart, *The Tanks* vol 1 p 194.
16  Maj Gen Sir Louis Jackson in lecture to RUSI Nov 1919, Ibid p 201.
17  Haig, Col Comdt Neil, Journal of the Royal United Service Institute (JRUSI) Feb 1921.
18  JRUSI May 1920.
19  Chevenix Trench, Maj R JRUSI May 1922.
20  Fuller, *Tanks in the Great War* pp 302-315.
21  Fuller, *The Reformation of War* p 100.
22  Ibid, p 150.
23  *The Tanks* vol 1 op cit p 219.
24  Parliamentary Debates Commons 5th Series Vol 139 12 Mar 21 Col. 1288. HMSO.
25  Liddell Hart, *Memoirs* Vol 1 p 109.
26  *The Tanks* vol 1 op cit pp 251-2.
27  Ibid, p 255.
28  Collins, *Lord Wavell* p 130.

29  Divine, *The Blunted Sword* p 158.
30  Ibid, p 159.
31  Liddell Hart, *The Remaking of Modern Armies* p 15.
32  Ibid, p 59.
33  Ibid, p 93.
34  Germains, *The Mechanisation of War* pp 109-110.
35  Ibid, pp 160-1.
36  Ibid, pp 180-7.
37  Liddell Hart, *Memoirs* Vol 1 p 161.
38  Macksey, *Tank Warfare* p 85.
39  *The Tanks*, vol 1 op cit p 273.
40  Letter Rochenback to Lt Col Joseph W Viner (Army Service Schools, Fort Leavenworth), 5 Sept 19. Viner Papers, Patton Museum, Fort Knox, Kentucky, USA.
41  Weigley, *The American Way in War* p 216.
42  *Patton Papers* op cit p 720.
43  Ibid, p 736.
44  Millis, *American Military Thought* p 355.
45  Wheldon, *Machine Age Armies* p 43.
46  Green, Thomson and Roots, *US Army in World War II: The Technical Services* p 190.
47  *Infantry Journal May 1922.*
48  Yale, White and Manteuffel, *Alternative to Armageddon* p 76.
49  *Infantry Journal Jan 1930.*
50  *Infantry Journal Jan 1928.*
51  *Cavalry Journal* Jan 1926.
52  *Armor* Sep/Oct 1973.
53  *Cavalry Journal* Oct 1921.
54  *Cavalry Journal* Jan 1922.
55  *Cavalry Journal* Jul 1922.
56  Ibid.
57  *Patton Papers* op cit p 946.
58  *Cavalry Journal* Jan 1928.
59  *Cavalry Journal* Jul 1928.
60  *Cavalry Journal* Jan 1930.
61  Stubbs & Connor, *Armor Lineage Series* p 55.
62  *Infantry Journal* Nov 1930.
63  Chapman, Guy, *The French Army and Politics* from Michael Howard ed *Soldiers and Governments* p 67.
64  *Royal Tank Corps Journal* Dec 1927.
65  Seeckt von, *Thoughts of a Soldier* pp 62-3.
66  Guderian, *Panzer Leader* p 24.
67  O'Neill, Robert, *Doctrine and Training in the German Army 1919-1939* from Michael Howard ed *The Theory and Practice of War.* p 146.
68  Best account of these negotiations is given in Carsten's *The Reichswehr and Politics.*
69  Manchester, *The Arms of Krupp* p 397.
70  Gartoff, *Soviet Military Doctrine* p 66.
71  Kournakoff, *Russia's Fighting Forces* p 66.
72  Erikson, *The Soviet High Command* p 267.

# 3
# Forging of a Weapon

**Britain**
In May 1930 there appeared in the Journal of the Royal United Service Institute (RUSI) an article by Brigadier Wavell (later Field Marshal) entitled *The Army and the Prophets*. It was a significant piece of writing in that he attempted to review dispassionately the arguments of the 1920s on the subject of reformation of armies and air forces. He spelt out the dilemma of the practical reformer as follows:

'The problem which faces the reformer of armies in peace might be likened to that of an architect called on to alter and modernise and old-fashioned house without increasing its size, with the whole family still living in it (often grumbling at the architect's improvements, since an extra bathroom can only be added at the expense of someone's dressing-room) and under the strictest financial limitations.'

Although the World War 1 had produced clear lessons in the context of the vulnerability of infantry, the need for tanks and artillery to aid the offensive, the development of aviation and poison gas and the importance of industrial power, there were good reasons why these lessons had not been acted upon. He believed that governments were only concerned with immediate military problems at the end of the war, such as garrisoning enemy territory and internal security at home and overseas. 'These called for considerable numbers of armed men, but not necessarily for a high degree of technical efficiency or scientific equipment.' Secondly, financial stringency acted as a brake on reform, and, finally, the military administrators themselves were too close to the event to judge the lessons clearly. He felt that post-war armies '. . . came to differ from those in 1914 in detail rather than principle.' The increase in machine guns had augmented defence and, because the foot soldier was still the basic element on the battlefield, efforts in the 1920s had been directed towards improving his mobility and protection on the modern battlefield rather than attempting to find a substitute for him, as Fuller had advocated. He argued that large conscript armies would cause a return to trench warfare because their level of training would be low, leading to a loss of efficiency, and slow reactions. He showed himself in favour of the development of armoured forces, discounting the argument that they were limited by terrain by saying that: '. . . since all great civilisations have established their centres in open plains,

66

decisive battles will usually be fought in those plains and fighting in mountains and forests will be subsidiary.' However, he believed, like the Vickers designer Carden, that tanks must be designed for speed and firepower rather than 'armour and bulk'. The development of anti-tank guns would lead to an increase in protection, which would limit mobility, but 'that speed is often a better protection than armour can be instanced throughout military history.' He also felt that armoured forces could only be manned by professional long-service armies, because the high level of training required would be difficult to achieve by conscript armies. As regards airpower, Wavell felt that civil aviation must be developed with a view to winning the industrial power race, which was so decisive in wartime (both Lufthansa and Aeroflot were doing this). There must be close air-ground co-operation, and this was best achieved by having air squadrons integrated as part of the land force, however a separate air force was better for technical development. He finished his article with a warning:

> 'In the past, armies have at the beginning of hostilities at any rate, been able to interpose as a shield between the enemy and the nation; with the invention of the aeroplane and the prospective mechanisation of land forces this is no longer so. [1]

These words were prophetic when applied to the French efforts to create such a shield in the shape of the Maginot Line. This point of view represented the views of the moderate reformers, or, as has been described, the 'conservative reformer' versus the 'radical' reformer like Fuller [2]. Certainly Wavell's argument is more carefully considered and much less unbalanced than Fuller's writings, which tended to irritate by their extremism.

Meanwhile attempts had been made to set up an armoured brigade on a permanent footing. Charles Broad, the author of the 'Purple Primer', had been asked by the CIGS, Milne, to write a paper looking five years ahead to a new modernised army. Broad advocated the setting up of four armoured brigades, each of 89 tanks, of which two thirds would be light tanks, thus accepting the Vickers preference for this type. This was submitted in June 1930, but found little favour with the pacifist-influenced Labour administration of the time. At the same time another *ad hoc* tank brigade of a mere two tank battalions was set up for trials. It was used with horse-cavalry brigades and both ordinary and lorried-infantry brigades in various combinations. An atmosphere of intense caution hung over the exercises and at no time was there an attempt to use the tank brigade en masse. Liddell Hart, writing in the RUSI Journal, had some bitter comments to make. He complained of the issues being obscured by 'misdirection of the armoured strokes.' He criticised the neglect of strategic objectives and the tendency to strike at the front rather than rear of enemy positions. In effect, lack of imagination was at the base of his criticisms. The infantry had shown little drive in their attempts to pick up the mantle of motorisation, and Liddell Hart gloomily predicted that the state of affairs as it stood would mean trench warfare 'within a week if (the armies of today) ever got to grips.' In conclusion he stated:

'Thus the problem today is not merely what tanks can do, but what mental and moral effect they can have. And here lies the ground for declaring that talk about 'gradual mechanisation' is merely a soothing draught, which though innocuous in itself, is indirectly perilous to a grave cause. The need for thorough conversion is urgent.' [3]

Nevertheless, the next year, 1931, did see a significant advance in the evolution of armoured formations. A tank brigade was set up on a temporary basis (for six months only). It consisted of three tank battalions and Broad, after some wrangling, was appointed to command it. Simultaneously, a revised edition of *Mechanised and Armoured Formations*, entitled *Modern Formations*, was published. It laid down that the Army would consist of 'mobile divisions and divisions'. There would be three types of the former — cavalry divisions, divisions consisting of tank brigades and motorised infantry with perhaps cavalry and, finally, independent formations consisting only of tanks and armoured cars. Unfortunately, because the new force fitted the last category only, the Royal Tank Corps was about to become carried away in its thinking. It would forget thoughts of combined arms and would become mesmerised by the 'all-tank' idea. Broad, who had written the revised version, started with good intentions. Because of the negative results produced by the 1930 exercises he felt that the tank brigade should start its training from scratch. Emphasis was placed on quick reaction with tanks going into the attack off the line of march without halting. Wireless was brought into widespread use for the first time, and Broad showed that it was possible to 'drill' 180 tanks using just his own voice over the radio. Tactics were evolved to deal with anti-tank guns, practice carried out in attacking enemy artillery, administrative concentrations and infantry columns on the march and in a fast moving advance in contact with the enemy. The results of these exercises can be summed up in the 1st Tank Brigade Training Report for 1931, where the evolved role of the brigade was stated as being '. . . to find the enemy (with the assistance of aircraft if possible), to ascertain the direction from which tank attack is least expected and to attack him from that direction.' It was the concept of Liddell Hart's 'Indirect Approach' par excellence. Speed of reaction and flexibility of response, two essential qualities for blitzkrieg, had been recognised. In the same year Wavell's 6th Infantry Brigade had also been undergoing mechanisation trials. This enabled Wavell to crystallise further his thoughts on the employment of tanks. He believed that the tendency to try and concentrate tanks and keep them for a decisive blow was wrong. Rather, it would be better to spread tanks more generously along the front. They could be used to achieve local tactical success and then withdrawn under cover again for further operations. Anyway, there was the problem of finding a suitable objective for a mass tank thrust and quite often their efforts would be wasted. He saw the company, as opposed to battalion or brigade, as the basic tank element in a field force. This view showed more concern for the use of combined arms, and was suitable for the second type of mobile division, but was unpalatable to the Royal Tank Corps because it dissipated the effect of concentrated shock action which could be produced by the complete brigade acting as one.

Yet another point of view was put across when Martel, the self same officer who had advocated an 'all-tank' army back in 1916, published a book in 1931 entitled *In the Wake of the Tank*. Martel, although a Sapper, had maintained close ties with tank development and had commanded the engineer company attached to the original Experimental Mechanised Force. He had spent much time in the 1920s designing what he called 'tankettes', which were small one and two man tanks armed with machine guns. He envisaged the conversion of existing infantry divisions into mechanised divisions consisting of nine infantry battlions each equipped with 250 two-man tankettes. They would remain mounted for the attack, but would dismount in defence, thus recognising that tanks on their own could not hold ground. He believed that there was danger in becoming carried away by the independent tank brigade concept.

'Until such time as we have progressed further and been able to try out this more independent role, it is by the co-operation of those mixed tank battalions and infantry that we are most likely to achieve rapid success when attacking main positions.' [4]

However infantry, artillery and engineers must be able to operate in the same environment as the tanks. Hence they should have the same mobility and protection. In other words he believed that these arms should be mechanised as opposed to motorised. He also accepted that the British Army was most likely to have to fight in hot climates against armies with little mechanisation, but:

'We do not want to have two armies, one for a possible but remote continental war and the other for the everyday needs of foreign service. All machines have therefore to be tested and tried out for both purposes.' [5]

This last proposal would become a major bone of contention in a few years time when the shape of the British Expeditionary Force (BEF) for the Continent was being debated.

The next two years were gloomy ones for progressive military thinkers. It was hoped that, as a result of the success of the 1931 tank brigade, a permanent tank brigade would be formed immediately. This was not to be so. Firstly the brunt of the world economic crisis had hit Britain in 1931, causing the collapse of the Labour Government and the formation of a National Coalition. Cuts in public spending had to be instituted and, although the permanent formation of a tank birgade would cost little extra, it gave the Government a good excuse to postpone any decision. In addition, an international disarmament conference, likely to be the most important to date, had been convened to open at Geneva at the beginning of February 1932. The line the conference was likely to take was that all offensive weapons should be banned. Besides the military aircraft, the medium tank was also considered a likely offensive weapon. Therefore it seemed an inopportune moment to form the permanent brigade. However, a temporary formation was set up on the same lines as 1931. The theme of the previous year was continued, but this time the exploitation of a break-through and movement over long distances were practised. In the former the tanks were used to infiltrate the enemy defences, leaving other troops to mop up points of resistance in much the same manner as the Germans had done on foot in 1918. The complete brigade did a march of 50 miles in nine hours, including a long midday halt. As one observer of this move put it:

'Such is the difference between manoeuvres in tank-time and old time. Tank-time gains time so quickly, that it can gain a decision. And it is the only rate of manoeuvre which has such promise in modern war.' [6]

In 1933 the tank brigade was not even formed on a temporary basis. Perhaps part of the reason is attributable to the arrival in office of a new CIGS. Milne, in spite of his cautious approach during the latter half of his time in office, had appreciated the need for mechanisation. His successor, Sir Archibald Montgomery-Massingberd, proved to be an ultra-conserva-tive.* When Liddell Hart had asked him back in 1926 whether he had read Fuller's *Foundations of the Science of War*, Montgomery-Massingbred had replied: 'I have not read Fuller's book! And I don't expect I ever shall. It would only annoy me.' [7] Small wonder that Liddell Hart wrote gloomily to Hankey (still Secretary to the Committee for Imperial Defence (CID)) on hearing of Montgomery-Massingbred's appointment:

'. . . I anticipate that he will not favour, still less initiate, steps towards the necessary reorganisation of the Army; that he will be antipathetic to the extended use of tanks, and also of aircraft; that he will discourage, if not penalise, independence of view and freedom of speech among the younger officers; that he will endeavour to check critical examination of the history of the War . . . What I fear most is that his regime will lead to influential posts being increasingly filled with officers who are either unprogressive or skilled in hiding their own opinions at the expense of the more constructive-minded . . . I shall be pleasantly surprised if Fuller is not squeezed out of the Army without further employment.' [8]

His last observation soon became fact. After turning down command of the 1927 Experimental Mechanised Force Fuller had been successively a divisional

---

*It is perhaps strange that he agreed to accept the honorary appointment of a Colonel Commandant of the Royal Tank Corps.

staff officer and then an infantry brigade commander. During the winter of 1929, when he was commanding his brigade in the North of England, he gave all officers of his brigade a series of lectures on *Field Service Regulations*. From these lectures he wrote his last major contribution to the mechanisation argument, *Lectures on FSR III*. He had become even more firmly wedded to the 'all-tank' idea. 'To combine tanks and infantry is tantamount to yoking a tractor to a draught horse.' [9] He envisaged a mechanised army as being split into two parts; one, the tank force, which would provide the offensive power, while an anti-tank force gave protective power in the form of mobile anti-tank weapons established in a 'waggon laager' close to the tank force. Infantry would only be used in country unsuitable for tanks. Perhaps less fanciful was his idea that aircraft should be used to 'threaten the enemy's mobility on the ground rather than attempting to destroy him.' Looking into his crystal ball he wrote:

'. . . in future warfare co-operation between tanks and aeroplanes is likely to prove far more important than co-operation between tanks and infantry. So important that we may see tanks and aeroplanes forming one force and infantry a completely separate force. [10]

He believed that any future British British Continental force should consist of a highly mechanised army of some 30 000 men. There should be a strong air element, but its major roles would be reconnaissance and the maintenance of air superiority. There is no mention in his book of the idea of ground attack aircraft giving close air support to the ground forces. Towards the end of the book he relapsed into pure Douhetism with the idea that the air force would be responsible for the counter-offensive, concentrating on breaking the morale of the civil population. All in all, a muddled book, which showed Fuller to be past his prime. Although, he was promoted Major-General in September 1930, the only job offered to him was command of a Second Class District in India. He turned this down, hoping for something that might bring him back into direct contact with mechanisation. It was not to be, and after three years on half-pay he was placed on the retired list in December 1933. Fed up with what he called 'panic-stricken' governments, 'press-shackled' peoples and a 'loan-shackled' world, Fuller took up the creed of Fascism, and little more was heard from him for the rest of the decade. Fuller's contribution to the crusade for mechanisation had been immense. Plan 1919, and his fearless writings of the early 1920s had done more than anything else to encourage progressive thinking both in the British and foreign armies. Without his inspiration it is likely that there would have been no mechanisation experiments in the 1920s. His tragedy was in his character. He was the worst type of zealot, convinced that he was right and incapable of listening to the views of others. Hence he was bound to make many enemies and bound to be thwarted in his designs, particularly in the political and economic environment of the time.

In the meantime, Montgomery-Massingberd did his best to discourage progressive thought, going to the extent of changing the subject of the military history paper of the Staff College entrance examination from the American Civil War to Gallipoli so as to avoid using Liddell Hart's *Sherman* and Fuller's *Grant and Lee*. While presiding over the Fifth Annual Haldane Lecture in May 1933 he argued that the prime responsibility of the British Army was still 'policing the Empire' and therefore there was no need to increase the rate of mechanisation as the likely battlefields would be unsuitable for mechanised warfare. Yet, later that year the CID Defence Requirements Sub-Committee was set up and concluded that Germany was ' . . . the ultimate enemy against whom our "long range" defence policy must be directed.' They believed that a Continental Expeditionary Force was essential:

'If the Low Countries were in the hands of a hostile power, not only would the frequency and intensity of air attacks on London be increased, but the whole of the industrial areas of the Midlands and North of England would be brought within the area of penetration of hostile air attacks.' [11]

There was nothing new in the idea of the enlarged threat from the Continent produced by the aeroplane. Milne had stated in 1925 that ' . . . the true strategic position of Great Britain is on the Rhine.' [12] There was then, a case for switching priorities. Yet, the Chiefs of Staff, although acknowledging the potential threat from Germany believed that war in Europe meant trouble elsewhere. Because, anyway the British Army could only raise two divisions at the most for a continental expeditionary force, they concluded that:

' . . . we should be able to do little more than hold the frontiers and outposts of the Empire during the first few months of the war.' [13]

Thus priority, as far as they were concerned, still remained with the Empire, and the Army should continue to be shaped for this role. Duff Cooper, when introducing the Defence Estimates for 1934-35, argued in this context that the Army must be balanced, hence:

'On Salisbury Plain or even on the fields of Flanders the tank is no doubt the most powerful weapon you can possibly use, but it is not necessarily the most powerful in the North-West Frontier, or in the swamps and ditches that surround the suburbs of Shanghai.' [14]

Out of this arose the Doctrine of Limited Liability. If the Army's first duty was towards the Empire, then it was no good expecting it to be able to mount a modern European-style of expeditionary force for the Continent as this meant widescale mechanisation which was unsuitable for imperial defence. Yet, because of the importance of the Low Countries it was essential that Britain should show herself prepared to help her Continental Allies,

72

who were assumed to be France and Belgium. If the Army could not do it, the RAF certainly could. Chamberlain, the Foregin Minister was a proponent of this, writing in his diary in February 1936, said:

'I cannot believe that the next war, if it ever comes, will be like the last one, and I believe that our resources will be more profitably employed in the air, and on the sea, than in building up great armies.' [15]

Liddell Hart too gave his support in an article in *The Times* of November 25th, 1935, saying that there was no point in sending an expeditionary force until the situation became clearer. An air component would be much more sensible. In January 1936 he wrote to Lord Halifax recommending that priority be given to air production to this end. Thus the Army found itself in the mid 1930s lying a poor third behind an RAF committed to strategic bombing and a Royal Navy which still retained its traditional roles.

Against this background it is somewhat surprising that the decision was taken in November 1933 to finally form a permanent tank brigade, 1st Tank Brigade. Its charter was encouraging:

'A Tank Brigade may be employed on a strategic or semi-independent mission against some important objective in the enemy's rearward organisation . . . Such employment of the Tank Brigade thus differs fundamentally from that of an Army Tank Battalion, which latter is normally employed only after an opportunity for decisive action has been found and fixed by other arms . . . The Tank Brigade should avoid strength and attack weakness . . . In addition it must be capable of more intimate co-operation with other arms where the situation demands such action.' [16]

Its first commander was Hobart, an ex-Indian Army Sapper, who, after a distinguished record of service on the Western Front and in Palestine during World War 1, had become a convert to the tank, while serving in India in the early 1920s. His views were formed in the course of a protracted correspondence with Lindsay in 1925-6, while Hobart was an instructor at the Indian Staff College at Quetta. Thus, while Hobart wrote:

'Why limit ourselves to a 3000-4000 yards advance . . . Why piddle about with porridge-making of the Third Ypres type? When one is possessed of modern weapons one shoots a tiger in the brain, heart, or spine. One doesn't painfully hack off a foot at a time 'consolidating' as one goes.' [17]

Lindsay replied that:

' . . . the war will be won, or lost, as far as military operations go, by the Mechanical Force, in the air and on the ground, working in co-operation. The ground troops, present infantry and cavalry, will occupy, administer, and police, the areas conquered by the Mechanical Force.' [18]

This sample of their correspondence showed that, although they appreciated Liddell Hart's psychological disclocation, they veered more towards Fuller's 'all-tank' doctrine. Indeed Hobart had much of Fuller's aggressiveness in his character, although, at the same time, he had a charisma that made him a leader of men.

Hobart set about training the brigade, which consisted of three medium and one light tank battalions, by first holding a staff exercise at Cambridge in early May 1934. From this it was concluded that the task given to the Tank Brigade was feasible provided that it could be supported logistically. Another interesting conclusion was: 'The co-operation of the RAF at all stages appears to be a factor vital to success.' In connection with this was the suggestion that aircraft could be used to provide a 'covering barrage for tank attack.' [19] The Tank Brigade itself carried out exercises on Salisbury Plain during August and early September. The theme of these exercises was the infiltration by the complete brigade deep into the enemy's lines. The use of feints, long marches under the cover of darkness and close co-operation with aircraft all helped towards this end. In mid-September Hobart had his chance to try co-operation with other arms when his brigade was exercised with the 7th Experimental Infantry Brigade, a motorised formation under the command of none other than Lindsay. Burnett-Stuart, the forward-looking General Officer Commanding (GOC) Southern Command, was the exercise director and Wavell the chief umpire.

The origins of this exercise lay in an exchange of letters between Lindsay and Hobart at the end of 1933. They started with the concept of the second type of 'Mobile Division', as taken out of *Modern Formations*, with a cavalry brigade, tank brigade and motorised infantry brigade. The cavalry brigade was to be the 'eyes' for the tanks, while the infantry provided a firm base from which both could operate on 'tip and run' raids. The latter was on much the same lines as Fuller's 'wagon laager'. In February 1934 Southern Command ran a war game in which the idea was tried out. The main conclusion reached was that it was feasible, except that horse cavalry did not have the speed, endurance or armament for the task, and their place was taken by an armoured car battalion for the September exercise. The picture painted for the exercise was that the Mobile Force, starting from near Gloucester, was to make a raid on a series of objectives near Amesbury on Salisbury Plain. These were protected by the 1st Infantry Division and the 2nd (Horsed) Cavalry Brigade. Unfortunately every obstacle was placed in the way of Lindsay and Hobart. The strict timings they were given prevented any significant move by night. They were told that they must not risk such losses or expenditure of energy that they would be unfit to take part in the main battle, which was supposed to take place immediately after the raid. As Lindsay remarked, 'that was like telling a jockey that while trying to win a race he must take care to keep his horse fit to run again immediately afterwards.' [20] Each side was given an equal number of aircraft, leaving no chance to gain air superiority, and the nature of the countryside forced the Force to advance on one route only. In the event, 7th Brigade was used to seize and hold crossings over the Kennet and Avon Canal, while the tanks passed over 24 hours later and then hid up until the third day when they were actually to execute the raid. Unfortunately Burnett-Stuart called the raid off before the third and most spectacular phase could be executed. The Mobile Force was then invited to extricate itself, with the knowledge that the opposing commander had slipped motorised infantry in behind them to man road-blocks and set up minefields. At this stage the proceedings took on the attitude of a farce. As one young tank officer described it:

'The infantry were allowed by the umpires to surround the area and lie on the road like the members of Gandhi's 'disobedience campaign' in India. They were guided by officers' wives who had arrived by car earlier. As we closed in on them they would not move, and others attempted to climb on to the tanks, while the artillery were allowed to bring up their field guns and block the roads at point blank range, in full view.' [21]

Yet, in spite of all this, the Mobile Force did succeed in extricating itself. Unfortunately a number of senior officers had witnessed this last part of the exercise, having had little idea of what had gone on before. Hence they had seen the Mobile Force in the worst possible light, and the idea that it could be employed on deep penetration raids found only lukewarm favour. The exercise turned out to be no more than an effort to boost the morale of the infantry, and did much to prevent the setting up of British armoured divisions for the next three years. Its effect on Hobart was to drive him even more firmly into the 'all-tank' school. In his report on the 1934 exercises he made the point that the problem of co-operation with infantry had resolved itself ' . . . into a study of how best to use motorised forces in co-operation with the Tank Brigade without handicapping the mobility, power and great moral and material potentialities of the latter.' Yet the attitude of the infantry was that they only wanted tanks to support them in the set-piece attack. It was the same with co-operation with the RAF. Hobart had spelt out the role of the RAF co-operation in his report. He saw the air tasks as being reconnaissance, bombers operating behind the enemy's lines, replacing long range artillery, while fighters maintained air superiority and carried out low flying attacks against key points in the enemy's forward areas. This was the blitzkrieg concept, yet the Air Ministry was still under Trenchard's shadow and Hobart experienced the same obstructiveness as Broad had a few years before. The RAF were still interested only in strategic bombing.

In spite of these frustrations the decision was taken in the autumn of that year to replace horse cavalry divisions by Mobile Divisions, consisting of a reconnaissance, fighting and support groups. Cavalry armoured car regiments would provide the reconnaissance element; a tank brigade and mechanised cavalry brigade the fighting element; and, the Support Group would be made up of artillery, engineers and possibly a cavalry machine gun regiment. At the same time, the transport of infantry divisions was to be motorised, a tank battalion would be allotted to each infantry division, and each infantry brigade would consist of three rifle battalions and one machine gun battalion mounted in armoured machine-gun carriers. When these proposals were introduced, at a lecture at the RUSI in November 1934, the CIGS emphasised the need to proceed cautiously and slowly with mechanisation. This was reinforced by the Army Estimates for 1935-36, which allowed an increase in forage by £44 000 to £400 000, while the increase for petrol was merely £12 000 to a total of £121 000. The effects of the September 1934 manoeuvres were illustrated when the CIGS laid down that the Tank Brigade must concentrate on actions in conjunction with the main force. It was not going to be allowed to slip away on its own as in the previous year. Even worse, it was temporarily broken up in September so that its battalions could play at the role of support to the infantry divisions. After the hopes of 1934 it turned out to be a frustrating year, which was reflected in Hobart's report, included in which was the plea that the RAF should provide permanent co-operation with the Tank Brigade, again to fall on deaf ears in the Air Ministry.

## Germany

Meanwhile in Germany there were quite different developments in the first half of the decade. For a start it saw Hitler's rapid rise to power. Before examining German re-armament in the years up to 1936 it is necessary to dip into the pages of *Mein Kampf*, written while Hitler was imprisoned in the fortress of Landsberg after the failure of his 1923 Munich *putsch*. Some historians have considered this book as merely being indicative of Hitler's frustration in his failure at Munich and not as a blueprint for his long term aims. It was not a blueprint as such, but there is little doubt that it was written with the idea of setting out a strategy in broad terms for the future of Germany. Although there are few direct illusions to military strategy, Hitler was quite clear on the form future war would take. He spoke of 'the general motorisation of the world, which in the next war will manifest itself overwhelmingly and decisively.' [22] In this context he maintained that a strong industrial base would be even more important than in World War 1, in which Germany had had to prop up her allies because of their lack of such a base. By 1930, the Nazis had become the second largest party in the Reichstag with 107 seats, and Hitler could afford to be more specific in his views. He immediately set about urging the Government to concentrate on rearmament to a far greater extent than they had hitherto. Addressing an open letter to the Chancellor, Bruning, he wrote:

'For us the Army is the expression of strength of the nation for the defence of its natural interests abroad. For you, Herr Chancellor Bruning, it is in the last resort an institution for the defence of the Government at home.' [23]

Yet, much at the same time he had written:

76

'It is impossible to build up an Army and give it a sense of worth if the object of its existence is not the preparation for battle. Armies for the preparation of peace do not exist; they exist for triumphant exertion in war.'[24]

In 1932 he crystallised his thoughts still further when he declared:

'The next war will be quite different from the last world war. Infantry attacks and mass formations are obsolete. Interlocked frontal struggles lasting for years on petrified fronts will not return. I guarantee that . . . we shall regain the superiority of free operations.' [25]

Thus, by the time that Hitler came to power in January 1933 he was clear in general terms what he wanted — an army which would be highly mobile and capable of a quick devastating strike at the enemy. As he said: 'I shall never start a war without the certainty that a demoralised enemy will succumb to the first stroke of a single gigantic stroke.' [26]

By 1930 the Reichswehr was still theoretically tied to the limitations imposed by the Treaty of Versailles, or the *Diktat*, as the National Socialists referred to it. The major threat to the Reich still remained Poland, and in 1928 a five year plan was drawn up to expand the Reichswehr to 17 divisions to counter it. At the same time, however, there was a shortage of raw materials and the plan was never put into effect. But, progressive thought, aided by co-operation with Russia, continued to synthesise and fashion what was ultimately to become the blitzkrieg. Guderian had the chance to carry out some of his ideas in practice, when he appointed at the beginning of 1931 to the command of the 3rd (Prussian) Motorised Battalion, which was made up of a company of armoured reconnaissance cars, a company of dummy tanks, an anti-tank company and a motor cycle company. This helped him to develop further his ideas on combined arms. But he remained convinced that armoured forces were to be the decisive weapon of the future. Yet, not everybody believed him. Even his superior, Von Stulpnagel, the Inspector of MT Troops, on his retirement in Spring 1931, remarked to Guderian: 'You're too impetuous. Believe me, neither of us will ever see German tanks in operation in our lifetime.' [27] Although the Allies had relented to the extent of allowing the Reichswehr to possess four-wheeled armoured cars, albeit without machine guns, they had never relented on tracked vehicles. The clandestine construction of tanks at Gasonwerk did not produce a tank until April 1930, and by the spring of 1931 the Reichswehr possessed the princely total of six medium and four light tanks, which went under the cover names of 'light' and 'large' tractors. The shortage of raw materials prevented an accelerated programme of tank production, and many saw this as a major flaw in the new style of mechanised warfare in that a large industrial base was required to support it. One such wrote:

'Mechanised armies with a high degree of motorisation and using chemical weapons are far more dependent on raw material supplies than were the armies of the world war.' [28]

Even so, the Reichswehr, small as it was, had become efficient and up-to-date in thought, if not in equipment. Liddell Hart, wrote in 1932:

'The German Army, converted unwillingly into a small professional army, has as rapidly acquired a new faith, that of the superiority of such an army, highly trained and mobile, over the unwieldy masses of a conscript army.' [29]

In that same year the Reichswehr's autumn manoeuvres involved whole battalions of armed motor cycle and motorised reconnaissance units. Several cavalry detachments were motorised, and the manoeuvres marked the first appearance of multi-axled vehicles, in defiance of the Versailles Treaty.

Meanwhile the embryo Luftwaffe also had been slowly growing in strength. The secret manufacture of aircraft in the USSR, Sweden and Switzerland had boosted the force from four squadrons in 1926 to fifteen in 1931. In 1930 it was calculated that 22 squadrons would be needed in the event of mobilisation. However there was no question that the air force would be placed under other than army command, and it was planned to deploy one reconnaissance, two fighter and one night bomber squadron to each formation headquarters from corps upwards. It was felt that the formation of an independent air force was out of context in a peacetime environment, although the force was divided into two, a combat force operating under the army, while a defence air force was put under naval control. There was, however, growing interest in building up a strategic air potential, and from 1927 effort was put into the development of a four-engined night-bomber, but this took time because of the need to camouflage this work against the prying eyes of other European nations. Lipetsk contributed much to the development of the groundwork of the Luftwaffe, and by the time Hitler came to power there were no less than 550 trained pilots available. The Germans themselves, both before the after World War 2, liked to claim that the Luftwaffe had been created out of nothing from 1933 onwards. This was not so, and if other nations had been aware of the clandestine developments of the 1920's and early 1930's the official unveiling of the Luftwaffe in 1935 would not have produced the shock it did. With the coming to power of Hitler the pace of rearmament merely quickened rather than being begun from scratch. Just before he became Chancellor a revised mobilisation plan had been produced envisaging a wartime military strength of 21 divisions, instead of the 17 planned for in 1928. By December of 1933 the *Truppenamt* was submitting plans for a peacetime army of this strength by 1937. To aid this, a secret law was introduced to cut down the length of service from twelve years to one in order to produce a sufficient large reserve of trained manpower. By April of the next year, Hitler pronounced himself dissatisfied with progress and decreed that the target

78

must be brought forward by three years to autumn 1934. It was the same with the Luftwaffe. In 1933 Goering planned to have 1 000 aircraft by 1935, but in 1934 a new plan was introduced calling for 4 000 by autumn 1935. By the end of 1934, 2 000 of these had materialised.

Hitler quickly saw the attraction in tanks. Visiting the weapons-proving establishment at Kummersdorf in the year of his accession to the leadership of Germany, he was given a demonstration of some Mark I Light Tanks (Panzer Kampfwagen (PZ KW) I). He remarked to Guderian 'That's what I need! That's what I want to have!' [30] Krupps immediately set up a programme of tank production, producing five tanks by August 1933, and 100 in 1934. The first tank battalion was formed in 1934 under the camouflaged name of 'Motor Transport Training Unit'. In the same year a Motorised Troops Command Staff was set up with General Lutz in command and Guderian as his chief of staff. This headquarters would co-ordinate the development of the panzer arm and command it. But there were some in high places who doubted the efficacy of wholesale mechanisation. Beck, the chief of the *Truppenamt*, and in 1935 to become Chief of the Army General Staff, believed that in the end the ultimate decision on the battlefield would not be gained by the panzers, but by having sufficient mass of infantry divisions. His pamphlet *Die Truppenfuehrung* produced in 1933 showed little advance from the tactics of 1918. The only difference was that the storm troop units or *Kampfgruppen* would include tanks, or even have tanks alone if the circumstances permitted it. However, he did accept that mechanised forces should not necessarily be tied to the apron strings of the foot marching and horsedrawn 'mass of decision'.

'If tanks are too closely tied to the infantry, they lose the advantage of their speed and are liable to be knocked out by the defence.'

Beck and many others thought of the tank as a useful weapon, but not a decisive one. It was merely an addition to the family of combined arms. There was another school which opposed the mass development of the panzer arm because they saw it as a direct threat to the cavalry, which in the Reichswehr had made up a significant proportion of the army. In addition, Guderian's school might see, like their British counterparts, the tank as restoring mobility to the battlefield and thus preventing a return to trench warfare, but here again a powerful opposition led by no less a personage than Ludendorf opposed them. Ludendorf postulated:

'In view of the mass mobilisation of armies, the extent of the reserves available for a defeated enemy, and the highly developed railway network which permits the rapid concentration and movement of military forces, it is unlikely that it will be possible to obtain a decision in the first battles of the war.' [31]

The editor of the influential military journal *Militar-Wochenblatt* gave another reason why static warfare was likely to recur:

'In view of the fact that all States, both big and little, are guarding their frontiers even in peacetime by military fortifications of all kinds, it appears very doubtful whether a war of movement on the 1914 scale will ever be possible again.' [32]

This was perhaps influenced by a *Truppenamt* appreciation of the potential of Germany's neighbours made at the beginning of 1935. This concluded that recent work on the Maginot Line had increased France's defensive power by a factor of three. There was too the realisation that a mechanised army needed a large industrial base to sustain it, an aspect of which Hitler himself was well aware.

Hitler, having gone through the horrors of the Western Front, realised only too well the dangers inherent in static warfare. Appreciating the concern of many of the military hierarchy, he believed that blitzkrieg was the only way to avoid such a war. Speaking at the 1935 Nuremburg Party Rally to foreign delegates of the League of German Girls he said:

'I shouldn't negotiate for months beforehand and make lengthy preparations, but — as I have always done throughout my life — I should suddenly, like a flash of lightning in the night, hurl myself upon the enemy.' [33]

This is the first recorded illusion to the term blitzkrieg. Shortly afterwards Guderian gave an idea of the shape this 'flash of lightning' would take:

'One night the doors of aeroplane hangars and army garages will be flung back, motors will be tuned up, and squadrons will swing into movement. The first sudden blow may capture important industrial and raw-material districts or destroy them by air attack so they can take no part in war production. Enemy governmental and military centres may be crippled and his transport system disorganised. In any case, the first strategic surprise attack will penetrate more or less deep into enemy territory according to the distances to be covered and the amount of resistance met with.

The first wave of air and mechanised attack will be followed up by motorised infantry divisions. They will be carried to the verge of the occupied territory and hold it, thereby freeing the mobile units for another blow. In the meantime the attacker will be raising a mass army. He has the choice of territory and time for his next big blow, and he will then bring up the weapons intended for breaking down all resistance and bursting through the enemy lines. He will do his best to launch the great blow so suddenly so as to take the enemy by surprise, rapidly concentrating his mobile troops and hurling his air force at the enemy. The armoured divisions will no longer stop when the first objectives have been reached; on the contrary, utilising their speed and radius of action to the full they will do their utmost to complete the breakthrough into the enemy lines of communication. Blow after blow will be launched ceaselessly in order to

*Above*: The start of it all — Little Willie's successor, *Mother*, on trials in February 1916. The wheels at the rear were to assist steering./*Royal Armoured Corps Tank Museum, Bovington*

*Below*: Cause — British 8-inch howitzers in action on the Somme, August 1916./ *Imperial War Museum (IWM)*

*Above*: Effect — Clapham Copse, Passchendaele, September 1917./*David Higham Associates*

*Below*: General von Hutier (nearest camera) mastermind of the new German assault tactics 1917-8./*IWM*

*Above*: German *sturmtruppen* in action June 1918. They advanced in short rushes, covering each other with fire./*IWM*

*Below*: Sopwith Camel — used extensively in the ground support role 1917-8./*RAF Museum, Hendon*

*Left*: 'Boom' Trenchard in full dress uniform just before World War 1./*RAF Museum, Hendon*

*Above*: General Guilio Douhet./*Rivista Aeronautica*

*Above right*: General Billy Mitchell./*US Air Force*

*Right*: 'Boney' Fuller in 1920./*David Higham Associates*

*Right*: Basil Liddell Hart in 1957./*Lady Liddell Hart*

*Below*: Johnson's Medium D, the basis for Plan 1919, undergoing amphibious trials. The figure on the tank in the soft hat is Martel./*RAC Tank Museum, Bovington*

*Above*: The start of mechanisation for the US Cavalry — an armoured car troop on manoeuvres, 1929./*Patton Museum of Cavalry and Armor, Fort Knox*

*Left*: General Estienne, the French tank enthusiast./*Etablissement Cinematographique et Photographique Des Armées (ECPA)*

*Left*: Pétain, who so influenced French military thought between the wars, inspecting artillery officers, 1921./*ECPA*

*Far bottom left*: French Renaults exercising in the Rhone Valley, 1921 (Weight 6.7 tons, Speed 5mph, 2 man crew, 37mm gun and coaxial machine gun)./*Radio Times Hulton Picture Library*

*Below left*: The Reichswehr training with one of the dummy tanks./*RAC Tank Museum, Bovington*

*Right*: Hans von Seeckt, *eminence grise* of the Weimar Republic./*Bundesarchiv*

*Below*: Beginnings of Red Army mechanisation. Russian Renaults in the early 1920s./*Radio Times Hulton Picture Library*

Cavalry

Horse-mounted sabre-troop with accompanying lorry reducing weight carried by the horses.

Machine-Guns & Crews in Fast Lorry.

15 h.p. Car. (O.C. Column)

Mechanised Anti-Aircraft Guns

6-Wheel Lorry. (Packs)

Forward Control Lorry. (Regimental Stores)

6-Wheel Lorry. (Personnel)

Standard Type Medium Tank with Wireless Signal Control.

6-Wheel Lorry. (Great Coats)

6-Wheel Lorry. (S.A.A.)

6-Wheel Lorry. (Hay)

7 h.p. Car. (Section Commander)

Mobile Anti-Tank Gun.

New Type Medium Tank.

Artillery

6-Wheel Lorry. (Oats)

Backing Field Gun into position

Infantry

Tractor towing Field Gun.

Infantry Tank

Lorry & Trailer. (Petrol) No.1

7 h.p. Car. (Section Commander)

6-Wheel Lorry. (Biscuits)

Mechanised 60 pr. gun. ← Lorry carrying Field Gun.

Tracked-Train (Troops & Machine-Guns)

Mechanised Machine-gun & Crews.

Tank Corps

"In-Fighter" Tankettes

Lorry & Trailer. (Petrol) No.2

Howitzer.

G. HAWKINS 1930.

*Top:* A fanciful view of British Army mechanisation which appeared in the *Illustrated London News* in July 1930./*London Electrotype Agency*

*Above:* 1st Tank Brigade on Salisbury Plain in 1934. The Carden-Lloyd carriers represented light tanks./*RAC Tank Museum, Bovington*

*Far left*: 'Hobo' Hobart (right) when commanding 2nd Battalion Royal Tank Corps with his adjutant in front of his Vickers Medium./*RAC Tank Museum, Bovington*

*Left*: General Wever, who wanted a balanced Luftwaffe./*Bundersarchiv*

*Below left*: The Panzer arm unveiled. Pz Kw Mk 1s (Weight 5.75 tons, two man crew, Speed 22mph, two machine guns) at the 1935 Nuremburg Rally./*Radio Times Hulton Picture Library*

*Below*: Marshall Tuchachevski on a visit to France in 1936./*Radio Times Hulton Picture Library*

*Left*: ' . . . the worst we saw was a few engines missing fire . . . ' Soviet BT-7s (weight 13.5tons, speed 36mph, three-man crew, 45mm gun and two machine guns)./*RAC Tank Museum, Bovington*

*Below left*: Part of the Maginot Line./*IWM*

*Right*: Lt Gen Daniel Van Voorhis — Father of the US Armored Force./*US Army*

*Below*: Curtiss F-11C-2 Hawk (or Goshawk) the first operational dive-bomber./*J.W.R. Taylor*

*Left*: Wolfram von Richthofen, who perfected the Luftwaffe's ground support tactics in the Spanish Civil War./*Bundesarchiv*

*Below*: Hitler watching Pz Kw Mk Is during the 1937 Wehrmacht manoeuvres in Mecklenburg./*Barnaby's Picture Library*

roll up the enemy front and carry the attack as far as possible into enemy territory. The air force will attack the enemy reserves and prevent their intervention.' [34]

Thus, here in 1935 was a German recipe for the blitzkrieg technique; a mixture of Douhet, Liddell Hart and Fuller's Plan 1919. Yet Guderian appreciated that an enemy could not be beaten merely by the use of an elite regular armoured force, for it could not hold ground. It must have the backing of a mass army. Thus he agreed with Beck to a certain extent, but whereas Beck believed that it was the mass follow-up army which would inflict the decisive damage, Guderian thought the opposite. At the same time Hitler, conscious of the importance of having a sound industrial base, decided in August 1936 that while the Army must be prepared for a war in four years, so must the economy be put on a war footing within this time. Yet he doubted that any state, Germany included, could stockpile enough munitions and raw materials for more than a year's worth of modern war, and thus blitzkreig became not just an attraction but a necessity. In the meantime the German Armoured Force grew. By March 1935 an improvised panzer division had been set up for exercises, and in October the first three panzer divisions were formed, with Lutz becoming Commander of the Panzer Corps. The interest which the Germans had shown in the British 1st Tank Brigade is illustrated in that the tank brigade in each panzer division had the same organisation of three medium tank battalions and one light tank battalion. However, in accordance with Guderian's emphasis on combined arms, the other elements of the division were a motorised rifle brigade of two rifle battalions and a motorcycle battalion, an anti-tank battalion, a reconnaissance battalion, two artillery light howitzer battalions, a signal battalion and a light engineer company. They had made the Lindsay-Hobart Mobile Division of 1934 a standard formation. Yet, Guderian did not have things all his own way. In 1936 it was decided to form panzer brigades for the infantry support role in much the same way as the British had done at battalion level. Also, in order to pacify the cavalry elements, who felt that they were losing their role, light divisions were formed, consisting of some tanks, motorised rifle battalions, artillery and reconnaissance elements to take on the cavalry's traditional roles of reconnaissance and security. Furthermore, four infantry divisions were motorised. Guderian himself was aghast at this dissipation of effort and believed that all available industrial backing should be concentrated on the panzer divisions. What he wanted for them was:

'. . . the ability of the infantry, artillery and other divisional arms to follow them in an advance across country. We wanted lightly armoured half-tracks for the riflemen, combat engineers and medical services, armoured self-propelled guns for the artillery and the anti-tank battalions, and various types of tank for the reconnaissance and signal battalions.' [35]

These were to be slow in coming. It is however significant that, in spite of the existence of three panzer divisions, the Vogelsang manoeuvres of September 1936, the largest held since 1913, with 80 000 troops taking part, only involved the use of one panzer battalion, and that was used in the infantry support role. It was adjudged to have suffered badly at the hands of the anti-tank guns, which added ammunition to the critics of wholesale mechanised warfare. Instead, the manoeuvres themselves concentrated on Beck's 'mass of decision' with the infantry committed to long marches on their feet.

The first half of the Thirties saw considerable debate as to the major role of the other main ingredient of blitzkrieg, the Luftwaffe. Hitler, before coming to power had determined on a large air force. Milch, soon to become State Secretary for Air, records a conversation with him in April 1932:

> 'Hitler then spoke at length on the ideas of General Douhet. As early as this he was principally interested in bombing warfare as the best means of deterring an aggressor. He talked of the importance of powerful armed forces, in which he saw the air force as occupying a position equal to the army's; this was the only way for Germany to rid herself of the shackles of Versailles short of war itself.' [36]

The army remained convinced that the air force should operate under military command and control. Goering, appointed to command it, had other ideas. He wanted to see it as a separate service, which being new and thus untainted by reactionary ideas, could become part of the National Socialist ideal. On the other hand he did not see the Luftwaffe as a Douhet type of force. He gathered around himself initially his old flying companions of World War 1, and they were incapable of seeing roles other than those to which they had been used — maintenance of air superiority and direct support to the ground troops. However, there was one exception, Wever, the Chief of Staff of the Luftwaffe, who was a follower of Douhet, in that he appreciated the need for a strategic bomber force. But, he believed, unlike Douhet, that the Luftwaffe should be a balanced force. In 1934 a special Air Ministry Staff was set up under Wilberg (the officer who had looked after air affairs in the early days of the Reichswehr) to investigate the conduct of air warfare. Their findings were issued as a Luftwaffe field manual in 1936. In essence they recognised four offensive air missions — the gaining and maintaining of air superiority, strategic or independent air operations, battlefield interdiction and close support for the ground troops. To this end Wever saw a need for heavy bombers, medium bombers, ground attack aircraft and fighters. Earlier, in 1933, Milch had developed the concept of the *Risikoflotte*, whereby the Luftwaffe would be built up as a deterrent against any possible aggressor. The idea of a bombing force fitted nicely into this concept. However, Wever believed that strategic bombing was not the whole answer, although it could make a significant contribution to victory. In an address given in November 1935 he showed himself still to be a believer in defeat of the enemy's armed forces as the key to victory:

'The object of any war is to destroy the morale of the enemy. The morale of the leader and of a nation is reflected to a great extent in the armed forces of that nation. Thus, in the war of the future, the destruction of the armed forces will be of primary importance.' [37]

This ran contrary to Liddell Hart's and the air power theorists' definition of the moral objective.

Meanwhile Hitler was careful not to show his hand too early and, although he had withdrawn Germany from the League of Nations and the Geneva Disarmament Conference in October 1933, he continued to develop an air force in secret. He was not prepared to reveal it to the world until it was a reasonable deterrent. When the opportunity arose in March 1935 he took care to let other countries think that it was larger in size than it actually was. In the same year the Wehrmacht, as the old Reichswehr had now come to be called, carried out a strategic study. It concluded that Germany's most likely enemies were France, Belgium, Poland and Czechoslovakia, all having common borders with Germany. In this context the main roles of the Luftwaffe were seen as reconnaissance, the achieving of air superiority and support of the ground forces. Little was made of strategic air warfare. Military bases and industrial targets were listed, but were only to be attacked as reprisals for the bombing of German civilian targets. The overriding principle was that the Luftwaffe was not to be the aggressor, and it was assumed that hostilities would open with the enemy mounting a surprise air raid. The long term significance of this study was that it marked the beginning of the Luftwaffe's swing away from the idea of the long range strategic bomber in favour of the medium tactical bomber.

Hitler's policy of bluffing other nations as to the strength of the Luftwaffe paid off when he decided to march into the demilitarised Rhineland in March 1936. Although there were at the time only three modern fighter squadrons in existence in Germany, Hitler was able to bluff the French into raising little objection to his flagrant violation of the Versailles Treaty. The concept of the *Risikoflotte* had been shown to work. Two months later Wever and Wilburg produced the first Luftwaffe training manual, based on the findings of Wilburg's 1934 study. The manual emphasised that 'air power carries the war right into the heart of enemy country from the moment war breaks out. It strikes at the very root of the enemy's fighting power and of the people's will to resist.' But it was quite categorical in ruling out attacks against the civil population. [38]

Thus by mid-1936 Germany was already shaping the tools for blitzkreig. The mailed fist of the Panzer Corps and the thunderbolt of the Luftwaffe were now in development and had been given priority over the remainder of the Wehrmacht and the navy. They would act as the spearhead, while the remainder of the Wehrmacht was to be trained up as a mass army, reliant on traditional weapons and transport, which would consolidate the lightning successes of the blitzkrieg.

## Soviet Union

Meanwhile developments in Germany's compatriot 'in the cold', Soviet

Russia, were growing in even more remarkable fashion. In 1930 the Red Army experimental mechanised force was expanded into a brigade size formation consisting of two tank battalions, two motorised infantry battalions, artillery and reconnaissance elements. Instead of following the British 'all-tank' idea, the Russians continued to exercise their doctrine of combined arms. Towards the end of the First Five Year Plan, in 1932, sufficient material had been manufactured to produce a mechanised corps of two mechanised brigades, a rifle brigade and an anti-aircraft battalion. In the same year the Stalin Academy of the Mechanisation and Motorisation of the Red Army was opened, and it was quite clear that the Red Army had already outstripped the West in terms of mechanisation. The Japanese Naval Attaché in Moscow had written in 1932:

'It is not merely the great number of tanks which is important, but the fact that an enormous number of them are of the most modern type. The mechanisation of the Red Army astonishes all the foreign attaches at its parades.' [39]

This is indicative of the success of the First Five Year Plan. In 1933 a significant series of military exercises were held in the two frontier military districts. Tuchachevski had already introduced paratroops into the Soviet order of battle by 1931, and these were combined with cavalry and mechanised units, supported by artillery and infantry to practise his concept of offensive operations, using the encirclement technique. It was becoming clear, however, that as with the Wehrmacht, the Red Army was splitting into two separate armies. On the one hand were the mechanised and motorised forces, while on the other the mass of the Red Army still consisted of infantry on their feet. Marxist doctrine had ruled out the idea of a small all-regular modern army, but industrial resources were not sufficient to produce a modernised mass army.

With Hitler's coming to power the decision was made to cease active training and participation in research and development with the Soviet forces, although the 1922 Pact still remained on the statute book. This did not deter Soviet development. Some 2 000 tanks existed by the end of 1933, but the Second Five Year Plan envisaged even greater expansion. Whereas tank production for 1930-31 was 740 tanks, that for 1931 rose to 3 371. They concentrated on the T26, a 6-ton tank with a 45mm gun, based on a Vickers design which had not found acceptance in the British Army, and the BT, a fast tank mounting a 37mm gun, based on the concept of the American designer Walter Christie. The former was designed for infantry support, while the BT was employed with the mechanised brigades. In addition, two other models found their way into the Soviet armoury, the T28 with a 76mm gun and the T35, a heavy tank with the same calibre of gun. Both these types were domestic designs and owed little to foreign influence — another measure of the development of Soviet mechanisation.

There was, however, a continuing debate as to how far mechanisation and motorisation should go. Tuchachevski wanted to take them as far as

Russia's industrial potential would allow, but not all agreed with him. There was still a large body of opinion, albeit obsolescent, led by Budenny, the commander of the Red Cavalry in the civil war, which believed in cavalry as the *arme blanche*. As far as they were concerned the tank was useful for supporting the cavalry, but it would never do to replace the horse by the tank. Budenny saw the question as being '. . . not whether we need cavalry but whether we can solve the concrete problems of its combat potentialities and modernise its tactics.' [40] In other words, this school favoured only partial mechanisation. They saw no reason why tanks and horse cavalry should not operate together. As one of them, Krivoshrin, wrote:

'Just as for cavalry, the pursuit of a defeated enemy is one of the most fruitful tasks of mechanised troops. The great mobility of cavalry is supplemented by the impetus and manoeuvring capacity of the tanks, and therefore a mixed formation of cavalry and mechanised troops represents a very effective instrument of pursuit.' [41]

They believed that the key tactic of encirclement would be carried out by cavalry, supported by aircraft and mechanised forces. Tuchachevski disagreed, seeing the mechanised forces as the key. The manual *Tactics of Mechanised Higher Formations*, which had appeared in 1932, prepared by S. N. Ammosov under Tuchachevski's direction, stated:

'Wiping out the combat forces and reserves, destruction of the combat forces and army depots together with enemy aerodromes, the mechanised forces could be reinforced with support from the air, motorised units and in some cases cavalry.' [42]

For the time being a compromise was arrived at, whereby cavalry divisions had tank units placed within them, and the mechanised formations would, if need be, co-operate with the cavalry. Yet at the same time Voroshilov had warned that:

'First and foremost, it is necessary to put an end once and for all to the wrecking 'theories' on the substitution of machines for horses, on the 'withering away' of the horse.' [43]

Tuchachevski continued to labour towards his ideal. Addressing the 7th Congress of Soviets in January 1935, he spoke of the difficulties in trying to get his ideas accepted:

'. . . The problem is not a simple one. During the civil war we became accustomed to cavalry as the most rapid arm, while the majority are accustomed to infantry actions, and to be able to adjust ourselves to a new level, to be able to utilise the mobility of aviation and our mechanised troops and tanks is not so simple.' [44]

He then went on to decree that 'the axis of our military training in 1935 is to master the technique and art of commanding the swift-moving forms of engagements involving every kind of arm.' The Red Army manoeuvres of that year certainly impressed the French. General Loizeau, head of the French military delegation attending the manoeuvres, wrote in his report:

'The technique of the Red Army is on a particularly high level . . . To achieve this level of armaments in three or four years not only demonstrates the power of Soviet industry, it also establishes the immense superiority of the Red Army over all other European armies, which are often forced, and for a long time to use old material.' [45]

It would seem that Tuchachevski's ideas were winning through. The culmination came with the introduction of the Field Service Regulations of 1936. In his foreward, Tuchachevski remarked that military thought in capitalist countries seemed to have fallen on barren ground. The British were ignoring Fuller and Liddell Hart, the French were doing the same to the 'brilliant' writer de Gaulle, and even the Italians showed little interest in carrying out the ideas of Douhet. He then went on to discount the popular communist idea of the 'special manoeuvrability' of the Red Army, which, rather like the French interpretation of Ardant du Picq's ideas in the years leading up to 1914, would have one believe that the Red Army was invincible because of its revolutionary ardour alone. At the same time he poured cold water on the all-tank idea, saying that it did not take into account '. . . the anti-tank operations of the opponent, and the failure to appreciate that like infantry, tanks cannot operate without the powerful support of artillery . . .' The Regulations began with the premise that:

'Every war, offensive and defensive, has the aim of defeating the enemy. But only a decisive offensive in the main direction concluding with persistent pursuit, leads to complete annihilation of the forces and means of the enemy.'

To this end, Tuchachevski saw the battle taking place in four stages. Assuming that the enemy were holding some sort of fixed line, the first stage would be an attack by assault groups, consisting of infantry, tanks and artillery, on the weakest point in the enemy's line. Where initial success was achieved support groups with additional artillery would be pushed through. The third stage was to be the decisive breakthrough. Tanks, cavalry and motorised infantry would split up enemy units and form local encirclements, which would be subjected to artillery fire and ground attack from the air. Finally, there would be the pursuit phase when paratroops and airmobile forces would join the mechanised forces and cavalry for a penetration deep into enemy territory. There were similarities to Plan 1919 in this doctrine, but there was less emphasis on the effect of attacks on enemy headquarters and lines of communication. Also, until such time as an effective breach had been made the pace of the battle was that of the infantryman on his feet, only in the latter stages would it quicken. Thus unlike the German concept of using the 'mass' in the follow-up role, the Soviets used the mass first, but then the doctrine unlike that of the Germans, started with the premise that static conditions of warfare would exist initially.

The first chance the Red Army had to try out these new tactics was in the September 1936 manoeuvres, which two British officers experienced in mechanisation, Martel and Wavell, attended. One side, the aggressors, had three infantry divisions, two cavalry divisions, five mechanised brigades, a tank brigade (four battalions, each of 32 T28 tanks) and six air squadrons. The other had a corps of two infantry divisions with two mechanised brigades, another infantry division, a cavalry corps of two divisions with a mechanised brigade and a motorised brigade, and also six air squadrons. Martel was not impressed with the tactical handling of the tanks. Describing a battle between one aggressor mechanised brigade and two similar defending brigades, he wrote:

'There was little skill shown in the handling of these forces, which appeared just to bump into one another! Nevertheless, it was interesting to see such large tank forces in contact, and one was impressed with their power when employed in such suitable country. The use of horsed cavalry on the battlefield, however, and in the presence of tanks on this open country seemed quite impossible.' [46]

Yet, he was impressed with the mechanical efficiency of the tank forces:

'We have seen some 1 200 tanks of all kinds covering considerable distances during the four days of the manoeuvres, and with practically no mechanical trouble . . . On the first day over a thousand tanks marched past us on a parade, and the worst we saw was a few engines missing fire a little at times.' [47]

At the same time, they saw an impressive demonstration whereby an airborne force of infantry, lorries, light tanks, armoured cars and field guns were dropped. Although they saw aircraft being used to attack front line positions, Martel was surprised not to see them employed in attacking targets further to the rear. All in all, although the Russians had the equipment, which in quality was up to, and in quantity greatly exceeded that of Western countries, it was clear that Tuchachevski's high sounding ideas had not really percolated down to the more junior ranks. As Martel wrote in summary:

'The Russian Army was still a bludgeon, quite incapable of rapier work; it had the armoured spikes put on the head of the bludgeon and would strike a deadly blow when it binded; but an active and well-equipped enemy should often be able to avoid or counter the blow and would at least inflict heavy damage on a clumsy opponent.' [48]

With regard to Martel's surprise at the employment of the Red Air Force, it is important to realise that the VVS was not just employed as Martel saw it. The early 1930s saw the Red Air Force become much more of a service in its own right. For a start, there was an increasing tendency to concentrate air resources at the highest level of military command, and to use the advice of air force officers attached to military headquarters. There was also a significant drift away from the idea that airpower's prime use was in close support of the ground forces. As early as 1926, A. N. Lapchinsky had stressed the importance of strategic air operations, and, although he had dismissed the Douhet concept of airpower being the decisive weapon, the value of having a strategic air force became more attractive. At the beginning of 1935, the VVS Chief of Staff, Kripin, came to the conclusion that modern warfare could not be waged without a strategic air arm, and from then on there was a gradual shift in emphasis towards the long-range bomber. Even between the years 1929 and 1931 there had been a change in the proportion of bombers in the VVS from 16% to 30%, but it was not until 1935 that an independent bomber force was formed directly under the control of the VVS Headquarters in Moscow. But, this force was not in the Douhet mould. Its role was still in support of the Red Army, by interdiction deep into the enemy's territory as opposed to destroying his industrial effort. Thus the VVS assisted the Red Army in two ways. It gave close air support on the battlefield, especially during the early phases of the Tuchachevski attack doctrine, and it helped the breakthrough and pursuit phases by attacking targets further behind the enemy's front.

### France

The majority of Frenchmen entered the 1930s convinced that the Maginot Line was the answer to their country's problems of defence. This is not to say that the French Army was entirely blinded to the need for mechanisation. Estienne's parting words on his retirement from the Army in 1930 were a final plea to make the French tank force an independent arm, arguing that '. . . it has not the least analogy to the infantry.' [49] Yet in the same year the manual *Instructions for the Employment of Tanks* continued to make the point that 'Tanks are only supplementary means, put temporarily at the disposal of the infantry. They strengthen considerably the action of the latter but they do not replace it . . . the progress of the infantry and its seizing of objectives are alone decisive.' Pétain's successor, Weygand, although a cavalryman, was not opposed to mechanisation, but, like his British counterpart Milne, believed in proceeding with caution. In 1931 he advocated the partial mechanisation of the cavalry divisions. This produced the retort from General Dufieux, Inspector of Infantry and Tanks, that:

'In my opinion, there is no possibility that a mechanised combat detachment can ever be used to lead a complete operation by itself . . . I cannot understand therefore why the Mechanised Cavalry Division is being formed as if it were sufficient to itself in all circumstances.' [50]

In spite of this opposition from the infantry, 1932 saw exercises taking place with mechanised infantry and cavalry detachments. This led to the formation of a completely motorised cavalry division the following year. In 1934 this formation was designated as a *Division Legere Mecanique* (DLM). It was made up of a reconnaissance battalion, a tank brigade of two regiments, each equipped with eighty 1933 Model Renault light tanks, a motorised rifle brigade of three battalions, each including 20 light tanks, a towed artillery regiment and an engineer battalion. In organisation it was remarkably similar to the 1935 pattern Panzer Division, but, unlike the latter, it maintained the traditional cavalry role of reconnaissance and security.

Meanwhile, de Gaulle, having finished commanding his infantry battalion, was posted to a staff job in the Levant. On his return in 1932, he was posted to the general secretariat of the Higher Council for National Defence, where his role was to study French war plans. In that year he published his first full length book *Le Fil de l'Epée* (The Edge of the Sword), a philosophical piece of writing based on his lectures to the Ecole de Guerre. It was however in the following year that he wrote the book *The Army of the Future* (*Vers l'Armée de Metiér*), which was to make his reputation as a protagonist of armour. The main thesis of the book was the need to form a small professional army, which would be superimposed on the existing conscript army. De Gaulle believed that such a force was necessary in order to ward off surprise attacks and gain time. He argued that France was now short of manpower brought about by a drop in the birthrate and could no longer rely on a mass army. 'It is none the less certain that future French victories will no longer be those of the big battalions.' [51] De Gaulle's élite force of 100 000 men needed the ability to react quickly to a threat and to move fast to counter it. To do this it would have to rely on the internal combustion engine:

> 'Six divisions of the line completely motorised and 'caterpillared' and partly armoured, will constitute an army suitable for carrying through a campaign. It will be an organisation whose front, depth and means of protection and supply will allow it to operate independently.' [52]

Each division would consist of a heavy brigade of 500 medium guns, 400 light guns and 600 machine guns, a tank brigade of one heavy regiment, a medium regiment and a reconnaissance battalion, and an infantry brigade with 40 light guns, 40 anti-tank guns and 600 machine guns. The role of the infantry would, as Fuller had envisaged, to be 'occupying, mopping up and organising the territory which the terrible but temporary power of the tanks will have virtually secured. [53] Each division would have an artillery group of two regiments in direct support, together with an anti-aircraft group. There would also be a light division, carrying out the same role as the new DLM. As part of the general reserves for the army there would be a brigade of very heavy tanks for attacking permanent fortifications, along with an artillery brigade of ultra heavy guns. He emphasised the need for the tanks to push through to the final objective and made much of the need for the artillery to be self-propelled in order to support them. His fixation with heavy artillery shows that he had not thrown off the spectre of the Maginot Line or indeed the establishment view that maximum concentration of firepower was the essence of success. He hardly mentioned the use of aircraft. He did at one point suggest that they might be useful for laying smokescreens to cover the advancing tanks, but otherwise he passed them by. It was only later, after his bitter experiences in May 1940, that he published a new edition giving them a more positive role in his scheme.

Only a quarter of the book actually dealt with de Gaulle's concept of armoured warfare, the remainder was concerned with justifying the need of a professional army. This was an anathema to the majority of Frenchmen, who had always viewed such an army as a threat to the constitution of France. Hence *Vers l'Armée de Metiér* was virtually ignored in France, only selling 750 copies in its first edition. The Germans thought it of little consequence, and Lindell Hart for the British commented that: 'So far as can be deduced from his hazy outline, the division he pictured would have been a clumsy monstrosity, impossible to manoeuvre . . .' [54] Only in Russia was it well received. At this time the Left was in the ascendant in French politics and relations with the USSR were improving dramatically. Hence there was a new interest in things French. Also, Tuchachevski, whether he remembered the days when he and de Gaulle were fellow prisoners of war or not, liked the book. It did provide a suitable concept for the expanding Soviet armoured force. However, in spite of the general lack of enthusiasm for de Gaulle's book in France, he did gain himself one ally, the eminent politician Paul Reynaud, who agreed to air de Gaulle's views in parliament.

It so happened that in March 1935 an important debate took place on the subject of raising the length of service for conscripts from one year to two. Reynaud drew the attention of the deputies to Germany's rising military strength, especially her panzer forces. He spoke of the German determination to begin and end a future war with one massive stroke. In this context it was not increased length of service, but a regular armoured force, which would be the only means of defeating such a blow. In reply, General Maurin, the defence minister, said:

'How can anyone believe that we could again think of taking the offensive when we have spent milliards to establish a fortified barrier? Are we to be so mad as to advance in front of this barrier — on, I do not know what kind of adventure? That, Gentlemen, shows you the mind of the Government. For the Government, at least as far as I am concerned, knows perfectly well what the plan of the next war will be.' [55]

This effectively killed any possibility of official acceptance for de Gaulle's ideas. Yet, the soldiers themselves were well aware that France's military situation was serious. Weygand had said as much to Pétain, the then War Minister, at the beginning of 1934:

'The Army has sunk to the lowest level that the security of France can allow, in the present state of Europe . . . it just barely satisfies the needs of National Defence as set by the international political situation in accordance with which it was created and on which our security in part depends.' [56]

The problem was that the French Army was organised to deal with a German Army of the size of that laid down by the Treaty of Versailles. By 1934 it was common knowledge that the terms of Versailles had been completely disregarded. More and more officers realised that something other than concrete defence works, which anyway did not cover the whole of the French frontier, were needed. As one high-ranking officer put it: 'We should be deceiving the country if we said that defensive works were in a position to guarantee complete security.' [57] Perhaps then there was something in de Gaulle's ideas, but no official doctrine could be based on the idea of a professional armoured force, because that would be politically unacceptable. De Gaulle's old patron, Pétain saw the need for a new doctrine, but not on the basis of armour. He was still convinced that the tank was the servant of the infantry, and also saw de Gaulle's force as being entirely offensive. Instead he nailed his colours to the mast of air power. It took the German re-occupation of the Rhineland to shock France into action. As de Gaulle ruefully remarked after it had happened:

'It is a disaster, probably an irreparable one. The general staff and the government hesitated. They refused to resort to general mobilisation. If we had had my professional army and my tanks, mobilisation would not have been necessary. We should have advanced and the Germans would have retreated. If we had done our duty, peace would have been assured.' [58]

Nevertheless, the groundwork for an armoured force had been laid in 1935 when orders were finally placed for Estienne's Char B, which had been on the drawing board since 1921. But French industry was to be slow to adapt to an increase in military orders. Time was needed for re-tooling, industrial disputes proliferated and the system of ordering was inefficient.

If the Army was slow in stepping into the present, the Air Force did react more quickly. In 1934 the *Armée de l'Air* became an independent service under the ministry of General Denain. He set about shaping a positive air doctrine based on the premise that war against Germany and/or Italy would come sooner or later, and that because the air force was now independent it could prepare for roles independent of the army. Thus, he came up with the idea of a strategic bomber force and a tactical air force, the latter supporting the army. The new doctrine was summed up by General Fequant its commander:

'The task of our air force will not be limited to defending our country from air attack. It already has sufficiently powerful weapons to give it the

91

upper hand in the event of a conflict, and by its offensive operations it will break the will of the enemy and pursue him to the very sources of his power. Our air squadrons will strike far behind the enemy lines and attack the material sources indispensable for the supply and continued existence of his armies. And further, when it has weakened the enemy by such attacks, it will be in a position, thanks to the wide radius of action and high speed of its machines, to assemble its forces from all sectors of the front and to concentrate its fighting strength at the critical moment on any one point of the front and thus effect a breakthrough for the land forces.' [59]

In essence, his plan was for an initial Douhet type of stroke against the enemy, followed by tactical support for the ground forces. Unfortunately, as with the Army, his words seemed impressive on paper, but France had few modern aircraft. Although she possessed some 4 300 aircraft at the beginning of 1936, the majority were obsolete, and bombers and fighters accounted for less than a quarter of the total, the majority being reconnaissance aircraft and trainers. The truth was that the aircraft industry was, as with the rest of the armaments sector, hopelessly inefficient. In August 1936 it was nationalised but the beneficial effects of this would not show themselves for another three years, by which time the prospect of war was more than a first small cloud on the far horizon.

The year 1936 marked another landmark with the introduction of a new set of *Instructions* to replace Pétain's 1921 version. If anyone had hoped for radical changes they were disappointed. General Georges, who had chaired the board which had drawn them up, wrote:

'The Committee which has drawn up the present instructions does not believe that this technical progress sensibly modifies the essential rules hitherto established in the domain of tactics. Consequently it believes that the doctrine objectively fixed at the end of the war (1918) by the eminent chiefs who held high commands must remain the charter for the tactical employment of large units.' [60]

Although the *Instructions* accepted that 'only the offensive can produce decisive results', it emphasised that in order to take to the offensive overwhelming superiority was essential. Looking at this truism in the context of the Maginot Line, Weygand speaking to the British Military Attaché in 1934 had complacently remarked that:

'Before she could attack France with any certainty of success, Germany would need an overwhelming margin of superiority; the increase in French armaments sufficient to meet a German attack would therefore be very considerably less than that required by Germany before she could launch it. The position was therefore safe for a considerable time without great effort by France, unless, of course, some new scientific development capable of revolutionising warfare were to be discovered. The existence

92

of this possibility was an additional reason for preserving liberty of action.' [61]

The infantry were still to be the predominant arm.

'Protected and accompanied by its own guns and by the guns of the artillery, and occasionally preceded by combat tanks and aviation, etc., it conquers ground, occupies it, organises, and holds it.'

The manual indicated that the power of the anti-tank gun precluded the operation of tanks on their own, and they could be used '. . . only in an attack after the protection and support of a very powerful artillery.' There was little or no attempt to restore the art of manoeuvre to the French Army and 'the battlefield was conceived as a corps-à-corps struggle, a wrestling bout rather than a boxing match.' [62]

By the mid 1930s France was starting to wake up to the potential threat of Germany, but it had taken the Rhineland episode to do this . Although she had realised a need for up to date weaponry her inefficient industry needed to be reformed before the necessary armaments could be produced in any quantity. Her air force was trying to face up to the realities of the possible European wars of the future, but her army high command still remained firmly wedded to the doctrines which had brought success in 1918. Those who were rash enough to speak out against this, were censored and the country at large continued to be led to believe that the Maginot Line was a sufficient deterrent to German warlike ambitions.

## United States
The American protagonists of armoured warfare greeted the start of the 1930s with hopes held high. Summerall's decree that a permanent mechanised force should be formed made it seem that at long last the US Army could take its place among the modern armies of the world. The 1930 force itself was on more modest lines than its predecessor, being made up of a mere company of tanks and one of infantry machine guns together with a troop of armoured cars and a self-propelled artillery battery. Once again it contained the same motley collection of vehicles, still being based on Renaults but with a mixture of experimental tanks and armoured cars. Summerall had intended, however, that it should be re-equipped within three years. Colonel Daniel Van Voorhis was assigned to command the force with Lt Col Sereno Brett, a tank veteran of World War I, as second-in-command. After a short time Chaffee replaced Brett. The force mission was laid down optimistically, in view of its size, as,

'. . . to provide higher commanders with a powerful weapon of tactical and strategic opportunity, when the mission indicates the desirability of employing a force whose characteristics are highly tactical and strategic mobility, hard hitting power, high mobile defensive power, limited holding power, and one which is capable of sustained independent action.' [63]

The major difference between this and the 1928 mission lay in the emphasis on independent operations as opposed to those in co-operation with cavalry and infantry formations.

All seemed set fair but unfortunately MacArthur, Summerall's successor as Chief of Staff, decided to countermand the order late in 1931. Instead he directed that each branch of the Army should pursue mechanisation on its own with whatever limited facilities, in terms of money and material, were allotted to it. Thus the 1930 experiment went to a premature grave with little more to show in the way of tangible results. Yet, if nothing else it had fired the imaginations of both Van Voorhis and Chaffee. As Chaffee himself said after the closing down of the experiment:

'If fast tanks can operate in this manner, we will greatly aid in restoring mobility to warfare, in keeping with the doctrine of operating on the flanks and rear and through the gap. In forcing the enemy to make detachments to guard his line of communication, important bridges, airdromes and bases, we would so weaken his main forces in battle that a quicker decision will be reached.' [64]

This was in effect Liddell Hart's 'Indirect Approach', but the inference was that mechanised forces would act merely as a threat on the periphery of the battlefield, leaving more orthodox forces to make the main attack. This idea was to predominate in the thoughts of the American protagonists of armour throughout the decade.

MacArthur, by reason of his disbanding of the 1930 force, has been held up by some as a reactionary and a 'doubting Thomas'. In view of the circumstances surrounding the disbandment this criticism is hardly fair. For a start, money was even scarcer than it had been in the previous decade, as a result of the aftermath of the Wall Street crash of 1929. Whereas $542 000 had been allocated for tank development for the fiscal year 1931-32, for the next year there was only one million dollars available for development as a whole in the US Army. The Ordnance Board decided that the top three priorities were semi-automatic rifles, 3-inch anti-aircraft guns and the tank. The rifles were the cheapest to produce, and the belief of the time that air power was a formidable threat justified developments in air defence. The tank was regarded by the politicians as an offensive weapon, and President Hoover was about to put forward the motion at the disarmament conference that all offensive weapons should be banned. Thus it found itself a poor third. MacArthur believed that to try and run a mechanised force experiment without modern equipment was senseless. He could also point to the British who had been unable to continue their experiments with a tank brigade after 1931 because of financial restrictions. There was, too, the spectre of a bitter struggle growing between the infantry and the cavalry over the tank. The infantry felt that they alone should be the possessors of the tank and could point to an Act of Congress to prove their case. Both Van Voorhis and Chaffee were cavalrymen, and the infantry saw this as a prelude to a cavalry takeover of the weapon. Even more aggravating to them had been an article by Summerall in the February 1931 issue of the *Cavalry Journal*, in which he wrote: '. . . it will follow that from being an immediate auxiliary of the infantry, the tank will become a weapon exercising offensive power in its own right.' It was thus necessary for MacArthur to try and reconcile the two branches. His compromise was to allow the cavalry to experiment with light tanks, as an aid to their traditional reconnaissance role, while the infantry retained the bulk of the tanks for use as infantry support. The tanks already in the 1930 force were handed over to the cavalry, which absorbed them into the 1st Cavalry Regiment (Mechanised). In order to circumvent the 1920 Act they were called 'combat cars'.

Undoubtedly MacArthur at the beginning of his term in office was against the Fuller idea that the tank could conquer all. In his Annual Report for 1931 he wrote:

'To the greatest extent possible machines will be used to increase the mobility, security, and striking power of the ground arm, but no separate corps will be established in the vain hope that through a utilisation of machines it can absorb the missions, and duplicate the capabilities of all others.' [65]

In the next annual report he did make it clear that he foresaw the eventual wholesale mechanisation of the Cavalry, but only when '. . . machines have been developed capable of performing every function heretofore devolving upon the horse, and these machines will have been made available in adequate quantities.' [66] Since there was not the money available for the wholesale equipment of units with modern tanks, emphasis would have to be placed on the production of prototypes,

'making precise arrangements for speeding up their production in emergency; procuring annually sufficient numbers for thorough tactical test and for developing tactical doctrine for mechanised units; and indoctrinating the whole army in methods of co-operation so as to capitalise fully the inherent capabilities of these machines and make allowances for their inherent weaknesses.' [67]

This explains why the US Army continued to be dilatory in introducing new tanks into service. Not that MacArthur had not tried. Appearing before the Congressional Appropriations Committee in November 1932 he had pleaded for more money for the raising of mechanised forces. 'They suffer tremendously from one thing and one thing only — that Congress will not give them enough money to equip them properly with modern tanks.' [68] But to a Congress still wedded to the principle of isolationism his words fell on deaf ears.

American tank design in the late twenties and early thirties was dominated by one man, J. Walter Christie. Christie believed that mobility and agility were far more important than protection and firepower. In 1921 he had produced a design for a fast medium tank, which was not taken up because of its mechanical unreliability. Later, in 1928, he introduced a new design for a tank which could travel on tracks and wheels. Even more revolutionary than this was its speed. Powered by a 338bhp Liberty aircraft engine it was capable of speeds of 70mph on wheels and 42mph on tracks, far faster than anything which existed at the time. Both the cavalry and infantry became interested, and in 1931 seven of an improved version were brought by the US Army for evaluation. Unfortunately the Ordnance Board, in view of the limited funds available, decided that it was too expensive to produce, and in 1936 the concept was dropped. Only the Russians immediately pursued it further with their BT tank. As a result, only sixteen new tanks were accepted into service up to 1936, and the Army continued to rely mainly on its stock of vintage World War 1 Renaults.

Meanwhile, elements within the cavalry became unhappy about mechanisation. Most realised that it would certainly aid the cavalry, but the majority looked on the idea that the machine would eventually replace the horse with abhorrence. One officer went so far as to claim that a cavalry force with 'all the light cannon and heavy machine guns of large caliber that it can handle without loss of its essential mobility' would 'certainly take care of itself' if it came up against a mechanised force of equal numbers of men. [69] Patton, working in the Office of the Chief of Cavalry, was in an invidious position. On the one hand, he had successfully commanded tanks in action and had seen their potential, and on the other he had his loyalty to his own arm and to his chief. Although he welcomed the introduction of mechanisation into the cavalry, he was worried by the lowering of morale within the ranks of the cavalry, who began to think that the days of the horse were numbered. Ideally Patton hoped that the two would be able to operate together, although this had been shown to be wishful thinking on the Western Front. He attacked the idea of large independent mechanised formations, saying that 'Men not machines win battles' [70] and 'the army exists to kill men — not to groom vehicles.' [71] Mechanised forces were there to assist the older arms, not to replace them or act on their own.

The neglect of the Army Air Corps was even more startling. The MacArthur-Pratt Agreement of 1931 laid down that the Army Air Corps would assume coastal defence while its naval counterpart was given primarily offensive roles, making use of aircraft carriers. This gave the impetus to the Mitchell school to proceed with bomber development. Later, in 1934 the Baker Board recommended that control of the Army Air Corps should be centralised as opposed to the existing system of being split up among the military regions. It did not however recommend an independent air force. These recommendations were adopted in 1935. In the meantime President Roosevelt had decided that the Army Air Corps should be given the additional responsibility of carrying the nation's air mail. The result was a disaster, eight aircraft were wrecked during the first week of the scheme, which showed up the low standards of training and maintenance. Now that the Corps had more control over itself it was determined to push through the Mitchell concept of the strategic bomber. While Congress did not like the idea because of its offensive connotations, the army liked it even less because it was robbing them of tactical air support. Yet, the Army Air Corps got its way, and in 1935 the first B-17 bomber was produced.

## Other Nations

Of the other nations, the Italians used tanks, light two-man L/3s, and the Regia Aeronautica was employed on both tactical and strategic missions during the invasion of Ethiopia, but little worthwhile experience was gained, apart from technical evaluation, against a primitive and ill-equipped enemy. The Japanese started to produce their own tanks in 1931, and by 1935 had the makings of an armoured force. However, they continued to employ tanks solely in support of the infantry during their operations in Manchuria and China. The Poles, too, in spite of their neighbours' pre-occupation with armoured forces, continued to develop their own slowly. By 1935 they only had some nine battalions, mainly made up of Vickers 6-ton tanks. As yet there was no thought of developing a proper armoured force. The Japanese air force copied the American idea of having an army and naval component, and they did contemplate the idea of strategic bombers. The small Polish air force was dedicated to support of the army and defending Polish air space. The emphasis was therefore on fighters and reconnaissance aircraft.

By mid-1936 the Germans had fashioned a blitzkrieg weapon. The Russians with the largest mechanised force were planning to employ it in a counter-offensive role, supported by the Red Air Force. The French were attempting to overhaul their armaments industry, and were introducing gradual mechanisation, although their main hopes were still pinned firmly on the Maginot Line. They were, too, trying to develop a dual role air force. The British tank enthusiasts were going off on a tangent with the 'all-tank' idea, while the RAF remained committed to the strategic bomber. The American militants continued to struggle against the policy of isolationism, and although they had produced a strategic bomber still did not have a true mechanised force.

### Notes

1   JRUSI May 1930.
2   Bidwell, *Gunners At War* p 59.
3   JRUSI May 1931.
4   Martel, *In the Wake of the Tank* p 228.
5   Ibid, pp 386-7.
6   *The Tanks* vol 1 op cit p 301.
7   Luvaas, *The Education of an Army* p 352.
8   Ibid, pp 245-6.
9   Fuller, *Armoured Warfare* p 16.
10  Ibid, p 27.
11  Dennis, *Decision By Default* p 35.
12  Howard, *The Continental Commitment* p 94.
13  Ibid, p 104.
14  Dennis, op cit p 45.
15  Ibid, p 61.

16  *The Tanks* vol 1 op cit p 306.
17  Macksey, *Armoured Crusader* p 82.
18  Ibid, p 83.
19  *The Tanks* vol 1 op cit p 307.
20  Ibid, p 333.
21  Ibid, pp 333-34n.
22  Hitler, *Mein Kampf* p 603.
23  Bullock, *Hitler* p 189.
24  *National-Sozialistiche Monatshifte* No 3, 1930 p 101.
25  Strawson, *Hitler as Military Commander* p 36.
26  Ibid, p 39.
27  Guderian, op cit p 24.
28  Metzsch, *Wie weirde ein neuer Krieg asseben?* p 34.
29  Liddell Hart, *The British Way in Warfare* p 126.
30  O'Neill, *The German Army and the Nazi Party 1933-39* p 94.
31  Ludendorff, *Der totale Krieg* p 110.
32  *Militar-Wochenblatt* 4 Jun 36.
33  Muller, *Germany's War Machine* p 30.
34  *Militarwissen Schlaftliche Rundschau* Dec 1935.
35  Guderian, op cit p 37.
36  Irving, *The Rise and Fall of the Luftwaffe* p 27.
37  *Military Affairs* Spring 1960.
38  Irving, op cit p 47.
39  Kournakoff, op cit p 68.
40  Garder, *A History of the Soviet Army* p 84.
41  Werner, *Military Strength of the Powers* p 98.
42  Garder, op cit p 84.
43  Gartoff, op cit p 316.
44  Erikson, op cit p 381.
45  De La Gorce, *The French Army* p 258.
46  Martel, *An Outspoken Soldier* op cit p 144.
47  Liddell Hart, *Memoirs* Vol 1 op cit p 390.
48  *An Outspoken Soldier* op cit p 144.
49  Shirer, *The Collapse of the Third Republic* p 175.
50  Ibid, p 176.
51  De Gaulle, *The Army of the Future* p 91.
52  Ibid, p 100.
53  Ibid, p 101.
54  Crawley, *De Gaulle* p 72.
55  Reynaud, *Venu de ma Montagne* p 434.
56  De La Gorce, op cit p 254.
57  Allehaut, *Etre Prêt* p 218.
58  Tournoux, *Pétain and de Gaulle* p 80.
59  *Vu* 14 Nov 36.
60  Shirer, op cit p 180.
61  Bankwitz, *Maxime Weygand* p 136.
62  Chapman, *Why France Collapsed* p 38.
63  *Cavalry Journal* Jul/ Aug 1931.
64  Whitehouse, *Tank* p 129.
65  Waldrop, *MacArthur on War* p 51.
66  Ibid, p 127.
67  Ibid, p 129.
68  Watson, *US Army in World War II: Pre-War Plans and Preparations* p 22.
69  *Cavalry Journal* Sep/ Oct 1931.
70  *Patton Papers* op cit p 906.
71  Ibid, p 909.

# 4

# Dress Rehearsals

**The Spanish Civil War**

In July 1936 civil war broke out in Spain between the forces of the Right, representing the Church, the Army and the industrialists, and the Left, an amalgam of republicans, socialists, syndicalists, anarchists and communists. Although Great Britain, France, Germany, Italy and Russia signed an agreement of non-intervention in August, this was not upheld. In November Mussolini reached an understanding whereby Italy would supply Franco, leader of the forces of the Right, with men, arms and money in return for concessions in the Western Mediterranean. In October, Russia moved in to support the Left, and Germany followed Italy's lead. Spain quickly became a laboratory where the new techniques of warfare could be tried out.

The German contribution remained small in terms of numbers of men and amount of material. Perhaps their most far-reaching form of aid was the unofficial loan of twenty JU 52 transport aircraft which ferried some 4000 of Franco's troops, together with almost 300 tons of stores from Tetuan in Spanish Morocco across to Seville during August and September 1936. The remainder of the air element came to be known as the Condor Legion, which initially reached a strength of 30 JU 52s in the bomber role, three squadrons of He 51 fighters, and some assorted reconnaissance aircraft. Later the opportunity was taken to try out more modern aircraft in the shape of the He 111, Do 17, Me 109 and Ju 87 and reached a total of some 200 aircraft. The ground element was even smaller. Colonel von Thoma arrived in Spain in September with two companies of Pz Kw Mk Is and an anti-aircraft battery. By the end of intervention in 1938 this had risen to four tank battalions, each of 45 tanks, and 36 gun batteries of 37mm anti-tank guns. However, no heavier tank than the Pz Kw Mk I was ever sent.

The Italian contribution was very much larger — a complete Corps known as the *Commando Truppe Volontarie* (CTV). However, although it had plenty of infantry and some motor transport columns, it had few tanks. Initially the latter were represented by four companies of L/3 tanks, and an armoured car company. Later, a tank group of two L/3 battalions, a motorised infantry battalion, and a support battalion of machine guns, flamethrowers, anti-tank guns and 65mm howitzers was formed. They sent over 700 aircraft throughout their period of intervention, being made up in the main of Fiat CR 32 fighters, Savoia-Marchetti SM 81 bomber transports and Savoia-Marchetti SM 79-1 bombers. The Russian effort was also large.

99

Exact figures are impossible to identify, but it would seem that a total c 700 tanks and 1 500 aircraft would be a reasonable estimate. The tank were made up of T-26s and BT types, while the aircraft were Tupolev SB twin-engined bombers and stubby I-15 biplane and I-16 monoplane fighters The Russian forces were initially led by Pavlov, and other notable figure who took part were Schtern (codenamed 'Kleber'), Rokossovsky, Koniev Malinovsky and Rodimtsev, all of whom would become Marshals of th Soviet Union, and Krivoshein, who had commanded the first Soviet tan brigade.

The first occasion on which the foreign powers had a chance to emplo their new weapons in action was at the Battle of Esquivas on October 29th 1936, a Republican effort to throw back the Nationalists south of Madrid Heralded by an announcement over Madrid Radio, which said 'At dawn our artillery and armoured trains will open fire. Immediately, our aircraf will attack. Tanks will advance on the enemy at his most vulnerable point [1], a group of less than 50 Russian tanks under Pavlov attacked Nationalis cavalry in the streets of the town. Infantry were supposed to follow up th tanks, but soon got left behind. After initial success the tanks, unable t hold ground on their own, were forced to withdraw. If nothing else this ha shown that tanks operating on their own could bring only temporar success. In March 1937 it was the turn of the Nationalists to emplo mechanised forces. Having failed to cut off Madrid from the south, a attempted in the Battle of Jarama in February 1937, the Nationalists nov resolved to attack from the north-east. The first objective was the provincia capital of Guadalajara. The bulk of the attackers were Italians, who wer organised in four divisions. One of these, the Black Flames Division unde General Coppi was composed entirely of lorried infantry and armoure cars, supported by tanks. It led the initial assault which was successful i breaking through the Republican lines. The advance however soon slowe to a halt. Vile weather and the inability of Nationalist aircraft to take of because of fog, while their opposite numbers were not so hindered, took it toll of the advancing troops. After five days the Italians had managed t advance 20 miles down the main Barcelona-Guadalajara-Madrid road Since the main thrust was tied to the axis of this road Pavlov's tanks ha plenty of time to concentrate for the counter-stroke. On March 13th the attacked supported by infantry. Once again the tanks outstripped thei supporting infantry and although the Russian armour penetrated to a dept of 25 miles it was forced to retire. The net Nationalist gain at the end of th battle was a salient some 30 miles wide and ten miles deep. Although haile by the Republicans as a great victory, in truth neither side could call i such. It merely showed that the Italians did not understand that ope terrain and good weather conditions were essential conditions for a successfu blitzkreig, whereas the Russians still had not appreciated the need fo combined arms, operating closely with one another. Colonel F. O. Miksche who fought on the Republic side as an artillery commander, commented:

'This battle, more than any other in Spain, struck the imagination c

Europe and led to an underestimation of the power of motorised infantry. Most of the armies of Europe judged from this battle, with some relief, that motorised forces were not as necessary as progressive theorists had made out. The German General Staff, on the other hand, were perhaps armoured against this feeling by the depth of their contempt for the Italians as soldiers. They did not say 'it can't be done'. They said 'Naturally, these people can't do it'. [2]

By this stage in the war two things had become clear to observers. The first was the use of aircraft in support of ground operations. The Nationalists, in particular, employed their air power as a form of aerial artillery to soften up the enemy prior to an attack. Adolf Galland, one of the most renowned Luftwaffe fighter pilots of the Second World War, won his spurs with the Condor Legion in Spain, flying an He 51 in support of the ground troops. He saw his role as follows:

'The task of the *cadenas* or *trabajadores*, as they called us, was to provide air cover for infantry attacks, hold down movements behind enemy lines, silence artillery, prevent reserves from being brought up and foil any possible counter-attack. German fighter support became an essential requisite for any Nationalist operation.' [3]

It was during the Spanish Civil War also that the Ju 87 Stuka divebomber was blooded.

The idea of vertical bombing had been experimented with during the World War 1. Its attraction lay in increased accuracy over horizontal bombing using the primitive bomb-sights of the time. The Germans continued to experiment with the technique in the 1920s in Russia, but when Hitler came to power, Wolfram von Richthofen, cousin of the famous fighter ace of World War 1, and head of the newly formed Technical Office of the Air Ministry, went against the idea, believing that to go under 6 000 feet in the face of anit-aircraft defences was suicidal. But, across the Atlantic, the US Navy had taken up the idea. Admiral Moffett, Head of the Naval Bureau of Aeronautics in the 1920s, had been impressed by Mitchell's successful trials into the bombing of ships. He saw that the combination of aircraft carriers and bombers would give the Navy greater flexibility in dealing with any threat to the American seaboard than would land-based aircraft. The first US carrier was launched in 1925, and by 1930, the carrier-based attack squadrons had developed the dive-bombing technique using the Curtiss Hawk biplane. It so happened that they were in the habit of giving public displays, and one of these was seen by a German ex-fighter ace turned stunt pilot and film star, Ernst Udet, who became a convert. When, in 1933, Udet came under pressure from Goering to join the Luftwaffe he was bribed by the purchase by Goering of two Hawks for investigation by the Luftwaffe. Although the majority of those in the top echelons of the Luftwaffe were not impressed, Udet continued to champion the cause of the dive-bomber. He approached aircraft firms privately to take the idea up, and this resulted in the firm of Junkers designing the Ju 87. Udet and his disciples used as the argument that one dive-bomber could knock out a pinpoint target, which would take a whole squadron of conventional bombers. This appealed to Goering as well as to Wever in terms of cost-effectiveness and a contract for development was offered up to German industry in January 1935. Within a few weeks the first Ju 87 prototype had been produced. This lost its tailplane in a dive in the autumn of that year, but tests were pursued with further prototypes. In January 1936 Udet was appointed Inspector of Fighters, but devoted most of his attention to dive-bombers. Arado, Blohm & Voss and Heinkel all produced versions, but in the end the Ju 87 won out after Udet had succeeded in crashing the Heinkel version, He 118. By now he had taken over command of the Technical Office, while von Richthofen had been sent to Spain as Chief of Staff to the Condor Legion. The first Ju 87s made their appearance in this theatre at the end of 1937, although in March 1937 von Richthofen had organised He 51s, which had been outmatched as fighters by the Russian I-15s and I-16s as fighters, into ground attack units (*Schlachtflieger*). During the next year von Richthofen was able to perfect the technique of vertical dive-bombing, which was to become an essential element of blitzkrieg.

Although the figures are difficult to substantiate, Miksche asserts that during the Nationalist offensives of August to October 1938 the weight of bombs used almost equated to the weight of artillery [4]. One who fought on the Nationalist side as a British volunteer in the Spanish Legion describes the effect of a combined artillery and air bombardment prior to one of these attacks:

'Soon after nine o'clock the first squadron of bombers flew over us towards the enemy, and our artillery opened fire with a barrage far more powerful than that which we had witnessed in the Sierra Palomera. The bombardment continued for over two hours with constant relays of aircraft and incessant fire from our batteries; if the enemy had any artillery it was silent. Beyond the low ridge of hills in front of us, which hid the enemy from view, we could see columns of smoke and dust drifting upwards. Shortly before noon we heard the rumble of engines as our tanks moved into position; a few minutes later the advance began . . . Our bombs and shells were no longer falling on the *Fronton*, but small units of our fighters were diving on the position, raking the trenches with machine-gun five.' [5]

The Nationalists, unlike Pavlov, kept their tanks close to their infantry even during an advance, as opposed to set-piece attack, as Peter Kemp illustrates:

'Our manoeuvres followed a familiar pattern: preceded by an advance-guard of tanks we marched at a forced pace along the road; ahead of us flew fighters for reconnaissance and protection. At the first sign of resistance we would deploy across country in battle order, the tanks extending in line abreast in front of us; if the position was strongly defended there would be a brief artillery preparation before we went into the assault, in the same manner as on previous days.' [6]

There was no attempt to bypass strong opposition, which was to be a tactic of the German armoured spearheads in the years 1939-42. Yet, although commentators wrote about the employment of air power in the ground support role, it was not this that caught the imagination of the world as a whole.

On April 26th, 1937 at 4.30pm the small town of Guernica, which lies some ten kilometres from the Northern Spanish coast and thirty kilometres from Bilbao, was attacked from the air by He 111s and JU 52s of the Condor Legion. At this stage in the war it formed part of a Republican enclave some 150 miles wide by 25 miles deep, which was entirely cut off from the main part of Republican Spain. The attack lasted some three hours and by the end of it over 1 500 people had been killed and the centre of the town was gutted. An immediate outcry rippled through the headlines of the world press. Picasso was moved to paint one of his greatest masterpieces on the subject. It brought home to people once again the threat of strategic bombing against the civil population, and, because this was naturally of more immediate concern to people at large, the significance of tactical air operations in Spain was forced into the background. Only the Germans appreciated the value of the lessons learnt in this field.

The other misconception to arise from the Spanish Civil War was over the employment of tanks. Those who had been against the idea of giving tanks a role other than infantry support had used as one of their arguments the threat of the anti-tank gun to the tank. They foresaw a race between the two and likened it to the gun-armour race which had occurred with the battleship. Sooner or later an anti-tank gun would force the tank to take on so much protection in the form of armour that it would become impossibly heavy. It so happened that one of the many contemporary accounts of the war in Spain was a book by a German emigré, Helmuth Klotz, entitled *Lecons Militaires de la Guerre d'Espagne*. He concluded that the anti-tank gun had outstripped the tank and that power once more rested with the defensive. 'Whenever a tank attack has met with strong, well-handled anti-tank defences, it has been annihilated or immobilised and has failed to accomplish its task.' [7] This seemed to vindicate France's obsession with defence as based on the Maginot Line and the book received wide publicity. Yet many other observers came to the same conclusion. Even the Royal Tank Corps Journal commented that 'From the experiences in the Spanish Civil War it appears that the defence against tanks has developed more rapidly and effectively than the tank itself.' [8] One French military writer put it even more strongly:

'The antidote to the tank has been found. It can no longer count on technical surprise. It fights on equal terms with anti-tank defence, and the theories advanced on the devastating power of the 'Panzer Division' and other armoured formations, employed in isolation, have been over-taken by events.' [9]

However he did not go so far as a British Member of Parliament, who declared that:

'It is hardly fashionable to mention it in this country just now, but the fact remains that cavalry have been the successful arm of the current war in Spain. One does not see many tanks there; nor are they highly thought of . . . ' [10]

Unfortunately none of these 'experts' had taken into account certain important factors. Firstly, much of the terrain was unsuitable for tank warfare. Large areas of the country are mountainous, which naturally suits the defender more than the attacker. Secondly, the number of tanks available to both sides was relatively small, and the types of tank used, especially on the Nationalist side, were neither the most modern nor did they carry much armour protection. Also, they were often used inefficiently and the crews were poorly trained. Indeed, the Germans complained that it was almost impossible to teach the Spanish how to handle tanks.

While Germans were careful to regard the Spanish Civil War as a technical as opposed to tactical laboratory, the Soviet Union made a fundamental change of course with regard to the employment of tanks. Their attempts to use tanks on their own had proved to be disastrous. This resulted in Pavlov taking the message back to Russia that tanks should only be used in the infantry close support role. Yet, how much he genuinely believed this is not clear, for when he returned to Russia Stalin was in the midst of his great purges. These had started with the murder of Kirov head of the communist party in Leningrad in December 1934. After the liquidation of his potential political opponents, Stalin moved on, in 1937, to tackle the armed forces. The main object of his attack was the 'Tuchachevski Circle', which he seems to have seen as a threat because of its independent line of military thought. Tuchachevski himself, having at the last moment been prevented from attending the coronation of King George VI as the official representative of the Soviet Union, was arraigned in June 1937. During the next year the purge worked its way down from the very highest to the lowly company officers. Almost all those who had been identified with Tucha-chevski's doctrine were liquidated. Khalepsky of the armoured forces, Alksnis and Khripin of the VVS, and Yakir were some of the cream of the armed forces who were executed. Only the Far Eastern Army under Bluyker did not suffer for the time being. In a short time Stalin had succeeded in getting rid of no less than two thirds of the senior officers down to and including brigade commanders by execution or imprisonment. The few that dared warn against the decrease in war-preparedness were themselves quickly purged.

Tuchachevski's ideas of an elite mechanised army were eradicated over-night. Although he had written a month before his trial that to use tanks on

104

their own was wrong, this very technique was laid at his door. The emphasis which he had placed on the use of combined arms within his mechanised formations was forgotten. The Red Army reverted back to the old Marxist idea of the mass army, with the tanks being dispersed in support of infantry formations. The Far Eastern Army would shortly demonstrate the soundness of Tuchachevski's ideas just as the Russo-Finnish War and the German invasion of Russia in June 1941 would demonstrate the effects of the purges on the Russian Armed Forces.

## Britain

The year 1935 finally saw Britain shake off the constraints of the Ten Year Rule. Although it had been formally rescinded in 1932, the Government showed no inclination to increase the Defence Budget. The East Fulham by-election of October 1933 when a National Government candidate advocating rearmament had been heavily defeated by a Labour candidate opposed to rearmament, and the Peace Ballot of the following year had convinced Baldwin, the Prime Minister, that the British public would not yet stand for rearmament. He was well aware of Germany's resurgence under the Nazis, but was inclined to think that it would be better to let Germany rearm to an extent rather than attempt to prevent her. Not until the Conservatives had convincingly won the General Election of November 1935 did Baldwin feel that he could proceed cautiously with British rearmament. Priority went to the RAF, although at this stage the Air Staff still remained committed to strategic bombing. But they had been given priority over the other two Services not so that they could make themselves into an effective strategic bombing force, but because by the mid-1930s most people had come to the conclusion that only a strong fighter-orientated air force could defend a country against strategic air attacks. Thus, while the earlier RAF rearmament plans still showed emphasis on the strategic bomber, by the end of 1937 the pendulum was swinging in favour of the fighter. The theorists were also moving away from the ideas of Douhet. In fact, it became fashionable to criticise Douhet and thus indirectly Trenchard. General Golovine, a Russian emigré who enjoyed RAF patronage wrote: 'The fundamental error in General Douhet's works is that his whole doctrine has been built up mainly by deduction.' [11] He dismissed Douhet's idea of a single all-purpose aircraft as nonsense, and argued that:

' . . . air supremacy is inextricably mingled with superiority on land or on the sea and, therefore, the Air Force alone cannot attain absolute superiority in its element without decisive action on the part of surface forces.' [12]

In 1936 Wing Commander (later Marshal of the Royal Air Force Sir John) Slessor published a book *Air Power and Armies*. He wrote that:

'The first and most important commitment of the Royal Air Force is, of course, the defence of Great Britain against air attack; and ultimately connected with this commitment is the provision of an air expeditionary force to co-operate with the army in a campaign overseas.' [13]

This statement on the surface was an anathema to the Trenchard influenced Air Staff, but it was this role of support to the ground forces, which Slessor now examined. He put forward the hypothesis that the major role of the ground forces was to 'ensure the integrity of the Low Countries' in order to prevent a Continental enemy from setting up bases from which an aerial assault on Britain could be mounted. Once this task had been successfully achieved the emphasis would change. From now on the RAF would take over the predominant role of 'the ultimate reduction of the enemy'.

'That is to say it will become an air campaign, and the task of the army will be simply to protect the air bases. When that happens then it is arguable that a decision may be secured by action against enemy air forces — since the complete defeat of those forces would place the enemy nation at the mercy of unrestricted air action. As a matter of fact it is more likely that even in an air campaign action against air forces will remain only subsidiary, and the decision will only be gained by direct action against the hostile vital centres.' [14]

However, like Golovine, he did not see that air supremacy was possible. The very best that could be hoped for was neutralisation which would reduce enemy air interference to a minimum. He believed that the main weapon of an air force should still be the bomber and that there were two types of decisive objective for it, troops on the ground and supplies. The latter could be sub-divided into production and supplies in the field. To any land battle there were three phases, inactivity, preparation and the actual joining of battle. These phases could be matched in the air by attacking production during inactivity, supplies in the field during preparation and the fighting troops once battle was joined. It was at this stage in the book that he came to realise that the campaign could not be won by air action alone, especially in the face of a land invasion 'perhaps by great armoured forces supported by air action'.

' . . . it is vain to pretend that the situation could then be dealt with entirely by air measures against an enemy country, or the invading army defeated by attacks on its supply at the source — because these measures would not have time to take effect.' [15]

Air action against production could only limit the effectiveness of a ground offensive — it could never replace troops on the ground. The twin principles of selection of the aim and concentration at the decisive point were paramount. An air force to be effective in the land battle must concentrate on one objective, and that objective must be the decisive one.

When battle was joined and the air force was supporting the ground troops, aircraft should not be used in the immediate battle area. ' . . . The

106

aeroplane is not a battlefield weapon — the air striking force is not as a rule best employed in the actual zone in which the armies are in contact.' [16] Instead it should take on targets beyond artillery range. He observed that low flying action was not practised by the RAF except in emergencies, but noted that dive-bombing was

' . . . likely to become increasingly popular for engaging strongly defended objectives where the presence of anti-aircraft artillery makes accurate precision bombing from a height a matter of increasing difficulty and danger.' [17]

It is interesting to note that von Richthofen used exactly the same argument against the introduction of this technique into the Luftwaffe. Suffice to say that the British Air Staff were also not impressed with this argument. When Vickers' chief test pilot visited Germany in October 1937 he was given the opportunity to test fly the Stuka. He was deeply impressed by it and the Vickers Chairman passed his views onto the Secretary of State for Air, who replied somewhat forcibly: 'My dear Archie, kindly tell your pilots to mind their own bloody business . . . ' [18] Thus the Royal Air Force went to war in 1939 without a dive-bomber.

Slessor's book is noteworthy in that it does show how the more forward-thinking RAF officers of the 1930s managed to throw off the shackles of Trenchard and Douhet. By the end of the book he was taking a realistic and balanced view of the RAF's capabilities in support of the land battle. His dislike of aircraft being employed in the ground attack role in the forward areas is understandable. No pilot who had flown on the Western Front in 1917-18 had enjoyed 'ground strafing'. What is surprising was that he did not, in view of his argument for it, take his remarks on the dive-bomber to their ultimate conclusion, that they should be employed for close support of the Army. Yet within a year, in Spain, Stukas were being employed as aerial artillery in direct support of the fighting troops. In spite of this Slessor's ideas found support in the ranks of the two older services. Both strived during the 1930s to get the RAF to apportion part of its strength to support of the land battle. One who worked as a junior staff officer in the Director of Military Operations' office just prior to the outbreak of war records:

'A constant bone of contention in our discussions was the role to be played by the Air Force. Both the General Staff and the Naval Staff opposed the fanatical efforts of the Air Staff to press upon us their theory that the war would be decided by the action of air forces, almost unaided by the other two Services. We fought hard and unsuccessfully for the provisio of adequate specialised air forces, properly trained and equipped for the support of naval and military operations. The introduction of such a policy was regarded by the Air Staff as a 'prostitution of the Air Force' so a senior officer in the Air Ministry once expressed it to me.' [19]

All that remained specifically allotted to the Army were the Army co-operation squadrons, whose role was strictly reconnaissance, and whose pilots included a significant number of seconded Army officers.

In November 1936, Winston Churchill said in the House of Commons:

'Nothing has been done in "the years that the locust hath eaten" to equip the Tank Corps with new machines. The medium tank which they possess, which in its day was the best in the world, is now long obsolete. Not only in numbers — for we have never tried to compete with other countries — but in quality these British weapons are now surpassed by those of Germany, Russia, Italy and the United States.' [20]

The Royal Tank Corps reached its nadir in 1936. Out of 209 light and 166 medium tanks, two thirds of the former and all but two of the latter were obsolete. At the same time Germany could boast of 1 600 light (PZ KW I and II) and 3-400 medium tanks (PZ KW III and IV). The problem was essentially one of money. The lead time for introducing a new tank into service increased as technology grew more advanced, and time meant money. Although the Army Estimates of 1936 had shown a step forward when two million pounds was allocated to mechanisation, to invest this in better tanks was seen as a risky business. For it cost time and money to produce prototypes, and there was always the danger that they might be found unsuitable, hence money invested in development would have been wasted. A better prospect financially was to concentrate on motorisation rather than mechanisation. Wheeled vehicles gave the possibilities of sales on the civilian market, whereas tanks would only be of interest to the military customer.* Hence nearly half the money allocated to mechanisa-tion went on replacing the infantry's horsedrawn transport. The Germans were concentrating their energies on mechanising from the front, while the British motorised the rear.

Another reason for this low ebb was the inability of the Army to decide on the type of tank it wanted. In 1934 Elles, who had caught so much of the world's imagination by leading the attack of the Tank Corps in person on November 20th, 1917, was appointed as Master-General of the Ordnance (MGO). This gave him, amongst other responsibilities, the task of weapons procurement for the Army. This might have seemed welcome news to the Royal Tank Corps. Perhaps they would at last get modern tanks suitable for armoured warfare. But it was not to be. Elles was not the same man as he had been in 1917. Like many others he believed that the tank had been outstripped by the anti-tank gun. He also did not believe in the type of warfare preached by Fuller, Liddell Hart and others, but saw the tanks being employed in infantry support as they had been in the First World War. He accepted the need for light tanks for reconnaissance, but was not

---

*Indeed civilian firms which bought military lorries were given a government subsidy. Not many firms took up this offer because the extra ruggedness, and hence weight, required by military transport made it uneconomical to run commerically.

interested in any ideas of a tank having speed and adequate firepower for use in armoured formations. Vickers, who had the monopoly for tank construction therefore concentrated their efforts into producing infantry tanks. The first was a two man model, heavily armoured, but only armed with a machine gun, which became known as the Infantry Tank Mark I, while the later model was larger, with a crew of four, having a high velocity 2 pounder gun. It was designated the Infantry Tank Mark II, and later became affectionately known as the 'Matilda'. The problem with both these tanks was that they were slow. The former had a top speed of only 8mph, while the latter was restricted to 15mph. But as they were designed to work with infantry on their feet it was not considered necessary to make them any faster.

It is quite likely that, but for one man, the British Army might have been forced to go to war in 1939 equipped with light and infantry tanks only. Martel had been favourably impressed by Russian tank design as a result of his visit to Russia in 1936. He held the vital job of Assistant Director of Mechanisation and as such had particular responsibility for tank development. It was the Russian BT tank which had impressed him most. Its 37mm gun and top speed of 36mph seemed the right characteristics for a successor to the Vickers Medium. Having had his suggestion for the development of a British tank along the same lines turned down by Elles he resolved to go it alone. Sir John Carden, the chief Vickers tank designer, had shortly before his death in an air crash in 1935, produced two designs for a medium, or 'cruiser' tank as they were now called, designated A-9 and A-10. Neither was fast enough for Martel's requirements. Instead he contacted the American tank designer Walter Christie and managed to arrange for the British Army to purchase his one remaining prototype. At the same time he received some guidance from Hobart, who at the end of his 1936 report on the Tank Brigade had produced a specification for a cruiser tank. Martel then persuaded Lord Nuffield, head of the Morris motors group, to purchase the patent rights from Christie, and to undertake the development of the tank. After some fifteen years the Vickers monopoly in tank design had been finally broken. This tank was to become the A-13 mounting a two pounder (40mm) gun with 14mm of armour and a speed of 30mph. The first prototype was produced in November 1937 and became known as the Cruiser Tank Mark III. Thus by 1939 the British Army had three types of tank — light tanks for reconnaissance, infantry tanks for infantry support and cruisers, whose duty was to act in armoured formations in a more independent role.

The three types of tank were reflected in the new armoured formations which made their appearance in the late 1930s. These were developed in the context of the British Army role in the increasing likelihood of another war in Europe. By the end of 1937 the Cabinet had reached the conclusion that Britain's Armed Forces were not strong enough to cover all possible commitments in another global war. It also concluded that the Army's prime role was still to be Imperial and Home Defence. In addition, in order to aid it in the latter, the responsibility for anti-aircraft defence was also given to the Army. Yet, at the same time, Britain was also honour-bound to go to the assistance of her Continental allies. Although Chamberlain had believed that an air element only should be sent, Vansittart, the Permanent Under-Secretary of State for Foreign Affairs, had argued that air power alone could not stop armies: 'Vide Spain. The Germans and Italians have learned from the Spanish experience that infantry is still the dominant factor.' [21] It was also unlikely that the French would accept merely an air contribution and hence ground troops would have to be sent to the Continent. It was at this stage that the 'Doctrine of Limited Liability' once again raised its head. It so happened that in May 1937 Chamberlain had become Prime Minister, and had chosen as his War Minister Leslie Hore-Belisha, a lawyer by profession, who entered office determined on wide-sweeping reforms for the Services, especially the Army. Shortly afterwards, Liddell Hart, who was *The Times* Defence Correspondent, was asked by Inskip, as Minister for the Co-ordination of Defence, to prepare a paper on the reorganisation of the Army. Having met Hore Belisha and explained the salient points of it to him, Liddell Hart sent him a copy. In the section dealing with the type of ground force to be sent overseas, Liddell Hart argued that 'the use of ordinary infantry divisions is not likely to have much effect on offensive operations' on the Continent. Rather, he argued:

'Because of financial and conventional limitations, however, it is unlikely that any ally will possess more than a small proportion of fully mechanised divisions. Hence a contribution of this kind might count for much more than its mere numbers implied — e.g. in August 1914 the 4 British divisions despatched to France represented barely 6 per cent of the forces deployed to meet the invaders, whereas two armoured mobile divisions to-day would increase by 66 per cent the forces of this kind available in France. They would combine high mobility and concentrated fire-power with economy of men.' [22]

He then went on to say that two such armoured divisions should be formed in Britain and one in Egypt. The paper made a deep impression on Hore-Belisha, who made Liddell Hart his unofficial adviser. Significantly, the French had requested the pledge of two armoured divisions at the beginning of 1937. Yet, by the end of 1937 the British Army had not a single armoured division in existence. Thus the stark choice remained of either sending no ground troops or conventional infantry divisions. The latter could only be of limited number because of the priority towards Imperial and Home Defence and, anyway, neither the Government nor the Chiefs of Staff were prepared to allow the British commitment on land to the Continent to grow to anything like the size that it had in World War 1. No wonder Hore-Belisha wrote, while visiting the French Army manoeuvres in Normandy in September 1937 that:

'I was informed that the Maginot Line only required 100 000 men to hold it, which left a large reserve for the French Field Army. When the

French realise that we cannot commit ourselves to send an Expeditionary Force, they should be all the more induced to accelerate the extension of the Maginot Line to the sea.' [23]

In late 1934 the decision had been taken to replace horse cavalry divisions by mobile divisions. It was, however, not until the Autumn of 1937 that this step was taken. Initially there was a tussle as to who should command it. Hore-Belisha, egged on by Liddell Hart, wanted a tank officer to command, but Deverell, who had replaced Montgomery-Massingberd, insisted on an aged cavalryman. In the end a compromise was reached whereby an artilleryman, Major-General A. F. Brooke (later Lord Alanbrooke) was given command. He stepped across from being Director of Military Training, which job, on the insistence of Hore-Belisha, was given to Hobart. The latter was not to last long in his new appointment. His reforming zeal did not go down well with the more cautious approach of those above him on the Army Council. In particular, he attempted to exert much influence on the training of the Mobile Division and to get is members to think 'tank' rather than 'horse'. But, as he wrote to Liddell Hart at the end of May 1938 after six months in office:

'The attitude of those in authority — well, one point is that so long as you continue to provide the cavalry officer with 2 free chargers although his unit is equipped with tanks, so long psychologically, will he be wedded to the horse and indifferent or averse from 'getting down to' the machine.' [24]

Very soon afterwards he was offered command of the Mobile Division about to be formed in Egypt, which he accepted. Hore-Belisha, again prompted by Liddell Hart, had insisted that this was the price that the Army Council would have to pay if he was to acquiesce to their wish of removing Hobart.

The new Mobile Division could do little more than operate in the cavalryman's traditional role of reconnaissance. Over 80% of its tanks were suitable for no other role. Indeed, there was a move to rely entirely on the light tank and to do away with the one medium tank brigade altogether. Once again Liddell Hart used his influence on Hore-Belisha to see that this did not happen. It was finally confirmed in November 1937 that the Mobile Division would consist of the 1st Tank Brigade and 1st and 2nd Cavalry Brigades, both mechanised. The influence of Liddell Hart on Hore-Belisha became even more marked when, in the course of introducing the Army Estimates for 1938-9, Hore-Belisha declared that it was now the intention to convert the British Army into two types of division only: 'One type, a motorised division based on the light machine-gun, and the other a mechanised armoured division, based on the tank.' [25] Yet, the Mobile Division was still only in the process of being formed and such a programme would take years to achieve at a time when war seemed almost daily more imminent. The only immediate step taken, in the face of continued conservatism among the General Staff was the setting up of a second Mobile

Division in Egypt, to which, as has been mentioned earlier, Hobart was appointed to the command. The mobility of infantry battalions was increased only by the addition of a platoon of armoured carriers. By 1939 the term 'motorised division' had been dropped in favour of 'infantry division' with only sufficient mechanical transport to lift one out of three brigades at a time. Simultaneously a large proportion of the Royal Tank Corps found itself still committed in the role of infantry support, three battalions out of the eight now in existence being equipped with infantry tanks to form the 1st Army Tank Brigade.

With Hobart now the only serving officer of the apostles of tank warfare in a position to influence events, it might have seemed that the laboratory of tank doctrine had moved to Egypt, and that here further revolutionary developments would take place. It was not to be. Ordered to form the Mobile Division from scratch by Gort, the new CIGS, Hobart arrived in Egypt at the end of September 1938. It was a critical time with Chamberlain just back from Bad Godesburg and the Cabinet having decided to oppose Hitler's demands on Czechoslovakia. War seemed close and the potential threat from the Italians in Libya on Egypt was taken seriously. Yet the first words of Gordon-Finlayson, the GOC, to Hobart were: 'I don't know what you have come here for and I don't want you anyway.' [26] The troops available for the Division consisted of a supposedly mechanised cavalry brigade, (one regiment in light tanks, one in Ford trucks and the third in vintage Rolls-Royce armoured cars), a tank group of two RTC battalions, an artillery regiment with eighteen howitzers and a solitary infantry battalion. Hobart set to with his customary zeal, but found himself obstructed at every turn by the apathy of Headquarters in Cairo. He sought to concentrate initially:

' . . . on dispersion, flexibility and mobility . . . to try and get the Division and formations well extended, really handy, and under quick control. To units unused to the speed and wide frontages made possible by mechanisation these matters present considerable difficulties.' [27]

His single-mindedness of purpose permeated all ranks of the Division as it had done in the 1st Tank Brigade, but it had the opposite effect on Gordon-Finlayson. After giving him an adverse confidential report, Gordon-Finlayson returned home to become Adjutant-General. His successor, Wilson (later a Field-Marshal) was as averse to Hobart's extremism as Gordon-Finlayson had been and in November 1939 Hobart was sent home in disgrace and placed on retired pay the following March. In spite of this, Hobart's spirit lived on in what was to become one of the most famous formations of the World War 2, the 7th Armoured Division, the Desert Rats.

In 1939 the two Mobile Divisions were redesignated Armoured Divisions and the Cavalry and Royal Tank Corps combined into a single corps, the Royal Armoured Corps. Seven territorial battalions of the Royal Tank Regiment, as it had now become, were raised from existing infantry attalions, and these, together with the now eighteen mechanised cavalry regiments should have provided a powerful foundation for a proper armoured force. Yet only two armoured divisions were in existence when war broke out, and the 1st Armoured Division was still not sufficiently trained to join the British Expeditionary Force in time for the debacle of May 1940. A significant part of the available armour remained tied up in the army tank brigades committed to infantry support. Yet Hore-Belisha in the 1939 Army Estimates had spoken of sending an expeditionary force to the Continent comprising of nineteen divisions, including two regular armoured divisions, a territorial armoured division and three territorial motorised divisions.

Liddell Hart now relinquished his position of influence over Hore-Belisha. Although in his *Memoirs*, he makes much of the increasing divergence of views between himself and the War Minister, especially over the decision to double the size of the Territorial Army and introduce conscription, both of which Liddell Hart opposed, there is no doubt that their relationship was an invidious one. That it should be common knowledge that the Minister of War was using a journalist as his primary adviser could not but excite adverse comment however sound was the advice. It was not as though Liddell Hart was used just to advise on military doctrine. Hore-Belisha's questions to him covered the whole gamut of military affairs. Perhaps most pernicious of all was that Liddell Hart's advice on appointments to the higher positions in the Army should have been eagerly sought. No wonder that by the mid-Summer of 1939 Liddell Hart had been pushed firmly into the background. His last flourish before the outbreak of war was a rush into print on a book entitled *The Defence of Britain*. The book's two main themes were firstly, that the only way to deal with an attack by mechanised forces was to adopt a mobile defence reliant on swiftly moving mechanised formations of one's own, and secondly to strike a blow against the Trenchardist doctrine of the Royal Air Force with its continued emphasis on the bomber. It was fighters and not bombers which were needed to defend Britain in the event of air attack.

Although the RAF remain wedded to Trenchard's doctrine, the first expansion plan of the 1930s, Scheme A of July 1934, had provided for a ratio just over three fighters to every five bombers. By January 1937 with Scheme H the proportion had changed to only one fighter to every four bombers. At this stage Dowding was appointed to head Fighter Command, and during the next two and a half years he fought virtually a single-handed battle to get the proportion of fighters raised again. Scheme M, introduced after Munich, showed that he had been partially successful in that it allowed for 800 fighters as opposed to 1360 bombers, but Dowding by then had become the arch enemy of many on the Air Staff, and constant efforts were made to get rid of him, culminating in his sacking in the hour of victory in October 1940.

There was too, the shape and role of Britain's air contribution to the Continent. The French wanted it to act in support of the ground forces by concentrating on the German military bases and lines of communication.

The Air Staff would have liked to have used it in a strategic bombing campaign against the Ruhr, but the French, fearful of the Luftwaffe's retaliation, were opposed to this. Indeed, Air Ministry studies had shown that the RAF's available resources were not enough to ensure significant damage to Germany's war industry. Hence by March 1939 the British and French had agreed that the Advanced Air Striking Force (AASF) would act in support of the ground forces rather than carrying out an independent role.

**France**
In October 1936, Gamelin, presiding over a meeting of the Army Council stated:

'One must have the implements to match the technique. The Germans have invented the Panzer division, which is the tool of a sudden attack followed by exploitation in depth . . . We do not have the instrument of attack . . . necessary for attack or counter-attack in force . . . We need an instrument stronger than the Panzer division.' [28]

This was the first indication that the French High Command were having second thoughts on de Gaulle's proposition for the formation of a proper French armoured force. Although the majority of the War Council were still against the idea, the Minister of War, Daladier ordered the General Staff to carry out a study into armoured divisions. These produced little in the way of concrete conclusions, apart from the fact that the light Renault 35 was unsuitable for such a formation. The politicians, the military establishment and the public at large continued to remain transfixed by the idea of Maginot, believing that its concrete and steel emplacements were sufficient to keep out whatever the Germans might bring against France. But, in 1936 the new *Tactical Instructions* had provided for tank groups, which were to be used for long range and relatively independent action. They were termed *Chars de manoeuvre d'ensemble*. The next year, 1937, however had seen the emergence of the false lesson from Spain that the anti-tank gun had now outstripped the tank. Thus the 1937 manual on tank employment emphasised that tanks could only really be used on their own once the enemy had been disorganised. Infantry support was still listed as the highest priority, with action against enemy tanks second, and exploitation in conjunction with the *Divisions Légères Mécaniques*, the lowest priority. In any case, because of the threat of the anti-tank gun, which was parallel to the threat of the machine-gun to the infantryman in World War 1, the manual stated that tanks should never move out of the range of artillery support.

In spite of all, Gamelin persisted in his quest to get the armoured division concept off the ground. In December 1937 he took his question of the year before a stage further, when he asked the Superior War Council to consider whether heavy tank battalions should be maintained as part of the general reserves or placed together in an independent group. Dufieux, the Inspector of Infantry, who had so consistently opposed the idea that tanks should be

114

used for other than infantry support, maintained his opposition, but the Council agreed to investigate further. It was not however until December 1938, well after Munich, that the decision was finally taken to form two armoured divisions, both to be ready for 1941.

In the meantime de Gaulle had been appointed in November 1937 to the command of the 507th Tank Regiment stationed at Metz. Daladier was supposed to have remarked to him on taking up his appointment: 'You've given us enough trouble with your paper tanks. Let's see what you make of the metal sort.' [29] Although his Regiment was part of an infantry division it did give de Gaulle the opportunity to attempt to confirm his theories. Writing to a friend he said:

'After some detailed experimentation, I find myself more than ever convinced of the soundness of my ideas which I tried to spread and which, alas, have up until now been listened to far more willingly by the Germans than by my own compatriots. The possibility of manoeuvre and attack can no longer be demanded on land except as a defensive arm. Artillery keeps its relative value but from now on it is in support of tanks that it must be used before all else. It remains to recognise these facts and to organise the French army accordingly, making it an instrument of manoeuvre and shock attack based on tanks, that is to say an armoured corps. Moreover this corps, given its relative importance and the cost of the material devoted to it, can only be formed for the moment out of specialists like the navy and aviation.'[30]

Two significant points arise from this extract. Firstly, there is his conviction that he was influencing German military thought. *Vers Le Metier* had made little impression on the Germans. Guderian did not read it until 1937 and thought then that it contributed little new. The second point is de Gaulle's belief that the armoured force should take priority over even the needs of aviation. As yet he still thought little of air power, and also, when taken in conjunction with his mistaken belief of the impression his book had had on the Germans, it was clear that he had not entirely grasped the German blitzkrieg doctrine.

In direct opposition to de Gaulle's views, there appeared in 1939 a book written by General Chauvineau entitled *Invasion est-elle encore possible?* The foreword was written by no lesser personage than Pétain. In it he stated that tanks:

' . . . are expensive, rare and relatively slow to move into position. The time necessary for them to develop their action can be used by the defence to bring up their reserves. There is also, on the ground, the mortal barrage which can destroy them, a combination of mines and anti-tank weapons.' [31]

Chauvineau himself put forward the thesis that:

'In France, the war of invasion at a rapid pace, which is called the war of movement, has had its day . . . To-day, when progress has multiplied tenfold the strength of the defensive, the nation that prepares for a short war is heading for suicide . . . If our neighbours have any notion of causing trouble on continuous fronts . . . the little flame they will stumble upon will knock the vain glory out of them in a few weeks . . . As for the tanks, which were to bring a new epoch of short wars, their inadequacy is patent . . . It is the continuous front . . . which breaks the wings of offensive operations . . . the fear of the continuous front has become a factor for peace.' [32]

This made comforting reading to the majority of Frenchmen, both civilian and military, encouraging still further their false sense of security. Unfortunately both they and the author had conveniently forgotten that the Maginot Line only covered part of France's eastern frontiers.

Meanwhile the French Air Force struggled to modernise itself. In spite of the nationalisation of the French aircraft industry, by 1939 only 600 aircraft a year were being produced, as compared with the 3 000 for the Luftwaffe. Vuillemin, now commander of the air force, made a tour of Luftwaffe installations in August 1938 at Milch's invitation. Milch, furthering his doctrine of the *Risikoflotte*, made certain that Vuillemin saw nothing but the most modern aircraft in the Luftwaffe armoury. His carefully prepared programme had the right effect. Vuillemin privately told the French Government that he did not think that the French Air Force would last more than a week against the Luftwaffe. In particular he realised that France did not possess any fighter modern enough to stand up to the Me 109E or 110. In desperation one hundred Curtiss Hawk 75A-1s were ordered from the USA. On the tactical side, Vuillemin lacked the foresight and drive of his predecessor Fequant. This was aggravated by the fact that Gamelin, as Chief of the Defence Staff, although responsible for the Air Force, was not interested in air power. Thus, while the 1936 *Instructions* might talk of the Air Force being used in support of ground forces on interdiction tasks behind the immediate battle area, they also said that: 'It is convenient to leave the air force commanders the initiative for launching the attack.' The Army expected the Air Force to support it, but was not prepared to spell out how this should be done.

France drifted towards war in 1939 fully conscious of what Germany might throw against her. Yet the ghost of Verdun still walked the corridors of the Ministry of Defence. The incomplete shield of the Maginot Line continued to be held up as France's salvation. It was incomprehensible that it could be penetrated. Thus the High Command did not think it necessary to set up anything on the lines of de Gaulle's armoured force, which would have the speed, flexibility and firepower to counter any such penetration. For one thing, too much money had been invested in the Maginot Line and for another, the French people must not think that their Government was prepared to risk them in another slaughter on the scale of 1914-18. The attitude of the French High Command cannot be better summed up than in the words of an unidentified French general, speaking at the end of a day's manoeuvres in May 1938:

'I am happy to have been through a day of defensive strategy. For we shall make defensive war. We will not have the French people slaughtered.' [33]

## Germany

By the autumn of 1937 the Wehrmacht possessed 39 Divisions. Of these three were panzer divisions, there being no change in the quantity of the latter since 1935. Yet the major manoeuvres of that year, unlike the Vogelsang manoeuvres of the previous year, did utilise all three panzer formations. Von Rundstedt's 'Blue Army' was allocated them, and on the final day of the manoeuvres they executed a mass attack on the 'Red Army', turning its southern flank. Hitler and Mussolini who were present, were much impressed. Yet, not all went well with the new arm. The manoeuvres showed up grave deficiencies in the supply and repair system, and in spite of remonstrations by Lutz, the Panzer Corps commander, nothing was done to rectify these problems. This was to cause embarrassment the following year. However, the panzer school were able to use these manoeuvres to show that some of the lessons apparently coming out of the Spanish Civil War were not valid. As the military correspondent of the *Frankfurter Zeitung* put it, in an article on the manoeuvres:

'. . . it was easy to realise that experience in the Spanish Civil War can hardly be regarded as decisive for the use of the tank in modern warfare. There has never been any attack in Spain carried out by a really large number of tanks.' [34]

But in spite of the apparent success of the Panzer Corps, not all were convinced. Most of those in the Wehrmacht High Command were still perturbed about the extent of the French and Czech fortifications and thought that they would render mechanised forces incapable of movement. There was a continued reluctance to expend too much effort in mechanisation and motorisation at the expense of conventional infantry, which it was still believed provided the 'mass of decision'. In any event, Germany was limited in the extent of mechanisation which she could carry out by her shortage of oil and steel.

Nevertheless, by the end of 1937 Hitler was ready to flex his muscles, and looked first southwards to Germany's old ally of World War 1, Austria. At a meeting on November 5th, 1937 he outlined his plans for the annexation of Austria and Czechoslovakia to the heads of the armed services and Baron von Neurath, the Foreign Minister. Blomberg, Fritsch (Commander-in-Chief of the Army) and von Neurath were horrified. They believed that Germany was nowhere near ready for war and that Hitler's plans were bound to create a large scale war because they did not see how Britain and France would be content to remain on the sidelines. Within three months all three had been removed from their positions and Hitler had installed himself as Commander-in-Chief of the Armed Forces in place of Blomberg. By March

1938 he felt ready to deal with Austria. Schuschnigg, the Austrian Chancellor, was ordered to legalise all Nazi activity in Austria and bind foreign and economic policies to those of Germany or face invasion. Three Army Corps and the Luftwaffe were mobilised, Schuschnigg was forced to resign and German troops entered Austria without a shot being fired. Contrary to the belief of Blomberg and others, neither Britain, because she thought that union was inevitable, or France, in the middle of a political crisis, did anything to help. The operation went smoothly on the surface, but Lutz's concern over the performance of the panzer divisions in the 1937 manoeuvres had not been without foundation. Guderian, newly appointed to command of the XVI Panzer Corps of two divisions, led the spearhead of the advance into Austria. On his own admission no less than 30% of his vehicles broke down or ran out of petrol. Jodl, testifying at Nuremburg put the figures even higher, at 70%. The main problems were brought about by lack of organisation of fuel supplies, inexperience of the crews, many of whom were still undergoing recruit training, and the fact that all major repairs could only be carried out at the tank factories in Germany. One result of this was that Hitler to his displeasure was forced to postpone his triumphant entry into Vienna by 24 hours. In any event it showed that the panzer arm had still a long way to go before it could be considered to be ready for war, particularly for the type of war which Hitler wished to fight.

Within a month of *Anschluss* Hitler turned his attention to Czechoslovakia. Plans for the invasion of Czechoslovakia had been drawn up by Blomberg in June 1937 under the codename of Case Green (Fall Grun). In the event of war in the East Blomberg had suggested that:

> 'The war in the East can begin with a surprise German operation against Czechoslovakia in order to parry the imminent attack of a superior enemy coalition. The necessary conditions to justify such an action politically and in the eyes of international law must be created beforehand.' [35]

The 'justification' for this act was the existence of three and a half million Germans in the Sudetenland. The local Nazi party were emboldened after *Anschluss* to demand separate autonomy for the Sudetenland and a redirection of Czech foreign policy, and, in the early summer of 1938 it seemed that Hitler was preparing for a lightning blow against Czechoslovakia. Detailed plans were drawn up for an invasion starting on October 1st, including the stepping up of production in the air industry through the introduction of ten hour shift working. Twelve hundred bombers and fighters were allocated to this operation and, in addition, 250 Ju 52s were allocated to the 7th Airborne division for attacks on Czech strongpoints. Even more significant was a demonstration in mid-August laid on at the Juterborg artillery range outside Berlin where heavy artillery bombarded concrete replicas of the Czech fortifications in an effort to impress upon the Wehrmacht High Command that these fortifications were not impregnable. But there was, in view of pacts between France, Russia and Czechoslovakia, a more real danger that Hitler might find himself at war against Russia,

Britain and France, than at the time of *Anschluss*. However, with the continuing neutrality of Poland, Belgium and Holland it was not considered that Britain and Russia could take effective reprisals for geographical reasons. It was hoped that Vuillemin's visit to Germany in August 1938 would put the French off any attempts to counteract German moves, and hence Hitler was prepared to call the bluff of Czechoslovakia's protectors, both to the east and west. In the event the Allies gave Hitler *carte blanche* to move into the Sudetenland at Munich, and in the following March Hitler polished off the rump of the country with a peaceful entry into Prague. Besides the territorial and strategic gains which he had been able to make, Hitler was also able to seize the highly reputable Czech armament industry.

In the meantime the panzer arm expanded. By January 1939 there were five panzer divisions in existence. In addition, there were four Light Divisions and four motorised infantry divisions, the former having grown out of the cavalry's own efforts at modernisation. Their main task was medium reconnaissance, and for this they were equipped with four motor rifle battalions, a PZ Kw Mk II battalion of approximately 90 tanks with reconnaissance, engineer and artillery support. There is however evidence that Hitler, whether as a result of the misconceptions to come out of the Spanish Civil War or because of the logistic problems of the panzer divisions, did not think that massed armour was totally invulnerable. At a conference held in late August 1938 to discuss Czechoslovakia he indicated that he believed that the tank as a weapon of attack was not as powerful as it had been, and would only be effective against a disorganised enemy. Certainly he was content to leave a concentration of anti-tank guns and fields of anti-tank mines but no tanks to guard against any French counter-stroke in the West during operations against Czechoslovakia. On the other hand, he could not afford to disperse his then limited armour. Nevertheless, Hitler's doubts about the effectiveness of the panzer arm in the attack would show themselves not so much in Poland, which could be considered as a weak enemy taken by surprise, but certainly during the planning for and execution of the invasion of the Low Countries.

Not all German thinking during the later 1930s was directed towards the attack. In 1936 von Leeb, who was to lead Army Group North in the attack in Russia, published a treatise on defence in the periodical *Militarwissenschaftliche Rundschau* ('The Scientific Military Review'). This was expanded into book form two years later under the title *Die Abwehr*. Von Leeb's thesis was that the blitzkrieg form of attack must be met by a similar type defence.

'Operative defence must meet the threat of offensive by using the same weapons and the same means. The stronger and more mobile are its land and air formations, the better it can face a mobile enemy utilising the element of surprise.' [36]

He argued that the tanks and aircraft assisted defence just as much as attack. They prevented defence from becoming merely a war of position as the Western Front had been in 1914-1918. In addition the new weapons

119

provided generals with ' . . . greater combinations of forces and liberty o
action. They will tend to repel the danger of paralysis at the front.' [37] He
was supported in his arguments by a number of his fellow countrymen
One, a Colonel Foertsch wrote that a strong reserve was essential in
defence, and that this should consist of strong formations of aircraft and
tanks for 'considered as a weapon of attack, they accrue to the benefit of
the defensive as a whole, quite as much as of the offensive.' [38] Yet he
pointed out that the 1914-18 war of attrition was not yet dead. 'Any interva
in the fighting, the result of material exhaustion, can lead to a stabilisation
of the front such as we witnessed in the World War.' [39] Both de Gaulle
and Liddell Hart had written on these themes, but although ignored in thei
own countries it is surprising that France and Britain should have taken so
little notice of a German antidote to blitzkrieg. Within the Wehrmach
itself the emphasis on training was on the attack. Defence was covered, bu
it was only considered to be a temporary phase, while withdrawal, the mos
difficult of military operations, was hardly touched on.

The Luftwaffe, although essentially committed to operations in suppor
of the Wehrmacht, did have second thoughts on the requirement for a
strategic bomber. In the mid 1930s, particularly after the death of Wever
the idea of a strategic bomber, or 'Urals' bomber in that its main task had
been seen as attacking Soviet industry beyond the Urals had waned. The
reasons for this were threefold. Firstly, by the end of 1935 Germany's
potential enemies had been seen as being her immediate neighbours, and
hence a long distance bomber was not necessary. Secondly, in order to give
the idea of the *Risikoflotte* credence it was essential to have quantity. Many
more two-engined bombers could be built than heavy four-engined ones and
hence Hitler himself lost interest. Finally the influence of Udet's ideas on
dive-bombing had become all prevalent. But the planning for Case Green
had had to take some account of possible reaction by Britain as well as
France. The only way that Britain could be effectively attacked was from
the air. General Felmy, appointed in February 1938 to make a study of the
inferences of war against Britain, concluded that she could only be
attacked if the Luftwaffe established forward airfields in Belgium and
Holland. The existing Luftwaffe bombers only had a radius of action of 430
miles with a bombload of ½ ton. As a result Udet, in mid-1938, commissioned
work to commence on a new four-engined bomber, the He 177, which would
replace the Do 19 and Ju 89, which had been scrapped finally in 1937
Unfortunately Udet insisted that this bomber have a dive-bombing capability
and the technical problems caused by this meant that the Luftwaffe would
not have a four-engined bomber in service until 1942 and then in only
very limited quantities. At the same time Udet became carried away by the
Ju 88, originally Wever's brainchild, having a radius of action of almos
1000 miles with a 2-ton bombload, was converted to a divebomber in the
final stages of development. Goering then insisted that this should replace
the He 111 as the standard Luftwaffe bomber, and maximum priority was
given to it. Thus, in spite of efforts to give the Luftwaffe a strategic
capability, the insistence that dive-bombing and quantity as opposed to

quality restricted the Luftwaffe's roles even more closely.

## Soviet Union

In Russia the shadow of Stalin's purges hung over the armed forces, apart from the Far Eastern Army under Bluyker, which was now to show that Tuchachevski's doctrine had been on the right lines. The Japanese had invaded Manchuria in 1931 and set up the puppet state of Manchuckuo. As far as the Soviet leaders were concerned, it was quite likely that Japan might well turn her attention to the Soviet satellite of Outer Mongolia, or even Russia's Far Eastern territories. Hence the Far Eastern Army was kept strong and well supplied with modern equipment. By 1936 it had grown to 20 Rifle Divisions and three cavalry divisions with some 900 tanks and in mid 1938 it was split into three independent armies. In August 1938 a Japanese column invaded Soviet territory on the Manchurian border in the area of Lake Khasan. Although, the resultant action with Bluyker's troops was a stereotyped head-on battle, leading to the repulse of the Japanese, certain lessons came out of the action, which showed that the ideas propagated in the 1936 *Field Service Regulations* appeared correct. Air power had been found to be unsuccessful on its own against a dug-in enemy. Infantry and tanks still needed heavy artillery support, and tanks on their own were prey to anti-tank guns, and the taking of prepared defensive positions was a combined arms task. But, as yet the encircling operations envisaged by Tuchachevski, with their reliance on mechanised forces had not come to fruition. Stern, who took over from Bluyker on the latter's liquidation during the later stages of the short campaign, drew the politically acceptable lesson that:

' . . . the action at Lake Khasan has once more confirmed that the organisational structure of the Red Army is fundamentally right. It has confirmed the fact that, in addition to powerful technical equipment, aircraft, artillery and tanks, a strong and well-trained infantry is of the highest importance for military success and continues to be the principal and decisive arm.' [40]

Attempts might be being made to make the Far Eastern Army toe the post-purges line that armour was once more only subsidiary to infantry, but Lake Khasan did show that the standards of training of the Soviet tank crews had improved. The diary of a Japanese battalion commander, killed during the operations recorded that:

'We have had to suffer quite a lot from Soviet tanks. They made use of the terrain to come to close quarters and fire at us. The firing was terrific and very accurate. Adapting themselves to the terrain, Soviet tanks frequently displayed only their turrets when they wanted to fire. Our fire was not sufficiently effective.' [41]

The following year showed, however, that Tuchachevski's more grandiose tactics had not yet been totally ignored. In May 1939 the Japanese made another major incursion, this time seizing a piece of Outer Mongolia which

121

lay between the frontier with Manchuria and the River Khalkin. The next three months saw a build-up of strength by both sides. By August, Zhukov, who was later to be one of the major architects of Soviet victory on the Eastern Front in the years 1942-45, had concentrated a force of 35 rifle battalions, 20 cavalry squadrons, 500 tanks and 500 aircraft. Although many of the tanks had been split up among infantry in accordance with post-Tuchachevski doctrine, Zhukov did retain one tank brigade in its own right. The Japanese were well dug in with 25 infantry battalions supported by 17 cavalry squadrons, 180 tanks and 450 aircraft. Since, as a rule of thumb, the attacker should be stronger than the defender in a ratio of at least 3:1, the Japanese appeared well placed. On August 20th, Zhukov attacked all along the Japanese front, but unlike the action at Lake Khasan where all the attacks had been frontal, he used his independent armoured brigade to break through the Japanese defences at their extreme ends. It then executed a Tuchachevski type of double encirclement, cutting the Japanese forces off from their lines of communication back into Manchuria. He also used his air power in an interdiction role to prevent the Japanese moving up reinforcements to break Russian armoured ring. By August 31st the Japanese had been driven back across the frontier, leaving behind 40 000 casualties, while their opponents only lost 10 000. This might have been the vindication of Tuchachevski's ideas, but back in Moscow Stalin did not see it that way. The breaking up of the mechanised formations continued until, what had been at its peak in 1937 of four mechanised corps and 25 tank brigades was reduced to 38 mechanised brigades by 1940, with the remaining tanks being broken up among the conventional infantry divisions. The whole concept of blitzkrieg was dismissed as so much bourgeois nonsense.

The lessons brought out of the Spanish Civil War by the Red Air Force were similar to those of the Luftwaffe in that value of close support to the ground forces was recognised. But belief in strategic bombing waned. No Russian heavy bombers had been employed in Spain, and German attempts at bombing targets well behind the front line had not produced the desired effect, especially on the civil population. Stalin himself had finally put paid to any thoughts of Douhetism when he had declared in his speech on May Day 1937:

> 'Whoever thinks that one can win a war with mighty aviation alone is deeply mistaken. If we look back into history we see what an important role artillery has played in all wars.' [42]

The result was that by 1939 bombers made up only 26% of the Red Air Force, a reduction of 4% from 1935. However, although the proportion of bombers might not have changed much, no effort was made to produce new types, which was to cost the Soviet Union dear in 1941.

## United States
Like other nations, the United States read the wrong lessons from the Spanish Civil War. General Malin A. Craig, who had taken over from

122

MacArthur as Chief of Staff in Autumn 1935, stated in his Annual Report to the Secretary for War in 1938 that:

'The current operations in Spain and China illustrate from day to day the greatly increased power of these new defensive weapons. They have restored to the defence the superiority it seemed to lose with the advent of the new offensive arms [tanks and aircraft]. It is largely because of these new defensive weapons that we find current operations confirming anew the testimony of history that the infantry is the core and essential substance of an army. It alone can win a decision. Each of the other arms is but an auxiliary — its utility measured by the aid it can bring to the infantry.' [43]

This had come at a time when the tank school in the US Army had been gaining momentum. The 7th Cavalry Brigade (Mechanised), although officially called into existence in 1932, was finally about to become fact in the shape of two mechanised cavalry regiments, each with 56 combat cars, supported by an artillery regiment with towed 75mm howitzers. As yet no infantry were allocated to it, but then it was officially only designed to carry out the traditional cavalry tasks of limited exploitation and raids. But, two years earlier than this the Commander of the VI Corps, reporting on the 2nd Army manoeuvres of 1936, although not considering that armour would have a key role in the attack, had said that in defence mechanised forces were capable of blocking the attacker by ' . . . rapid movements threatening in succession many vital points' thus forcing the attacker to divert troops from the main attack. [44] He thus reorganised the suitability of mechanised forces in the 'Indirect Approach'.

The problem was that Van Voorhis and Chaffee were at odds with the rest of the Army as to how mechanised cavalry should be employed. The remainder of the cavalry and the infantry saw the mechanised cavalry as a means of supporting horse cavalry as the infantry tanks did with the infantryman on foot. No wonder did Van Voorhis rather ruefully state in a lecture to the Army War College in 1937 that whereas the strength of mechanised units lay in their mobility and firepower, both of which required the ability to make prompt and quick decisions in order to exploit them:

' . . . to develop this faculty one of the greatest problems that confronts us is making the mobility of the mind equal to the mobility of the machine.' [45]

Van Voorhis' fellow-thinkers in Britain and France would undoubtedly have and indeed did echo these words at this time. Even more frustrating was the attitude taken by the Chief of Cavalry, Herr, who had taken office in March 1938. Although prepared grudgingly to accept the Mechanised Cavalry Brigade, he ruled that there should be no expansion of it at the expense of the horse. Major-General Harmon, who was to command both the 1st and 2nd Armored Divisions with distinction during World War 2, recounts an interview he had with Herr, which sums up the latter's attitude:

'At the end of my service with the General Staff I was called in by General John Herr, the Chief of Cavalry, who generously asked me where I would like to be assigned. This was a painful meeting for both of us. General Herr, who had always been kind to me, still believed that the horse had an important part to play on the battlefield. I did not. It hurt me as much as it hurt him when I said I wanted to go to tanks to learn about the new type of combat. General Herr told me I could expect no more friendship from the Office of the Chief of Cavalry.' [46]

Patton, with perhaps a shrewder eye on his future prospects, welcomed Herr's arrival in office by presenting him with three prototypes of a sabre-cum-bayonet, which he had designed for the cavalry. Within three months Patton found himself promoted to full colonel and given command of the 5th Cavalry. The time for his return to tanks had still not yet arrived. At the same time tank development did take a step in the right direction. One of the few lessons, which the Americans deduced rightly from the war in Spain was that the light tank was of little use on the battlefield other than for reconnaissance. Hence the decision was taken in 1938 to concentrate on medium tank development.

But, although events in Europe and China became of increasing concern to President Roosevelt's administration, the USA still remained in a dilemma as to who to consider as potential enemies, particularly when the policy of isolationism was still paramount. The planning difficulties of the armed forces were well summed up by General George C. Marshall when, as Deputy Chief of Staff, he addressed the Air Corps Tactical School in October 1938:

'The most difficult problem for the War Department is the determination of the best organisation for the Army, within the limits of the funds available . . . With us, geographical location and international situation make it literally impossible to find definite answers to such questions as: who will be our enemy in the next war; in what theatre of operations will it be fought; and what will be our national objective at the time? These uncertainties lead inevitably to the conclusion that the only sensible policy to follow is to maintain a conservatively balanced force for the protection of our own territory against any probable threat during the period to the vast but latent resources of the United States, in men and material, are being mobilised.' [47]

The fact that the United States could do no other than prepare for the defence of her own territory also restricted aircraft development. Although Mitchell's disciples had developed the B-17 under the umbrella of a coastal defence aircraft, they received a setback when General Craig directed that the Air Corps must confine its research and development to ' . . . types of aircraft for the close support of the ground troops. No funds to be set up for the development of heavy bomber types.' [48] But this ruling was not made because Craig was considering adopting a form of blitzkrieg, but rather that bombers could be considered only as offensive weapons and that they were expensive to produce. In any case the responsibility for defence of the seaboard, other than coastal areas, was that of the Navy, and to use a heavy bomber for coastal defence was not considered cost-effective. The result of this was to slow down procurement of the B-17, and to hold up development of its successor, the B-29.

**Notes**

1   Thomas, *The Spanish Civil War* p 316.
2   Miksche, *Attack: A study of Blitzkreig Tactics* pp 21-2.
3   Galland, *The First and the Last* p 29.
4   Miksche, op cit p 78.
5   Kemp, *Mine were of Trouble* pp 159-60.
6   Ibid, p 167.
7   Klotz, *Lecons Militaires de la Guerre D'Espagne* p 83.
8   *Royal Tank Corps Journal* Sep 1937.
9   Miksche, op cit p 107.
10   JRUSI Feb 1939.
11   Golovine, *Air Strategy* p 4.
12   Ibid, p 167.
13   Slessor, *Air Power and Armies* p vii.
14   Ibid, p 3.
15   Ibid, p 80.
16   Ibid, p 90.
17   Ibid, p 99.
18   Scott, *Vickers: A History* pp 212-3.
19   Kennedy, *The Business of War* p 9.
20   Churchill W. S., *While England Slept* p 328.
21   Dennis, op cit p 94.
22   Liddell Hart, *Memoirs* vol 2 p 5.
23   Minney, *The Private Papers of Hore-Belisha* p 59.
24   Macksey, *Armoured Crusader* op cit p 157.
25   *The Tanks* vol 1 op cit p 397.
26   *Armoured Crusader* op cit p 157.
27   Ibid, pp 159-60.
28   De La Gorce, op cit p 276.
29   Tournoux, op cit p 276.
30   Nachin, *Charles de Gaulle* p 88.
31   Chauvineau, *Une Invasion est-elle encore possible?*
32   Ibid.
33   Bankwitz, op cit p 166.
34   Werner, op cit p 149.
35   Shirer, *The Rise and Fall of the Third Reich* p 304.
36   Leeb von, *Defense* p 110.
37   Ibid, p 120.
38   Foertsch, *The Art of Modern Warfare* p 254.
39   Ibid, pp 235-6.
40   Voroshilov et al, *The Red Army Today* p 70.
41   Kournakoff, op cit p 115.
42   Gartoff, op cit p 301.
43   Millis, op cit p 428.
44   Pogue, *George C. Marshall* p 292.
45   *Armor* Sep/Oct 1973.
46   Harmon, *Combat Commander* p 57.
47   Frye, *Marshall — Citizen Soldier* p 260.
48   Reinhardt & Krimer, *The Haphazard Years* p 182.

# 5

# The Weapon is Proved

## Poland

Two weeks after German troops had entered Prague, Chamberlain, the British Prime Minister, announced that he had made a bilateral agreement with Poland that, in the event of a German attack against her, Britain was pledged to go to her assistance. The policy of appeasement, which had so influenced Britain in the 1930s was now dead. This step aggravated Hitler who had been hoping to recover Danzig, lost to Germany at Versailles, and secure road and rail access through Poland to it, without the threat of war. On April 3rd, 1939, with Poland now encouraged to resist his demands, he ordered the army to be ready to invade her by September 1st. The directive itself was codenamed Case White, and in it Hitler stated that:

'The isolation of Poland will be all the more easily maintained, even after the outbreak of hostilities, if we succeed in starting the war with sudden heavy blows and in gaining rapid successes . . . '

The task of the Wehrmacht was given as ' . . . to destroy the Polish armed forces. To this end a surprise attack is to be aimed at and prepared.' [1] While military planning went ahead Hitler kept Poland isolated on the diplomatic front with a series of non-aggression pacts made with her neighbours, culminating in the prize of a ten year pact with Russia, which was signed, in the teeth of attempts by Britain and France to do the same, on August 23rd. The stage was now set for the first of the blitzkrieg operations of World War 2.

On June 15th Hitler had received the military plan for Case White from the Commander-in-Chief, von Brauchitsch. Von Brauchitsch had refined Hitler's aim into one of destroying the Polish forces on the West of the Vistula-Narew Line by two army groups. Beck's Army Group North, consisting of the Third and Fourth Armies was to drive into East Prussia and then to turn south towards Warsaw. Army Group South under von Rundstedt, with the Eighth, Tenth and Fourteenth Armies was to move through Silesia and occupy the Vistula both sides of Warsaw. In effect, von Brauchitsch envisaged a giant double encircling movement. Once the Polish forces had been caught in the trap created by the two army groups, their systematic destruction could take place. The total German force available for Cast White was 40 infantry divisions, six panzer, four light and four motorised divisions. Two panzer and two motorised divisions were allocated to Army Group North and all of these, less one panzer division, were placed under XIX Corps commanded by Guderian. It must be emphasised however that, mechanised and motorised formations apart, the Wehrmacht still relied heavily on its feet and horse-drawn transport. Only the point of the sword was harnessed to the internal combustion engine. No wonder that the one section of the Army General Staff which was pessimistic about the forthcoming war, particularly if it should involve Germany in a wider conflict than just Poland, was the Transport Department. Its Chief declared bluntly in June 1939 that: 'In the transportation sphere Germany is at the moment not ready for war.' [2]

The Luftwaffe's contribution to Case White consisted in essence of Kesselring's Luftflotte 1, and Lohr's Luftflotte 4. This made up a total of some 1 300 aircraft, mainly He111s, Ju87s, Me109s and Me110s. In addition, a further 400 machines were retained under Goering's direct command or handed over to the army. However, the latter were mostly reconnaissance and communications aircraft. The Luftwaffe had two major roles. Firstly it had to achieve immediate air superiority, and it was intended to do this by catching the Polish Air Force on the ground. Thus its first priority targets were the Polish airfields. Once air supremacy had been achieved it would then turn its attention to support of the army and navy. However, it was not intended so much to involve itself in close air support*, taking on targets in the immediate battle area, but rather in interdiction, whereby it would attack targets behind the enemy's front lines in order to disrupt his lines of communication with a view to hindering the movement of troops and supplies. When not engaged in interdiction, the Luftwaffe was to carry out attacks on the Polish war industry, but it was categorically laid down that attacks on wholly civilian targets were prohibited. Thus, as far as the Luftwaffe were concerned, the ideas of Douhet hardly applied. The panzer divisions may have ironed out many of their doubts and problems during the 'dry runs' of Anschluss and Czechoslovakia, but the Luftwaffe were not so confident. Spain may have acted as a useful technical laboratory, but it had not taken them much further in the realm of tactics. As Kesselring wrote:

> 'For us of the Luftwaffe war meant war in the air. But except for individual experiences in Spain we had no practical experience. We had evolved our own basic principles of air warfare and appropriate rules of strategy and tactics to the best of our knowledge, and these were in our bones. Yet there were no international prescriptions for air warfare.' [3]

But, if the German armed forces had their worries, the situation facing the Poles was very much grimmer. With the occupation of Czechoslovakia, the Poles found themselves having a common frontier with Germany of some 1 750 miles. Both flanks were exposed to invasion, from Pomerania in the

---

* Only 36 Henschels (ground attack biplanes) were permanently allocated for close support.

north and Czechoslovakia in the south. In order to defend her territory Poland could put into the field 30 infantry divisions, 11 cavalry brigades, but only two motorised brigades and a single armoured brigade. The motorised brigades each consisted of one company of Vickers 6 Ton tanks, and two companies of tankettes, which were a version of the British Carden-Lloyd Mark VI. In addition, each had two motorised cavalry regiments, which were nothing more than lorried infantry, and motorised battalions of artillery, 37mm anti-tank guns and engineers. The armoured brigade had two battalions of 7-TP tanks, an improved version of the Vickers 6 Tonner, having thicker armour and a high velocity 37mm gun, and one battalion of Renault 35s. In addition, eighteen independent companies, each of thirteen tankettes were attached to the infantry divisions, and each horse cavalry brigade had a reconnaissance squadron of thirteen tankettes and eight armoured cars. In all this represented some 660 tanks, but none, other than possibly the 7-TP and Vickers 6 Ton, could be classified as other than light tanks. In comparison, the Germans were pitting against them some 2 000 tanks, although the majority were Pz Kw Mk Is and IIs mounting only a machine gun. There were however some Mk IIIs with a 37mm and MK IVs with a low velocity 75mm. The Polish Air Force could put up some 450 aircraft against the Luftwaffe, but only their Los B bombers of which they possessed a mere 36, could be said to be modern. The backbone of their fighter force was the PZL P.11c, a single-seater with open cockpit, braced wings and a top speed of only 242mph. Nevertheless, the Poles seemed to have been surprisingly confident in their ability to turn back the invader, relying on the Polish national spirit in place of machines to fulfill the task. They organised their army into seven individual armies. Five were placed to cover their joint border with Germany proper, and the other two were echeloned back to face East Prussia. With such a long frontier to defend and only limited forces available, defence could be little more than linear.

On August 15th, German mobilisation plans were set in motion. The date for invasion was brought forward to August 26th, in view of Stalin's assurance that Russia would remain neutral during the conflict. The propaganda campaign against Poland, part of Hitler's blitzkrieg technique, hotted up. But last minute attempts by the British Government to persuade Hitler to continue trying for a peaceful solution to the Polish problem, together with 'cold feet' on the part of Mussolini, caused Hitler to call for a postponement on the eve of invasion. Some units, who were already moving up to the frontier, did not receive the postponement order until late on the night of the 25th, and, in one or two cases, they had already attacked Polish blockhouses, but as so many incidents had recently taken place along the frontier, the Poles did not pay too much attention. After a few more days of desperate negotiation on the part of Britain and France, Hitler issued his final orders for Case White at 1230 hours on August 31st. His Directive No 1, the first of 75 which he would issue during the course of the next six years, stated:

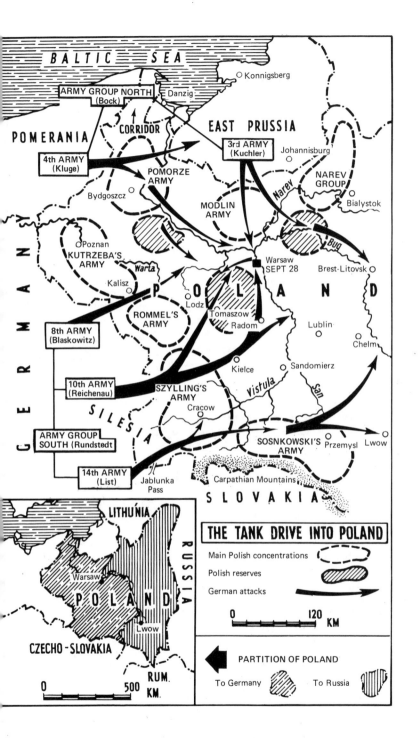

BALTIC SEA

Konnigsberg

ARMY GROUP NORTH (Bock)   Danzig

CORRIDOR   EAST PRUSSIA

POMERANIA

4th ARMY (Kluge)   POMORZE ARMY

3rd ARMY (Kuchler)   Johannisburg

NAREV GROUP

Bydgoszcz   MODLIN ARMY   Bialystok

Poznan   KUTRZEBA'S ARMY   Warta   Narev

Kalisz   P O L A N D   Warsaw SEPT 28   Bug   Brest-Litovsk

Lodz

ROMMEL'S ARMY   Tomaszow   Radom   Lublin

8th ARMY (Blaskowitz)   Kielce   Sandomierz   Chelm

10th ARMY (Reichenau)   SZYLLING'S ARMY   Vistula   San

ARMY GROUP SOUTH (Rundstedt)   Cracow   SOSNKOWSKI'S ARMY   Przemysl   Lwow

SILESIA

14th ARMY (List)   Jablunka Pass   Carpathian Mountains

S L O V A K I A

**THE TANK DRIVE INTO POLAND**

LITHUNIA

RUSSIA

Warsaw   P O L A N D   Lwow

CZECHO - SLOVAKIA

RUM.

0   500   KM.

Main Polish concentrations

Polish reserves

German attacks

0   120   KM

PARTITION OF POLAND

To Germany   To Russia

'The attack on Poland will be undertaken in accordance with th
preparations made for 'Case White', with such variations as may b
necessitated by the build-up of the Army which is now virtually com
plete. The allocation of tanks and the purpose of the operation remai
unchanged. Date of attack September 1st, 1939.' [4]

That night the troops of Army Groups North and South moved up to th
border prior to crossing it at 0445 hours next day. The world was about t
witness the 'first night' of blitzkrieg.

The first blow was struck by the Stukas, who attacked Polish demolition
at a bridge at Dirschau on the Vistula, which was to be a vital link in th
lines of communication from the Third Army in East Prussia with th
Reich. The attack went in at 0434 hours, but although successful, it did no
prevent the Poles from partially demolishing the bridge two hours later
However, in spite of the Luftwaffe being given the privilege of firing the firs
shots of World War 2, they did not achieve their main object of the firs
day's fighting, namely that of gaining complete air supremacy. Two factor
caused this. Firstly, fog dominated much of the battle area. This had beer
the great ally of the *sturmtruppen* of 1918 because, besides contributing t
surprise, it had prevented allied air power from interfering significantl
with the action of the assault divisions. It was not to Germany's advantag
on this first day of the new war in that it prevented many vital targets fron
being bombed until well after midday. Secondly, the Poles had taker
certain precautions to keep their slender air force intact. A Polish Air Forc
major explained:

'The German Luftwaffe did exactly what we expected. It attacked ou
airfields and tried to wipe out our aircraft on the ground. In retrospect i
seems quite naive of the Germans to have believed that during th
preceding days of high political tension, and with their own obviousl
aggressive intentions, we would leave our units sitting in their peace-tim
locations. The fact of the matter is that, by August 31st, not a singl
serviceable aircraft remained on them. In the previous forty-eight hour
all of us had been transferred to emergency airstrips. As a result th
Germans' opening air blast completely failed in its purpose.' [5]

Thus, the Luftwaffe attacked airfields, destroyed runways and hangars anc
knocked out already unserviceable aircraft, feeling able to report or
September 2nd that it had destroyed the Polish Air Force. In the event, th
Poles stayed their hand, and it was not until subsequent days, by whick
time the Luftwaffe was engaged on its second major task of interdiction
that the Poles began to make their presence felt. Although their fighter
suffered badly at the hands of the Me109s, their bomber force did much tc
hold back the German advance in the early days. However, the Luftwaffe'
interdiction battles had a greater effect than expected. Instead of jusl
disrupting the ground forces, they also had the effect of upsetting th
supply and communications systems of the Polish air force. Consequently

by September 8th Polish aircraft started to become grounded through lack of spares and orders took so long to get through that attacks were put in too late to have any effect. As a result, on September 17th the remaining serviceable aircraft, some 116, were flown across the Roumanian border and interned.

On the ground the situation was more straightforward. The main thrusts by the armies were led by the panzer divisions, which were followed by the Motorised and light divisions. If the tanks became held up by anti-tank guns or other fortifications, they paused until the lorry-borne infantry came up to deal with them. If it was available they could call on close air support and for this purpose a Luftwaffe officer with radio communication back to the supporting air division accompanied each mechanised formation. Behind the mechanised tip followed the conventional infantry divisions, whose task was to widen the initial penetration. For their part the long gruelling marches made on their feet during their training now paid off. In order to have any hope of keeping up with the tanks they were expected to cover at least 20-25 miles a day, besides whatever fighting they had to do.

It must not be imagined, however, that the operations on the ground proceeded entirely according to plan and that the mechanised divisions acted like some well-oiled machine. Most of the troops taking part had never been under fire, and during the first days there were mistakes, mis-understandings and hesitations. Guderian quotes several such examples with his own Corps. He himself was almost knocked out by the artillery of one of his own panzer divisions as he crossed the frontier on the first day, having specifically ordered his artillery not to fire. The same division had been ordered to get across the River Brahe, 20 miles inside Poland and the first significant river obstacle on Guderian's axis of advance, on the first day. Yet, by mid-afternoon, the divisional commander had ordered the divisions to rest on the near bank of the river because he did not believe that it would be possible to force a passage across it that day. And:

'During the night the nervousness of the first day of battle made itself felt more than once. Shortly after midnight the 2nd (Motorised) Division informed me that they were being compelled to withdraw by Polish cavalry. I was speechless for a moment; when I had regained the use of my voice I asked the divisional commander if he had ever heard of Pomeranian grenadiers being broken by hostile cavalry. He replied that he had not and now assured me that he could hold his positions.' [6]

Von Mellenthin, who was the Intelligence Officer to III Corps operating to the south of Guderian's Corps, records a similar experience:

'A low-flying aircraft circled over corps battle headquarters and everyone let fly with whatever he could grab. An air-liaison officer ran about trying to stop the fusillade and shouting to the excited soldiery that this was a German command plane — one of the good old *Fieseler Störche*. Soon afterwards the aircraft landed, and out stepped the Luftwaffe

131

general responsible for our close air support. He failed to appreciate the joke.' [7]

But certainly, in Guderian's case, he was able to react quickly to these indications of nervousness. He believed that the commander of a mechanised formation could only influence events if he was well forward. He used an armoured command vehicle (ACV) equipped with radio communication to his divisions and his corps headquarters. Thus he, as the formation commander, was always in touch with the latest situation, and had the ability to influence events personally by moving to the trouble spot. In a fast moving battle information is often out of date by the time it gets back to the commander. It is often difficult for him to make a sound decision relying merely on stale information and the use of a map. If he can get forward in time and see the ground in question his reaction is very much more likely to be the correct one. The *sturmtruppen* of 1918 had got round the problem by delegation of command in allowing junior commanders to make decisions on the spot. But then the communications of 1918 bore little resemblance to those of 1939, and thus there was no other solution if the momentum of the advance was to be maintained. There were of course dangers in Guderian's command style. If he got out of radio contact he lost his ability to command, and there was always the danger that he might be tempted to take over the job of the leading platoon commander, thereby causing resentment among the junior commanders and, even more serious, finding himself incapable of 'seeing the wood for the trees'. One of the few major criticisms of Rommel was that in North Africa, by adopting this method of command from the front, he was frequently out of contact with his main headquarters, thereby forcing comparatively junior staff officers to make major decisions which should have been taken by himself. Nevertheless, the panzer commanders and later Allied armoured commanders, especially Patton, adopted this method of command up to and including divisional level, and sometimes up to Corps level.

In spite of the shortfalls in the inexperience of the troops, the German plan worked well. The Poles, although they fought with almost fanatical bravery, were bemused by the pace of the German advance. A subaltern in a motorised regiment advancing from Slovakia in the southern part of the Fourteenth Army's area of operations wrote:

'The whole thing was so like an occupation or a manoeuvre that we could hardly believe this was really war; it all seemed too well-ordered and familiar. There was virtually no resistance, and for days on end we advanced towards the Polish Ukraine. There were rumours of sharp shooters and partisans, but I never saw or heard anything of them, except for the occasional sound of a shot in the distance. There was a certain amount of sporadic fighting when we got to the river barriers, but the Luftwaffe cleared the way for us. Their Stuka dive-bombers were deadly accurate, and as there was no opposition they had it all their own way. The roads and fields were swarming with unhappy peasants who had fled in panic from their villages when the bombing began, and we passed hundreds and hundreds of Polish troops walking dejectedly towards Slovakia. The Poles seemed to be completely apathetic, and there were so many prisoners that nobody bothered to guard them or even tell them where to go.' [8]

By September 6th von Rundstedt's Army Group South had broken through or bypassed the three Polish armies facing it, and was driving across the Polish plain towards Warsaw. In the north, von Bock's two armies, spearheaded by Guderian's XIX Corps, had cleared the Polish corridor, thereby linking East Prussia with the Reich, and were now turning south to the east of the Vistula. Hitler, meeting Guderian on that day, showed himself amazed at the damage wrought by Guderian's tanks and also at the small number of casualties suffered by the Germans. But, in spite of Hitler's marvelling, there was a tendency at times to hold back the panzer divisions. The German High Command showed a certain nervousness in allowing them to get too far ahead of the main body. Although this reduced their shock potential, this reluctance was understandable in view of the fact that the main body was on its feet, which severely limited its rate of advance. If the panzers got too far ahead there was a grave danger of them becoming cut off. Although they were able to look after themselves for a limited length of time, lack of fuel and ammunition would soon have made them powerless. This tendency would manifest itself even more strikingly in May 1940. Nevertheless, by September 8th, the 4th Panzer Division in von Reichenau's 10th Army, finding a gap in the Polish defences, had raced ahead and reached the outskirts of Warsaw, having covered 140 miles in a week.

On September 10th Army Group South had two major Polish concentrations trapped east and south of Warsaw with their backs to the Vistula. While Fourth Army closed the trap to the east of the Vistula, Guderian's Corps, which had been placed under direct command of Army Group North and had received a second panzer division in place of one of its motorised divisions, crossed the River Narev 70 miles north-east of Warsaw and drove towards Brest-Litovsk, some 100 miles to the south-east. The next day, Marshal Smigly-Rydz ordered the Polish forces to withdraw to south-east Poland, but the order had come too late for many Polish formations. On September 17th Guderian linked up with armoured spearheads of Army Group South at Wlodawa on the River Buq, and the Poles found themselves trapped by an inner cordon on the Vistula and an outer on the Buq. All that now remained was to mop up the pocket. What it was like during the final stages is described by a member of the Leibstandarte SS, which fought as a motorised rifle regiment in Army Group South:

'Our advance took us across that part of the battle-field which had been held by the so-called Pomorze Army. The whole area was a scene of death and destruction. The bloated bodies of men and animals blackening under the hot sun, smashed carts, burnt out vehicles and those most tragic victims of war, the wounded horse, waiting for the mercy shot. Now I understand what the words of our song mean "Man and horse and wagon, the Lord God struck them down . . ."' [9]

Any hopes which the Poles might have had for prolonging the struggle were dashed also on the 17th when the Russians crossed the Polish frontier from the east. Stalin, surprised by the rapidity of the German advance and still very mistrustful of Hitler in spite of their non-aggression pact, did not want German troops sitting on the Russian border, and needed some of Poland to act as a buffer.

Although Warsaw continued to hold out until September 27th, the Polish campaign was to all intents and purposes over in three weeks. Blitzkrieg had lived up to its name. The Poles had lost an army of almost 800 000 men and their air force was either interned or lay in ruins about the Polish countryside. The Germans had only suffered some 40 000 casualties, including 8 000 dead. They had lost no more than 285 aircraft and 217 tanks — a small price to pay for such a victory. The ideas preached by Liddell Hart, Fuller, Guderian, De Gaulle, Tuchachevski and others of that small band of prophets in the wilderness had been vindicated. Now, having achieved victory in the east, Hitler could now turn westwards and try his new weapon on a tougher nut.

## Scandinavia and France

The reactions to Hitler's overrunning of Poland were strangely muted in the West. Britain and France had declared war on Germany on September 3rd. To the British public nurtured on twenty years of the cry 'the bomber will always get through!' there was much concern that Hitler would unleash a Douhet type of air attack on London and other major cities at the start of the war. Poland seemed a long way away, as had Czechoslovakia, and few thought that it was possible to give her direct assistance. Franco-British Staff discussions during the Summer of 1939 had expressed the hope that Poland would be able to keep some 35 German divisions tied up while Britain and France mobilised and deployed their forces, and during the first few days of the war the British Government took an optimistic view of events in Poland. Thus, on September 11th, the day Smigly-Rydz had given the order to withdraw to south-east Poland, Ironside, the British CIGS, reported to the British Cabinet:

'The Poles are putting up a good fight and are defending Warsaw vigorously. Their main army is still intact. Eight divisions have been caught in the Posen salient, but it is hoped that some might break through. A line of defence has been taken up on the Vistula.' [10]

Not until September 14th did the tenor of Ironside's reports change. To most the implications of the speedy defeat of Poland had not got through. Liddell Hart, writing to his publisher on September 11th expressed his frustration thus:

134

'The prevailing mood of the moment, and the widespread loss of all sense of the realities of the situation give one the sense of being confined in a mad-house. It is obviously impossible to write the truth, and to write anything less would only make one an accomplice in maintaining a dangerous state of illusion, so that it is better to keep silence . . .' [11]

Much the same attitude was apparent in France. Gamelin expressed the optimistic opinion to the Premier, Daladier, when the latter was making up his mind as to whether to declare war, that Poland would resist long enough to prevent the bulk of the German forces being turned westwards before Spring 1940. In fact, German troops commenced their deployment westwards towards the end of September.

Meanwhile the British and French carried on with the task of deploying their forces. Full staff talks between the French and British did not get going properly until after Hilter had moved into Czechoslovakia. Before this time the British Government, intent on its policy of appeasement, had not wished to advertise the formation of any sort of military alliance with France. Although prior to this, following the 'Doctrine of Limited Liability', they had agreed that British bombers would operate against Germany from French soil until such time as there were enough long-range British bombers available, but they would only commit two regular divisions as a ground contribution. At their first session they agreed that the first phase of the war in the west would necessarily be a defensive one against an enemy with superior land and air forces, but weaker at sea and in economic strength. Time would be needed to set their respective war machines in motion, but this could only be through the ability to prevent any early major German incursion into France. 'In other words they had to presume that the Allies could force Germany to accept a repetition of the static warfare of 1914-1918, in spite of the fact that mechanisation, tanks and air forces had made obsolete the pedestrian pattern of the First World War.' [12] The weak area of the French defences was recognised as being the Franco-Belgian frontier which was not covered by the Maginot Line. The Germans, therefore were quite likely to move against Holland and Belgium rather than combat the strength of the Maginot Line. Although nothing could be done to save Holland, it would be possible to meet any German attack through Belgium before it reached French territory, by forestalling it on the line of the Albert Canal. The problem was that Belgium, as in 1914, was adopting a neutral posture, and would on no account agree to France and Britain moving their forces into her territory unless she had actually been invaded. Thus the British and French Armies had to be content with preparing for a move forward into Belgium without being allowed to make any reconnaissance or preparation of the positions which they would have to occupy should the German Army move in that direction.

The French expected to be able to mobilise some 85 divisions, of which 15 would be tied to manning the Maginot Line, and a further 12 would be required to guard the Franco-Italian frontier. This left some 58 divisions to cover the expected move through Belgium and to provide a reserve. In addition, the British agreed, in April 1939, to increase their contribution to four regular divisions. At the same time conscription was introduced with the object of creating an army of 32 divisions. Britain also promised to provide her two projected armoured divisions, but the first of these would not be ready before the end of 1939. There would also be an air component operating in support of the British Expeditionary Force (BEF). Its strength would be two light bomber squadrons, six army co-operation squadrons, whose role was reconnaissance, and four fighter squadrons with the task of giving air protection. The other RAF contribution, the Advanced Air Striking Force, was controlled by Bomber Command in England, and would concentrate its attacks on the German lines of communication when Germany invaded. Its strength would be ten bomber and two fighter squadrons. The French Air Force numbered some 1 300 aircraft of all types at the outbreak of war, but only 50% could be considered modern, and of these there were only 11 bombers. It could do no more than try to defend French air space. It was estimated that the Germans could field 3 700 aircraft of all types and Italy, if she entered the war, a further 1 400.

On the day Britain declared war Lord Gort, a Guardsman with a distinguished fighting record in World War 1, was appointed to command the BEF, and the movement of troops across the Channel began. Two days later the French, as agreed in the joint staff talks commenced a cautious advance up to the German border. This was supposed to have the effect of relieving pressure on the Poles, who by now were pleading for a bombing campaign on Germany, which was met with deaf ears. Neither the British or French were prepared to bomb targets in Germany for two reasons. Firstly, it seemed that the Germans themselves had been very careful to restrict aerial targets to those of a military nature only. This was a correct supposition, only broken with one raid on Warsaw, which was after an ultimatum to surrender the city had been given. Secondly, the Allies, in particular the French, had no wish to bring down German retribution in the shape of air attacks on civilian targets at this stage. In any case, Air Staff appreciations in the 1930s had shown that Bomber Command would not be capable of mounting a strategic air offensive against Germany until a considerable time after the outbreak of war. In the event, the Advanced Air Striking Force initially contented itself with leaflet raids over Germany. On September 11th the French advance ceased, having closed up to the Siegfried Line, the German equivalent, although not so elaborate, of the Maginot Line. The Phoney War, or *Sitzkrieg* as the Germans called it, had now started.

Hitler had hoped that the quick defeat of Poland might make the Western Allies reconsider the decision to wage war on Germany. In early October he went as far as putting out peace feelers, but meeting no response, he resolved to attack westwards at the earliest opportunity. His first instructions to this effect were given in Directive No 6, dated October 9th, 1939. The plan was called Case Yellow. As deduced by the Allies in their pre-war staff talks, Hitler envisaged a repeat of the Schleiffen Plan of 1914, the only difference being that he allowed himself more elbow room by taking in Holland as well as Belgium and Luxembourg. The offensive was to be launched 'at the earliest possible moment and in the greatest strength'. The three main aims of the offensive were the defeat of the Allied forces, the gaining of territory in the Low Countries to act as a base for 'the successful prosecution of the air and sea war against England' and to act as a buffer for the 'economically vital Ruhr'. The Luftwaffe's roles were purely tactical — air protection for and direct support to the ground troops, and the prevention of British landings and establishment of Anglo-French air bases in Holland and Belgium. There was no mention of attacking Allied war industry, as there had been prior to the Polish campaign. But then this would only have a long-term effect, which would not begin to bite before the end of the short campaign envisaged by Hitler. In any event, the destruction of Allied war industry would also deny its use to the Germans once they had captured it. The timing of the attack was to depend, besides the weather upon '. . . the readiness for action of the armoured and motorised units involved. These units are to be made ready with all speed.' [13]

Although some divisions had been transferred westwards during the latter stages of the Polish campaign, the mechanised formations did not move until early October. But, however highly successful they had been in their debut, they still required several weeks in order to make them fit for what would cerainly be a much tougher campaign. Much maintenance needed to be done on the vehicles, and the crews needed recuperation. More important were changes in organisation and equipment. The main lesson to come out of Poland was that the light divisions were unsatisfactory, being too cumbersome for reconnaissance, but not having sufficient tank strength to be capable of much else. The decision was therefore made to transform them into panzer divisions. This would mean that ten such divisions would be available for Case Yellow. However, the ex-light divisions were weaker in tanks than the original panzer divisions, having three tank battalions only, and in the case of 9th Panzer Division two battalions only, as opposed to the four battalions of the six original divisions. The motorised divisions were also found to be too unwieldy and were reduced by one regiment each. A few of the infantry organic to the panzer divisions were given half-tracks as opposed to lorries so that they could keep up closer with the tanks. Poland had also shown that the PZ Kw Mk I, of which there had been over 1 400 at the start of the campaign, was useless in modern combat, being too lightly armoured and having only two 7.92mm machine guns. The Mk II was only suitable for reconnaissance, and hence it was essential to give the panzer divisions more punch. Ideally it would have been sensible to concentrate tank production on the MK IV with its 75mm gun, but the decision was taken to rely mainly on the MK III with the smaller 50mm gun. In addition there were also Czech 35t and 38t tanks available, which mounted a 37mm, and these were used to equip the newly transformed Panzer Divisions. All this naturally took time, but Hitler was impatient. He had made it quite clear in a secret memorandum, issued at the same time as Directive No 6, that he was relying on the panzer divisions to lead the breakthrough. He also laid down how they were to be handled:

'They are not to be lost among the endless rows of houses in Belgian towns. It is not necessary for them to attack towns at all, but . . . to maintain the flow of the army's advance, to prevent fronts from becoming stable by massed drives through identified weakly held positions.' [14]

The generals, however, were pessimistic, and did not believe that the Army would be ready before the end of 1939, or that Hitler's plan would succeed. Hitler, however, laid down the law at a conference on October 27th, and decreed that Case Yellow would be put into operation on November 12th.

On October 28th Hitler decided that the primary task was the defeat of the Anglo-Belgian forces as opposed to the capture of territory. Although this would still be achieved by attacking through the Low Countries, the main thrust, which had been planned to proceed on a line Brussels-Ghent-Bruges, would now be split into two. The northern arm would strike north of Liege, while the southern would pass west and south of Liege with the object of breaking through the Allied Line towards Rheims and Amiens. Army Group B under von Bock was given the leading role in this plan and was allotted all the armour. Von Rundstedt's Army Group A would guard von Bock's southern flank, while von Leeb with Army Group C contented itself with feint attacks against the Maginot Line. Von Manstein, who was Chief of Staff to von Rundstedt, objected to this plan because he felt that central Belgium would be strongly defended, and also because the Allies would be expecting the major thrust through the Low Countries. He argued that a more effective thrust could be mounted through the Ardennes, north of Sedan. This would split the Allied front in two. Guderian, invited to approve the plan, concurred, having decided that, although seemingly impassable to tanks, it would be possible to mount an armoured thrust through here, provided that all the armour was allocated to this thrust. In the meantime Hitler had been considering a subsidiary operation in this direction, and it was agreed that one panzer division would be allocated to von Rundstedt. Simultaneously he started issuing orders delaying the attack by a week at a time, perhaps finally realising that the Army was still not ready. These delays culminated in Directive No 8 dated November 20th, which did not give a date for the attack, but merely ordered the armed forces to remain at a high state of readiness. Also indicative of the growing influence of von Manstein's plan was an amendment to the operation order of October 29th:

'All precautions will be taken to enable the main weight of attack to be switched from Army Group B to Army Group A should the disposition of enemy forces at any time suggest that Army Group A could achieve greater success.' [15]

A few days earlier Hitler had agreed to transfer the whole of Guderian's XIX Corps, which now consisted of three panzer divisions and a motorised rifle regiment, to von Rundstedt.

Von Manstein was still not happy. He requested that the role of flank

138

protection to Army Group B be dropped, and an additional army be given to Army Group A. Both these requests were turned down. In spite of having the support of von Rundstedt, von Manstein had become so unpopular with the High Command that he was removed from his job of Chief of Staff to Army Group A and sent to an infantry corps. Finally, on December 28th Hitler gave the order that the campaign would start on January 17th, 1940. It so happened that on January 10th a staff officer from Luftflotte 2 at Munster was flying to attend a conference at Cologne to discuss ways and means for relieving the 7th Air Division and 22nd Infantry Division (Airborne) once had completed their Case Yellow plan of capturing the Ghent fortifications, the fortress of Eben-Emael and bridges over the Albert Canal by airborne attack. Although the weather was foggy he accepted a lift by aircraft, an Me 108 communications plane. Unfortunately the pilot got lost in the fog, suffered an engine failure, and was forced to land near Mechelen in Belgium. Among the papers which the staff officer was carrying was the Luftflotte 2 order for Case Yellow. Although he tried to burn this and the other secret documents which he was carrying, he only partially succeeded and they fell into the hands of the Belgian authorities. When Hitler heard of this he was furious and ordered an indefinite postponement of the offensive. Yet, he did not immediately change the plan. It was only after a series of war games played throughout January and February, together with Hitler hearing about the von Manstein plan from its author in person, that Hitler decided that the Sedan attack was the correct course of action to adopt.

The final plan was issued on February 24th, 1940. The new aim was now to cut off the Allied armies north of the Somme and annihilate them. Whilst Army Group B with three panzer divisions, one motorised and twenty-four infantry divisions overran Holland and Northern Belgium, Army Group A with seven panzer divisions, three motorised and thirty-four infantry divisions was to advance on a front from south of Aachen to inclusive of Luxembourg, break into France between Namur and Sedan, and then cut the Allies off north of the Somme by capturing Amiens and Abbeville on the Somme. Army Group C, with seventeen infantry divisions, remained with its task unchanged from the original plan, namely to mask the Maginot Line. In addition there was a reserve of forty-four infantry divisions and one motorised division. In support of Army Groups A and B would be Luftflottes 2 and 3, under the command of Kesselring and Sperrle respectively. This combined strength of the two airfleets on May 10th, 1940 was to be 1 120 bombers, 324 dive-bombers, 1 264 fighters, together with reconnaissance and transport aircraft.

The main question of concern to the British and French during the autumn of 1939 was how far the Allies should advance into Belgium once the Germans started to attack. The troops involved in this operation would be three French armies and the BEF. The French came to the conclusion that there were only two courses open — either to advance to the River Scheldt (called the Escaut by the French), which was known as Plan E, or Plan D, which involved advancing to the River Dyle, Wavre, Namur and then along the River Meuse. Plan D was the more attractive in that it was a shorter line to hold, with defence in depth behind it, as well as covering more of Belgium. But the Belgians were not prepared to hand over any details of their defences on the Dyle. In the event, it was decided that it would all depend on the extent of resistance which the Belgians offered to the Germans as to which plan was adopted, although 'if circumstances permitted' Plan D would be the one used. It is significant that at no stage was any other German plan contemplated. Even the 'Mechelen Incident' did not make Belgium move closer to France and Britain, both of whom considered the documents captured as fake, and therefore continued to ignore the possible German approach through the Ardennes. In the meantime, the British steadily reinforced the BEF and constructed defences, while the French appeared to do little but wait.

Hitler had ordered the redeployment for the final version of Case Yellow to be completed by March 7th. But, before he could decide on a date for attack another more pressing problem arose. Russia, having partitioned Poland with Germany, also wanted to create a buffer on her northern flank in case of invasion from the west. Having virtually annexed the Baltic states of Latvia and Estonia, she turned her attention on Finland. Her demands were a thirty year lease on the island of Hango at the entrance of the Gulf of Finland, the western part of the Rybachi peninsular, which extended into the Barents Sea, and part of the Karelian Isthmus, which lay north of Leningrad. The occupation of these territories would enable the Russians to ward off better any attack from the Baltic and around northern Scandinavia. The Finns refused these demands and the Russians attacked along the length of their common frontier on November 30th, 1939. The Finns were outnumbered by ten to one, but succeeded in putting up a brave showing against the Russians. If nothing else, it showed the effect the purges had had on the Soviet forces. The bravery of the Finns caught the imagination of the British and French, but the only way they could provide material assistance was by going through Scandinavia, in particular Norway, which at that time was neutral. At the same time there was concern in the Allied camp over the supply of Norwegian iron-ore to Germany, and the possible use by the Germans of Norwegian naval bases with which to threaten British trade routes with North America. In fact, Admiral Raeder had been pressing Hitler over the latter possibility in the context of U-Boat bases since the beginning of October 1939. But it was not until approaches had been made to Raeder by the Norwegian Quisling, whose name was to become a household word, that Hitler set in train a study on the possible invasion of Norway. He did not begin to take up the possibility seriously until December 1939 when it was clear that the British and French were actively considering using Norway as a base from which to support the Finns. After the Mechelen incident, and the decision to change the emphasis of Case Yellow, Hitler, with time on his hands, took personal responsibility for the planning of Case Weser-exercise as it had come to be called. Hitler issued a detailed planning directive on March 1st, 1940, which also included an invasion of Denmark, which would have to be accomplished

140

if secure lines of communication with Norway were to be set up.

The Allies had planned to land in Norway by the end of March, and then move across to help the Finns. The latter part of the plan, however, was forestalled by the Finnish surrender to the Russians on March 13th. Nevertheless, there was still concern at the possibility of the Germans seizing Norwegian iron-ore. Mining of Norwegian water was scheduled to commence on April 5th, followed by landings in Norway a few days later. In view of Allied plans, Hitler finally made a decision on April 1st, that Case Weser-exercise should be mounted in the early hours of April 9th. Meanwhile French hesitancy caused the postponement of the Allied operation by three days, enabling the Germans to strike first.

This was a different type of blitzkrieg. Two essential ingredients, common to the more conventional form, speed and surprise were present, but, for obvious reasons, this operation was unsuitable for the mechanised formations. It relied on a massive concentration of air power, the use of airborne troops, and a limited naval presence. It was, however, the Luftwaffe, which tipped the scales — not with its physical but its psychological effect which paralysed the opposition. Indeed, Hitler, in his order of March 1st, had specified that, in the case of Denmark, the Luftwaffe's primary role was '. . . demonstration and for dropping leaflets.' [16] With the Luftwaffe hovering up above like the sword of Damocles, the Germans were able to sail three small transports into Copenhagen harbour at first light and land a small force with no opposition from the bemused Danes. Although the Norwegians, aided by Franco-British forces did put up some resistance, a mixture of speed, surprise and bluff on the part of the Germans enabled them to seize and hold key ports and population centres in Norway from the start. The Allies could have done more by cutting off the German sea communications across the Skaggerak, but the presence of the Luftwaffe dissuaded the British Admiralty from sending in warships other than submarines. The last Allied troops were not evacuated from Norway until June 7th, but the Germans had, to all intents and purposed, won the battle in the first few hours.

The only effect that Case Weser-exercise had which could be deemed beneficial to the Allies was that it caused Hitler to delay further his invasion of the Low Countries. But the Allies, who were committed to an advance into Belgium for which little preparatory work could be done before invasion actually took place, derived little benefit from this.

The Allied dispositions on May 10th, 1940 showed that they were still firmly wedded to the idea that the Germans would repeat their strategy of August 1914. Billotte's First Army Group of 23 divisions, organised into three French armies and the BEF, was poised to move up to the Dyle line, where they would join 14 Belgian divisions. Forward of this on the Albert Canal and Meuse were a further ten Belgian divisions. Above the northern limit of the Maginot Line lay Huntziger's French Second Army with seven divisions. To guard the Maginot Line were two army groups, the Second and Third with a total of 50 divisions between them. Expecting the brunt of the fighting to take place in the north, Gamelin had placed the BEF and the two best equipped and trained French armies, Giraud's Seventh and Blanchard's First, in the north. The weak part of the front lay with Corap's Ninth Army, which was to guard the southern flank when Billotte moved forward, and the Second Army. Both contained a high proportion of low grade reserve divisions. Thus Plan D played into the Germans' hands by drawing the best of the Allied troops, like a matador's cloak, as Liddell Hart described it, so far into Belgium that it would be impossible for them to assist their weaker brethren to the south, who would bear the brunt of the German attack. The situation was even more aggravated by Gamelin's decision that aid must be given to the Dutch. To this end, the Seventh Army was to advance well beyond the Dyle line into Holland, thus putting it out on a limb.

The Allies had greater strength in armour than the Germans. The latter deployed some 2 570 out of an available strength of 3 380 available. Of these, just under 1 000 mounted a 37mm gun or larger. The French put 3 285 into the field, but one third of these were parcelled out into non-divisional tank battalions for infantry support only; 110 were split up among the five horse cavalry divisions, *Divisions Cuirassées* (DLC), while the three DLMs accounted for a further 582. There were, however, by May 1940 three armoured divisions (DCR) in existence, and a fourth was about to be formed. Each consisted of two demi-brigades, each of one battalion of 34 Char B's, the same tank that Estienne had designed back in 1921, and one of 45 Hotchkiss light tanks equipped with a 37mm gun. These two demi-brigades were supported by one motorised rifle battalion and two 12-gun *groupes* of motorised artillery. They were retained as part of the Allied reserve of 22 divisions. It might be thought that the DCRs had been so positioned in deference to de Gaulle's arguments for keeping armour concentrated, but this was not so. Two had been formed only in January, and the other as late as April. Their training was not finished and their equipment incomplete, and hence it was not considered worth deploying them further forward. The role of the DLMs and the cavalry divisions was to provide the advanced guard and covering force for each army.

The BEF was in an even worse state with regard to tanks. By May the 1st Armoured Division, which should have formed the backbone of its armoured strength, was still training in England. This left the bulk of the armour available in the form of seven regiments, cavalry and yeomanry, equipped with Mark VI Light tanks, armed solely with a machine-gun for reconnaissance duties only. Until the first week in May there was only one other unit, which could boast of anything more powerful, and that was 4th Royal Tank Regiment, which had 50 Infantry Tank Mk Is, the brainchild of Elles when he was MGO. This was part of the 1st Army Tank Brigade, nominally of three regiments, whose role was infantry support. The delay in sending across the other two battalions was because of the slow production of the Infantry Tank Mark II, which mounted a 2-pounder gun as opposed to a 0.50 inch machine-gun of the Mark I. Just before the Germans invaded, the second regiment of this brigade, the 7th Royal Tank Regiment arrived in France, with seven light tanks, 27 Mark Is, and 23 Mark IIs. The latter was all that the BEF had to stand up to the PZ Kw Mk IIIs and IVs. In addition, the slow speeds of the infantry tanks severely restricted the mobility, and hence flexibility of the Brigade. Thus, while the Allies had dissipated their armour along the whole front, the Germans kept 70% of their armour concentrated for their main thrust through the Ardennes.

The deployment of armour was not the only disadvantage under which the Allies suffered. The Allied command structure was too cumbersome for the quick reactions required in mobile warfare. Gort, commanding the BEF, had nominally to go through two intermediary headquarters, those of Billotte and Georges (commanding North East Theatre) before he could reach Gamelin. The latter relied solely on the civilian telephone system to connect him with Georges' headquarters. Gamelin, too, saw himself merely as an adviser, and once he had given the order to cross the Belgian frontier felt that he could hand over the function of command entirely to his subordinates. French teaching between the wars had so emphasised methodical preparation before the battle that few, if any of the French commanders were capable of thinking in 'tank time'.

Unsatisfactory command arrangement were also present in the organisation of the Allied air forces. Air Marshal Barratt, in command of the British Air Forces in France, found himself in a dilemma. Although under Gort's command for the operational use of the Air Component, he was also expected to work in close conjunction with General Vuillemin, in charge of the French Air Force. At the same time, the Advanced Striking Force was controlled from London, and arguments between the Air Ministry and War Office as to how it should be employed caused nothing but confusion. The French Air Force was similarly split. The North-East Theatre was divided into Zones of Air operations, which followed the army group boundaries. These were under the command of General Têtu, the Officer commanding the Air Cooperation Forces, who had his headquarters close by that of General Georges. Consequently air formations found themselves often getting two sets of orders, sometimes contradictory, form both Vuillemin and Têtu. This was not helped by the lack of attention paid to air-ground cooperation in the years immediately preceding 1939.

The Phoney War had also acted like a canker on the French troops. In many formations little training was carried out. Little was done to keep the troops busy, and this led to boredom, leading in turn to discontent and absenteeism. Alanbrooke, commanding the British II Corps, describes a parade he was invited to by General Corap, commanding the French 9th Army, in November 1939:

'. . . Corap requested me to stand alongside of him whilst the guard of honour, consisting of cavalry, artillery and infantry marched passed. I can still see those troops now. Seldom have I seen anything more slovenly and badly turned out. Men unshaven, horses ungroomed, clothes and saddlery that did not fit, vehicles dirty, and a complete lack of pride in themselves or their units. What shook me most, however, was the look in the men's faces, disgruntled and insubordinate looks, and although ordered to give 'eyes left', hardly a man bothered to do so.' [17]

These were the troops who would face the main German onslaught. The British, too, spent more time preparing defensive positions rather than training for a mobile war, which, considering that less than a third of the troops were regulars, was a grave error. In addition, some BEF divisions were only partially equipped. It was hoped that their equipment would catch up with them in France. Meanwhile, they were deployed on the lines of communication, where it was thought they would be safe from any sudden German attack.

After several last minute postponements, Hitler finally gave the codeword 'Danzig' on the evening of May 9th, 1940. Shortly after receiving 'Danzig' the commander of 7th Panzer Division, an ex-infantryman called Erwin Rommel, sat down to write a short note to his wife:

'Dearest Lu,
We're packing up at last. Let's hope not in vain. You'll get all the news for the next few days from the papers. Don't worry yourself. Everything will go alright.' [18]

At 0300 hours on May 10th German bombers crossed the frontier, and an hour later were reported to be attacking Dutch and Belgian airfields and, shortly afterwards, airfields around Arras. The first phase of the Luftwaffe operation, that of gaining air superiority was under way. At 0630 hours Gamelin ordered Plan D to be executed.

Holland, with its numerous dykes and ditches, was not good tank country, and success hinged on the initial operations by Student's 7th Air Division, Germany's only parachute formation at the time, and the 22nd Infantry Division, which was to be airlanded. Their tasks were to seize vital bridges along the main roads through Holland and to hold them intact long enough to link up with the ground troops of Army Group B, as well as capturing the Dutch machinery of government in The Hague. In effect, they were to ensure the mobility of the leading elements of Army Group B, in particular the spearhead, 9th Panzer Division, and to aim at immediate dislocation of Dutch control on the battle. This latter task recalled the prime objective of Fuller's Plan 1919, which called for disorganisation of the enemy's command structure before the main attack was launched. In the event, the majority of bridges were captured and held and by the afternoon of May 13th Hubicki's 9th Panzer Division was approaching the outskirts of Rotterdam. The operation against The Hague failed mainly because the Dutch, aware of the German airborne operations against Norway, had taken the precaution of putting obstructions on the airfields to be used by the Ju 52s to air-land 22nd Infantry Division. This resulted in heavy casualties to the Germans. However, in the event, the speed of the German advance, together with the paralysis caused by the airborne and air operations made this operation superfluous. The final act in the overrunning of Holland was the bombing of Rotterdam on May 14th, an operation which should never have taken place in view of the fact that negotiations between General Schmidt, commanding XXXIX Panzer Corps, and the Dutch authorities were under way at the time for the surrender of the city. It was brought about by misunderstandings between the ground commanders and Luftflotte 2, all wanting to finish off Holland quickly so that more troops could be transferred to the main thrust. But, regardless of the attack on Rotterdam, which completely destroyed the old part of the city, the Dutch surrender was forthcoming on the evening of 14th May.

To the south the Allies closed up to the Dyle Line, relying on the Belgians on the Albert Canal to hold the Germans up long enought for them to get into position. But this was not to be. The key to the Belgian defences on the Albert Canal-Meuse Line, Fort Eben-Emael south of Maestricht, thought by the Allies to be impregnable, fell to a small band of parachute engineers. At the same time the two key bridges over the Albert Canal were captured intact, again by airborne assault. Twenty-four hours later the attackers had linked up with the 3rd and 4th Panzer Divisions from Reichenau's 6th Army, the southern of the two armies in Army Group B. This forced the Belgians to pull back just as Billotte's troops were arriving on the Dyle. Although they were still holding firm on the Dyle on May 15th, the hurried withdrawal of the Belgian forces convinced the Allies even more that this was where the main German effort was. They continued to look towards the Dyle when they should have been worrying about the Ardennes to the south.

The seven panzer divisions with Army Group A were split into three panzer corps, XIX Panzer Corps (Guderian with the 1st, 2nd and 10th Panzer Divisions) with the major task of seizing crossings over the Meuse near Sedan. To Guderian's north was XLI Panzer Corps under Reinhardt (6th and 8th Panzer Divisions), which was to cross at Montherme. Both of these formations came under Panzer Group Kleist, which was answerable to the Twelfth Army. Behind them followed von Wietersheim's XIV Motorised Corps of five motorised infantry divisions. On their right Hoth's XV Panzer Corps (5th and 7th Panzer Divisions) was to make a subsidiary thrust towards the Meuse between Givet and Namur, as well as guarding the right flank of Panzer Group Kleist. Once across the Meuse, the Panzers were to assist the infantry across, but beyond that they were given no orders, although the overall plan was for Army Group A to swing round behind Billotte's forces in Belgium and cut them off.

To Guderian, it was essential to reach the Meuse before the French had time to react. Once there he was relying heavily on the continuous support of Loerzer's II Air Corps and elements of Richthofen's VIII Air Corps, which was the main close support force of the Luftwaffe. To this end, he ensured that the Luftwaffe were intimately involved in all stages of planning. Rather than using his air support in one massive blow against the French defences on the Meuse, Guderian and his close air support commander, General Loerzer, agreed that continuous attacks would be made in accordance with a detailed fire plan. Guderian was intending to use his aircraft as aerial artillery, working to the same fire plan as his ground artillery. In the event, Guderian's superior, von Kliest wanted to employ the 'one time only' Luftwaffe attack, and then leave it to the panzers, but in the event the various Luftwaffe groups did attack at different times much to Guderian's relief.

By the evening of May 12th the panzer divisions were closing up to the Meuse. Corap's 9th Army defended bravely, but the speed of the German advance, together with constant air attacks by the Stukas, which were fitted with sirens to increase the terror effect, proved too much. Every time the panzer divisions came across any resistance, it was subjected to air and artillery bombardment, while the reconnaissance elements picked out routes round it. Once it had been softened up the tanks and motorised infantry went in to the attack. Much of the secret of the success of the panzer divisions was the ability to bring down heavy fire quickly. As Rommel found very quickly:

> '. . . the day goes to the side that is first able to plaster its opponents with fire. The man who lies low and awaits developments usually comes off second best . . . It is fundamentally wrong simply to halt and look for cover without opening fire, or to wait for more forces to come up and take part in the action.' [19]

It was not necessary for this fire to be particularly accurate; as long as it was fire in the general direction of the enemy it was usually enough to prevent the enemy from bringing down effective fire by virtue of making him keep his head down. The key to success was to beat the enemy to the draw, something which the Panzer formations were good at because they were trained to react quickly — far more quickly than their opponents.

Yet even on these first days there were indications of nervousness among the higher German commanders, similar to those during the Polish campaign. Guderian recounts that on the night of May 10/11th von Kliest suddenly became alarmed at the threat to Guderian's left flank of French cavalry advancing from Longwy and ordered him to divert 10th Panzer Division in this direction. In Guderian's view cavalry was of little threat to tanks, and, more important, the diversion of a third of his forces at this juncture might seriously jeopardise his main objective, that of seizing bridgeheads across the Meuse as soon as possible. In the event, he merely pulled 10th Panzer Division in closer to his main axis of advance. However, there were grounds for the concern of the higher commanders. The left flank of Army Group A would become more exposed as the invasion continued. The plan still relied on the capability of the conventional infantry divisions to be able to advance on their feet fast enough to cover this flank. It was known too that the French did possess armoured divisions, and there was always the danger that a determined French attack could cut the panzer head off from the infantry body. True, the French had begun to deploy their DCRs, but two had been committed to the support of Billotte, leaving only 3rd DCR in the south. Meanwhile, de Gaulle had finally had his ideas recognised to some measure, mainly thanks to his old political ally Paul Reynaud, who had been prime minister since the end of March. Reynaud, shortly after coming to office, had told de Gaulle that he

146

ould give him 4th DCR, which was yet to be formed. On May 11th he
:ceived his orders to take over this new division, now still only partially
rganised.

The Allies did what they could in the air to try and slow down the panzer
rive through the Ardennes, but confusion over command and roles, lack of
iitable aircraft and the initial Luftwaffe attacks on airfields, put them at a
:vere disadvantage. Perhaps the most tragic example was the employment
f the British Fairey Battle squadrons. This aircraft was a three-seat
ngle-engine light bomber, having the same engine as a Hurricane, but
ith twice the weight. It was perhaps the nearest aircraft to a Stuka that the
AF had in that it was designed for daylight bombing and employed in
ipport of ground operations, but that was where the resemblance ended. It
id no dive-bombing capability, and even by 1937 it was regarded as being
nsuitable for war against Germany. In spite of causing the Germans some
ritation, the eight Battle squadrons in the Advanced Air Striking Force
st 35 aircraft out of 63 employed during the first five days alone. Most of
e Battle attacks were on bridges along the German line of advance, but
erman air superiority and the effectiveness of local air defence resulted in
w successes. There was also the lack of fighter cover to support these
llied interdiction attacks. The French fighters were almost wholly employed
combating Luftwaffe bombing attacks on airfields and communication
ntres, leaving the few Hurricane squadrons of the RAF to lend support to
llied bombing operations. The demand for them was so great that
owding was forced to hand over more and more of his precious fighter
juadrons allocated for the defence of Britain.

The Germans succeeded in getting their bridgeheads across the Meuse on
ay 13th. However, it was no easy operation, and three of the seven
tempted crossings by the three panzer corps failed. The French had
cceeded in blowing all the bridges, and the Germans were forced to rely
a rubber assault boats to gain an initial toehold on the west bank.
evertheless, by the evening of May 13th each Corps had established
idgeheads, although these were tenuous footholds with no tanks across.
w would have been the time for the French to counter-attack, and indeed
ders to this effect went out on the evening of the 13th. Unfortunately, six
urs of air bombardment had had its effect on morale and rumours began
multiply that the Germans had succeeded in getting tanks across. The
ench front began to crumble, and on the 14th, in spite of Allied artillery
d air attacks on the German pontoon bridges, the Germans were able to
ss across their tanks. It was on this day that the French did attempt to
t a mechanised corps to attack. Flavigny's XXI Corps consisted of 3rd
CR, 3rd DLM and 5th DLC and was ordered early on the 14th to relieve
e shattered X Corps opposite Sedan. A counter-attack was planned
ainst Guderian's forces for noon but it never took place. The slow
ssage of orders and the exorbitant time taken to refuel caused 3rd DCR
be four hours late in arriving on the start line. By that time Flavigny had
anged his mind and ordered the Corps to take up defensive positions
ere they were. Even the French mechanised formations were incapable of

147

thinking and acting at anything like the speed required in fast-movir
mechanised warfare. The chance to throw back Guderian's forces across tl
Meuse had been lost.

By first light on the 15th Guderian was poised to break out of his bridg
head, and had met up with von Wietersheim, whose mechanised divisior
were to take over in the bridgehead. Leaving 10th Panzer Division to cov
the left flank until such time as there were enough of von Wietersheim
troops to take over this task, Guderian prepared to push on. At this sta₁
there was another manifestation of German higher command nervousnes
Von Kleist gave orders that there was to be no further advance or extensic
of the bridgehead. After furious arguments with him, Guderian was able
reach a compromise whereby he would advance for a further 24 hours
order to make more room for the relieving mechanised infantry formation
Linking up with Reinhardt's left hand division, 6th Panzer, in Montcorne
Guderian gave orders for the 1st and 2nd Panzer Divisions to push on
long as their fuel lasted. By evening, when the panzers had run dry, the
had advanced 40 miles in the day. French resistance had been well ar
truly broken, and the panzer divisions could roam almost at will, provid₁
of course that petrol and ammunition supplies could be maintained.

It was on this day, the 16th, that de Gaulle's 4th DCR had its first brus
with the enemy. Symbolically it was to find itself pitted against tl
spearheads of Guderian's Corps in Montcornet. De Gaulle had base
himself in Laon on the 15th and was awaiting the last units to join h
division. Realising that he had the chance to taking the Germans in tl
flank he attacked next day. He attacked with three tank battalions whic
reached Montcornet, but were halted there by the Germans. Having ı
infantry with which to support his tanks he found himself forced to pt
back, leaving one company of tanks in German hands. This perhaps help₁
to reinforce von Kleist's fears of opening up too long an exposed flank, f
early on the 17th he ordered Guderian to report to him in person ar
categorically ordered him not to continue with his advance. Guderian, in
fury, handed in his resignation there and then. It transpired, however, th
the order had come from Hitler himself. Von Rundstedt, hearing
Guderian's stand, agreed that he could continue to reconnoitre in force,
long as his corps headquarters remained in its present position. Guderi₂
accepted back his command, regarding this as permission to continue. Y₁
what was really worrying Hitler was that the panzer advance was proceedir
so rapidly that the mass of infantry divisions were unable to keep u
Consequently he was applying more and more pressure on von Rundstedt
slow down. He was, in effect becoming fearful of his own success. Bt
regardless of Hitler's qualms, Guderian continued to press onwards.

In order to keep the cream of the Franco-British Armies tied up
Belgium, Hitler, in his Directive No 11 dated May 14th ordered Arr
Group B to continue to apply pressure, although acknowledging that t
main advance was to be made by Army Group A, to whom all panzer ar
mechanised divisions would be transferred as they became available. I
keeping Billotte tied down in Belgium there was no chance of the remnar

148

f the Second and Ninth French Armies being reinforced, and the Panzer ▪rmations of Army Group A could sweep round behind Billotte and cut ▪m off from France. Although the 7th French Army was quickly forced out f Holland, the Allies held on the Dyle Line until the 15th, when they were ▪dered back by easy stages to the River Escaut, which was the original ▪an E. With the gradual realisation that the main German effort was in ▪e south, the Seventh French Army was ordered to the rear of the BEF to ▪ver the threat from this direction. This had become essential in view of ▪creasing pressure from Hoth's Panzer Group on the French First Army, ▪ the right of the BEF, and by May 17th it was echeloned back from the EF on the Canal du Nord. On this day General Georges realised that there ▪as a yawning gap between Douai, where the First Army sector ended, and ▪e River Somme. All that could be spared to cover this gap were two ▪-equipped British territorial divisions. Both were under strength and both ▪cking in any organic artillery, apart from the thirteen 'scrounged' 25 ▪unders. By the evening of May 18th five panzer divisions in line were ▪aking for this gap. Although they resisted bravely both divisions had ▪ased to exist by the end of the 19th. 1st Panzer Division had captured ▪miens and was facing south, while in the north Rommel's 7th Panzer ▪ivision was preparing to attack at Arras early next morning, leaving 2nd, ▪h and 8th Panzer Divisions to dash for the Channel coast between ▪bbeville and Etaples and so cut off Billotte's forces.

Gamelin had finally come to the conclusion that the only way to defeat ▪e panzer thrust was by coordinated armoured thrusts from the British ▪d French in the north and de Gaulle in the south. His final order before ▪ was replaced by Weygand on May 19th was to this effect. De Gaulle had ▪en harrying Guderian's left flank with limited success, but by the time ▪amelin had sent out his order, and the reins picked up by Weygand, the ▪p was too wide and coordination with the topheavy Allied command ▪ructure impossible.

The 20th was a crucial day. While the three panzer divisions continued ▪eir gallop towards the coast, and indeed reached Abbeville, Lord Gort ▪ceived orders from England that the BEF was to move southwards from ▪miens and attack any enemy forces encountered. These orders had been ▪ought by Ironside, the CIGS, in person. Gort, now anxious that his line of ▪treat to the Channel might be cut off, chose to ignore them. However, ▪ommel had become slowed down in front of Arras. His tanks had got well ▪ead of his organic motorised infantry, and the French had managed to ▪filtrate his line of communication. Hence his attack on May 20th did not ▪cceed. Gort, aware of the necessity to hold Arras, in order to prevent his ▪rces from becoming entirely cut off, ordered the commander at Arras, ▪eneral Franklyn, to block the roads south of Arras, in order to cut off ▪ommel's communications from the east. Franklyn had at his disposal two ▪eak infantry divisions and the 1st Army Tank Brigade. The commander of ▪e of the two infantry divisions, 50th Northumbrian TA, was none other ▪an Martel. This was the setting for the only significant British tank action ▪ the campaign.

The tragedy of the Arras counter-attack, as it came to be called, was tha the 1st Army Tank Brigade was entirely unsuited to the type of operation was being expected to perform. Trained specifically for infantry support, it officers were used, like the French, to set-piece attacks with their implie careful and methodical preparation. At Arras, the Brigade had just come the end of a frustrating five day road march covering 120 miles along route heavily congested with refugees. Franklyn had wanted the attack to go in a 0500 hours on the 21st, but as the last tank did not arrive at Vimy, eigh miles away from the start line, until that time this was clearly not possible Martel, who was to command the attack, could only scrape up tw battalions of tanks and two of infantry. He attempted to organise them int two battle groups, each of one battalion of tanks, one of infantry, a field battery, anti-tank battery and machine-gun company. He agreed with Prat commanding the 1st Army Tank Brigade, that an attack would not b possible before 1500 hours, especially as time for rest, maintenance an reconnaissance was required. Franklyn insisted that H-Hour must be earlie and 1400 hours was agreed on, although the infantry did not arrive in tim and Martel had to release the tanks on their own. The first phase was a advance of ten miles, followed by a second phase of three miles. Thus, t start with, only 70 slow infantry tanks were available to capture some 4 square miles of ground.

The attack hit Rommel just as he was setting off to loop round th north-west of Arras:

'. . . the enemy tank fire had created chaos and confusion among ou troops in the village and they were jamming up the roads and yards with their vehicles instead of going into action with every available weapon t fight off the oncoming enemy . . . About 1 200 yards west of our position the leading enemy tanks, among them one heavy,* had crossed the Arras Beaumetz railway and shot up one of our Panzer IIIs. At the same tim several enemy tanks were advancing down the road from Bac du Nor and across the railway towards Wailly. It was an extremely tight spot, fo there were also several enemy tanks close to Wailly on its northern sid . . . With the enemy tanks so perilously close, only rapid fire from ever gun could save the situation.' [20]

Rommel himself supervised the laying of the anti-tank guns, and they succeeded in knocking out the leading British tanks. Elsewhere one of hi motorised infantry battalions had also suffered badly and had been forced to fall back to the south, along with other units of the division. Only by deploying the fire of the divisional field artillery and 88mm anti-aircraf guns, which were soon to make a name for themselves as anti-tank guns was he able to halt the British attack. He then launched his 25th Panzer Regiment, which had already reached its objective to the north-west o Arras, to counter-attack to the south-east. Again he speaks of the Regiment

---

* Infantry Tank Mark II, 'Matilda'.

engaging 'a superior force of heavy and light tanks'. However, this move succeeded in driving the remnants of the 1st Tank Brigade back towards Arras, although not without the cost of three Mark IVs, six Mark IIIs and a number of light tanks.

On the other side Pratt, writing shortly after the event, recorded that:

'We got about four miles forward before any infantry of ours appeared in sight. During this time we played hell with a lot of Boche motor transport and their kindred stuff . . . His anti-tank gunners, after firing a bit, bolted and left their guns . . . None of his anti-tank stuff penetrated our Is or IIs . . . The main opposition came from his field guns, some of which fired over open sights. Also the air dive-bombing on the infantry — this, of course, did not worry the tanks much.'

In conclusion, he wrote:

'The whole show was appallingly handled by 'the powers that be', but we did learn that our tank armour is good at present, and that our 2-pounder is quite sufficient also for the present.'

and:

'Had we only been allowed to stage a methodical battle with a series of reasonably short objectives with some artillery support and even a little air support and no frantic rush we should have done far better and saved many lives of fellows we cannot afford to lose.' [21]

This last sentence neatly sums up the outlook of a tank officer trained in the infantry support, as opposed to the independent tank role. The type of battle he envisaged bore little relation to the fast moving shock action as preached by Liddell Hart, Fuller, Hobart and even Martel. It typified the inflexibility of mind of the Allies, which made them so ill-equipped to deal with the blitzkrieg attack.

However, in spite of the small scale of the attack, its effect reverberated right up to Hitler's own headquarters, and produced the biggest scare for the Germans of the whole campaign, It was, as before, the fear that the panzer divisions had got too far ahead of the infantry and were in danger of becoming cut off. The brake was applied, thus slowing down the rate of advance to the Channel, which gave the British a valuable breathing space in which to fortify the perimeter at Dunkirk, to which the BEF was now withdrawing intent on evacuation. But this was not all. Closing up to the Dunkirk perimeter, the panzer divisions were ordered not to attack. The task of destroying the Allied forces at Dunkirk and preventing the evacuation was handed over entirely to the Luftwaffe. The Wehrmacht was merely to '. . . prepare to destroy in the shortest possible time the remaining enemy forces in France.' [22] The reason behind this plan was not so much that the area around Dunkirk was unsuitable for tanks. Nor was it that tank casualties, both from enemy action and mechanical troubles, had been getting dangerously high resulting in a need for the Panzer Divisions to pause before they turned south to deal with the remainder of France. These reasons contributed to the decision, but were minor. Goering had become jealous of the success of the Wehrmacht during the past two weeks. It seemed to him that the Luftwaffe had played but a minor role and must have its rightful share of the limelight. On May 23rd he saw his chance to persuade Hitler and returned to his own headquarters to inform Milch: 'We have done it! The Luftwaffe is to wipe out the British on the beaches. I have managed to talk the Fuhrer round to halting the army.' [23] It proved an expensive mistake. Three days fog at the beginning of the operation, the fact that the Luftwaffe's bomber airfields were too far from Dunkirk, and the superiority achieved by the Spitfire over the Me 109 enabled the British to carry 338 000 British and 139 000 allied troops back from the beaches to England by June 4th, although they were forced to leave their equipment behind. The Luftwaffe had had to learn the hard way that they could not destroy an army on their own. It was another nail in the coffin of Douhetism.

It was just at the start of the evacuation from Dunkirk that the British 1st Armoured Division finally put in an appearance on the battlefield. It was not however the same division as that planned for at the end of 1937. It had been reduced to two armoured brigades only, and one of these, 3rd Armoured Brigade, had only two tank battalions, instead of the customary three. Almost 50% of the division's tanks were light, and many of the cruisers had only been recently issued and lacked essentials such as wireless and gun sights. Even worse, its infantry and field artillery had been taken from it and besides tanks, all it had was one combined anti-aircraft and anti-tank regiment. In conjunction with de Gaulle's 4th DCR, 1st Armoured Division was ordered to advance towards St Pol to relieve pressure on Dunkirk. Initially all went well, but as soon as they came up against opposition the French general under whose command they were, ordered them to take up a defensive position rather than push on. Other French attempts to reduce the German bridgeheads over the Somme during the next few days also failed, although de Gaulle succeeded in pushing the Germans back 14 kilometres at Abbeville. Indeed, in spite of having no air support, he captured some 500 prisoners, and a German who was present wrote of 'a profound terror of the tanks' which '. . . got into the bones of our soldiers'. [24]

On June 5th the Germans launched Operation Red aimed at annihilating the remaining Allied forces in France. XV Panzer Corps crossed the Somme at Abbeville and by June 19th had cleared Normandy and Brittany, forcing the evacuation of the British 1st Armoured Division and taking the surrender of, among other formations, the 51st Highland Division, which had been detached to the French since the start of the campaign. Panzer Group Kleist with the XIV and XVI Panzer Corps drove southwards from the Aisne, while Panzer Group Guderian (XXXIX and XLI PZ Corps) swung round behind the Maginot Line to bottle up the French 2nd Army Group in

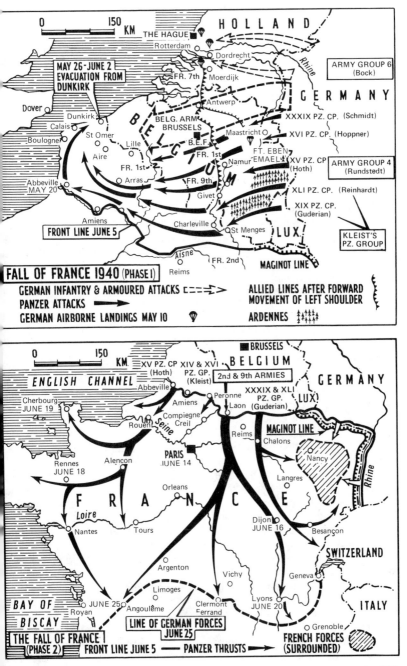

## FALL OF FRANCE 1940 (PHASE I)

**Map labels (top map):**

HOLLAND
THE HAGUE
Rotterdam
Dordrecht
Moerdijk
FR. 7th
Rhine
ARMY GROUP 6 (Bock)
GERMANY
MAY 26-JUNE 2 EVACUATION FROM DUNKIRK
Antwerp
Dover
Dunkirk
Calais
Boulogne
St Omer
BELGIUM
BRUSSELS
BELG. ARM.
B.E.F.
Maastricht
XXXIX PZ. CP. (Schmidt)
XVI PZ. CP. (Hoppner)
Lille
Aire
FR. 1st
FR. 1st
Namur
FT. EBEN EMAEL
XV PZ. CP (Hoth)
ARMY GROUP 4 (Rundstedt)
FR. 9th
Arras
Abbeville MAY 20
Givet
XLI PZ. CP. (Reinhardt)
Amiens
FRONT LINE JUNE 5
Charleville
St Menges
XIX PZ. CP. (Guderian)
LUX.
KLEIST'S PZ. GROUP
Aisne
FR. 2nd
Reims
MAGINOT LINE

GERMAN INFANTRY & ARMOURED ATTACKS ⊏===➤
PANZER ATTACKS ➤
GERMAN AIRBORNE LANDINGS MAY 10 ☐
ALLIED LINES AFTER FORWARD MOVEMENT OF LEFT SHOULDER
ARDENNES ♠♠♠♠

**Map labels (bottom map):**

BRUSSELS
BELGIUM
XV PZ. CP (Hoth)
XIV & XVI PZ. GP. (Kleist)
2nd & 9th ARMIES
GERMANY
ENGLISH CHANNEL
Abbeville
Amiens
Peronne
XXXIX & XLI PZ. GP. (Guderian)
LUX.
Cherbourg JUNE 19
Laon
Compiegne
Creil
MAGINOT LINE
Rouen
Seine
Reims
Chalons
Nancy
PARIS JUNE 14
Rennes JUNE 18
Alencon
Orleans
Langres
FRANCE
Rhine
Loire
Dijon JUNE 16
Besançon
Nantes
Tours
SWITZERLAND
Argenton
Vichy
Geneva
BAY OF BISCAY
Limoges
Angoulême
Clermont Ferrand
Lyons JUNE 20
ITALY
Royan JUNE 25
LINE OF GERMAN FORCES JUNE 25
Grenoble
THE FALL OF FRANCE (PHASE 2)
FRENCH FORCES (SURROUNDED)
FRONT LINE JUNE 5 — PANZER THRUSTS ➤

153

a repeat of the Prussian victory at Sedan in 1870. Weygand in an attempt to slow down the Germans had, on May 26th, issued orders that there would be no retreat, and that his troops should form a series of 'hedgehogs' or strongpoints. Unfortunately this merely gave the panzer divisions an even freer rein, because the French had no armoured formations left to counter them. The panzers bypassed the strongpoints in their usual manner leaving the following infantry to reduce them. By June 25th the French had had enough and an armistice had been signed.

In a little less than seven weeks the Germans had overrun Belgium, Holland and the northern half of France. They had driven the British back across the Channel and had forced the surrender of the Maginot Line whose guns had hardly fired a shot in anger. It was a dazzling performance costing the Germans a mere 156 000 casualties against the Allied bill of 2 300 000. The fact that the German casualties were small, and that two million of the Allied casualties were prisoners showed more than anything else that it was the psychological dislocation of the Allies which had brought about their defeat. The psychological effect on the higher headquarters is well described by André Beaufre, who was a junior staff officer at Georges' headquarters:

'At the switchboard, which was receiving bad news at monotonous one-minute intervals, there was no longer any reaction: one officer would acknowledge messages in a quiet, soft voice, another with an almost hysterical giggle — 'Ah, yes, your left has been driven in; oh, I see, they're behind you. I'll make a note of it!' Everyone else in the room, prostrate and silent, was sitting about in armchairs.' [25]

The root of the problem was that the Allies had trained themselves to fight a battle in slow time compared with the Germans. Hence they were unable to think at the required pace in order to react to the German moves in time. As Lord Gort, in his official despatch on the campaign, ruefully wrote that the German success showed '. . . the advantage which accrues to the commander who knows how best to use his time and to make time his servant and not his master.' [26]

Unlike its predecessor in 1914, the German plan had worked like clockwork. Poland had taught the Germans much, particularly in the field of logistics. In order to maintain the speed of advance of the panzer divisions they adopted re-supply by air. Remembering how they had employed their JU 52s in Spain, they used these to fly in fuel and ammunition into forward airfields, from which it could be collected by the lorries of the panzer formations. Panzer divisions, after the experience of the march into Austria in 1938, now had mobile field workshops, which enabled tanks to be recovered and repaired in the minimum length of time. The only uncertainties in the German technique were the nervousness which manifested itself from time to time in the higher headquarters that the panzer divisions were in danger of being cut off by getting too far ahead of the mass of the infantry. Indeed there were some justification for this. The British counter-attack at Arras and de Gaulle's attack at Abbeville had

154

shown that the German soldier was not impervious to whatever might be thrown against him. But, because of the Allied inability to think quickly and to concentrate sufficient forces in time, these attacks were only pinpricks, and only momentarily threw the Germans off balance. Yet, it did give a glimmer of what might be done to counter the blitzkreig.

The Luftwaffe had operated well. Often, although they had little experience of the technique, they found themselves guarding the long exposed flanks thrown up by the speed of the Panzer Divisions and thwarted counter-attacks on their own. Their only failure, albeit a major one, was in allowing the Dunkirk evacuation to take place. The blame for this lies at Goering's door. It was simply a matter of jealousy in that he felt that the Army was getting all the publicity, and that the Luftwaffe, whose role was support of the Army, was playing only 'second fiddle'. However, the casualties in the air were very much closer between the two sides than on the ground — the Luftwaffe losing some 1 300 aircraft to the Allies 1 500. Although the Luftwaffe gained air superiority it had to fight to maintain it, and in the skies over Dunkirk, the air fighting between the Luftwaffe and the RAF was evenly balanced.

After the signing of the Armistice there was a pause while Hitler waited for Britain to come to terms. Only the Luftwaffe remained engaged — against British shipping in the Channel. But, in Britain itself, Churchill, who had replaced the ailing Chamberlain as Prime Minister on May 10th, was hurriedly preparing his country for the battle he knew was to come.

Across the Atlantic, the United States was slowly awaking from her isolationist sleep. The outbreak of war had caused Roosevelt to make small increases in the regular army and National Guard. The Polish Campaign showed that American ideas had become stagnant, and the result was the organisation of the first fully-fledged corps manoeuvres since 1918. These took place in Louisiana in April-May 1940. Among the troops taking part was an improvised armoured division made up of Chaffee's 7th Mechanised Cavalry Brigade and a Provisional Motorised Tank Brigade formed by the infantry. Sponsored by the Third Army, the object of the manoeuvres was to test doctrine, organisation, movement over long distances against a mobile enemy, and the co-operation between mechanised forces and aircraft. Patton was an umpire, and saw with his own eyes how the mechanised forces completely dominated the horse cavalry. While General Embick, commanding the Third Army, was recommending that, as a result of the manoeuvres, the two mechanised brigades be expanded into armoured divisions, Patton was turning his eyes again from the horse to the tank. In mid-July, after the fall of France had confirmed the growing conviction that mechanisation was essential for modern war, Chaffee was appointed to command the newly formed 1st Armoured Corps, consisting of the 1st and 2nd Armoured Divisions. Patton, to his delight was given a brigade consisting of two light tank and one medium tank regiment, a field artillery regiment and an engineer battalion. His first reaction on taking over command was:

'The whole thing is most interesting as most of the tactics have yet to be worked out and there is a great chance for ingenuity and leadership. As I see it we must be able to fight any place and in any manner either alone or in close association with infantry and cavalry.' [27]

Although it would be some sixteen months before the United States would enter the war, the success of the German blitzkrieg had galvanised her into finally making amends for the locust years.

### The Battle of Britain

Hitler, having tried to persuade Britain to come to terms, even using the offices of the USA, Sweden and the Vatican, without success, decided somewhat reluctantly that no other alternative existed apart from the invasion of the country. On the July 2nd he issued his first directive on the subject, declaring that: '. . . a landing in England is possible, providing that air superiority can be attained . . .' [28]. On July 16th he gave details of Operation Sealion, as the invasion was codenamed. While the Wehrmacht was to concentrate on the actual crossing of the Channel, the navy was to procure the means necessary for invasion, and in conjunction with the Luftwaffe and the Italians, was to seal the Straits of Dover with mines on both flanks and tie down the British fleet in the North Sea and the Mediterranean. But, in Hitler's eyes, the key task lay with the Luftwaffe. Complete air supremacy must be attained before any attempt at invasion was made. Hitler's Directive No 17 dated the August 1st stated how the Luftwaffe was to achieve this, and was the executive order for the Battle of Britain to commence:

'The German Air Force is to overpower the English Air Force with all the forces at its command, in the shortest possible time. The attacks are to be directed primarily against flying units, their ground installations, and their supply organisations, but also against the aircraft industry, including that manufacturing anti-aircraft equipment.' [29]

In past operations the Luftwaffe had gained air supremacy by attempting merely to destroy the enemy's air force on its airfields. This was suitable for what was strictly a tactical air force, but to include the destruction of industry was to ask of the Luftwaffe a strategic capability which it did not have. This was the fundamental reason why the Germans lost the subsequent battle.

The decision taken in 1936 to halt development of the 'Urals' 4-engined bomber in favour of the dive-bomber now came home to roost. The Do 17, He111 and Ju88 were too light with not enough payload or range to be effective in the way that Hitler now required. The German fighters again lacked the range to cope with both protection of the bombers and tackling the RAF in the air. But there were other reasons. Goering constantly changed the tactical aim of the operation, thereby contravening an elementary principle of war. First he attacked the radar stations along the south coast, realising quite rightly that herein lay the key to Britain's air defences, but before this task had been completed, he switched to attacks on airfields. Then, after the Luftwaffe had bombed the outskirts of London in error and the RAF had retaliated with a raid on Berlin, Hitler ordered the Luftwaffe to switch to the bombing of London itself, firstly by day, and later because of the high aircraft casualties, by night. Attempts to halt British production of aircraft failed dismally; indeed the production rate increased during the Battle and it was loss of pilots rather than aircraft which became crucial to the RAF. Although the battle rumbled on until the Spring of 1941, the Germans had effectively lost it in September 1940. The bombing of British cities lowered but did not break the spirit of the British people, and as Guernica had done, indicated again that Douhet's theory did not stand up in current practice.

## North Africa

British attention now turned to North Africa, where the Italians, who had entered the war in June 1940, were bent on wresting Egypt and the Suez Canal from British hands in order to expand their North African empire. The North African campaign, which was to last for the next three years, was unique in its setting and conduct. Although it was a war of mechanised forces and air power it was not typical of the blitzkreig campaigns. The geography of North Africa, with the sea on the one side and almost impassable desert, as typified by the Quattara Depression, less than 100 miles inland, resulted in a long but narrow area of operations. Although air and ground forces co-operated closely, the priority for air power was not in the immediate battle area. For the campaign was more than anything a battle of supplies. Time and again, supplies were unable to keep up with the rate of advance, and the main air and naval effort was directed towards keeping one's own lines of communication open, while disrupting those of the enemy. The desert itself did provide the ideal laboratory for tank warfare, with infantry being reduced to holding ground. But, although much technical experience was gained, particularly by the British, the campaign conditions were tactically misleading when put in the context of a European battlefield. It was the nearest that tank warfare came to Martel's 1916 idea of fleets fighting on land. The armoured division became the decisive formation and, by 1942 the British version showed marked similarity to the panzer division. In 1940 the organisation had shown an imbalance with only two lorried infantry battalions to six tank battalions. These, along with a field artillery battalion, engineer element and anti-tank battalion made up the Support Group. In 1942 all this was changed when it was realised that the closer country of Tunisia, together with the likelihood that the Allies would sooner or later set foot again on the Continent, called for a higher ratio of infantry. The second armoured brigade was thus replaced by a motorised infantry brigade of three battalions. An infantry battalion had been added to each armoured brigade after the fall of France, one of these coming from the Support Group. The battalion was retained in the one remaining armoured brigade, thus achieving a ratio of four infantry battalions to three tank battalions. In addition, a second field artillery battalion was added. The pre-war plans for allocating the majority of tanks to infantry support and only creating three armoured divisions were revised. The immediate target was set at nine with more to be added in the long term. Hobart, who had trained the 7th Armoured Division so successfully, was brought out of retirement where he had been languishing as a lance-corporal in the Home Guard, to raise and train one of these new divisions. More striking, was the drawing together of the British Eighth Army and Desert Air Force. The latter became a proper tactical air force and, after Montgomery assumed command of the Eighth Army in August 1942 the army and air force headquarters were co-located to ensure the closest co-operation. This was in complete contrast to the Air Ministry attitude of 1940.

**Notes**

1   Shirer, *The Rise and Fall of the Third Reich* op cit p 468.
2   Ibid, p 498.
3   Kesselring, *Kesselring: A Soldier's Record* p 39.
4   Trevor-Roper, *Hitler's War Directives* p 4.
5   Bekker, *The Luftwaffe War Diaries* pp 49-50.
6   Guderian, op cit p 71.
7   Mellenthin von, *Panzer Battles* p 7.
8   Flower and Reeves, *The War 1939-1945* p 11.
9   Lucas & Cooper, *Hitler's Elite* p 61.
10  Minutes of a War Cabinet Meeting, 11 Sep 39. Public Record Office.
11  Liddell Hart, *Memoirs* vol 2 op cit p 258.
12  Ellis, *The War in France and Flanders 1939-40* p 4.
13  Trevor-Roper, op cit p 16.
14  *Rise and Fall of the Third Reich* op cit pp 645-6.
15  Trevor-Roper, op cit p 16.
16  Ibid, p 24.
17  Bryant, *Turn of the Tide* p 71.
18  Liddell Hart, *The Rommel Papers* p 6.
19  Ibid, p 7.
20  Ibid, pp 31-3.
21  Liddell-Hart, *The Tanks* vol 2 pp 14-15.
22  Trevor-Roper, op cit p 27.
23  Irving, op cit p 90.
24  De Gaulle, *War Memoirs* vol 1 pp 52-3.
25  Beaufre, *1940: The Fall of France* p 204.
26  Supplement to the London Gazette 10 Oct 41. HMSO.
27  *The Patton Papers* op cit p 956.
28  *The Rise and Fall of the Third Reich* op cit p 751.
29  Trevor-Roper, op cit pp 37-8.

# Blitzkrieg Meets its Match

Hitler had always had the defeat of Russia and the annexation of her territory as *lebensraum* for the German people as his ultimate objective. He had made this clear in *Mein Kampf*. In October 1939 he had instructed the Wehrmacht to regard Poland as an assembly area for future operations. A month later he told his generals that: 'We can oppose Russia only when we are free in the West.' [1] By July 1940, he had made it clear to his commanders that he was considering attacking Russia in the Autumn of 1940 should Operation Sealion not materialise. The General Staff saw the military aim as being the defeat of the Red Army and the seizure of enough territory for the Luftwaffe to be able to attack Soviet industry behind the Urals, while at the same time preventing Russian bombers from reaching Germany. They estimated that the campaign would last four to six weeks, and that 110 infantry, 24 panzer and 12 motorised divisions would be required. By the time this appreciation had been made, the Battle of Britain was reaching its height, but it was already too late in the year to launch an attack in the East. Nevertheless, by the end of October, several divisions had been transferred from France to Poland as part of the preparations.

The original plan, which was drawn up by General Marcks of the Army Branch of Hitler's own staff (OKW), called for two main thrusts. The northern attack was to be directed on Moscow, while the southern drove through the Ukraine with Kiev as the final objective. Two subsidiary operations would clear the Baltic coast up to Leningrad, and drive from Roumania through Bessarabia to link up with the southern thrust at Kiev. With Moscow and Kiev captured, the two army groups would turn south and north respectively in order to seal the Russian armies in one vast pocket. Marcks submitted his plan to the Army High Command (OKH), who had been drawing up their own appreciation of the situation. While agreeing with Moscow and Kiev as main objectives, they also added a third — Leningrad, although they regarded Moscow as the key, and designated the centre thrust as the main axis. This plan was presented to Hitler on December 17th, 1940, and was followed next day by Hitler's own Directive No 21 for Case Barbarossa. But overnight, he had made some radical changes to the plan. Instead of retaining Moscow as the main objective, he laid down that once the centre thrust had reached Smolensk it should detach part of its forces to the north to assist in the reduction of Leningrad. Only when this had fallen would Moscow be taken. Herein lay the first fatal mistake in Hitler's conduct of the campaign. Moscow, as the seat of

159

government and the key communications centre, would if captured be more serious loss to the Russians than any other single objective. Th German failure to take the city in 1941 meant that it became a symbol an stirred the Russians to renewed effort during the winter of 1941-2.

Hitler, in his directive, laid the intention down as:

'The bulk of the Russian Army stationed in Western Russia will t destroyed by daring operations led by deeply penetrating armoure spearheads. Russian forces still capable of giving battle will be prevente from withdrawing into the depths of Russia.'

The final objective would be to 'erect a barrier against Asiatic Russia on th general line of Volga-Archangel.' This he felt was far enough to prever Russian aerial attacks on Germany. Once this line had been establishe the Luftwaffe could then deal with the industrial centres in the Urals, bu 'in order that we may concentrate all our strength against the enemy a force and for the immediate support of land operations, the Russia armaments industry will not be attacked during the main operations.' On after 'the conclusion of mobile warfare' would such attacks take place. [2 Thus the Russians were able to continue the manufacture of armament without being disturbed — another contributory factor to Hitler's eventua defeat in Russia. More than ever were the Germans to regret their lack of strategic air force.

The very vastness of the operation meant that the ten panzer divisions i existence after the fall of France would not be enough. In September 1940 rapid expansion of the panzer arm was called for, but lack of sufficien numbers of tanks meant that new divisions could only be formed at th expense of reducing the tank strength from four battalions to two in som divisions. The rifle brigade was reorganised into two motorised rifle battalions which being lorry-borne still had to dismount to fight, and a motor-cycl reconnaissance battalion. Another field artillery battalion and an anti aircraft battalion, equipped with 88mm guns was also added. Although, b June 1941, the Germans had 21 panzer divisions, thus doubling the numbe from the previous summer, there was an increase only of 11 tank battalion on the 35 of 1940. Yet, these new battalions were more powerful than thei predecessors because they were equipped with PZ Kw Mk IIIs and IVs, th Mk II being retained only in the divisional reconnaissance battalions Simultaneously there was an increase in motorised divisions. Here agai there were reductions in strength from the 1940 division, but there were 1 such in existence in June 1941. Meanwhile the bulk of the Wehrmach continued to be made up of infantry divisions, 163 in number, still relyin on their feet and horse transport.

Hitler's directive had called for all preparations to be completed b mid-May 1941. This was crucial. The duration of the Russian summer wa bounded at one end by the spring thaw, which usually meant that th country would be insufficiently dried out until May, and at the other end b the autumn rains, which usually started in October and continued until th

160

*Risikoflotte* demonstrated. A fly past of He 111s during the visit of Prince Paul of Yugoslavia to Germany, June 1939./*Barnaby's Picture Library*

*Above left*: Colonel Charles de Gaulle and his officers, 507th Tank Regiment. Left hand tank is a medium D-2, the right a Renault 35, both armed with a 47mm gun./*ECPA*

*Left*: Char Bs on parade during the State Visit to Paris of King George VI, July 1938./*Barnaby's Picture Library*

*Above*: General Adna Chaffee, Commander US 1st Armored Corps, with Secretary of War Stimson, in 1940./*Keystone Press Agency*

*Right*: General Heinz Guderian.//*WM*

*Above left*: The gaining of air superiority — a French airfield in May 1940. Wreckage of a Blenheim IV./*Zeitgeschichtliches Bildarchiv* (*ZB*)

*Left*: The Fairey Battle, which suffered so severely in operations against the Meuse crossings./*Royal Aeronautical Society*

*Above*: Panzers on the rampage, May 1940. Czech 38t tanks (weight 9.7tons, speed 21mph, 37mm gun and two machine guns, four-man crew) taken from Rommel's command vehicle./*Herr Manfred Rommel*

*Right*: Mechanised and motorised infantry of Rommel's 7th Panzer Division in the Somme Valley, June 1940. Fieseler Storch light aircraft overhead./*Herr Manfred Rommel*

*Left*: Abandoned Infantry Tank Mk IIs of 7th Royal Tank Regiment, Arras, May 1940. The crew of the lead tank had set it on fire, having failed to extricate the tank behind./*ZB*

*Below*: Knocked out Char B, victim of Rommel's 7th Panzer Division./*Herr Manfred Rommel*

*Above*: Junkers Ju87 Stuka releasing its bombload. The centre bomb is a 550lb HE, the others being 110lb. Alternatively one 1100lb HE could be carried./*IWM*

*Right*: Beck's 'mass of decision' France, Summer 1940./*ZB*

*Above left*: Russia 1941 — Knocked out BT-7s./*RAC Tank Museum, Bovington*

*Left*: Russia 1941 — A pause on the drive to Moscow. Pz Kw IIIs and Sd Kfz 250 half-tracks. Note the bullet holes in the nearest./*Centres des Recherches et d'Etude de la Seconde Guerre Mondiale, Bruxelles*

*Above*: Russia 1942 — Panzer Grenadiers in the attack supported by Sd Kfz 251 mounted 37mm tank gun, and 20mm cannon./*IWM*

*Below*: Tu34/76, which proved more than a match for the Panzers in Russia (weight 28tons, speed 32mph, four-man crew, 76mm gun and two machine guns)./*RAC Tank Museum, Bovington*

*Left*: Stormovik IL-2s in action. The ability to carry a variable weapon mix — cannon, rockets, HE bombs, anti-tank and anti-personnel cluster bombs — made them very effective in the ground support role./ *Novosti Press Agency*

*Below*: Allied aerial artillery (1) — US B-17F Flying Fortresses in box formation/ *IWM*

*Right*: Allied aerial artillery (2) — Hawker Typhoon./*RAeS*

*Below right*: Allied aerial artillery (3) — The Falaise Pocket. Note the German dependence on horse transport.//*IWM*

*Left*: General George Patton./*IWM*

*Below*: Poised for the Allied blitzkrieg. A British troop of M-4 Shermans await the order to break out over the Seine, August 1944. The second furthest is a Firefly, with significantly longer gun barrel./*IWM*

*Right*: The everstretching Allied supply lines. Canadian built Dodge 3-ton lorries of the British XXX Corps./*IWM*

*Below right*: Last Bow — a 'brewed up' Panther, Ardennes, December 1944./*IWM*

*Left*: Dan Tolkowsky, who resolved on a strictly tactical Israeli Air Force./*Israeli Defence Ministry* (*IDM*)

*Below*: Captured Egyptian equipment in the Gaza Strip 1956. Left, two British made Archer 17pdr SP anti-tank guns; Right, Russian built SU-100 SP gun; Rear, Russian BTR-152 wheeled APCs./*Radio Times Hulton Picture Library*

*Above*: Israeli Shermans with 90mm guns drive on towards Suez, June 1967./*Central Press Photographs Ltd*

*Right*: Israeli Air Force strike 1967 — an Ilyushin IL-28 of the Egyptian Air Force burns on the runway./*IDM*

*Above*: Centurions, backbone of the Israeli Armoured Corps./*Central Press Photographs Ltd*

*Left*: General Arik Sharon after his dramatic crossing of the Suez Canal, October 1973./*Camera Press Ltd*

vinter set in. It was therefore essential that the Germans had established themselves on their final objective, the Volga-Archangel line by the end of September. Calculating that this would take them some nineteen weeks to achieve, they had left themselves precisely this length of time and no more. Unfortunately for them, events elsewhere forced a postponement of the date of the attack by five weeks.

Mussolini had, on entering the war, coveted the Balkans as part of Italy's sphere of influence. But Hitler was also interested in this area, particularly in Roumania which contained oilfields vital to the German war effort. In August 1940, having warned Mussolini not to meddle in the Balkans, Hitler sent troops into Roumania. Mussolini, goaded to a fury by this, launched an attack on Greece at the end of October in order to even the score. Within a week, the dogged Greek defence had not only stopped the Italian invasion, but had thrown it back into Albania. At the same time, Mussolini had also suffered defeat in North Africa, where his army had been forced to retreat by O'Connor's small Western Desert Force culminating in the debacle at Beda Fomm at the beginning of February 1941. At the beginning of January, Hitler resolved to send a small force to help the Italians in Albania and another, under Rommel, to North Africa. At the same time he ordered preparations to be made for a plan which he had formulated in November for the occupation of Bulgaria and Greece in order to protect the Rumanian oilfields from attack by the RAF from bases in the eastern Mediterranean. He hoped that the occupation would take place with little or no fighting. However, at the end of February the Greeks accepted Churchill's proposal to divert British troops from North Africa to assist them against the Italians. Then at the end of March there was an anti-German coup in Yugoslavia, which previously had leant towards the Axis powers. Hitler immediately resolved to crush Yugoslavia with a lightning blow and then move into Greece.

The troops involved in this operation had to be taken from those preparing for the invasion of Russia. The Second and Twelfth Armies, together with Panzer Group Kleist were deployed for the invasion of Yugoslavia, whose army possessed little modern equipment. As in Poland and France, the German force was supported by von Richthofen's VIII Air Corps. The invasion was launched on April 6th, with the Twelfth Army and Panzer Group Kleist attacking Yugoslavia and Thrace from Bulgaria. Two days later Second Army launched an attack on northern Yugoslavia from Austria. Yugoslavia, ill-equipped to face a blitzkrieg and politically rent by internal divisions, capitulated on April 17th. It was, according to von Mellenthin, who was on the staff of Second Army, ' . . . virtually a military parade.' [3]

Greece was a tougher nut to crack. The Greek Army, after its success against the Italians, was in good shape psychologically. In addition, it had been reinforced by an Australian division, a New Zealand division and a British armoured brigade. The mountainous terrain which abounded in the country was also ideally suited to defence. Unfortunately the Greeks had pinned their hopes on the Metaxas Line, which guarded their common

161

frontier with Bulgaria. The border with Yugoslavia had few defences, and while the bulk of the Twelfth Army masked the Metaxas Line, the 2nd Panzer Division turned its left flank, at the same time threatening the rear of the Greek forces facing the Italians in Albania. The Allies then hoped to hold up the German advance in the difficult country around Mount Olympus, but brilliant handling of the 2nd Panzer and 6th Mountain Divisions enabled the Germans to outflank the Australian and New Zealand positions. Indeed the official New Zealand pamphlet, written after the war commented:

'Seldom in war were tanks forced through such difficult country, or had foot soldiers, already with over 500 kilometres marching behind them, pushed forward so rapidly under such punishing conditions; it was a record of which any soldier might be proud.' [4]

Although the Greeks signed an armistice on April 23rd, the Germans failed to prevent the bulk of the British and Anzac troops from being evacuated by the Royal Navy, in spite of overwhelming Luftwaffe superiority. The British, however, still held Crete, and it fell to the Luftwaffe to capture this important island. The airborne assault of Crete, which was launched on May 20th, came as a complete surprise to the British, and in the space of eleven days they were cleared off the island. However, German casualties were high, and although parachute divisions remained as part of the German order of battle for the rest of the war, they were never used on such a large scale again. The loss of transport aircraft would also affect events in Russia.

Nevertheless, with the Balkans now secure, Hitler could turn back once again to Russia. But, at the end of April he was forced to postpone the invasion date until June 22nd, to enable the troops and aircraft used in the Balkans to be redeployed.

The Germans had allocated 105 infantry, 17 panzer and 12 motorised divisions to Barbarossa. They were split as follows:

*Army Group North* (von Leeb)
Eighteenth Army (von Küchler)
Sixteenth Army (Busch) — 20 infantry divisions
4 Panzer Gruppe (Hoepner)      3 Pz and 3 Motorised divisions
Luftflotte 1 (Keller)          400 aircraft (five Ju87 wings, one plus Me 109F wing, a Stuka squadron and miscellaneous reconnaissance aircraft)

*Army Group Centre* (von Bock)
Ninth Army (Strauss)           12 infantry divisions
3 Panzer Gruppe (Hoth)         4 Pz and 3 Motorised divisions
Fourth Army (von Kluge)        21 infantry divisions
2 Panzer Gruppe (Guderian)     5 Pz, 3 motorised and one cavalry divisions

162

| Luftflotte 2 (Kesselring) | 1000 aircraft (three Ju87, two Me109E/F, two Me110, one plus Ju52, one plus Do17Z, one Ju88 and one He111 wings) |
|---|---|
| *Army Group South* (von Rundstedt) | |
| Sixth Army (von Reichenau) | 12 infantry divisions |
| Panzer Gruppe 1 (von Kleist) | 5 Pz and 3 Motorised divisions |
| Seventeenth Army (von Stulpnagel) | 13 infantry divisions |
| Eleventh Army (von Schobert) | 13 infantry divisions |
| Third Rumanian Army ⎤<br>Fourth Rumanian Army ⎦ | 14 infantry divisions |
| Luftflotte 4 (Löhr) | 600 aircraft (three Ju88, three Me 109E/F, two Ju52 and two He111 wings) |

The panzer groups were directly answerable to Army Group Headquarters, and had wings from the Luftflottes attached to them to provide intimate close support. Army Group Centre was by far the strongest, but then it was tasked to switch forces, including both panzer groups, to Leningrad.

On the eve of invasion the Germans estimated that the Red Army in Western Russian had some 154 rifle (infantry) divisions and 25 cavalry divisions. Little was known about the Soviet tank organisation, but it was thought that 10 tank divisions and 37 mechanised. brigades would be a reasonable approximation. In fact, according to Marshal Zhukov, the Red Army strength in the border districts with Germany, Hungary and Rumania was 150 divisions, including 36 tank, 18 motorised rifle and 8 cavalry divisions. [5] The Red Air Force was considered to have some 4000 first-line aircraft in the west, although this was an underestimate, the strength being more like 6000. The Red Army was initially organised into four fronts. The Northern Front under Popov, which covered Leningrad and the Finnish Border; North-West Front (Kuznetsov) the Baltic; West Front (Pavlov) * Belorussia to north of Pripet Marshes; South-West Front (Kirponos) the Ukraine. Much has been written of the Russian unpreparedness for the German attack. From early 1941 onwards, both the British Government and the Soviet spy rings in Occupied Europe and elsewhere had sent repeated warnings to Moscow, which appeared to fall on the deaf ears of Stalin. Indeed, the accusation had been levelled at Stalin that he did not prepare for invasion because he was afraid of becoming embroiled with Germany, and thought that any defensive precautions that he might take would be provocative in Hitler's eyes. A detailed discussion of Stalin's attitudes is outside the scope of this book. The fact remains that the Russian defensive posture played into the hands of the Germans.

Defences on the border with German-occupied Poland were non-existent,

---

*The same officer who had been present in Spain and made erroneous deductions from the fighting there.

with only the River Buq providing any form of natural obstacle. A defensive line, the Stalin Line, had been constructed in the late 1930s along the pre-1939 western border. Apart from in Bessarabia, however, this was almost 300 miles behind the new frontier and could play no part in the initial stages of the battle. To compound the error of failing to build defensive positions the Russians, instead of using the depth of the country to draw the German mechanised formations in so deep that their supply lines became overextended, and then counter-attacking, deployed the bulk of their forces in the frontier districts. As one former Red Army General put it:

> 'There were no reserve echelons backing up the front-line troops, because defence in depth was waved aside as sheer nonsense. No defensive war plans were made or even contemplated. Giant supply depots were filled to bursting with arms, ammunition and fuel not in the safe rear, but so close to the frontier as to be within range of Nazi heavy artillery.' [6]

But, to be fair to the Russians, the German invasion caught them in the middle of a reorganisation. As a result of the difficulties which they had experienced against the Finns, and also the German successes in Poland and France, the Red Army realised that they had drawn the wrong lessons from Spain in the drastic reorganisation of their armoured forces which took place at the time of Stalin's purges. The tanks which had been distributed among the infantry were not taken away, but during the latter part of 1940 the Russians did organise tank and mechanised rifle divisions. Following the German, and indeed Tuchachevski's emphasis on all-arms formations, the tank divisions were composed of two tank regiments, each of three battalions, supported by three motor rifle battalions and three field artillery battalions. The motor rifle divisions were similar, except that there were two motor rifle regiments and just one tank regiment. The idea was that two tank divisions and a mechanised rifle division would form a mechanised corps. Organisation of the tank divisions had been only partially completed in the border districts by June 1941, and although some had been organised into mechanised corps there was still a miscellany of tank and mechanised brigades, some banded into old-style mechanised corps (a mixture of mechanised brigades and tank brigades), but otherwise independent.

It had been planned to form twenty new-style mechanised corps by the autumn of 1941, but there was not the industrial capacity to meet this requirement. While the infantry formations would retain the new obsolete T28, T35 and BT models, it was hoped to equip the new formations with a fair proportion of T34s, a medium tank with a 76mm gun, which was to prove, in terms of mobility, protection and firepower, one of, if not the outstanding, tanks of World War 2, and the heavier KV series. But, although there were some 1 000 T34 and 400 KV tanks deployed in June 1941, supply could not keep up with demand. Thus many of the tank divisions were hopelessly under-strength. One mechanised corps, which was under the West Front, faced Guderian and Hoth with 508 BT tanks only instead of an establishment of 1 025 tanks, of which 420 should have been T34s and 126 KV1s. There was too a problem of training, which had been low in existing tank units since the demise of Tuchachevski and his disciples. The massive expansion of the armoured forces resulted in a large intake of soldiers to man the new tanks, which diluted the low standard of training even further. At the outbreak of the invasion it was common for tank drivers to have had no more than two hours of driver training, and for tank commanders to have had little or no practice in the art of commanding a tank.

The Red Air Force was in a similar state. Their main fighters were still the Polikarpov I15 and I16, which had been outclassed by the Me109 in the Spanish Civil War. The Yak 1, Lagg 3 and Mig 3 were coming into service, but were still inferior to the Me109. Although the VVS was now a tactical air force with its formations under command, as well as in support of the army, it still retained the lumbering TB heavy bomber series of the early 1930s, albeit mainly in the supply and parachute roles. For bombing it relied on the medium-range SB1 and SB2, which had performed usefully in Spain. The Petlyakov Pe2, similar in appearance to the Me110, was just starting to make its appearance in service, as was the 'Stormovik', the Ilyushin IL2* the Soviet ground attack aircraft. Thus, like the armoured forces, the VVS was caught in June 1941 in the process of re-equipping, but at an early stage with too many obsolete aircraft still on its hands.

On the evening of June 21st Stalin appears to have finally relented and ordered all units to be warned that the Germans would invade before dawn on the next morning. At the same time, remembering the Luftwaffe technique of attacking airfields at the outset, all VVS units were directed to camouflage their aircraft. These orders were never to reach the headquarters below those at front level. On the German side all was quiet, the attacking troops remaining hidden in their assembly areas close up to the frontier. At 0200 hours on the 22nd a Soviet grain train, the last of many such since the signing of the Russo-German Trade Agreement in February 1940, chugged its way across the River Buq at Brest-Litovsk. One and a quarter hours later the German bombardment opened. Fifteen minutes after this the invasion started.

Although on some parts of the front the Russians fought fiercely from the start, in others the bombardment took them entirely by surprise. General Blumentritt, Chief of Staff to von Kluge's Fourth Army records:

'Almost at once our signals intercept listened in to a Russian message,

---

The term 'Stormovik' was derived from the German 'shturm' meaning 'attack'. It covered the Yak-1 and Pe-1, as well as the IL-2. All three were similar in appearance to the Hurricane. Later models of the IL-2 however had a crew of two and the aircraft therefore resembled the Fairey Battle, but with better performance, better armament and heavy protective armour. Its top speed of 300mph made it employable only in the ground attack role, in which it gained a significant reputation.

'We are being fired on. What shall we do?' They heard the reply from the senior headquarters to whom this request for orders was addressed. 'You must be insane. And why is your signal not in code.' [7]

Almost all the bridges across the Buq were captured intact, many being undefended from the start. The Luftwaffe, whose initial attacks had started at the same time as the opening bombardment, found much the same when they attacked airfields, coming across aircraft drawn up in serried ranks with no attempt to camouflage. Even the Russians themselves admitted that 1 200 Soviet aircraft had been destroyed by noon on that day, 800 of which never took off.

Army Group North had been given the task of destroying the enemy in the Baltic States and then linking up with the Finns. Von Leeb, having only one panzer group, ordered it to advance with both corps abreast, each followed by an infantry army. For the first few days all went well, but then friction arose between Hitler, von Leeb and Hoepner. Hitler's Directive No 21 had laid down that the overrunning of the Baltic States was to be followed by the capture of Leningrad. Von Leeb's understanding of this order was that he should complete the first task before continuing on to Leningrad. Hence he proposed to pause so that his infantry divisions, now strung out through Lithuania, Latvia and Estonia could catch up. It must be remembered that von Leeb was a conservative infantryman, who had retired from the Army in 1938. He was also the self-same author of *Die Abwehr* referred to earlier in this book. Aware of the existence of Russian armoured forces, he had no wish to be caught off balance. Unfortunately, although he saw the potential of his own armoured forces, he did not really understand them. Hence, while ordering the infantry to seal off the Baltic States from Russia, he ordered Hoepner to move north-east through the swamps and forests to Lake Ilmen, to cover against any Russian counter-attack. Hoepner was aghast at the prospect of moving tanks through such country. Moreover, he argued that any further advances by his panzer group should be in the direction of Leningrad, the next objective. At the same time, Hitler began to interfere with the detailed conduct of Army Group North's operations, worried, as he had been in France, that Hoepner was going to leave the infantry too far behind. In the event, after some days delay, Hoepner was allowed to press on towards Leningrad, while the two infantry armies, because of Hitler's concern that the Baltic ports were not being cleared quickly enough and von Leeb's concern that they were getting too strung out, remained tied up in the Baltic States. The delay in mounting Hoepner's drive, his lack of follow-up infantry, and increasing Soviet resistance lost him the chance of taking Leningrad, which was never to fall to the Germans. It is a classic example of what happens when commanders at different levels have differing ideas as to the conduct of operations. The other two army groups would not be free from these disagreements either.

In the centre the idea in Hitler's mind was for Hoth and Guderian to advance 250 miles until they were level with Minsk, and then turn to meet one another, thus creating a vast pocket of Russian forces, which could be

166

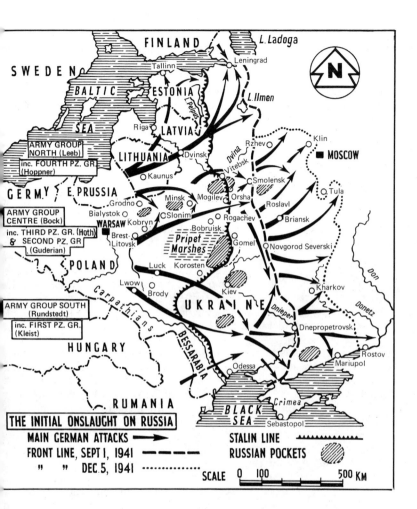

THE INITIAL ONSLAUGHT ON RUSSIA

MAIN GERMAN ATTACKS →
FRONT LINE, SEPT I, 1941 ─ ─ ─
   "     "    DEC. 5, 1941 ·········

STALIN LINE ▴▴▴▴▴▴▴
RUSSIAN POCKETS ▨

SCALE  0   100              500 KM

167

mopped up at leisure by the infantry armies. The army group commander von Bock had agreed with his panzer commanders that this was not deep enough, and had recommended to Hitler that Smolensk, another 200 miles further east, should be the eastern extremity of the pocket. He argued that the shallower the pocket the less troops would be trapped inside it, the less territory overrun, and that the drive on Moscow would be delayed. Also it would allow the Red Army elbow room in which to regroup. Von Bock represented this view as early as January 1941, but was not able to get a clear answer from OKH, and indeed did not have one when the campaign opened.

As with Army Group North, Hoth and Guderian had little problem at first in their respective drives. The latter had added to the initial surprise by sending his tanks across the Buq with schnorkelling equipment, which had been originally developed for Operation Sealion. But Guderian had had to argue to allow his panzer divisions to lead the attack. In the war games that had been part of the planning for Barbarossa:

'The generals who came from arms of the service other than the panzer troops were inclined to the opinion that the initial assault should be made by infantry divisions after heavy artillery preparation and that the tanks should only be sent to complete the break-through after a penetration to a specified depth had been made.' [8]

The same debate was to be repeated some 15 years later when the Israelis were planning the first of their pre-emptive attacks into Sinai. Nevertheless Guderian had his way, and the only notable strongpoint which he was forced to bypass initially was the fortress of Brest-Litovsk, whose defenders fought fanatically and which, as a result, did not finally fall until mid-July. The speed of Guderian's advance was such that he reached the River Beresina, some 250 miles from his start line, in six days. Hitler now insisted that Guderian link up with Hoth at Minsk rather than Smolensk. He was again showing signs of the same nervousness, with which he had been inflicted during the French campaign. Some 20 Russian divisions were estimated to be trapped between Hoth and Guderian, and Hitler was concerned that these might break out in the wake of the panzer groups cutting them off from the main body. Guderian reluctantly obeyed the order, and the Russians found themselves enclosed in two pockets, an inside one created by the infantry of Army Group Centre in the area of Bialystok Nowogrodek, and east of this, a larger pocket to the west of Minsk, held by the Panzer Groups.

The creation of these pockets on the Russian West Front showed up strikingly the error the Russians had made in deploying their troops so far forward. Pavlov aggravated the situation still further by ordering all his reserves forward to relieve pressure on the Bialystok pocket, not realising that by doing this he was leaving a vacuum around Minsk, and condemning his entire front to encirclement. Not surprisingly, he was relieved of his command on June 30th, summoned back to Moscow for court-martial and shot. Yet, the Russians did make determined efforts to break out, but there was little co-ordination. In one place Russian infantry would advance shoulder-to-shoulder entirely unsupported by artillery, tanks, cavalry or aircraft. In another, even an armoured train, a relic from the civil war, was used. Elsewhere the Russians mounted determined tank attacks. In one of these Guderian's 18th Panzer Division came up against the T34 for the first time. It proved impervious to the German tanks at any range above 200 yards. No wonder one German account spoke of it as being 'a wonder weapon . . . spreading terror and feared wherever it moved.' [9] But, because the Russian tanks were employed on their own without infantry support, against the German all-arms combat teams, and also the standard of training of the Soviet tank crews was so low, the Germans were able to contain and destroy these thrusts in spite of the T34, and its heavier companion the KV1. The Red Air Force, recovering a little from the initial onslaught by the Luftwaffe, did fly bombing attacks against the encircling Germans, but they flew unescorted by fighters and proved easy meat for the Me109s. Thus on June 30th wave after wave of bombers attacked the panzer troops around Minsk only to be beaten back by Colonel Werner Molders' *Jagdgeschwader* 51, which claimed 114 bombers shot down. No wonder the German fighter aces achieved such high scores on the Eastern Front.

On July 3rd the Russians in the Bialystok pocket surrendered to the Ninth Army, which had been tasked to clear it. The total bag from this pocket alone came to 290 000 prisoners, 2 500 captured or destroyed tanks and 1 500 guns. Meanwhile, for ease of control, the two panzer groups were formed into the Fourth Panzer Army under the command of von Kluge in preparation for the drive to the Dnieper. Guderian, who since the link up at Minsk had been impatient to push on, had been surreptitiously sending off panzer formations in this direction, which put him on bad terms with von Kluge. Nevertheless, on July 2nd, in spite of contradictory orders from above, which reflected Hitler's continuing concern that if the panzers were allowed to push on too early the Russians in the Minsk pocket might escape before the German infantry armies had caught up, Guderian and Hoth pushed on towards the Dnieper. They did, however, leave some formations behind to guard the pocket. Luckily, increasing Russian resistance in front of the Dnieper and Dvina rivers slowed down their advance, giving the infantry time to catch up, thus enabling the remaining panzer formations to rejoin their groups before the advance had proceeded very far.

Timoshenko had now taken over as commander of the West Front, and learning from Pavlov's mistakes had ordered the remainder of troops, including Budenny's Reserve Front, to concentrate along the Stalin Line. Soviet resistance had become noticeably stiffer, and Guderian, who considered that his next objective was Smolensk, hesitated before launching his troops across the Dnieper, on which the Stalin Line was based. On the one hand was the need to push on in order to reach Smolensk as soon as possible so that Moscow might be tackled before the autumn rains came. Yet he knew that the Russians were massing reserves behind the Stalin

Line, and there was the danger of his panzer forces becoming cut off especially as the Russians still had strong lodgements west of the river. The alternative was to wait for the infantry, and allow them to clear a path for him, as well as giving him a base from which to operate. But he estimated that it would be some 14 days before these would arrive, and in that time the defences on the Stalin Line would be immeasurably stronger. Believing speed to be the overriding factor, he decided to attack. Von Kluge, arriving in the midst of Guderian's preparations for the attack, was furious and ordered the attack to be cancelled. Guderian explained that preparations were too far gone, and pleaded that the operation was crucial to the object of ending the Russian campaign in 1941. Von Kluge grudgingly acquiesced, remarking: 'Your operations always hang by a thread'. [10] On July 10th and 11th Guderian crossed the Dnieper with comparative ease, and moved quickly towards Smolensk, easily warding off a Russian counter-attack from the south. Meanwhile, Hoth had passed through Vitebsk and was in a position to encircle Smolensk from the north by July 15th. On the next day Guderian reached Smolensk from the south, and once again he and Hoth joined hands to form another gigantic pocket.

Army Group South's initial objective was Kiev, the major city of the Ukraine. The main thrust was to be made by Panzer Group 1 and the Sixth and Seventeenth German Armies. They would advance eastwards, protected by the Pripet Marshes in the north, and by the Rumanians in the south. Von Rundstedt had two initial problems. For political reasons, he was not to mount any operations initially from Rumania. This restricted his axis of advance. Secondly, unlike Army Group Centre, he only had one panzer group to act as a pincer, with which he hoped to encircle Kirponos' South-West Front in front of Kiev. The other would have to be provided by von Schobert's Eleventh Army, which being an infantry formation did not have the same mobility. Although his initial break-in was successful his rate of advance was much slower than that of von Bock. The Soviet formations in the Ukraine were better trained, with more modern equipment than their compatriots to the north. In many ways this was not surprising because after all the Ukraine was Russia's main source of supply for food and thus important for the survival of the country. Von Rundstedt, try as he might, was unable to achieve a major encirclement. The Russians fought with great tenacity, but always seemed to slip away before the trap could be closed. Budenny, appointed to command of the South-West Theatre, and now Kirponos' superior officer, on July 10th, continued the good work by mounting a series of counter-attacks to keep the Germans off balance, and slow them down. Not until mid-July did the prospect of a pocket of significant size loom up in front of Kiev. Hitler himself had almost given up hope of such a thing happening and had tried to persuade von Rundstedt to split up his armour in order to create a series of small pockets instead of one large encirclement.

Thus, by mid-July Army Group North was pushing against steadily increasing Soviet resistance towards Leningrad. Army Group Centre was poised to reduce the gigantic Smolensk pocket, and von Rundstedt looked

170

like finally achieving his encirclement in front of Kiev. Hitler now issued another directive, No 33 for the continuation of the campaign. This was not before time. While the panzer group commanders in the north and centre had been keen to push on to capture the objectives laid down in Hitler's original directive, their superior commanders, including Hitler himself, had done much to interfere with this, because of their fears of the panzers over-exposing themselves. Indeed, it seemed that shortly after the campaign had started Hitler had virtually torn up his directive and was relying on sending telephonic daily orders to his army group commanders adjusted to suit the particular situation at the time. Thus, while the panzer group commanders thought they knew the main objectives, their superior commanders were kept increasingly in doubt. Nowhere had the effect of this been seen so clearly as in the failure to thrust on towards Leningrad in time.

The overall aim of Directive No 33 was still the same as its predecessor, No 21. It was still the destruction of the Soviet forces, and emphasised that 'further sizeable enemy forces' must be prevented from 'withdrawing into the depths of Russia'. But here the similarity virtually ended. Hitler ordered Army Group Centre to despatch part of its forces southwards to enlarge the size of von Rundstedt's pocket. In addition, von Bock was still expected to send forces northwards to assist Army Group North in the capture of Leningrad. Army Group Centre was expected to continue the advance on Moscow using infantry formations only. The only sop for the thrust on Moscow was Hitler's order for the Luftwaffe to bomb the city. In truth, Hitler was attracted to the Ukraine for economic reasons, and although von Brauchitsch, as Commander-in-Chief of the Wehrmacht, von Bock and von Rundstedt, objected that Moscow was no longer the main objective, Hitler remained adamant. Fourth Panzer Army was broken up and Hoth sent northwards and Guderian southwards. But Guderian still had a card to play. He got himself involved in a local battle south-east of Smolensk at the end of July, and this prevented him from moving south to combine with von Rundstedt for a time. This gave von Bock, Hoth and himself more time to persuade Hitler, but it was not until September 6th that Hitler, in Directive No 35, finally ordered attention again to be focussed on Army Group Centre. In the meantime, Army Group North became bogged down in the lakes and forests dominating the approaches to Leningrad. Hoepner's Panzer Group found it well nigh impossible to operate in this type of country, and having little infantry with them to flush the Russians out of the woods, they ground to a halt. As a result Hitler ordered the Luftwaffe to destroy Leningrad, in the same way as Moscow.

The Luftwaffe now found itself even further caught out by having adopted tactical posture from its inception. Whereas it had been able to give England its complete attention in 1940 because the army was no longer engaged on active operations, the situation was very different when it came to tackling Moscow and Leningrad. Because the Luftwaffe's primary role was support of the army, which was involved in intense fighting, the bomber wings had been split up among the air fleets. Consequently it was impossible to concentrate sufficient aircraft to make the raids effective. Thus the first attack on Moscow which was mounted on the night of July 22nd consisted of only 127 aircraft, a mere fraction of those used in raids against London. Both army and their supporting Luftwaffe commanders refused to offer up any more aircraft, believing their own sectors to be more important. After the first few nights the numbers of aircraft dropped below 100, and then declined even more rapidly. The situation was reached that, of 76 raids on Moscow during 1941, no less than 59 were made by a force of ten or less aircraft. The massive ground operations on the central and southern fronts simply sucked up all available Luftwaffe resources. The picture was the same with the attacks on Russian industry, which Hitler had also now ordered. However many tanks or aircraft were destroyed by the Germans, the Russian industry, from its comparative safety behind the Urals, manufactured more than enough to replace them. Again, the limited range of the German bombers meant that they could use only a limited number of forward airfields to attack strategic targets such as Moscow or the Urals industrial area. Hitler's original directive for Barbarossa had laid down that strategic targets would only be engaged once the objectives on the ground had been achieved. In that case the Urals industry would have been in range. The Luftwaffe was now forced to engage in strategic air warfare in order to achieve those objectives themselves, and lacking genuine 'strategic' bombers, found itself incapable of carrying out the task. Another aggravation was the decline in the proportion of serviceable aircraft on the Eastern Front. Lack of necessary spares had brought this about, caused more than anything else by bad administration. Milch, touring the Eastern Front in August, was horror-struck at the number of useless spares held by squadrons, who at the same time were screaming for essential items.

During August interest was centred on the southern front. Von Rundstedt using all three of his German infantry armies and von Kleist's Panzer Group sealed the pocket south-west of Kiev at the beginning of the month. Although some 100 000 prisoners were captured, many Soviet troops succeeded in breaking out eastwards to fight another day. However, his troops quickly closed up to the Dnieper, where it bends round eastward in a loop south-east of Kiev. This now gave the Germans the chance to bottle up all the remaining Russian forces around Kiev itself. It was for this purpose that the protesting Guderian was eventually forced by Higher Command to move south. Von Rundstedt now had two armoured pincers, with Guderian moving in from the north and von Kleist from the south. Playing into the Germans' hands, the Soviet High Command in Moscow, seemingly unaware of Guderian's move southwards, gave the order on August 19th for Kiev and the Dnieper to be held at all costs. Thus those of Kirponos' troops which had escaped or avoided the first encirclement now found themselves condemned to be trapped by this new threat. Guderian and von Kliest linked up at Secha, 100 miles east of Kiev and well in the Soviet rear on September 16th. The Russians, doing their best to hold the Germans back from crossing the Dnieper from the West, were powerless to prevent the completion of the encirclement. During the next ten days, despite repeated and, at times, fanatical efforts by the Russians to prise it open from the

172

ast, the pocket was reduced to yield 450 000 prisoners, larger even than the Smolensk pocket which had been cleared up by August 5th with a bag of 350 000 prisoners. But, although the success at Kiev had been spectacular and had cleared the Ukraine and the way forward to the Crimea and Donets basin, the advance on Moscow, which to Guderian was the key to victory, had been postponed until the beginning of October.

While the battle for the Kiev pocket was being fought the remnants of Army Group Centre had been involved in defensive operations against fierce attacks by Timoshenko's West Front. Although Timoshenko had been repulsed, the German infantry divisions had suffered heavy casualties, and the replacements were not available to restore them to their full strength. Their equipment too had suffered from the 400-mile advance which they had made into Russia. The panzer groups, although they had travelled more than twice as far as the infantry mass, were luckier in the state of their equipment because in August Hitler gave priority of production to tanks over all else. Thus, while the average tank strength of the panzer groups was down to under 50% at the end of August, a month later it was up to 75% of establishment. By the end of September the troops, both panzer and infantry, had been in action with little rest for over three months and exhaustion was setting in. For this reason, and because it was known that the weather would break in early October, to be followed by six weeks of frost before the snows came at the beginning of December, it was essential to push on and reach Moscow, 200 miles from Smolensk as fast as possible.

Between Smolensk and Moscow lay an estimated Soviet strength of eighty infantry and nine cavalry divisions, with eleven tank formations at divisional or brigade strength. Hitler, now favouring more limited encirclements as opposed to the deeper variety which had allowed too many Russians to escape, decreed that these Soviet formations must be destroyed before Moscow was reached, and ordered a pocket to be formed with its eastern extremity at Vyazma, 130 miles west of Moscow and 80 miles to the rear of the Soviet forces. Once again he formed the now familiar twin armoured pincers. The northern pincer was made up of Hoth's 3 Panzer Group, supported by Strauss's Ninth Army, while the southern had Hoepner's 4 Panzer Group and von Kluge's Fourth Army. Guderian's 2 Panzer Group, about to be redesignated as Fourth Panzer Army, and von Weich's Second Army, who were still involved in the Ukraine, would move north-eastwards to threaten Moscow from the south. At the same time, once the Vyazma pocket had been cleared, Hoth would move round to the north of Moscow to cut it off from Leningrad, while Hoepner approached from the west. Guderian would move off on September 30th, while the remainder set off two days later. Air support was to be provided by the 1 000 aircraft of Kesselring's Luftflotte 2. Hitler had now accepted that the capture of Leningrad had failed, and ordered the city to be closely invested by the infantry formations remaining in Army Group North, the panzer group having been transferred to Army Group Centre. In the south, too, the brake was applied. Although von Rundstedt had been allowed to keep his panzer group, he had lost one of his infantry armies, but in spite of this he was able to clear the approaches to the Crimea by the beginning of December.

Although the encirclement at Smolensk and the German air raids or Moscow had caused the Russians to expect an advance on the city from the end of July, their attention had been diverted by the German efforts in front of Leningrad and even more, by the operations of Kiev. Consequently they had continued counter-attacking and Guderian's advance on September 30th took them by surprise. They were off balance and their troops were disposed forward, thus once again falling in with German tactics. Once Operation Typhoon, as the advance to Moscow was designated, was under-way, the Russian formations were ordered to stand and fight where they were — again assisting the creation of pockets. But, at the same time reserves were scraped together to provide defence in depth. Thus Guderian's advance got off to a good start, advancing 50 miles on the first day. By October 5th he had got behind two Soviet armies situated around Bryansk and joining up with von Weichs, who had advanced north of Bryansk, and succeeded in closing the pocket by the 9th. Although casualties had been generally light, his troops were subjected to constant attacks by small groups of Red Air Force bombers. Also, on October 6th his XXIV Panzer Corps had a stiff fight with a brigade of T34s and KV1s, supported by infantry, which led Guderian to remark:

> 'The short-barrelled 75mm gun of the Panzer IV was only effective if the T-34 were attacked from the rear; even then a hit had to be scored on the grating above the engine to knock it out. It required very great skill to manoeuvre into a position from which such a shot was possible. The Russians attacked us frontally with infantry, while they sent their tanks in, in mass formation, against our flanks. They were learning . . . The danger suffered by the Russians was considerably less than that to our own tanks.' [11]

At the same time the first snow of the winter fell together with heavy rains, and this made Guderian aware of another problem, which affected all the land forces in Russia (but not the Luftwaffe, who thanks to Milch had taken the necessary precautions). This was the complete shortage of winter clothing. So optimistic had the German High Command been that the campaign would be concluded by the autumn, that no arrangements had been made to provide its soldiers with the necessary protection against the Russian cold. Furthermore, Guderian noticed that even the best of his officers and men were starting to become weighed down by exhaustion, both physical and mental. Problems of resupply of ammunition, fuel and spares were also making themselves felt, and Guderian was having to rely more and more on the good offices of the Luftwaffe to ensure that his tanks received sufficient to carry on the advance. None of these growing problems boded well for the future of Operation Typhoon.

To Guderian's north, the main attack was launched on October 2nd in fine weather, and both pincers forged ahead, linking up at Vyazma on

October 7th. Here too the Russians had been taken by surprise and resistance was weak with only a few scattered counter-attacks being attempted. During the next week this pocket, which contained the major part of five Soviet armies was reduced, yielding a record bag of 650 000 prisoners. Guderian's own pocket took longer to reduce because of the primeval forests and swamps within it. On October 14th OKH issued orders for the second and final phase, confirming that Moscow would be encircled rather than taken by an advance direct from Vyazma. Von Bock protested that this would disperse his troops over a 600 mile front and delay the capture of the city, but Hitler had now decided merely to surround the city rather than capture it. Meanwhile the Russians were taking desperate measures to defend the capital. Zhukov had now taken charge of operations and gathered the remnants of the West Front into defending the hastily dug Mozhiask Line, 80 miles west of the city. Additional troops were being transferred from the Far Eastern Armies, as well as other formations being drawn off the North-West and South-West Fronts. But even by October 8th German tanks had succeeded in breaching the Mozhiask Line in three places. It looked as though it was only a matter of time before the city fell.

At this stage, though, the autumn rains really took hold and the German advance became literally bogged down. The 112th Infantry Division, operating as part of the Second Panzer Army, reported:

'On October 22nd 1941 the advance began, and with it the period of the greatest difficulties of movement experienced by 112th Infantry Division. Even though the division had a good deal of experience in poor road conditions, what was now demanded of it vastly exceeded anything known in the past. The completely sodden forest paths, the areas of swampy marsh, and the sticky clay on open ground simply defy description . . . all motorised vehicles were hopelessly bogged down. Those which were not actually stuck in the swamp or on soft roads were unable to move through lack of fuel. The infantry regiments had spread out into unending long columns: the heavy vehicles were unable to keep up and had to be manhandled along. It was even worse for the artillery, which continually had to leave guns behind. Any normal supply of food-stuffs, fodder for the horses, and fuel was out of the question . . . The Panzer Army's motorised and armoured units had been almost entirely left behind on the soft roads, so that the advance was maintained exclusively by the infantry divisions.' [12]

By the beginning of November Guderian had come to a halt two miles short of Tula on the River Don. It was the same everywhere, and the infantry, now in front of and separated from the tanks, found it difficult to hold onto the ground they had already captured in the face of Russian tank and infantry counter-attacks. The bad weather also prevented the Luftwaffe flying. Thus, robbed of the mobile firepower provided by the close support aeroplane and the tank, the blitzkrieg was halted for the first time since the outbreak of war. In the meantime the Red Army had won a valuable breathing-space in order to prepare itself more thoroughly for the final battle for Moscow.

At the beginning of November the frosts arrived, making the ground passable to vehicles once again, and on the 7th the decision was taken to press on. But, by this stage an air of pessimism was permeating the minds of the German commanders. Even Guderian was moved to write: 'The unique chance to strike a single great blow is fading more and more, and I do not know if it will ever recur.' [13] At a conference held at the headquarters of Army Group Centre on November 13, which was chaired by Halder, the Chief of the General Staff, the Chiefs of Staff of both Army Groups North and South argued that the time had come to halt on all fronts until the spring. Only Army Group Centre, whose leading units were now 30 miles from Moscow asserted that the advance must go on rather than be left stranded in the snowy wastes with the prize so nearly in their grasp. In the face of this Halder concurred that the drive on Moscow should continue. On the 16th the panzer groups once more moved to the attack. At the start the Russians could not hold the German attacks, but as November wore on and temperatures plummetted, the Russian resistance, reinforced by more and more Siberian divisions, grew stronger until in the words of one German lieutenant:

'On the 30th we made our last attack — a hill known to us as Pear Hill and a village called Lneino. With artillery and mortar support we managed to take all the hill and half of the village. But at night we had to give it all up again in order to defend ourselves more effectively against the continuous Russian counter-attacks. We only needed another eight miles to get the capital within gun range — but we just could not make it.' [14]

With the Germans only 18 miles from Moscow von Bock was forced to write to Halder on December 1st that further offensive action was out of the question in view of the increasing strength of the Soviet forces. There was no longer the chance of reaching the objectives. But it was not until December 8th that Hitler agreed that Typhoon should be halted, when in Directive No 39 he ordered his forces to go over to the defensive, blaming the failure of the operation on 'the severe winter weather which has come surprisingly early in the East, and the consequent difficulty in bringing up supplies.' [15]

Although it was the weather which proved to be the immediate conqueror of the 1941 blitzkreig in the east, there were a multitude of other reasons which brought about its demise. Hitler's original aim, as laid down in Directive No 21, was wrong in calling for the destruction of Russian armed forces. This was the direct approach, which did not take account of the fact that blitzkreig was best used to dislocate the enemy psychologically. With this done, the destruction of his forces would automatically follow. Although the encirclement tactics used did bring about the destruction of a major part of Russia's forces in the west, they were able to recover by degrees

176

because the central command and control structure in Moscow was still able to function. Then again, Hitler changed his objectives during the campaign, becoming distracted first by Leningrad and then by the thought of the economic benefits to be gained in Southern Russia. This led to confusion among the various command levels.

But even more fundamental, was the fact that the Germans did not have the tools to take on such a vast undertaking. The Luftwaffe and the Wehrmacht had been built up during the 1930s only for war against neighbouring countries. Hitler may have always had the conquest of Russia at the back of his mind, but in his early years in power this was not an immediate objective, and many more years would have been required to create a weapon which could have coped with the very vastness of the Soviet Union. An air force tied to the tactical apron strings of the Wehrmacht had been shown to be unsuitable even against Britain, and was even less able to undertake strategic tasks in a country many times the size. The Wehrmacht, although well constructed for the comparatively limited campaigns in Poland and the Low Countries, was ill-equipped to tackle a heavyweight opponent like the USSR. The ratio between the mechanised forces and the mass of the foot-slogging infantry was too disproportionate. The one was not strong enough on its own to achieve what was necessary, while the other was too slow for the necessary momentum to be maintained. Thus, although the panzer groups were able to create the vast pockets, they were not able to reduce them on their own, and had to waste time awaiting the arrival of their slower compatriots, who were at times as much as two weeks' marching time behind. But, it is likely that Hitler subconsciously realised this, and hence his reluctance to allow the panzer commanders, who understood more than anyone as to how the blitzkrieg should be conducted, or at least thought they did, to push forward too far on their own.

There was too the problem of supply. The lines of communication were vast compared with those which the Germans had used previously. The supply of fuel, the most essential element to maintain a blitzkrieg, ammunition and spares dropped further and further behind demand the deeper the armoured spearheads penetrated into Russia. The poor road and rail system, together with the lack of air resupply resources brought this about. As the weather worsened, more and more reliance was placed on the Luftwaffe for this role, but they did not have the aircraft available, mainly because of the severe losses of transport aircraft suffered during the invasion of Crete and the high rate of unserviceability. Lack of administrative foresight in terms of making available the necessary stores and equipment also contributed. But, this was all part of the almost dreamlike optimism which infested Hitler's headquarters during the planning and execution of Barbarossa. The utter conviction that Operation Barbarossa could be successfully completed before autumn discouraged efforts to make a proper study of the implications of the geographical and meteorological factors peculiar to Russia.

No sooner had the German effort in front of Moscow died down than the Russians launched their first major counter-offensive. This was the brain-

177

child of Zhukov and was carried out in the main by divisions fresh from the Far East. On December 5th the first blow was struck by Koniev around Kalinin to the north-west of Moscow with the object of destroying the northern wedge created by 3 Panzer Group. Using tanks, infantry and ski troops supported by artillery and aircraft, Koniev managed to penetrate between 3 Panzer Group and Ninth Army to its north. The next day 4 Panzer Group, just to the north of Moscow was similarly attacked, while Guderian was forced to pull back towards the Don under pressure from a further attack. Down in Army Group South's sector, its northern army, the Second, also found itself threatened in the rear by a Soviet attack along its northern flank. In all sectors the Germans were forced to pull back, a tactic to which many of them were unused. The effect of this was recorded by General Schaal, commanding LVI Panzer Corps of 3 Panzer Group.

'Discipline began to crack. There were more and more soldiers making their own way back to the west, without any weapons, leading a calf on a rope, or drawing a sledge with potatoes behind them — just trudging westward with no-one in command. Men killed by aerial bombardment were no longer buried. Supply units, frequently without officers, had the decisive say on the roads, while the fighting troops of all branches, including anti-aircraft artillery, were desperately holding out in the front line. The entire supply train — except where units were firmly led — was streaming back in wild flight. Supply units were in the grip of psychosis, almost of panic — probably because in the past they had only been used to headlong advance. Without food, shivering with cold, in utter confusion, the men moved west. Among them were the wounded whom it had been impossible to send back to base in time. Crews of motor vehicles unwilling to wait in the open for the traffic jams to clear just went into the villages. It was the most difficult time the Panzer Corps ever had.' [16]

The need to pull back to positions more suitable to survive both the Russian attacks and the Russian winter became paramount.

In the meantime, the Soviet High Command, seeing the predicament which the Germans were in, resolved to turn what had been an operation merely to secure the safety of Moscow, into a counter-offensive with the object of encircling Army Group Centre to the east of Smolensk. In the south Zhukov and Cherevichenko were to swing towards Vyazma and Smolensk, while in the north two pincers, one under Koniev and a deeper one under Kurochkin, were to complete the encirclement. Pressure would also be maintained in front of Moscow in order to dissuade the Germans from withdrawing. For the first time the Red Army had the chance to try out Tuchachevski's encirclement doctrine against the Germans.

Von Brauchitsch had recommended to Hitler that, in view of the increasing Russian pressure and the German exhaustion, a withdrawal should take place to a line running east of Vyazma, 90 miles west of their line of furthest advance. This could be held during the winter prior to fresh

178

offensive efforts in the spring. Hitler was aghast at this and ordered that all troops should stand and fight where they were. There would be no withdrawal. He sacked von Brauchitsch and assumed personal command himself. Von Brauchitsch was not the only one to go, for von Kluge also relieved von Bock, who had fallen sick, and von Rundstedt and von Leeb also fell by the wayside. Russian pressure continued, forcing the Germans steadily back, and in cases surrounding them thus forcing them into pockets. Guderian, who had been conducting a skilful battle against superior Soviet forces fell foul of von Kluge once again, who accused him of evacuating a town unnecessarily. The result was that Guderian was sacked from his command and placed on the retired list.

The Russian counter-offensive continued for three months. Although, in some sectors the Russians penetrated as much as 150 miles, they did not succeed in carrying out their encirclement. The reasons were twofold. Firstly, Hitler's order of no voluntary withdrawal prevented the Soviet attacks from gaining momentum. The Germans held on to many key towns such as Vyazma, accepting Russian penetrations on either side. This had the effect of continuing to threaten the Soviet lines of communication and restricting axis of advance. It also enabled the Germans to cut in behind the Russians. Secondly, Stalin became carried away by the early successes of his counter-offensive, and ordered attacks at random along the whole length of the front. These attacks became less and less co-ordinated, leading to dissipation of effort. The Germans were thus able to hold out intact. But there was a price to pay. Casualties in men and materials were high, and replacements in no way kept pace with losses. Thus while the first five months of the campaign had cost the Germans 742 000 killed and wounded, the next four months up until April 1st, 1942 cost them a further 376 000. In this time only 450 000 replacements were received. Many divisions were to fight from now on at only a fraction of their authorised strength. The Luftwaffe too suffered heavily. The winter conditions, together with the fact that there were several small German pockets entirely surrounded by the Russians, meant greater reliance than ever on air resupply. At the same time the extremes of temperature produced enormous aircraft servicing problems, and only 25% of the total complement of aircraft on the Eastern Front were fit at any one time. Nevertheless, the Luftwaffe did succeed in keeping these pockets supplied, although at a cost in aircraft. The other problem was that the army needed offensive air support desperately in order to hold back the Russians. The Stukas found themselves unable to cope with the demands on their own and all the bombers were committed to close support on the battlefield itself, which prevented them from taking on the more important task of interdiction.

Planning for the 1942 offensive had started as early as November 1941, while the Germans were still hammering at the gates of Moscow. It was not until March 1942 that the plans were finally crystallised. The executive document was Hitler's Directive No 41 dated April 5th, 1942. He accepted that they had failed in the centre in 1941, and ordered attention for 1942 to be focussed in the south, where the objective was the seizure of the

179

Caucasian oilfields and the passes through the Caucasian Mountains. In the north, the object remained the same as in the previous year, the seizure of Leningrad and the linking up with the Finns, but this was to be regarded as a subsidiary operation. The centre was merely to remain on the defensive and no orders were given for it to mount any form of subsidiary attack in order to assist operations in the north and south. He proposed to achieve his objectives in the south 'by decisively attacking and destroying the Russian forces stationed in the Voronezh area to the south, west, or north of the Don.' But, instead of relying on the deep envelopment movements of the year before, Hitler decreed that:

'Experience has sufficiently shown that the Russians are not very vulnerable to operational encircling movements. It is therefore of decisive importance that, as in the double battle of Vyazma-Bryansk, individual breaches of the front should take the form of *close** pincer movements. We must avoid closing the pincers too late, thus giving the enemy the possibility of avoiding destruction. It must not happen that, by advancing too quickly and too far, armoured and motorised formations lose connections with the infantry following them; or that they lose the opportunity of supporting the hard-pressed, forward-fighting infantry by direct attacks on the rear of the encircled Russian armies.'

Much greater control was to be exercised over the panzers and there was no Guderian present to object. The Luftwaffe as before had as its prime role support of the ground forces, but Hitler did specify that the first step was to destroy the Red Air Force in the theatre of operations. He also laid down an interdiction task:

'If enemy forces are seen to be concentrating, the principal roads and railways serving the concentration area will be brought under continuous attack well in the enemy's rear. A first priority will be the destruction of railway bridges across the Don.' [17]

Because of the casualties during the previous nine months, Hitler was forced to rely more on the forces of his allies. Italian, Hungarian, Rumanian and even a Spanish volunteer division, became involved. Their role was mainly defensive, holding the flanks while the German formations did the actual attacking. The panzer divisions were almost all below their 1941 establishments, but nevertheless two more divisions were created. However, only in Army Group South did the nine divisions available have three tank battalions. In order to achieve this the divisions in the other two army groups were reduced to two, and sometimes one weak battalion. They still relied on the Pz Kw Mk III and IV, but there was a new heavy tank, the Tiger with its 88mm gun, designed specifically to combat the T34, which was to be introduced from September onwards. The Luftwaffe was not to be

*Author's italics.

180

as well equipped as in 1941. Calls for aircraft for the Mediterranean and home defence in view of the RAF bombing offensive on Germany, meant that the Eastern Front did not retain top priority for the supply of replacement aircraft. At the beginning of 1942 only 1 750 aircraft of all types, serviceable and unserviceable, were available compared with the 2 000 serviceable of June 1941. Although by mid-summer this total rose to 2 500, only 75% of these were serviceable at any one time.

While the supply of equipment to the Germans was lagging, that to the Russians was increasing. From the safety of the Urals Russian industry had turned out no less than 3 000 T34s in 1941. Because of the poor performance of their mechanised corps and tank divisions, they decided to make a brigade rather than a division the basic tank unit. This initially consisted of either two or three small tank battalions, each with 23 tanks, a motorised rifle battalion and supporting arms and services. It was hoped in this way to raise the standard of command and tactical handling of tank formations. At the same time the Russian aircraft industry easily outstripped that of its opponent, with effort being concentrated on the Yak fighter and the Stormovik. Indeed, the latter, although without the dive-bombing capability of the Stuka, showed itself to be a very versatile ground-attack aircraft, being able to carry a mixed armament of cannon, rockets and both high explosive, anti-tank and anti-personnel bombs.

While the Germans were making final preparations for the offensive in the south, the Russians launched a pre-emptive attack. At the end of March Stalin had called a session of the State Defence Committee to decide on the plan of campaign for 1942. While Zhukov and Shaposhnikov argued that the Russians should content themselves with aggressive defence until they were stronger, Stalin, supported by the remainder of the Soviet High Command declared that, with the Germans on the defensive the time had come to launch a counter-offensive before the Germans had time to strike. He ordered the recapture of Kharkov as the objective and Timoshenko, now commanding the South-West Theatre was entrusted with carying out the operation. Timoshenko planned to attack north-east and south-east of Kharkov, using 14 of the 20 new-style tank brigades then available to strike at the German panzer formations while they were concentrating for their own attack.

On May 12th Timoshenko attacked. Initially all went well with Timoshenko's tanks, supported by 23 infantry divisions, and 18 cavalry divisions, driving their way through six German and Rumanian divisions, which were without tanks. Von Paulus, commanding the German Sixth Army, was forced to commit all his reserves, but even then he could not stop the Russian onslaught. The planned role of von Paulus' army was to act as the northern arm of a German offensive intended to take out the Russian salient south of Kharkov, the very area over which Timoshenko's attack was now proceeding. The southern pincer was to be von Kliest's First Panzer Army, supported by Hoth's Seventeenth Army. The attack was due to be launched on May 18th. It was now clear that von Paulus was in no position to undertake his part of this attack, and hence, in order to relieve the pressure on him, von Kliest would attack on his own. The date was brought forward by one day in order to strike at Timoshenko. The effect of von Kliest's attack, which was made by two panzer, one motorised and eight infantry divisions, with an additional four Rumanian divisions covering his left flank, was to catch Timoshenko's forces in the flank, which had now become very extended because of the depth of penetration achieved. On that first day von Kliest cut through two Russian armies and penetrated the salient to a depth of 25 miles. There was little that Timoshenko could do since his armour was well away to the west, and he had not left himself an adequate reserve. He asked permission of the Russian High Command, the *Stavka*, to call off his attack and withdraw his forces eastwards before they became cut off, but Stalin refused to countenance this. The result was that the bulk of his forces were surrounded and the bill in prisoners alone came to 214 000, together with 1 200 tanks, most of which had been unable to escape because of lack of fuel, and 2 000 guns. It was a major disaster and seemed to bode ill for Russian fortunes. Indeed, Kruschev, who was the Politbureau representative at Timoshenko's headquarters, records that:

'Marshal Timoshenko told me that the army had been so utterly routed by the enemy that the only way to rally the troops was to set up mobile kitchens and hope that the soldiers would return when they got hungry.' [18]

This lack of confidence showed itself in June when von Kliest and Hoth in a mopping up operation around Kharkov captured a further 40 000 prisoners and the Soviet troops executed a precipitous withdrawal 30 miles eastwards.

While the battles around Kharkov had been taking place, von Manstein had cleared the Crimea, and the stage was now set for the last of the blitzkreig operations in the East. The capture of the Caucasus, Hitler's main objective for 1942, was codenamed Operation Blue. It laid down three main axes of attack, which would be mounted consecutively starting from the north. This was done so that the operation could get under way as soon as possible (Hitler wanted to start in mid-June) without having a long pause for deployment. Also, it meant that the Luftwaffe could concentrate its support on one thrust at a time rather than having its strength dissipated throughout the area of operations. In order better to allocate troops to tasks, von Bock, who had been in command of Army Group South since January 1942, split his command into two — Army Group A in the south, and Army Group B in the north. The first thrust was to be made by Hoth's Fourth Panzer Army, von Weichs' Second Army and Jany's Second Hungarian Army. Consisting in all of three panzer, two motorised and eighteen infantry divisions, this force had as its initial objective the capture of Vronezh. Hoth would then move south-eastwards down the Don and link up with the second thrust, which would be mounted from Kharkov. In this way it was hoped that the Russian South-West Front would be encircled and destroyed west of the Don. The second attack, starting two days later than the first, would be made by von Paulus's Sixth Army with two panzer

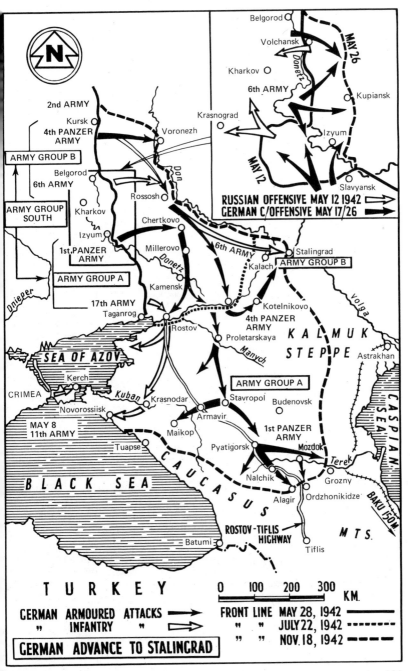

N

Belgorod

Volchansk

Kharkov

MAY 26

6th ARMY

Kupiansk

Krasnograd

Izyum

MAY 12

Slavyansk

**RUSSIAN OFFENSIVE MAY 12 1942** ⇨
**GERMAN C/OFFENSIVE MAY 17/26** ⬛➤

2nd ARMY

Kursk

4th PANZER
ARMY

Voronezh

ARMY GROUP B

Belgorod

6th ARMY

Rossosh

ARMY GROUP
SOUTH

Kharkov

Chertkovo

Izyum

Millerovo

6th ARMY

Stalingrad

1st.PANZER
ARMY

Donetz

Kalach

ARMY GROUP B

ARMY GROUP A

Kamensk

17th ARMY

Kotelnikovo

Taganrog

4th PANZER
ARMY

Rostov

Proletarskaya

Dnieper

Don

volga

K A L M U K

S T E P P E

Manych

Astrakhan

SEA OF AZOV

ARMY GROUP A

Kerch

Kuban

Krasnodar

Stavropol

Budenovsk

CRIMEA

Novorossiisk

Armavir

C
A
S
P
I
A
N

MAY 8
11th ARMY

Maikop

1st PANZER
ARMY

Tuapse

Pyatigorsk

Mozdok

S
E
A

C A U C A S U S

Nalchik

Terek

Grozny

B L A C K   S E A

Alagir

Ordzhonikidze

BAKU 150M.

ROSTOV-TIFLIS
HIGHWAY

M T S.

Batumi

Tiflis

T U R K E Y

0   100   200   300

KM.

GERMAN ARMOURED ATTACKS ➤

" INFANTRY " ⇨

**GERMAN ADVANCE TO STALINGRAD**

FRONT LINE MAY 28, 1942 ——
" " JULY 22, 1942 -------
" " NOV. 18, 1942 ----

183

and one motorised among its eighteen divisions. Once von Paulus had met up with Hoth, he was to take up position on his right, and then the two would continue southwards to link up with a third attack, which would start some days later. It was originally planned that this third thrust should be made from Taganrog, on the northern shore of the Sea of Azov, and would link up with the other two thrusts in the area of Stalingrad. However, on further consideration it was thought that Army Group A, which only had four panzer and two motorised divisions, did not have the strength to operate so far away to the south of von Paulus, and therefore the axis of advance was moved 150 miles north. But even then, half of Army Group A had to be diverted to cover the southern flank, leaving von Kliest, who was to make the attack, with only 15 divisions, including three panzer and one motorised divisions. Notwithstanding this, the Germans were committing eighty divisions to carve out a salient which would, all being well, have a perimeter of over 1 000 miles. Since Army Groups North and Centre needed 96 divisions to hold their 1 300 miles of front, there was a danger that the Germans could find themselves grievously overstretched.

Two factors set the operation off on the wrong foot. Firstly, Hitler was becoming increasingly mesmerised by the capture of Stalingrad itself. Admittedly, the city was an important communications centre, but its seizure would contribute little to the main objective, and it was not essential that the thrusts should link up precisely at this point. It would seem that his fixation with the city was psychological in that Stalin claimed to have defended it in the civil war, when it had been known as Tsaritsyn, and thus Hitler thought that its capture would be a bitter blow to Stalin himself. But, whatever Hitler's reasoning, the choice of Stalingrad as a key objective was to have disastrous results. The other factor was more immediate. On the June 19th, the chief operations officer of the 23rd Panzer Division, while on an aerial reconnaissance, was shot down and captured by the Russians. In his possession he had the XL Panzer Corps (of which 23rd Panzer was part) operation order for its role in Sixth Army's thrust from Kharkov. Although Sixth Army was notified that same night, no effort was made to change the plan and certainly by the 21st the *Stavka* knew of Voronezh as an objective, and the plan for the encirclement of the South-West Front.

On June 28th Hoth attacked, with the Second Army being used to cover his left flank. To support him was the entire weight of the VIII Air Corps, and all available air reconnaissance units, which were put directly under his direct command. Led by Kempf's XLVIII Panzer Corps with one panzer and two motorised divisions, the operation was initially very successful, evoking memories of 1940. A gap between the Thirteenth and Fortieth Soviet Armies was prised open, and indeed the headquarters of the latter army were almost captured intact on the first day, so speedy was the advance. The only pauses were caused by the need for replenishment and the occasional downpour of rain, but even then the halts were of minimal time and at the earliest opportunity combat groups were sent racing on again. Air reconnaissance, which gave early warning of Soviet moves, and the Soviet commitment of tanks piecemeal, enabled Hoth to ward off counter-attacks with ease. By July 2nd he had linked up with von Paulus, who had started two days later, at Staryy Oskol, and was pushing on towards Veronezh. Four days later he was across the Don and had captured Veronezh, which the Russians had evacuated. Meanwhile, the Russians, in spite of the capture of XL Panzer Corps' operation order, had remained convinced that Moscow was still the main objective. It was only the capture of Veronezh which caused them to move a tank army and two infantry armies down from the north. However, where they did benefit from knowledge of the German attack was by withdrawing the bulk of their troops before they became trapped. Thus the Staryy Oskol pocket was disappointing in terms of prisoners yielded, and there was a growing feeling among the Germans that their blows were landing on thin air.

The original plan had called for Hoth and von Paulus to move south down the line of the Don as soon as Veronezh had fallen. Yet as early as July 3rd Hitler, worried about the rapid withdrawal of the Russians, had told von Bock that the capture of Veronezh was not essential. All the same, the buildup of Russian forces gave von Bock cause for concern and he was loath to turn south immediately as Hitler wished. Only one corps of Fourth Panzer Army was initially sent southwards, but it was not enough to allow the Russian forces south of Veronezh to be trapped and they were able to escape. On July 8th more panzer formations were sent south, but the logistic pipeline had now become so overstretched that the tanks came to a halt through lack of fuel. The Luftwaffe did its best to harry the Russians as they crossed over the Don, but it was to little avail, and the bulk of the South-West Front got across safely and in good order, yielding only some 30 000 prisoners to the Germans.

Meanwhile, the third German thrust, lead by von Kliest's First Panzer Army, had been launched along the north of the Donetz River on July 9th. Hitler now deeply concerned that he was not going to achieve his primary aim of the destruction of the Russian forces, now drastically changed the original plan. He saw the only chance of achieving his aim was to create another pocket around Kamiensk, 200 miles west of Stalingrad. Sacking von Bock, because of his dilatoriness in moving south from Veronezh and replacing him by von Weichs, Hitler ordered Hoth to take command of von Paulus's only panzer corps and then move south to link up with von Kliest at Kaniensk. Thus he had abandoned the idea of a large pocket with Stalingrad as its apex in favour of a small one in an attempt to cut his losses. But, both Russian prisoners and Luftwaffe reconnaissance bore out the fact that few Russian troops now remained west of the Don, and hence it was another blow into thin air, giving the Russians a valuable breathing-space in which to regroup. The failure of the Kamiensk pocket made Hitler even more desperate, and operations now centred on the Lower Don, with Hoth being transferred to von List's command and ordered to advance south towards Rostov, while von Kliest crossed the Donetz and then about turned almost on his tracks to move on Rostov from the east, following the northern bank of the Lower Don. In the meantime, von Paulus, still without armour, was expected to continue on towards Stalingrad. Only after the

185

weather had broken and temporarily slowed up the movement of the panzers, did Hitler listen to his staff and allow von Paulus a panzer corps.

Undoubtedly the failure of the first phase of the campaign had been because the Russians, contrary to the past, had seldom stood and fought. For once the *Stavka* had realised that it was better to withdraw, and let the Germans expend their energies in striking into nothingness. Their withdrawals were too quick for the limited number of German mechanised and motorised formations, and the more these advanced, the graver the supply situation, on which the blitzkreig relied so heavily, became. At last, the Russians were realising that the way to defeat blitzkrieg was to use mobile rather than static defence, and to draw the Germans on in the same way that Kutusov had done to Napoleon in 1812. Hitler's previous victims had not felt that they could afford to sacrifice the territory to be able to do this, but the endless Russian steppes were ideal for the purpose. This new Soviet strategy quickly had its effect on Hitler, making him interfere more and more in the minutiae of the operations. Halder, writing in his diary on July 23rd, aptly sums up the atmosphere at Hitler's Headquarters:

'The situation is getting more and more intolerable. There is no room for any serious work. This 'leadership', so-called, is characterised by a pathological reacting to the impressions of the moment and a total lack of any understanding of the command machinery and its possibilities (i.e., Hitler is incapable of grasping that his constant interference is throwing everything in disorder).' [19]

The tragedy was that Stalingrad could have been taken in July if Hitler had allowed his original plan to proceed. Perhaps then there would not have been the disaster that was to occur later in the year.

In the meantime Hitler had also turned his eyes even further southwards, and on July 11th ordered von Manstein to move down the eastern coast of the Black Sea as a first stage towards seizing the passes over the Caucasus Mountains. But then, eight days later he countermanded this order, decreeing instead that this would be a task for the Rumanians. Then on July 23rd he issued Directive No 45 for Operation Brunswick. In his preamble he stated that: 'only weak enemy forces from the Timoshenko Army Group have succeeded in avoiding encirclement and reaching the further bank of the Don. We must expect them to be reinforced from the Caucasus.' This did not tie up with the facts, which Hitler had continually refused to accept. However, he did go on to forecast correctly that the Russians could be expected to hold Stalingrad tenaciously. He ordered Army Group A to complete the encirclement of the enemy forces around Rostov, then occupy the eastern coastline of the Black Sea, seize the passes through the Caucasus Mountains and then drive along the Caspian to overrun the Baku area. At the same time Army Group B were to secure the Upper Don and capture Stalingrad, blocking communications between the Don and Volga, and on the Don itself. Priority for air support was given initially to Army Group B. Thus, the two army groups found themselves moving in divergent

irections and a yawning gap opened up between them. This dispersion of
trength was to prove disastrous. Even worse, the fatal attraction of
talingrad was about to draw the Germans into a slogging match among
he streets of the city where their mechanised and motorised forces would
e of little use. Indeed Hitler, fully aware that the Russians intended to
efend the city, was inviting his troops to fight the type of battle which in
he past he had been so emphatically against.

On July 25th Operation Brunswick was launched. Von List had a total of
ree panzer, two motorised, eleven infantry and three Rumanian cavalry
ivisions, and he was faced with the daunting task of advancing 700 miles
n a front which would extend 800 miles along the line of the Caucasus
ountains. Initially the Soviet South Front under Malinovsky attempted to
efend in place. This, of course, played into the hands of von Kliest, and
on a breach 50 miles deep and 100 miles wide had been opened. By
ugust 9th von Kliest had advanced over 200 miles and was in the foothills
f the Caucasus. But, here the advance slowed down. It was the old story in
at supplies could not keep up with the rate of advance, and the tanks
round to a halt. In addition, the Germans found that they no longer
njoyed air superiority on this front, many of the Luftwaffe units supporting
on List being gradually drawn off northwards to the great battle for
talingrad. The Russians had raised fresh formations and the country
ecame more favourable to the defender the closer to the mountains the
ermans got. They were never able to seize the passes, although one small
roup actually reached the summit of the highest mountain in the range,
ount Elbrus. The only force to reach the Caspian was a reconnaissance
nit of 16th Motorised Infantry Division, which carried out a daring
econnaissance patrol as far as Astrakhan in September. Von List failed
ecause too many of his supplies and other support were diverted to
talingrad, which steadily became Hitler's prime objective.

Von Paulus's advance on Stalingrad did not proceed at the same pace as
rmy Group B's drive southwards. Although he had received XIV and
XIV Panzer Corps to replace his own XL Panzer Corps, which he had
iven up to Hoth, von Paulus was not able to get his advance moving
roperly again until the beginning of August because the bulk of the
uftwaffe transport force had been given over to Army Group B in
ccordance with Directive No 45. Hence he found himself starved of fuel.
y the time the administrative plan had been amended, all the Soviet forces
ere safely back across the Don, apart from a large pocket on the bend of
e Don in front of Stalingrad itself. This was held by four Soviet armies,
cluding a significant number of tanks and at least twelve infantry
ivisions. However, Stalin had issued an order on July 28th stating that
ere were to be no further withdrawals. Thus this pocket was waiting to
ll like a ripe plum into von Paulus's lap. Using the usual double
ncirclement, he reduced this pocket by August 15th and captured some
0 000 prisoners. This was small in comparison with the yields of 1941, but
arked an auspicious beginning to the Stalingrad offensive, especially
ecause the 'bag' was larger than any other so far since the start of the 1942

187

offensive. Indeed it imbued the Germans with a dangerous optimism whic
manifested itself in a noticeable decline in dash among the German tan
crews, who thinking that the city was about to fall, started to act in a ve
cautious manner verging on sluggishness.

By July 30th Hitler had decided that Stalingrad was definitely the ke
objective. To this end, Hoth was returned to the command of Army Grou
A on August 1st, being ordered to advance north-eastwards along th
Novorossik-Stalingrad railway. Again, initial progress was good and b
August 5th Hoth had breached the outer defences of Stalingrad, but again:
stiffening Russian resistance his thrust slowed to a halt four days late:
Nevertheless, the Germans were now in a position to attack Stalingrad fror
two directions, the north-west and the south-west. But from now on, th
closer the Germans got to the city the greater the intensity of the Russia
defence. By the beginning of September fighting was taking place withi
Stalingrad itself and was assuming the character of Verdun in 1916 wit
both sides throwing more and more men into the mincing-machine. Ther
was, however, one major difference. The Russians could afford to fight thi
type of battle because of their massive stocks of manpower. The German
did not have such limitless resources.

A detailed description of the fighting around Stalingrad, with the Russia
counter-attacks in November against the Rumanians on either side of th
city and the subsequent trapping of von Paulus's Army and his eventua
surrender would be out of context in this book. However, one or two aspect
cannot be ignored. Stalingrad was undoubtedly the turning-point of the wa
on the Eastern Front. From now on the Germans would be forced onto th
defensive. The blitzkrieg had met its match, not because it had bee:
defeated by superior tactics, but because it had become swallowed up in th
limitless Russian wastes. The German front in Russia had by Autumn 194:
become grieviously overextended because Hitler had taken on too man
objectives at once. Stalingrad merely aggravated the situation in that th
loss of 300 000 German soldiers was insupportable when there were les
than 3 000 000 men to hold a front which by the beginning of Novembe
1942 was 2 000 miles long. It has been argued that Hitler was correct i
ordering von Paulus to stand firm, when he could have extricated himself
because it allowed the Germans time to regroup and form a defensive front
But it is unlikely that this was what went through Hitler's mind. Mesmerise
by Stalingrad as he was, he could not psychologically accept any idea o
giving it up voluntarily. He was, too, encouraged by Goering's declaratio
that von Paulus could be resupplied by air, something which was entirel
beyond the capability of the Luftwaffe, and which merely led to anothe
large loss in transport aircraft, which had proved so vital to the blitzkrie;
effort.

The Russians, who by their usual tactics of attempting to stand and figh
regardless of the cost had played into the hands of the German blitzkrieg
were now able to catch the Germans making the very same mistake. I:
addition, although they had not designed it so, apart from the withdrawa
of the South-West Front in the Mid-summer of 1942, the Russians had

188

ealised that the Germans were over-extended. Thus, while they were still educing Stalingrad, they launched attacks on Army Group A, which was orced to evacuate the whole of the Caucasus, when a Russian drive on Rostov threatened its rear. The Russian counter-attacks around Stalingrad nd in the Caucasus showed that they had learnt much. For a start, ealising that the weakness of the German defence often lay in her allies, vhose formations were not so well equipped or trained, the Russians directed heir attacks on those parts held by other than German troops. Perhaps heir greatest art was that of infiltration. Taking advantage of the fact that he Germans did not have the troops to hold continuous lines of defence, elying instead on strongpoints with a mobile reserve, the Russians would lip units through the German lines at night, and establish a fortified base rom which they would attack the next day. But although these attacks were vell planned by the higher headquarters there were still weaknesses at lower evels:

'Russian tactics are a queer mixture; in spite of their brilliance and their exceptional mastery of field fortifications, yet the rigidity of Russian attacks was almost proverbial. (Although in some cases Russian armoured formations down to their lowest units were a conspicuous exception.) The foolish repetition of attacks at the same spot, the rigidity of Russian artillery fire, and the selection of the terrain for the attack, betrayed total lack of imagination and mental mobility. Our Wireless Intercept Service heard many a time the frantic question: 'What are we to do now?' Only a few commanders of lower formations showed independent judgement when faced with unforeseen situations. On many occasions a successful attack, a breakthrough, or an accomplished encirclement was not exploited, simply because nobody saw it.' [20]

By the end of January 1943 there was a significant change in the comparative make-up of the German and Soviet Armies. When the invasion of Russia had started in June 1941 the Germans had been able to field over 3 000 anks. Eighteen months later they had available on the Eastern Front a mere 495 fit for battle. Most of these were still the Mk IIIs and IVs which were inferior to the large numbers of T34s and KV1s now available. Hitler's insistence that no division should be struck off the order of battle meant hat instead of maintaining the strength of the panzer division by malgamating under-strength formations, the existing number of divisions was maintained but at a very much reduced strength in tanks. The Russians on the other hand were slowly increasing the size of their tank brigades as junior commanders became more experienced and the number of such brigades had shot up to well over 100 compared with the 20 available the year before. One battalion within the panzer division was now mounted in half-tracks, normally the Sd Kfz 251, which had two machine guns and a crew of six, and in 1943 motorised infantry units were designated Panzer Grenadiers. But in spite of this minor improvement no attempt had been made to increase the level of motorisation throughout the Wehrmacht as a

189

whole. Meanwhile the Red Army was now benefitting from Lend-Lease, an indeed before the end of the war would have received no less than 427 00 motor vehicles. The situation was thus being reached whereby:

'The German equivalent to the Red Army quarter-ton jeep for commande or messenger remained horse. The counterpart of the Studebaker or Dodg six-wheeled drive truck was the horse-drawn *panje* waggon.' [21]

The Wehrmacht was rapidly falling behind in terms of modern equipment The Luftwaffe, too, was suffering. They found themselves saddled with host of pre-war designs, which were now becoming obsolescent. Althoug] they were able to manufacture sufficient aircraft (in February 1943 alon some 1 500 were produced) there was no clearcut priority over the types o aircraft required. Too much effort was also wasted in impracticable investi gations such as the attempt to make the He 177, which could have been th Luftwaffe's answer to the Lancaster or American B-17, into a dive-bomber with the result that few ever flew on operations. In addition, there was nov a serious lack of trained crews to fly the new aircraft, and not sufficien emphasis on the production of fuel as opposed to more aircraft. Again th attacks by the RAF and USAAF on Germany itself were forcing th Luftwaffe to retain more and more aircraft in Germany and the West at th expense of the Russian Front. This enabled the Red Air Force to grov steadily more superior.

By March 1943 the German front in Russia ran from Leningrad down t west of Rostov on the Sea of Azov. Along it were two distinctive Germar salients, the northern with Bryansk as its base, while to the south of thi there lay another above Rostov. The latter might have lain even further tc the west if it had not been for a brilliant counter-stroke by von Manstein at Kharkov. In mid-January a Russian offensive mounted against the Second Hungarian Army south of Veronezh had opened up a gap 175 miles wide, and by February 21st the Russians had almost reached the Dnieper neai von Manstein's headquarters at Zaporozhe. Von Manstein, in spite of agitation from Hitler to recapture Kharkov immediately, held back until he thought that sufficient Soviet forces had passed westwards through the gap. He then unleashed Fourth Panzer Army from the south. The Russians were caught off balance and suffered over 20 000 killed, although there were only 9 000 prisoners. This enabled the Germans to restore their defensive line on the River Donetz and also brought an end to the 1942-3 Russian offensive. It was one of the last few glimmers of the blitzkreig in the east, and von Mellenthin concluded that it was successful for four reasons. High Command did not interfere with the panzer formations, allowing them to be given distant objectives, and also provided sufficient infantry to cover their flanks. The panzer commanders from corps level downwards led from the front, and finally the element of surprise was achieved. All these had been proved in the past to be essential for success in the blitzkrieg context. [22]

With the coming of the spring thaw Hitler, bearing in mind that Kharkov had shown that the Germans were capable of it, concluded that the only way to hold in the East would be to mount a limited offensive before the Russians had had time to wind up for their next major attack. It was the same line of thought which the *Stavka* had developed before Timoshenko's pre-emptive attack the year before. There was also the threat that the British and Americans would open a second front in Europe, and it was essential to mount any attack before this occurred. Looking along the front, the obvious place for this attack was the Russian salient around Kursk. The plan was simple. Model's Ninth Army, would attack from the north, while Fourth Panzer Army did the same from the south. It was hoped that this would cause the Russians such casualties as to make them incapable of further offensive action during the summer. The attack was originally due to be made in mid-April, but various factors brought about delays which were to be fatal to Operation Citadel, as it was called. For a start Model did not believe that he had sufficient troops for his task, arguing that the Russian defences in the salient had been under-estimated. The result of this was that Hitler committed no less than twelve panzer, and six panzer grenadier divisions to the operation, besides 25 infantry divisions. In terms of tanks this represented a total of some 1 900, or over two thirds of the number available on the Eastern Front. Guderian, now re-employed as Inspector-General of Panzer Troops, was horrified that so large a proportion of the existing tank force should have been committed to the operation and attempted to dissuade Hitler from mounting it. Hitler's reply was: 'You're quite right. Whenever I think of it my stomach turns over.' [23] Nevertheless his mind was made up. Even worse, he saw it as an ideal opportunity to try out new tanks in the German armoury, which he felt sure would turn the scale. Consequently the operation was further postponed while Panthers, which still had numerous problems to be ironed out, and Ferdinands, which although possessing a powerful 80mm gun and thick armour, had no machine gun and only limited traverse, making them useless for fighting other than at extreme range, were sent to Russia.

Consequently, it was not until July that the Germans were ready. In the meantime, the Russians had become aware of the German plan and took advantage of the delays to prepare accordingly. They resolved to wait for the German attack rather than pre-empt it, since they reckoned it would significantly weaken the German strength and thus make their own offensive more likely to succeed. Within the salient itself were two Soviet Fronts, Central Front with six armies, including one tank army and two independent tank corps, and south of it the Veronezh Front with four rifle armies forward, and one rifle and one tank army in reserve together with two tank and one rifle corps. These two fronts constructed an extensive system of fortifications including anti-tank strong points and minefields. However, this was not an end to the Soviet dispositions for the battle. To the rear of the salient a further defensive zone was constructed running north-south. This was held by the newly formed Steppe Front of five armies, including one tank army and a further tank, mechanised and three cavalry corps. The idea was that this front could counter-attack into the salient, but was far enough back not to get involved in the fighting before it chose to do so.

Precise figures of tanks and aircraft available to the Russians are difficult to come by, but it would seem that the Russians probably had of the order of 3 000 tanks and the same number of aircraft. The Germans had some 1 900 aircraft to support an equivalent number of tanks.

Thus the Germans were setting the might of their panzer formations against positions reminiscent to those of the Western Front 1915-17. It could hardly be called a blitzkrieg attack for surprise had been lost.

On July 4th, after a short sharp air and artillery bombardment, Fourth Panzer Army attacked at 1500 hours. This time was chosen rather than dawn in an effort to salvage some tactical surprise. Initially all went well, and XLVIII Panzer Corps succeeded in breaking into the positions held by the Sixth Guards Army. The Russians were slow to react and it was not until some hours later that their artillery opened up. In spite of this and an overnight thunderstorm which degraded the 'going', the first objectives were reached. But now the Russian defences and the weather took their toll. The minefields slowed down the advance, while torrential thunderstorms brought it to a halt. By the end of the second day Fourth Panzer Army had made three small penetrations, none more than six miles deep. There were still two more defensive zones to get through before the panzer formations could break out and fight the type of free-ranging battle to which they were used. It was the same story in the north, where Model had attacked twelve hours later than Fourth Panzer Army. On the first day he managed to penetrate to a depth of six miles on a twenty mile front, but was unable to get further in the face of ever increasing Russian resistance. By the third day he was running short of tank ammunition, and his tank losses were mounting. The Ferdinands in particular came to grief after their escorting tanks, which were supposed to protect them during the close-in fighting, had been knocked out and they became easy prey for the Soviet infantry. It was the same with the Panthers, which had an unfortunate tendency to 'brew up' at the slightest hit.

In the south, the Germans pushed on slowly. On the 6th, VIII Air Corps flew almost 1 700 sorties in support of XLVIII and II SS Panzer Corps, but against increasing Russian air opposition did not have the resources to support both simultaneously. By July 12th they had penetrated some twenty miles, but were still 55 miles from Kursk, and some 90 miles from Model. At this moment the Russians chose to counter-attack with the Steppe Front. The fighting which followed was centred on the village of Prokhorovka, and was the most intensive tank battle of the Second World War. Rotmistrov's Fifth Guards Tank Army with almost 1 300 AFVs attacked Hausser's II SS Panzer Corps, while to the west XLVIII Panzer Corps was engaged with the Sixth Guards and First Tank Army. In the air Stukas and Stormoviks also added to the carnage. Rotmistrov himself describes what the battle was like:

'The tanks were moving across the steppe in small packs, under cover of patches of woodland and hedges. The bursts of gunfire merged into one continuous, mighty roar. The Soviet tanks thrust into the German advance formations at full speed and penetrated the German tank screen. The T-34s were knocking out Tigers at extremely close range, since their powerful guns and massive armour no longer gave them advantage in close combat. The tanks of both sides were in closest possible contact. There was neither time nor room to disengage from the enemy and reform in battle order, or operate in formation. The shells fired at extremely close range pierced not only the side armour but also the frontal armour of the fighting vehicles. At such range there was no protection in armour, and the length of the gun barrels was no longer decisive. Frequently, when a tank was hit, its ammunition and fuel blew up, and torn-off turrets were flung through the air over dozens of yards. At the same time over the battlefield furious aerial combats developed. Soviet as well as German airmen tried to help their ground forces to win the battle. The bombers, ground-support aircraft, and fighters seemed to be permanently suspended in the sky over Prokhorovka. One aerial combat followed another. Soon the whole sky was shrouded by the thick smoke of the burning wrecks. On the black, scorched earth the gutted tanks burnt like torches. It was difficult to establish which side was attacking and which defending.' [24]

Although the Germans claimed the destruction of over 2 000 Russian tanks, they themselves lost approximately 1 000. The difference was that the Russians could afford these losses while the Germans could not. On July 10th the Allies had invaded Sicily, which meant that the long awaited second front in Europe was now a fact. Hitler realised that he would have to reinforce his troops in Italy and elsewhere. It was also clear that Citadel had failed, and hence on the July 13th he gave the order to halt the operation. This was the last time in which the Germans would attempt a major offensive in the East. It had been a gamble which had failed drastically. The losses in tanks would never be made up and from now on the Germans would remain entirely on the defensive. Kursk had been the very negation of blitzkreig. The Russian defences coupled with the lack of surprise had given the panzer formations no chance to work up the necessary momentum to achieve their objectives. The result had been a battle of attrition, which was the very thing which blitzkrieg had been designed to avoid.

The Russians went over to the offensive immediately, and from now on the pressure on the Germans would never let up. The strategic aim of the Russians was not so much the destruction of the German forces in Russia, but to clear them out of the homeland. Once this had been done, the destruction of 'Hitlerite Germany' could take place. Unlike the Germans, whose main objective had been the destruction of the Russian forces, the Russians did not concentrate so much on achieving double-encirclements. The pattern of their operations has been likened by Liddell Hart to that of Foch in 1918. [25] It consisted of a series of orchestrated attacks mounted concurrently all along the front. In this way the German reserves were kept tied down, and it ensured that the Russians retained the initiative for the Germans could never anticipate where the next attack was going to be. The

193

attacks themselves followed a familiar pattern. A massive artillery bombard-ment would be followed by infantry supported by tanks, which would achieve the break-in of the German defences. The attacks would be made by heavy concentrations of both infantry and armour on a very narrow front. If the attack failed, it would be mounted again and again, regardless of casualties, until success was gained. Meanwhile, the Red Air Force would add its weight to the attack, in the form of close air support. It is significant that the few attempts at strategic bombing, and even deep interdiction tasks. Seldom would it operate more than twenty miles behind the enemy lines. Once the breach had been made, more tanks and infantry, the latter normally riding on the backs of the former as the Russians lacked armoured personnel carriers (APCs), would push on to the next objective. This process would be repeated until the attack could go no further, and then it would be stopped and another attack mounted elsewhere. There was little finesse about these tactics. They relied on mass, and succeeded mainly because the Germans were forced to concede ground because of the pressure of sheer weight of numbers against them.

Encirclements were made, but these did not take up a distinct phase in the battle, unlike the doctrine of Tuchachevski, which called for encircle-ment and the reduction of the resultant pocket prior to pursuit. The encirclements were caused by the German defensive tactics, which relied on hedge-hogs, between which small mobile combined arms groups manoeuvred. Thus the Russians would surround these defensive networks to prevent them from interfering with the pursuit phase, which was launched at the same time as the encirclement. The Germans, because of the difference in mobility between their mechanised and infantry formations had been forced to pause until each pocket had been reduced before pushing on. The Russians did not need to do this, because their individual offensives had more limited aims than those of the Germans, and also the motorisation of the Red Army resulting from Lend-Lease meant that follow-up forces could keep up with the tanks. Finally, having far more mechanised formations available than the Germans did, they could pass fresh formations through immediately into the pursuit phase.

Much of the German defence in the East during the latter part of the war was conducted with great skill. As in the World War 1, they showed that they were still masters of the counter-attack, particularly in their ability to react quickly to a given situation and take the necessary steps to counter enemy moves. The panzer formations, although deteriorating in numbers of tanks, were used with great imagination, cutting in behind the Russian thrusts and disrupting them. Unfortunately the successful conduct of operations was repeatedly thwarted by Hitler. There was a continual need to shorten the front as casualties mounted. The only way to do this was to withdraw, but Hitler would seldom accept any voluntary surrender of ground. More and more he seemed to draw from his own limited experience of trench warfare. In the same way he often ordered formations to stand and fight when they were in danger of encirclement, which led to costly operations by both the Luftwaffe and the panzer formations to assist them to maintain themselves in their pockets and to breakout when Hitler finally gave them permission to do so. But, above all, it was the sheer mass of the Russian war machine which put paid to any hopes the Germans might have had in stabilising the Eastern Front more than very temporarily. After the Allied invasion of Normandy in June 1944 the superiority in numbers became even more marked, and the Germans faced a dilemma as to whether to concentrate on defence in the East or the West. They did not have the troops to be able to do both successfully.

**Notes**

1  *Rise and Fall of the Third Reich* op cit p 796.
2  Trevor-Roper, op cit pp 49-52.
3  Mellenthin von, op cit p 31.
4  Ibid, p 36.
5  Zhukov, *Memoirs* p 250.
6  Gartoff, op cit p 437
7  Westphal, *Fatal Decisions* p 47.
8  Guderian, op cit pp 146-7.
9  Orgill, *T34: Russian Armour* p 41.
10  Guderian, op cit p 169.
11  Ibid, pp 234-5.
12  Carell, *Hitler's War on Russia* vol 1 pp 162-3.
13  Guderian, op cit p 246.
14  Ibid, p 188.
15  Trevor-Roper, op cit p 107.
16  Carell, op cit p 339.
17  Trevor-Roper, op cit pp 117-120.
18  Crankshaw, *Kruschev Remembers* p 189.
19  Halder, *Diaries* p 358.
20  Mellenthin von, op cit p 186.
21  Seaton, *The Russo-German War 1941-45* p 352.
22  Mellenthin von, op cit p 209.
23  Guderian, op cit p 309.
24  Carell, vol 2 op cit pp 89-90.
25  Liddell Hart, *History of the Second World War* p 492.

# 7

# The Anglo-American Version and Final German Fling

While the Germans and Russians had been locked in battle on the Eastern Front, Britain and the United States had been preparing the way for re-entry into the continent of Europe. With North Africa and Sicily cleared of Axis forces, Italy was invaded, and Allied troops were steadily slogging their way northwards across terrain which overwhelmingly favoured the defender. Although these were campaigns on the periphery, there was one which was waged unceasingly against Germany herself from 1940 onwards. This was the strategic bombing campaign, something which neither the Luftwaffe after 1940, nor the Red Air Force, ever attempted seriously. This was waged by two air forces, the RAF and USAAF, both of which had been primarily designed, the one thanks to Trenchard and the other to Mitchell, for the strategic role. The effect of the strategic bombing campaign on Germany has been hotly debated ever since the end of the war. Undoubtedly it failed to bring Germany to its knees on its own, thus proving with the weapons of the period the Douhet hypothesis was incorrect. Indeed, during the years up to 1943 it was of indirect benefit to Germany, forcing her to put her industry on a proper war footing and paradoxically, it was not until 1944 that German tank and aircraft production reached its peak. Much of the reason behind the disappointing results of the allied air offensive was the constant changing of objectives. Those directing the campaign could never make up their minds as to which was the key range of targets. Thus, for a time attacks would be concentrated on industry, and then would change to the pure Douhet-like terror attacks on the civilian population, as typified by the raids on Hamburg and later, Dresden. Unfortunately, Harris and Spaatz, who directed the campaign were often misled by their own economic intelligence, which by over-estimating the damage caused them to cease attacking target systems before they had been completely destroyed. Attacks on the civilian population were also less effective in breaking morale than had been expected. The German people felt that, with the formulation of the concept of Unconditional Surrender at the Casablanca Conference in 1943, there were only two alternatives left open to them, victory or annihilation. Thus terror attacks on German cities, horrific as they were in their destruction, could produce no worse than surrender, and if the German people fought on there was always the faint hope that perhaps some miracle might take place, which would tip the scales in their favour again.

None of this is to suggest that the strategic bombing campaign contributed little to final victory. For a start, it gave the Western Allies the means of striking directly at Germany during the period before they were sufficiently strong to reopen operations on the continent of Europe. It also contributed to the rejection of Russian criticism of their apparent tardiness in opening the 'Second Front'. Indeed the campaign contributed to Russian success in the east because it forced Hitler to divert aircraft and artillery for the defence of Germany from the front line. It also resulted in fighters being given priority in production over bombers and thus blunted the Luftwaffe's offensive capability. Finally, it helped to establish air supremacy in the West prior to the invasion, although at a cost, sometimes almost insupportable, in bombers and crews.

On the ground, the British, as has been stated earlier, benefitted from their experience in the North African desert, both in terms of handling armoured formations and in air-ground co-operation. Experience in the close country of Tunisia, Sicily and Italy, and the realisation that much of the fighting to come on the continent was likely to be also in close country unsuited to the deployment of mass armour put a brake on the number of armoured divisions being formed. Thus, by the beginning of 1944 there were only five in existence, compared with the eleven which had been planned for after the debacle of 1940. Indeed, there were signs that the pendulum was swinging back the other way, for there was an increase in the number of armoured units dedicated to infantry support. Furthermore, by 1944 the role of armoured divisions was being considered as one of exploitation only. This changing policy was also reflected in the tanks in use. The categorisation of tanks into cruiser and infantry types still existed in 1944. The latter type was now represented by the Churchill tank, which had first been introduced into service in 1940. The Mk VII version mounted a 75mm gun and was heavily armoured, but still, in the best infantry tank tradition, only had a top speed of 15mph. The armoured divisions continued to rely on the American Sherman with which they had fought the larger part of the Desert Campaign. There was also the British Cromwell, which came into service in 1944, two years later than it was due. The problem was that these two types also only mounted a 75mm gun, and were thus hopelessly outclassed by the Tiger and Panther. This indicated that British tanks were not expected to become embroiled in tank v tank battles, and that the 75mm was felt quite sufficient for both infantry support and exploitation. To be fair to the Americans, the size of their tanks had been limited very early in the war by the fact that they had to be shipped to the theatre of war, and it was thought that unless restrictions as to size were laid down, the quantity of tanks available might be severely restricted. Nevertheless, in the months before D-Day there were hasty efforts to fit a 17-pounder to some Shermans. This became known as the Sherman Firefly. However, for much of the fighting in North-West Europe there were only enough available to provide one per troop of four tanks in the British Army.

The American Armored Force, like the British armoured divisions, was initially the subject of grandiose organisational planning. Many thought that the Americans would require at least 50 armoured divisions in order to win the war, and members of the Armored Force itself were quite clear that they were going to play the leading part in the fighting in Europe, with the infantry merely assisting them through obstacles and helping with re-supply. General Macnair, who as Chief of Staff of the Army General Headquarters, and later Commander of the Army Ground Forces (AGF), was responsible for the organisation and training of the US army for war, was not of the same opinion. He saw the role of the Armored Force as primarily exploitation, after the more traditional arms, the infantry and artillery, albeit with tanks and aircraft support, had broken through the enemy's defences. Thus, only 16 armoured divisions were eventually created, and Macnair thought that this number was a luxury. The armoured divisions themselves were organised by 1942 into two armoured regiments each of one light and two medium tank battalions, an armoured infantry regiment of three battalions, a 105mm howitzer regiment, again of three battalions, an engineer battalion and supporting services. What was novel about the US armoured division was the introduction of two tactical headquarters, designated Combat Commands A and B. These equated to brigade head-quarters, but the significant difference was that they commanded no laid down mix of units, but had units put under their command for a particular operation. As the tactical situation changed so did the mix and numbers of units in each Combat Command. In theory Macnair had wanted to see the corps as the basic unit, each having a number of divisional headquarters which would operate in the same way as the combat commands. Thus infantry would be always assured of armoured support. However, this situation was never reached in practice. The basic corps organisation for the fighting in Europe was set at two armoured and two infantry divisions, the latter including tank battalions for infantry support. In 1943, in order to give the infantry divisions integral tank support, the armoured division was reduced by three battalions, including both light tank battalions. This left it, apart from the 2nd and 3rd Armored Divisions, which retained the old 1942 organisation, with three tank and three mechanised infantry battalions. Indeed, the new reorganisation resulted in 60 tank battalions being allocated for infantry support, while only 50 were retained in the armoured divisions. As Macnair himself wrote:

'An armored division is of value only in pursuit or exploitation. For plain and fancy slugging against an enemy who is unbroken or at least intact the tank battalion or group is adequate.' [1]

The Allied invasion of Normandy and the subsequent fighting before the break-out gave little chance to practice mobile warfare. The closeness of the *bocage*, meant that it became an infantryman's battle, with the armour being mainly employed in infantry support. However, airpower did play a significant part in the success of the landings. From April 1944 the Allies earmarked 2 000 fighters and 700 medium bombers for an operation to seal Normandy off from the remainder of France. In addition, in spite of the protests of RAF Bomber Command, their available strength of 1 000 heavy

198

bombers was also on call for this operation. The Germans assisted the plan because of Hitler's insistence on keeping the bulk of the panzer divisions well back, instead of committing them close to the coast. Thus when the Allies landed on June 6th, 1944, the Panzer divisions were unable to move up to Normandy immediately to push them back into the sea because the road and rail communications were destroyed. It was a classic example of the successful use of interdiction. The overwhelming air superiority of the Allies, once they were established in Normandy, acted against them in some ways. The use of 'aerial artillery' was taken to extremes, whereby ground objectives were softened up by 'carpet bombing' before an attack was launched. This technique involved bombers flying in a close box formation pulverising the target with a massive concentration of bombs. Although it did much for the morale of the attacking troops to see waves of bombers flying over their heads, often the technique worked against them, in much the same way as the artillery bombardments on the Western Front 1915-17. The damage caused hindered the mobility of the attackers, and often a surprising number of enemy troops survived the aerial bombardment, and threw the attackers off balance by their unexpected resistance. Another luxury in which the Allies were able to indulge was the 'cab-rank' system. Fighters and fighter-bombers maintained a constant patrol over the battle area, and could be called in whenever a suitable ground target appeared. This added greater flexibility to close ground support, compared with that of the Germans, who never had the aircraft available to do this.

In Normandy the German Tiger really came into its own. The lighter Allied tanks proved no match for it, and it was reckoned that one Tiger was equivalent to a whole squadron of Shermans. Nowhere was this better illustrated than in Operation Goodwood, the British attempt to draw the available German tank strength onto themselves, to enable the Americans to breakout out from the Normandy bridgehead. The plan was for three British armoured divisions to attack southwards, from just east of Caen, in order to seize the gently rising and dominating Bourgebus Ridge which guarded the open and therefore good tank country to the south of Normandy. If successful in capturing the ridge, they were ordered to exploit southwards to Falaise. The Germans had three panzer divisions with a total of some 400 AFVs and three weak infantry divisions in the area. The attack was launched at 0745 hours on, after a concentrated air and artillery bombardment, but the narrowness of the front meant that only one armoured division, the 11th, which had been trained by Hobart, could attack in the first phase. Preceded by a rolling artillery barrage, the leading brigade advanced, with one regiment, 3rd Royal Tank Regiment, up. Initially the attack went well. The Germans had been numbed by the preparatory bombardment. However, after an hour, in which the advance had gone some four miles, German resistance stiffened the closer the 11th Armoured Division got towards the Bourgebus Ridge itself. The German Tigers, Panthers and self-propelled guns started to take their toll. An officer in the leading brigade of 11th Armoured Division describes what it was like:

'We had advanced about four miles without much trouble and reached the line of the main railway. So far so good! But we now had no air support and the artillery barrage had ceased. It was, therefore, a question of advancing across this open country with the Germans presumably in possession of the high ground, the village and any other cover, including clumps of trees and so on. A decision had therefore to be made to send a squadron either round to the right towards the high ground, or to the left to outflank the village and secure protection from that area . . . It was no good sitting where we were, and the fateful decision was made. C Squadron would advance over the brow of a slight rise to the left in the direction of the village of Fours.

Bill, my squadron leader, gave his orders over the wireless in an excited voice, but they were perfectly clear. They were to be his last . . . As soon as Bill had completed his orders, we started to move slowly forwards. Within a few seconds Peter Robson's tank was hit by an .88 and went up in smoke. All the crew baled out safely. The rest of the squadron moved on and I could hear Jock Addison reporting a Panther on the outskirts of the village, which he was trying to engage. This was almost the last coherent message to be heard from the rest of the Squadron. They were all brought under heavy and accurate fire and within a matter of minutes about five tanks were on fire and another three out of action . . .

Everything was now in a state of chaos and the Squadron on the right was also being rapidly engaged by the enemy and losing tanks rapidly. A general withdrawal in the direction of the railway line took place, but it seemed to be only a matter of time before the rest of the regiment was written off.' [2]

The attack by 11th Armoured Division had been halted, and by the end of the day the division was reduced to less than 50% of its tank establishment, 126 being out of action. The Guards Armoured Division, which came up on the left of 11th Armoured during the later stages, also suffered a loss of some 60 tanks. The attack was continued next day, but few further gains were made and more heavy tank casualties were suffered. The attack failed to take the Bourgebus Ridge, but did succeed in causing the Germans to concentrate some seven of their nine panzer divisions in Normandy against the British, leaving the Americans with the opportunity for a successful breakout in the West.

The American breakout from St Lô was to be Patton's moment. After having proved himself as an able commander in North Africa and Sicily, he had come unstuck for a time after the famous 'face-slapping incident' when he had set about a soldier suffering from battle fatigue in a field hospital during the closing stages of the Sicilian campaign. He was tasked with the setting-up of the US Third Army in England, which prior to D-Day was a 'dummy' formation designed to make the Germans believe that the invasion was going to take place in the Pas de Calais rather than Normandy. It was not until July 7th that he actually flew across to Normandy. His Third Army was to be tasked with Operation Cobra, as the breakout was called. The plan was for Bradley's First US Army to make the initial penetration from St Lo, with its objective as Avranches, the significance of this town being that it was the entry to Brittany, as well as having good routes running eastwards towards the Seine and Paris. Once Bradley had secured this stepping stone, Patton's Third Army would then clear Brittany, paying special attention to the ports, which would be used as the main means of supplying the US armies in France, and then turn eastwards. The nature of the country through which Bradley would have to operate, with only two reasonable north-south routes in it, meant that he was going to have a hard slog to reach Avranches. In order to make things easier for himself, he planned to saturate a small area of 2 500 by 6 000 yards, with bombs. In this way he hoped to literally blast his way through the German defences, which consisted of nine infantry and two panzer divisions. No less than 1 887 bombers and 559 fighter bombers were made available for this task. It was originally planned to mount the operation on July 24th, but bad weather forced a postponement until the 25th.

The massive aerial bombardment had the desired effect, apart from some bombs which had fallen short and caused damage and casualties to Bradley's army*— another drawback of 'carpet bombing'. The German troops were dazed and Bradley was able to push steadily forwards. Meanwhile Montgomery prepared to launch an attack by the Canadian First Army at Falaise in order to prevent the Germans from transferring any troops westwards. By the 28th the Americans had advanced 10 miles to Coustances, and the back of the German defences had been broken. Three days later a thrust by 4th Armored Division captured Avranches, and on the next day, August 1st, Patton's Third Army was formally activated as a force rather than a paper formation. The time for the Allied version of blitzkrieg had come.

Patton's planning for the breakout had been done off a Michelin road map. All he was interested in were the road and rail links, and the rivers. His plan was thus simple and daring. The first move would be to strike south from Avranches to Rennes and so cut off all the German forces in the Brest peninsular. He would then send an armoured division to Brest, driving the Germans into the ports to be dealt with by the infantry later. This achieved he would then turn his three corps eastwards towards the Seine. In truth, he was not interested in the need to capture the Atlantic ports to ease the logistic situation. He was after nothing more than the total destruction of the German Army Group B. This lack of appreciation of the logistic aspect would create problems later for the Allies. Brest would not fall until mid-September, and the other two ports of note, Lorient and St Nazaire would hold out until the end of the war. On the tactical level, Patton appreciated the need for maintaining momentum and laid down a drill whereby as soon as an advance guard bumped the enemy, they would

*Among these was General McNair the Commander AGF who was visiting Normandy at the time, and had come up to watch the opening of Cobra.

contain him, while another advance guard continued the advance. This
continual leap-frogging would keep the enemy off balance, thus preventing
him from mounting counter-attacks. Like Guderian, Patton insisted on his
subordinate commanders being well forward. He himself did the same, and
had a special unit which provided patrols equipped with radios, which
ranged across the whole of his front reporting back directly to him.*

Patton imprinted his personality on Operation Cobra, from the moment
he took over. His first problem was the deploying of the two armoured
divisions, 4th and 6th, of VIII Corps, which were to carry out the Brittany
operation. With only one bridge open in Avranches, together with the
damage caused by the carpet bombing, and the fact that the Germans
chose to launch one of their few major air attacks of the campaign down the
route which the two divisions had to move, made it appear almost impossible
to get them forward. Patton, by the sheer force of his personality had them
ready to jump off from south of Avranches in 24 hours, using himself and
his subordinate commanders as traffic controllers. The two divisions then
cleared Brittany in four days, but could not prevent the Germans from
withdrawing to and holding the ports, which the Americans lacked the
strength to reduce. Many have criticised Eisenhower for his insistence on
capturing the Atlantic ports, when the opportunities to destroy Army Group
B by an immediate thrust towards the Seine would have reaped greater
benefits. Indeed, no one was more bitter than Wood, commanding 4th
Armored Division, who stated that:

> 'There was no conception of far-reaching directions for armour in the
> minds of our top people, nor of supplying such thrusts. I was still under
> the First Army, and it could not react fast enough. When it did react, its
> orders consisted of sending its two flank armoured divisions back, 180
> degrees away from the main enemy, to engage in seige operations against
> Lorient and Brest.' [3]

Undoubtedly Eisenhower was in a dilemma. He realised the importance of
opening up fresh ports in order to be able to support the Allied drive
through France logistically. On the other hand, lay the possibility of cutting
off Army Group B and destroying it. In the end he tried to do both, but
because he was forced to disperse his troops in order to carry out both
tasks, he found himself with not enough to do either.

On August 3rd Patton was finally ordered to wheel eastwards towards the
Seine. The idea was that Allied air bombardment would have destroyed all
the bridges across the river, thus trapping the Germans. To the north of
him, Hodges, now commanding First Army in place of Bradley, who had
been promoted to command Twelfth Army Group, which was made up of
First and Third US Armies, would conform to Patton's movements. Patton
gave his leading corps, XV, orders to head for Le Mans, while XX Corps to
the south went for the River Loire. Meanwhile Hodges was to drive towards
Alencon. By the evening of August 6th First and Third US Armies were well

---

*Montgomery used the same system with Phantom, as well as having liaison officers
answerable to him personally.

202

to the rear of the Germans, and with the Canadians now attacking at Falaise there were hopes that the remanants of Army Group B would be trapped and destroyed. At this stage, the Germans realising the threat against them, chose to counter-attack. Hitler ordered von Kluge to deploy eight out of his nine panzer divisions in a thrust from Mortain towards the bottleneck at Avranches. But, because of the overwhelming domination of the Allied air forces, which were constantly pounding the German lines of communication, von Kluge was able to muster four panzer divisions, with a total strength of only 185 tanks between them. The attack was launched soon after midnight on the August 6th/7th, and although some initial gains were made, the Americans stood firm and fought, particularly the 30th Infantry Division, to the west of Mortain. Then at midday on the 7th the mist and low cloud, which had covered the battlefield up until then, cleared, and the Allied air forces attacked the Germans, stopping them in their tracks. Although the fighting continued for another two days, the German effort at counter-attacking was doomed on this very first day. As the German General Westphal claimed: 'This was the first time in history that an attacking force had been stopped solely by bombing.' [4]

By the end of the first week of August two German Armies, Fifth Panzer and the Seventh, were enclosed in a salient, with its apex on Mortain and its base on the line Argentan-Falaise. The US First Army lay to the east covering Avranches, while the British Second Army stood on the north side of the salient. Meanwhile, the Canadians were about to push southwards from Caen towards Falaise. The opportunity was now present to trap these two German Armies in a much tighter encirclement than that originally envisaged. Consequently, Patton was ordered to despatch his XV Corps, which had taken Le Mans on the 8th, northwards to link up with the Canadians at Argentan. The Canadian drive, however did not go well, in spite of having 1 000 bombers to pave the way. It took them eight days of hard fighting to reach Falaise, a distance of some fifteen miles from their start line, and it was not until four days later, on the 20th, that they actually linked up with Patton's troops east of Argentan. This enabled the Fifth Panzer and Seventh Armies to extricate themselves. Much has been written about the failure to close the gap earlier. Indeed Patton was so exasperated at the time, when ordered by Bradley to halt at Argentan, that he spoke to Bradley over the telephone saying, albeit jokingly: 'Let me go to Falaise and we'll drive the British into the sea for another Dunkirk.' [5] Undoubtedly he could have got to Falaise, but there were aspects which supported Bradley's halt order. Firstly, Montgomery, who was in command of the battle had made it quite clear that the link-up would take place at Argentan. A change of plan would have forced both Canadians and Americans to cut down drastically on air and artillery support for fear of causing casualties to each other. Secondly, XV Corps would have become very extended, and it is questionable whether it would have been able to resist a determined German effort to break out. Indeed, as events later turned out, the Allies probably gained more by not closing the gap earlier, and wasting valuable time in reducing the resultant pocket. For, it is very likely that the

Germans, although surrounded, would have continued to fight fiercely. But although the Germans were allowed to escape, they left most of their equipment behind. One American officer described the pocket:

'as far as my eye could reach . . . on every line of sight, there were . . . vehicles, wagons, tanks, guns, prime movers, sedans, rolling kitchens, etc. in various stages of destruction . . . I stepped over hundreds of rifles in the mud and saw hundreds more stacked along sheds . . . I saw probably 300 field pieces and tanks, mounting large calibre guns, that were apparently undamaged.' [6]

Some 50 000 Germans were captured and another 10 000 killed. By August 28th Fifth Panzer Army could boast of a strength of no more than 1 300 men and 24 tanks. Seventh Army was in much the same state.

The Allies now entered their most spectacular phase of the North-West Europe Campaign, and that most similar to the German blitzkrieg. The remnants of the two German Armies were making their way back to the Seine as best they could, harried continually from the air. While the pocket was being sealed, the remainder of Patton's Third Army had been continuing its advance westwards. Chartres had fallen to XX Corps on the 15th, and to the south XII Corps, driving along the north bank of the Loire, had reached Orleans on the 16th. Indeed, earlier, on the 14th Patton had boasted: 'As of today Third Army has advanced farther and faster than any army in history.' [7] On the 15th, too, Sixth Army Group, with one French and one US Army, had landed on the French Riviera and started to push northwards.

There now loomed a major difference of opinion between the Allies. This was the 'Broad Front' versus 'Narrow Front' argument. Montgomery still nominally in charge of the ground forces, proposed that once the Seine had been crossed 20th and 21st Army Groups should advance side by side towards Antwerp, with their right flank on the Ardennes. Bradley, on the other hand, favoured capitalising on Patton's success, and making the main thrust to the east, aiming at the Rhine south of Frankfurt. Eisenhower had to mediate, and was faced with two problems, political and logistic. If either Ally was given the decisive role to itself, there was bound to be trouble in the political camp of the other. Secondly, the Allies were still wholly reliant on Cherbourg and the Mulberry harbours off the invasion beaches for all their supplies. It was clear that there was not sufficient logistic support to allow both army groups their heads. Yet, the rate of advance of both Montgomery and Bradley was accelerating. Hence for the moment Eisenhower was prepared to shelve any decision, in the hope that advances both north and south of the Ardennes might be sustained for a little longer, but he did give Montgomery some priority on supplies at the expense of Patton, because of the importance of gaining Antwerp so as to reduce the ever-stretching lines of communication.

It took 21st Army Group a few days to sort itself out after the reduction of Falaise, and it was not until the 26th that it started to close up to the Seine. Meanwhile, Patton's troops, led by Le Clerc's 2nd French Armoured

Division, had entered Paris on the 26th. The US Third Army had now advanced 400 miles in 26 days, inflicting some 100 000 casualties, including prisoners, on the enemy, as well as destroying or capturing 500 tanks and 700 guns. All this had been done at a cost of 16 000 American casualties. Indeed, it was a spectacular success. Patton's dash and drive had put him in the forefront of mechanised commanders. Admittedly much of his success had been in the face of weak opposition, but this does not detract from the soundness of his generalship. He had grasped one fundamental principle of blitzkreig, maintenance of momentum, and used it to the full.

Yet, Montgomery was now to show that he was not necessarily the cautious methodical commander he appeared to be. Having closed up to the Seine, he was now ready for his breakout. The way would be led by the British Second Army, with two corps up. The initial objective was given as Amiens, with Antwerp the final objective. Montgomery laid down that:

'Any tendency to be 'sticky' or cautious must be stamped on ruthlessly . . . The proper tactics are now for strong armoured and mobile columns to bypass enemy centres of resistance and to push boldly ahead creating alarm and despondency in the enemy rear areas.' [8]

This was an order which could well have come from the pen of Fuller, Liddell Hart or Guderian. On the 30th XII Corps, led by 7th Armoured Division, and XXX Corps, led by 11th and the Guards Armoured Divisions, broke out of their bridgeheads on the Seine. At first the advance proceeded somewhat cautiously in view of the lack of enemy opposition, but this was the first occasion on which the British armoured divisions had had a chance to operate properly away from the confines of the *bocage*, and not surprisingly their joints were a little stiff. Nevertheless, Amiens, lying 70 miles north of the Seine, was reached two days later. The remnants of the German Seventh Army tried vainly to set up some sort of defensive line along the Somme, but the British armour was too quick for them, and they found themselves outflanked. But a more spectacular advance was to come.

On September 2nd, Horrocks, commanding XXX Corps was handed a brief pencilled note from the Second Army commander, Dempsey. It said: Dear Jorrocks, You will capture (a) Antwerp, (b) Brussels. M. C. Dempsey.' [9] By the end of that day the leading elements had reached the River Scarpe, and pushing on through the night 11th Armoured Division reached Antwerp itself on the early afternoon of the 3rd, while the Guards Armoured Division had liberated Brussels the day before. This leap forward had covered no less than 230 miles in seven days, even more impressive than Patton's advance to the Seine. There was, however, one aspect which was to detract from the success of this operation. Although the city of Antwerp and its port facilities were captured, no effort was made to clear the Scheldt which linked it with the sea. Consequently it could not be used as a port. The main reason was because Montgomery was now looking towards the Ruhr. Yet, he was now forced to halt his forces for three days in order to pause for breath and allow supplies to catch up. This gave the Germans a chance to regroup, and by the time Montgomery got going again they were strong enough to hold him temporarily on the Meuse-Escaut Canal, which he reached on the 10th.

The US First Army, on Eisenhower's orders, although not under Montgomery's operational control, had kept in step with the British advance, covering their right flank. Patton, had continued his drive towards the south of the Ardennes, reaching the Meuse between Sedan and Commercy on the 31st. He felt the effects of the now overextended supply line just before Montgomery, for Eisenhower had ordered the bulk of the US fuel supplies to be given to Hodges' First Army so that.it could support Montgomery. Thus on August 30th Patton only received 32 000 gallons out of the 400 000 which he had demanded. Although he managed to get across the Meuse, it was clear that he would not be able to get much further. This did not deter Patton. Firstly, he realised that if he did actually run dry, Bradley would be forced to divert fuel from Hodges. Secondly, he had captured some 1 000 000 gallons, about which he kept quiet, besides unashamedly poaching fuel off Hodges. He was therefore determined to push on to the Rhine, in spite of the fuel restriction. At this stage Eisenhower summoned the top American commanders back to Versailles, and ordered Patton to stand fast, while the administrative effort was concentrated in the north, but Patton was able to convince Eisenhower that the opportunities in front of Third Army were too good to pass up. Hence he was allowed to continue towards the Saar. At the same time Montgomery was also pressing once more for the single thrust on the Ruhr and thence to Berlin. In the event, Patton, although given a bigger slice of the logistic cake, now found himself passing through country less favourable for large-scale armour operations. The Germans had managed to scrape together sufficient troops to slow down his advance, and from now on it would be rather more of a slog.

Montgomery, frustrated by the lack of supplies coming to him and the increasing German resistance, was now regrouping for a new operation called Market-Garden. As a sop to him for not being allowed to pursue the idea of a single thrust on Berlin, he had been allotted the First Allied Airborne Army for an operation designed to enable him to outflank the German West Wall and get over the Rhine. The airborne troops had been used extensively on D-Day, but since then had been kept on stand-by in England for a series of operations, none of which had been put into effect because of the unexpected speed of advance of the ground forces. The idea now was for three airborne divisions simultaneously to seize crossings over the Maas and Waal Rivers around Nijmegen and the Lower Rhine at Arnhem. XXX Corps would then link up with each in turn. It was an imaginative plan, and the use of the airborne troops would obviously help to continue the psychological dislocation of the Germans. In the event, the plan did not succeed for several reasons. It took too long to mount the operation, ten days, during which little pressure was maintained on the Germans in front of 21st Army Group, giving them further time to reorganise. The intelligence picture, especially around Arnhem, was over-optimistic, and Dutch Resistance reports of two panzer divisions refitting in the area were ignored by the Allied intelligence staffs. Finally, XXX Corps were only given one route on which to advance. The Lommel-Nijmegen-Arnhem Road had on either side marshy fields, which made bad going for the armour. Hence much of the time the Corps advance was restricted entirely to this road. When the leading vehicle became engaged then the whole advance halted until the opposition was neutralised. The Germans, too, became quickly aware of how vulnerable this thin needle-like advance was, and caused constant disruption by molesting it on the flanks. Nevertheless, XXX Corps did achieve a link-up with the US 101st Airborne, which had seized bridges over the Wilhemina Canal, and the 82nd Airborne Divisions, the latter in the Nijmegen area. It was only the main prize of the Lower Rhine crossings, which slipped from Montgomery's grasp after very gallant efforts by the British and Polish paratroops at Arnhem. If the operation had succeeded it is probable that the West Wall would have been turned and the Allies would have crossed the Rhine in strength before the end of the year. With the supply situation as chaotic as it was, however, it is doubtful whether the Allies would have been able to maintain the momentum required to take full advantage of this. As it was, with the weather and the supply situation deteriorating the British were forced to concentrate their attention on clearing the Scheldt, so that the port of Antwerp could be brought into action to sustain what was likely to be a much tougher campaign in crossing the Rhine. This occupied them until the end of October.

The liberation of France had given the Allies the opportunity to use their armour and air power in the way in which the pre-war theorists had preached and the Germans had practised. Although the pre D-Day planners had taken a somewhat cautious view of the way the drive through France would go, when the opportunity presented itself, the British and American commanders had shown that the close-quarter fighting in the Normandy bocage had not dulled their senses. They had, particularly Patton and then Montgomery, taken the maximum possible advantage of that opportunity, and shown as much dash as Guderian and the other Panzer leaders had at the height of their powers. They failed to bring the war to an end in 1944 for logistic and political reasons. While most German commanders stated after the war that the single thrust would have worked, because it would have given no time for the Germans to throw up a proper defensive line, it was unacceptable politically and would have been difficult to support logistically. The former reason has already been touched upon. Eisenhower, as Supreme Allied Commander, had above all else to maintain cohesion between the Allies. With such strong personalities as Montgomery and Patton to contend with, his task was difficult at the best of times. Only one man could command the thrust, and be he British or American, he would naturally want his own country's troops to play the leading role. Thus only one country would get the limelight, causing resentment in the other. Hence Eisenhower was forced to compromise, which meant adopting the 'Broad Front' strategy.

207

The logistic aspect is similar to that which the Germans faced in Russia. But while in the German case, there was an increasing lack of understanding of the massive logistical requirements needed for the successful conduct of the blitzkreig, the Allies went wrong because they had not foreseen prior to the start of the campaign that the opportunities for blitzkreig would be so great. Thus the planners, although they had estimated that the Allies would close up to the Seine only thirteen days after they actually did so, did not expect the frontier with Germany to be reached until 300 days after D-Day, while Patton was on the Moselle in D+96. They had envisaged the Germans falling back in line, with the Allies steadily pushing them back. In this event of the flow of supplies through Mulberry and Cherbourg would have sufficed because there would have been no sudden stretching of the supply lines to the front. Admittedly the Allies, with their vast air superiority, could have done more than they did to keep the armoured thrusts supplied by air. As it was, a large proportion of the air transport fleet was earmarked for possible Allied Airborne Army operations. The Germans, too, aggravated the situation. Many have blamed Hitler for needlessly throwing away men by condemning them to hold out in 'fortresses' long after the Allied troops had passed them by. But, by doing this to the Brittany and Channel ports, their use was effectively denied to the Allies at the crucial time of the breakout over the Seine and beyond. The failure to clear Antwerp also magnified the problem. In addition, the continuous 'carpet-bombing' may have saved the Allies casualties and weakened the resistance of the Germans. But since much of it was concentrated on the German lines of communication, it acted against the Allies when they wanted to use these same lines in a hurry.

During the autumn and early winter the British and Americans slowly closed up to the West Wall, as the Siegfried Line was now called. The weather and the nature of the country gave them no chance to use armour *en masse*. But, during the months of October and November the Germans took advantage of the slow Allied progress to regroup for a counter-attack.

The origins of the Ardennes offensive, or the Battle of the Bulge as it has come to be called, lay in the halting of Patton's Army in mid-September, while Operation Market-Garden was being mounted. It had become increasingly clear in Hitler's mind that, with the Allied insistence on unconditional surrender, to remain on the defensive in both the East and West, might prolong the war, but could only lead to the eventual defeat of Germany. He therefore concluded that if he could mount a paralysing attack against the Western Allies, it would enable him to transfer sufficient numbers of troops in order to shore up his defences in the East. He realised the importance of Antwerp to the British and Americans, and hence considered it as the objective most likely to produce the required result. He was confident that this attack could be launched by mid-November, thus assuring a transfer of troops eastwards before Christmas. Indeed, winter had been slow coming on the Eastern Front, and hence the Russians were not expected to launch their next major blow until the new year, when they could be sure that the ground was hard enough not to affect mobility.

208

Hitler had ordered the formation of 25 new divisions at the beginning of September, and these were earmarked for the Western Front. Previous to this he had ordered 18 to be raised in July, of which two were to go to the West. The manpower for these new divisions came from scouring civilian occupations. The 27 divisions allocated for the operation were given the best equipment, apart from transport, for which they would be reliant on horse and bicycle. During the summer some 1 500 tanks had been built and these were all consigned to the West, where the panzer divisions, nine of which were earmarked for the operation, were slowly and discreetly drawn to the rear for refitting. In addition, ten tank brigades, built round a Panther battalion were formed — the only time during the war when the Germans formed independent tank formations at lower than divisional level.

Although Hitler had made up his mind in September that this operation was to take place, he maintained a veil of secrecy over it. Indeed, it was not until towards the end of October that he told von Rundstedt, the Commander-in-Chief in the West, about it. Von Rundstedt tried to find out during October as to why more and more troops were being drawn off to Sixth Panzer Army, newly formed for the counter-offensive, and why Fifth Panzer Army was withdrawn in toto. The only answer he could get was that these were to counter an expected Allied offensive in the Cologne-Bonn area. It was not until October 24th that he was let into the secret, and then he was flabbergasted. Hitler had decreed that the thrust would be made through the boundary between the US First and Third Armies in the Ardennes, but von Rundstedt reckoned that this could only be done with large well equipped forces with plenty of air cover. As he later declared at his trial at Nuremburg:

'My entire general staff training revolted against an operation of this sort. If old von Moltke thought that I had planned this offensive he would turn in his grave . . .

My lack of resources was such that I could not countenance the idea of this counter offensive. Our forces were far, far too weak for such immense objectives . . . With our Luftwaffe knocked out we had to move only at night, whereas Patton could wind up his tanks and move day or night right into our positions. Our man-power was all shot too. All we had was the rundown old men who could not fight and foreigners who kept deserting.' [9]

But, without listening to his objections Hitler despatched Jodl to the headquarters of Field-Marshal Model, now commanding Army Group B, to give the details of the operation.

In essence, Hitler based the success of the counter-offensive on five prerequisites. Firstly, von Rundstedt had to hold back the Allies without calling on the troops allocated for the counter-offensive, which was planned for November 25th. Complete tactical surprise must be achieved, and a period of at least ten days bad weather was needed in order to keep the Allied air forces grounded. There must be speedy exploitation of the breakthrough, and relative peace on other fronts. The idea was quickly to seize bridgeheads over the Meuse, and then, bypassing Brussels, drive for Antwerp. At the same time the lines of communication of the US First Army in the Meuse Valley, and those of 21st Army Group with Antwerp would be cut, as well as separating the British from the Americans. In many ways this plan bore marked similarity to Ludendorf's concept for March 1918. The reliance on bad weather to neutralise the enemy's air superiority, the driving of a wedge between Allies, and the speedy exploitation of tactical success were all hallmarks of March 1918. The Sixth Panzer Army under Sepp Dietrich would make the main effort, seizing crossings over the Meuse on either side of Liege then crossing the Albert Canal between Maastricht and Antwerp before advancing into the area north of Antwerp. For this task it was allocated four SS Panzer Divisions, which unlike their Wehrmacht counterparts had a guaranteed strength of two tank battalions and an additional two panzer grenadier battalions, and five infantry divisions. Von Manteuffel's Fifth Panzer Army with four panzer and three infantry divisions was to cross the Meuse to the south of Sepp Dietrich, and then cover his rear and left flank along a line Dinant-Namur-Brussels-Antwerp. Finally, the Seventh Army, commanded by Brandenburger, was to employ its one panzer and six infantry divisions to cover the southern flank of the operation, linking up with the northern flank of Army Group G to the south of Luxembourg. The northern flank would be taken care of by a subsidiary attack mounted by Fifteenth Army towards Maastricht from the north-east. Goering had promised to produce 3000 aircraft, including 100 Me262 jets, in support of the operation. But these aircraft had to come from Galland's carefully built up strategic fighter reserve for the defence of Germany against the strategic bombing campaign of the Allies.

Unlike operations in 1940, Hitler insisted that the infantry should be used to carry out the initial break-in of the enemy defensives. Once the gap had been made, the panzers would then be unleashed. He also laid down that a continuous three hour bombardment should be laid down all along the front, and that H-Hour should not be until 1100 hours. The generals who were to carry out this operation were all unhappy about the plan. They believed that Hitler was asking for too much, considering the limited forces available. Indeed Model had fewer troops than Army Group A had had in May 1940 to attack through the Ardennes. He lacked the air superiority that von Rundstedt had then had, and was also up against an experienced and strong enemy. Besides these handicaps, in 1940 there had been a reserve of 45 divisions, whereas the Germans were now hardpressed to raise more than four. Indeed Model argued fiercely for a more limited operation designed to cut off the Americans around Aachen, but Hitler would not countenance it. The Army Group commanders did, however, manage to persuade Hitler that November 25th was too early, and the operation was put back until December 10th. Hitler also agreed that H-Hour should be brought forward to 0530 hours in order to allow the attacking troops all available daylight hours in which to make the initial penetration. The bombardment was cut to three-quarters of an hour, and would concentrate merely on key points such as headquarters and communication centres in order to cause disruption of the American command structure.

While preparation for Operation *Wacht Am Rhein* (Watch on the Rhine), as it was called (although changed to the more apt title of Autumn Fog on December 6th), were underway, the Americans, had been maintaining continual effort all along their front in an effort to get to the Rhine before the end of the year. In particular there was fierce fighting around the River Roer, and that around the Huertgen Forest was paralleled by those that fought there to Verdun in 1916. The net effect of this was to prevent the Germans from giving adequate rest and training to many formations which were to take part in the counter-offensive. Notwithstanding this, some of the more mangled US formations were sent down to the Ardennes to regain their strength, little knowing what would be in store for them. Indeed, from the Allied point of view, the remarkable aspect of the battle was the failure of the Allied intelligence agencies to appreciate what the Germans were planning. Although, indicators such as low grade divisions holding the front line, and movement of tanks etc, were apparent, Eisenhower's intelligence officers chose to discount these, believing that the Germans were no longer capable of mounting a major offensive. Thus when the blow did fall it was to be left to a mixture of four tired and unblooded US divisions to bear the brunt of the attack. However, the Germans did take infinite pains to ensure secrecy. The troops taking part were not informed until the last possible moment. The wooded area of the Eifel, behind the German lines was an ideal assembly area, and they tried to restrict movement to the hours of darkness.

The heavy American pressure caused the attack to be postponed to December 16th. The detailed orders laid down that it was essential that the panzers did not become embroiled in eradicating isolated pockets of resistance. They must push on. Besides the reason of maintaining momentum, there was a logistical aspect to this. The panzer divisions only had two days of fuel, and, although it was hoped that this would be enough to get them across the Meuse, after that they were reliant on captured stocks. The longer it took them to get across the Meuse, the less the chance of getting hold of these stocks. They knew too that the American defence was based on a series of strongpoints supported by artillery and mechanised counter-attack forces — the ideal way to defend against a blitzkrieg attack. Another dark spot was that the Luftwaffe had not been able to produce more than a fraction of the aircraft promised, hence the attackers would just have to hope that the meteorologists were right in their predictions of bad weather.

At dawn on the 16th after an initial bombardment of three-quarters of an hour, elements of the Fifth and Sixth Panzer Armies infiltrated through the American front lines. Included among their number were a number of Germans disguised in American uniforms. Their object was to follow up the confusion caused by the initial bombardment, and to do all they could to disorganise the Americans. At 0730 hours, two hours after the initial bombardment had opened, the main attack went in. The weather forecasters had been right. The thick fog successfully kept all Allied aircraft on the

211

ground. But against this advantage was the fact that Russian pressure in the East had forced Hitler to transfer more troops there, which meant that the Fifteenth Army attack would not take place, and the strength of Seventh Army was reduced. Thus, Sixth Army quickly found itself held up on the right because the Americans were able to deploy reserves quickly from the north. In addition, the country over which Sepp Dietrich was expected to operate was not good tank country, consisting of areas of high ground surrounded by narrow river valleys. The mud and the slush helped little as well. Thus by midday on the first day of the offensive Sixth Panzer Army was already behind schedule. Von Manteuffel had better success. In his own words: 'My storm battalions infiltrated rapidly into the American front — like rain-drops. At 4 o'clock in the afternoon the tanks advanced and pressed forward in the dark with the help of 'artificial moonlight'*' [10] But, in the south, Brandenburger, robbed of his one panzer division, which had not materialised, had little success. This had the effect of exposing von Manteuffel's right flank.

During the next three days the Germans continued to attempt to push forward. Unfortunately they made two serious mistakes. Hitler was determined that the original plan, which called for Sepp Dietrich to take the leading role, be strictly adhered to. Consequently he refused to reinforce the success which von Mantueffel had had. Secondly, the key point in von Manteuffel's sector was undoubtedly Bastogne, which was the main communications centre in the southern part of the battle area. Any Allied counter-attack had to come through this town. It had been hoped to reach Bastogne in the first twenty-four hours of the attack, but it was not until the 19th that the Panzer Lehr Division, after suffering the frustrations of being held up by poor roads, reached the town. The original plan was for it to bypass the town, leaving it to be reduced by the follow-up Volksgrenadier Division moving behind it. But now von Manteuffel was not so sure:

'To invest Bastogne would mean a further draught on our already inadequate resources. Bastogne in American hands would remain a magnet for the enemy's forces, and thus a permanent danger for us, since were they to relieve the beleaguered town it would provide them with an excellent jumping-off point from which to imperil our entire offensive operation. On the other hand were we now to commit the whole XLVIIth Panzer Corps to the capture of Bastogne, it would mean that we had, at best temporarily, abandoned our offensive plans, since this would put a stop to any further advance westwards.' [11]

As so often happens in this sort of situation, von Manteuffel adopted a compromise; the panzers were to push on leaving the infantry to reduce Bastogne. This was the worst of both options, for the tanks were now unsupported, and the infantry, in the face of the US 101st Airborne

*A method of increasing the light over the battlefield at night by reflecting searchlight beams off clouds. This technique was also used by the Allies.

Division, which, with elements of the 10th Armored Division, was holding the town, were not strong enough to take it. The holding of Bastogne became an epic in the history of American arms, epitomised by the commander, Brigadier-General McAuliffe's reply of 'Nuts!' when called upon to surrender. With the thorn of Bastogne at his back, von Manteuffel, as he had feared, was finished. The furthest point westwards which he would reach would still be more than five miles short of the Meuse. By then Patton's Third Army was poised to drive up from the south to relieve Bastogne. Meanwhile, in the north Gerow's US V Corps continued to hold stubbornly onto the northern shoulder, thus limiting Sepp Dietrich's freedom of action. Although Group Peiper, which had been given the task of driving ahead of the main attack in order to seize bridges across the Meuse, actually seized Stavelot and came within an ace of capturing the American fuel depots south of Spa.

After two days, the low cloud and mist, which had hampered Allied air activity, started to clear, and more and more pressure was put on the German lines of communication as the days went by. In addition, the Americans, instead of panicking, had, although bypassed, fought on in isolated pockets, as well as destroying fuel stocks. Thus the panzer divisions began to run out of fuel, while the following infantry became involved in reducing these American pockets, and were thus unable to support the panzers. There was initially a difference of opinion between Montgomery and Bradley as to how to deal with the German assault. Montgomery was in favour of letting the Germans come on until they had over-extended themselves, before decapitating the penetration. In this way, the Allies would be saved casualties, and would be certain of dealing a death-blow. His experiences in North Africa, together with the realisation that too many casualties at this stage would only prolong the final battle cautioned him against any precipitate counter-attack. The Americans thought differently. To them it was a matter of honour that they should counter-attack straightaway in order to regain the ground which they had lost. Casualties were not so important, for there were still several more US divisions en route from the United States to the European theatre. To an extent, both pursued their own beliefs. Montgomery made little effort to counter-attack in the north, merely deploying his forces in blocking positions, while in the south, Patton switched his army through ninety degrees, and started to push northwards, relieving Bastogne on the 26th. In many ways, his drive was disappointing. He had hoped to cut right through the German salient, but such was his hurry to attack that preparations and planning were barely adequate, leading to considerable confusion, which slowed down the advance. Nevertheless, by December 26th, the Germans had realised that their offensive had failed. Dominated by the stupendous air power of the Allies, which had quickly driven the Luftwaffe from the skies over the Ardennes, and short of petrol and munitions there could be no more going forward. Model thus recommended to Hitler that he should merely consolidate his gains. Hitler, however, thwarted of his original objective of Antwerp, was determined to try elsewhere. Thus, while he agreed to Model's proposal, he

213

also laid down that another operation be mounted to the south in Alsace.

Known as Operation North Wind, this was launched on December 31st with eight divisions, but made little headway, in spite of provoking a row between Eisenhower and de Gaulle over the planned evacuation of Strasbourg. Its effect was merely to fritter away more German reserves, and divert badly needed supplies from the Ardennes salient. Here on January 3rd, Montgomery's troops joined in the counter-attack, and on the same day Hitler reluctantly agreed to a withdrawal. This was carried out slowly and skilfully by the Germans, who could now take advantage of the defensive possibilities of the close country over which they had tried to attack. They were helped too by the fact that bad weather again grounded the Allied air forces. The final blow came from the east on January 12th when Koniev launched his long-awaited offensive from the Baranov bridgehead. It was now essential that all possible troops were transferred eastwards, and the departure of Sixth Panzer Army followed almost immediately. This signalled the end of the Battle of the Bulge, and by the end of January the battle lines were back where they had been six weeks before, at the start of the operation.

The Germans failed because Hitler had set an objective which was beyond the capabilities of his troops in the context of late 1944. What had been possible in May 1940 was no longer the case four and a half years later. They were now facing an experienced, well-equipped enemy who would not panic if he was caught with his guard down. Guderian had proved that the Ardennes were passable for tanks in summer, but it did not follow that they would be so in the depths of winter. The Germans also lacked two essential elements for blitzkrieg, which they had possessed in 1940 — air superiority and sufficient fuel stocks. In addition, Hitler showed an inflexibility totally in opposition to the idea of blitzkrieg in his refusal to reinforce the early success of von Manteuffel at the expense of Sepp Dietrich. Thus, although the Germans succeeded in inflicting some 76 000 casualties on the Western Allies and postponed the final battle for a few weeks, their own losses of 100 000, together with 1 600 aircraft, and some 600 tanks could not be replaced. These losses merely had the effect at best of cancelling the delay in final defeat gained by mounting Operation Autumn Mist.

By the end of February the British and Americans were through the West Wall and closing up fast on the Rhine. First across were elements of the US First Army, which seized the bridge at Remagen before it could be blown on March 7th, but this could not be exploited, in spite of driving a crucial hole in the German defences, because of the nature of the countryside east of the river. Nevertheless, Hodges succeeded in drawing onto himself enough German forces intent on eradicating the bridgehead, that the defences along the Rhine elsewhere were seriously weakened. Three weeks later Montgomery was across the Rhine south of Wessel, and Patton, and Patch's Seventh US Army, south of Mainz. While Montgomery and Bradley sealed off the Ruhr, Dever's Sixth Army Group, moved south-eastwards towards the Austrian border. Meanwhile, in the East, the Russians reached the Elbe, 60 miles from Berlin, on April 11th. Two weeks later they had

Berlin surrounded, and had joined hands with the Western Allies. On May 8th the fighting in Europe came to an end.

The fighting in North-West Europe during the latter half of 1944, had shown that the British and Americans had profited much from the German experience. The break-out from the Normandy beachhead had once again shown how devastating the internal combustion engine in the air harnessed to that on the ground could be. But even then, the late summer of 1944 had shown that there were aspects of this type of warfare that the Western Allies, like the Germans, did not fully appreciate. In particular, the logistic problem dogged the British and Americans almost as much as it had the Germans in Russia. The war did not end in 1944 simply because the British and Americans could not provide sufficient logistic support in time. The 'Single Thrust' might have got to the Rhine by Autumn 1944, but would not have ended the war by the end of the year as Montgomery postulated. Even had it had the supplies to support it, the Germans, who in both wars had built up a reputation for quick reaction in defence, especially in mounting counter-attacks, would certainly have been able to muster sufficient forces to cut off the head of the Allied thrust once it was east of the Rhine. The Anglo-American effort fizzled out after Operation Market-Garden because not enough emphasis was placed on opening up the Atlantic and Channel Ports. As the Germans learnt at Bastogne, blitzkreig might mean speed, surprise, concentration of effort and maintenance of momentum, which demanded bypassing opposition in order to push to the rear so as to achieve the maximum psychological dislocation. There were however exceptions to this rule. Strongpoints which were either on the main axis of advance or able to influence the logistic plan must be cleared early, even at the cost of slowing down momentum temporarily.

A noticeable contrast between the Anglo-American and German methods was in the employment of airpower. The Luftwaffe was a first-rate tactical air force, but as had been found in Russia, was not capable of strategic interdiction, by which it is meant the interruption of supplies at their source. The RAF and USAAF were essentially strategic air forces, which were used tactically in Normandy. Their interdiction operations prior to Normandy were overwhelmingly successful in preventing the Germans from reinforcing their troops in Normandy after the initial landings, but when used in the strictly tactical role in the pre-break-out battles they became a two-edged weapon. Nevertheless, the ground troops continued to call for heavy bomber support in the aerial artillery role even after it had been removed from Eisenhower's operational control. Thus the strategic bombing orientated Allied Air Staff, who still believed that they could shorten the war on their own by continuous pounding of Germany, showed themselves more and more unwilling to divert strategic aircraft to a strictly tactical role. Used in the interdiction role there was also the drawback that once the break-out had occurred the same lines of communication as used by the Germans were needed in a hurry by the Allies, but the 'carpet-bombing' technique meant that it needed time for the necessary repairs to get them working to be carried out. The Luftwaffe-style tactical air force was not

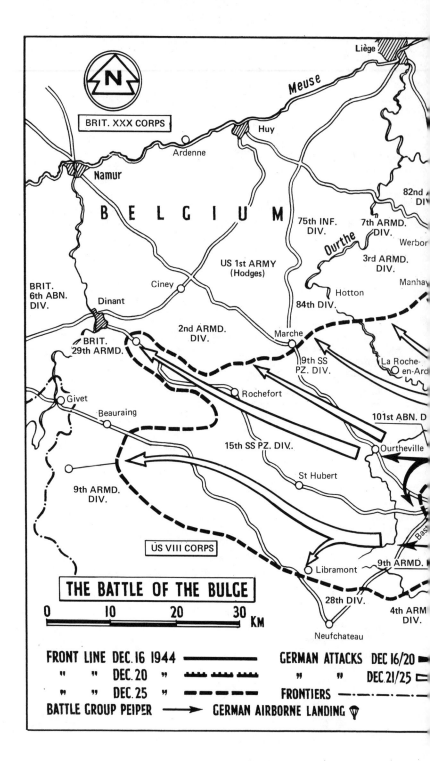

Liège

Meuse

BRIT. XXX CORPS

Huy

Ardenne

82nd A.
DIV

B E L G I U M

75th INF.
DIV.

7th ARMD.
DIV.

Werbor

Ourthe

US 1st ARMY
(Hodges)

3rd ARMD.
DIV.

Manhay

Ciney

Hotton

BRIT.
6th ABN.
DIV.

Dinant

84th DIV.

Marche

La Roche-
en-Ard

BRIT.
29th ARMD.

2nd ARMD.
DIV.

9th SS
PZ. DIV.

Givet

Beauraing

Rochefort

101st ABN. D

15th SS PZ. DIV.

Ourtheville

St Hubert

9th ARMD.
DIV.

US VIII CORPS

Bas

Libramont

9th ARMD.

THE BATTLE OF THE BULGE

28th DIV.

4th ARM
DIV.

0          10          20          30
KM

Neufchateau

FRONT LINE DEC. 16 1944 ——————     GERMAN ATTACKS DEC 16/20 ➤
   "        "     DEC. 20   "   ▰▰▰ ▰▰▰ ▰▰▰        "        "     DEC. 21/25 ⊏
   "        "     DEC. 25   "   – – – – – –    FRONTIERS —·—·—·—
BATTLE GROUP PEIPER ——➤     GERMAN AIRBORNE LANDING ⊽

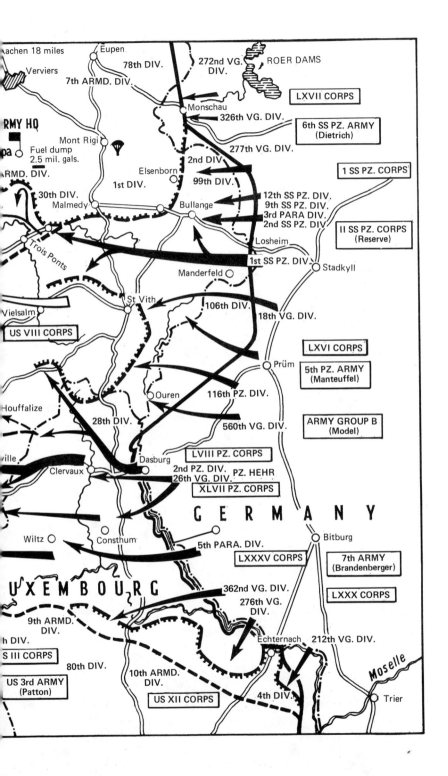

enough, but then neither was the sledgehammer strategic force. The answer lay in the middle — a balance between the two.

Nevertheless, in spite of these imperfections, the Allies produced commanders, especially Patton, who in execution if not deep thought, were on equal terms with Guderian and the other Panzer commanders. Yet, post-war practical experience in the art of blitzkrieg would not be given to any of those nations who had used it in World War 2.

**Notes**

1  Greenfield, Palmer and Wiley, *The Organisation of Ground Combat Troops* p 334.
2  Bishop, *The Battle* pp 45-7.
3  Liddell Hart, *History of the Second World War* op cit p 557.
4  Westphal, op cit p 196.
5  Essame, *Patton the Commander* p 167.
6  Blumenson, *Breakout and Pursuit* p 558.
7  Essame, op cit p 173.
8  *The Tanks* vol 2 op cit p 404.
9  Nobecourt, *Hitler's Last Gamble* p 52.
10  Liddell Hart, *The German Generals Talk* p 459.
11  Westphal, op cit p 243.

# The Sword is Handed On

Since 1945 the majority of wars have been of a counter-insurgency nature, usually following the four classic stages of revolutionary warfare — preparation, active resistance, insurgency and the open offensive. There have been exceptions. The Korean War, although a war of movement during the initial stages, soon settled down to resemble much of the Western Front 1914-1918 because of the terrain, which favoured the defence, and the United Nations policy which, after the counter-invasion of North Korea in 1950, was strictly defensive. The Indo-Pakistan War of 1965 was fought on very limited fronts, and although mechanised forces were used extensively by both sides, neither was prepared to fight for other than strictly limited objectives. Only in the Middle East has there been any resemblance to the blitzkrieg operations of World War 2. Here the Israelis have fought four campaigns against their Arab neighbours, employing in each many of the principles of blitzkrieg. Indeed, it is clear that the Israelis have to a large extent taken up the sword fashioned by the military thinkers of 1919-1939, and wielded by the Germans, and later the Allies, in 1939-45. However, Israel did not immediately adopt this technique on gaining her independence in 1948. She re-developed it from scratch, using not theory, but hard-gained practical experience as her baseline.

The origins of the Israeli Armed Forces lie in the formation of guards to protect Jewish settlements in Palestine from marauding Arabs at the end of the last century, when the area was still under Turkish rule. In 1907 these guards were organised into a body called the *Hashomer* ('watchmen'). After World War 1 this body was put on a more formal footing with an expansion in numbers and the formation of a small permanent cadre. It became known as the *Haganah*. However, it still remained strictly a police, rather than a military force. But, the Arab riots of 1929 forced it to pay more attention to military training, which was done in secret. It was the outbreak of the Arab Rebellion in Palestine in 1936, which caused emphasis to be given to creating a more military flavour. Having been a strictly defensive organisation, it began in a small way to take to the offensive against the Arabs. The man who stage-managed this shift in emphasis was Orde Wingate, a British Army Officer, who was later to win much fame as the leader of the Chindits in Burma during 1943-44. He organised what were called 'Special Night Squads', whose object was to counter Arab terrorism by aggressive means. They were made up of a mixture of *Haganah* members, Palestine Police and British soldiers. So successful were they, that

Jewish morale was considerably raised and Wingate himself became an Israeli folk hero. He also left a legacy in the form of principles of war, which were to be eagerly grasped by the Israeli forces some ten years later. Above all, he had emphasised the importance of mobility, surprise and aggressive action.

With the dying down of the Arab Rebellion in 1939, the *Haganah* became a proscribed organisation, and was forced underground. But, in 1941 when Rommel seemed to be knocking at the gates of Cairo, and German influence in Iraq and Syria was at its height, the *Haganah* was once more allowed into the open. For, in the event of Palestine having to be evacuated by the British, the latter resolved that a 'fifth column' should stay behind to harry the Germans. The *Haganah* was the natural body to fulfil this role. Later a Jewish Brigade was formed as part of the British Army and fought in Italy during 1944-45. With the coming of peace in 1945 the *Haganah* went voluntarily underground resolved to fight for independence. But, up until the end of 1947 the policy was defensive, and the Jewish Agency, which was the unofficial government until independence, concentrated on consolidating territory held by the Jews, and in smuggling illegal immigrants into Palestine. Meanwhile, the *Haganah* concentrated on military training, and made few aggressive actions, and then only to seize arms from the British.

On November 29th, 1947 the United Nations, after six months of debate, passed a resolution partitioning Palestine into a Jewish state and an Arab state, with Jerusalem being place under an international trusteeship with the United Nations being made the administering authority. In addition, the British mandate over Palestine would be terminated and British forces would be withdrawn by no later than August 1st, 1948. This Resolution was carried in the face of bitter Arab opposition to the whole idea of partition and the formation of a Jewish state. The result was that the Arabs, having been thwarted in the political arena, determined to achieve their objective of an independent Arab-dominated Palestine by force. The war that followed was to carry on until Spring 1949. It would consist of four distinct phases, and during this time the *Haganah* would develop from an irregular guerrilla force into a conventional army.

While the British remained in occupation, the Arab states of Egypt, Trans-Jordan, Iraq, Syria and Lebanon were not prepared to invade Palestine. Instead there was a period of minor battles fought for the control of roads and strongpoints, with the British taking on more and more the role of bystander. The main tasks of the *Haganah* were to hold onto remote settlements and continue the consolidation of those areas populated by the Jews. At the same time they were careful not to involve themselves in any major confrontation with the British or Arabs. Simultaneously the organisation had to be established on a proper war footing in order to face the Arab invasion which was bound to come once the British had withdrawn. It was this last task which was the most formidable. For a start, although by May 1948 the *Haganah* could boast of a strength of 35000, there were only sufficient small arms for 20000, and there were no heavy weapons available. There was as well a debate on the form that the *Haganah* should take. Here two extremes of thought existed. The one school, whose experience was drawn from the ranks of the Jewish Brigade argued that the force should be organised on conventional European lines. The other, drew on the existing offensive military arm of the *Haganah*, the *Palmach*, which was a commando-style organisation politically biased to the left and having little military discipline. The only common bond between the two was Wingate's 'legacy'. If the situation facing the new formed State of Israel had not been so grave this debate might have raged on for some time. As it was, Ben Gurion, the leading political figure, leant more towards the conventional force in terms of organisation, although the tactics of the Israeli Defence Force (IDF) would not bear much relation to those learnt by the Jewish Brigade in the relatively static conditions of Italy.

By the beginning of May 1948 the British withdrawal was complete and the time for 'Phase Two' had arrived. Israel was now subjected to invasion by five Arab regular armies operating on four fronts. Quite clearly, the IDF was not in a position to adopt successfully any form of static defence, having neither the men or the equipment to do so. Yet it was able to prevent the Arabs from making significant inroads in Israeli territory. They achieved this not by defeating the Arab armies, but by slowing them down and preventing any concerted action between them. This involved holding onto points of tactical importance in the path of the Arab axes of advance, and 'tip and run' attacks. It is unlikely that the Israelis could have successfully maintained this approach indefinitely, but in this instance they were saved by the imposition of a ceasefire by the UN on June 11th. The ceasefire allowed the IDF a valuable breathing-space. Its strength was growing and it was starting to obtain more weapons from Jewish sympathisers in Europe and America. However, this pause lasted only for four weeks. In spite of UN efforts to extend the ceasefire, the Arabs resumed their offensive on July 7th. But, in this short space of time the IDF had developed its tactics further, and mounted a series of very limited counter-offensives, constantly shifting the emphasis between the four fronts. This kept the Arabs off balance and again prevented any significant incursions into Israel. Ten days later the UN-invoked Chapter VII of the UN charter, ordering all parties to desist from military action. This resulted in a further ceasefire, which was destined to last longer than the first, giving more valuable time for the IDF to organise itself.

By this time the IDF had reached a strength of some 60 000 men and there were sufficient weapons to arm them all. The country was divided into four territorial commands, each with a small striking force of its own. At the same time some artillery, a few aircraft, and some tanks were obtained, and the Force started to take on the appearance of a proper military formation. In addition, it had obtained a motley collection of half-tracks, lorries and make-shift armoured cars, which improved its mobility.

The war entered its final phase when large-scale fighting broke out in the Negev area, just to the north and east of what was later to become known as the Gaza Strip. The major effect of the limited Israeli offensives during 'Phase Three' had been to force the Arabs onto the defensive. When the

221

fighting was resumed it was now the Israelis who took to the offensive from the start in a series of limited operations. The first of these, known as Operation *Yoav* ('Ten Plagues'), had as its objective the relief of the Jewish Negev, which had become cut off from the rest of Israel during the first Egyptian attack in May. The Egyptians could naturally expect the Israelis to attempt a relief operation, and had prepared comprehensive defences. Thus, wherever the Israelis attacked it would have to be frontal. However, all the Egyptian positions lacked depth, consisting of a number of strips, bounded by the sea in the West, the sandwich between Israel and the beleaguered Negev in the centre, and the mountains of Judea in the east. Consequently the Israelis resolved to disrupt the Egyptians by cutting their lines of communication within these strips. For this purpose the embryo Israeli Air Force (IAF) was used to transport a striking force into the Negev before the operation commenced, and on the October 16th this force virtually severed the Egyptian communications in the coastal strip. The day before the IAF had also struck at Egyptian airfields in Sinai, thus enabling the Israelis to have air supremacy throughout the operation. In addition, a series of commando raids were launched in the area of El-Arish to disrupt the enemy further. In the east another force seized dominating ground in the foothills of the mountains, thus threatening the eastern strip.

The time had now come to make the main assault from the north. This would be made by tanks and infantry. But it was the performance of the tanks in this operation, which would influence thought on their use for the next eight years. The only IDF tank battalion during 1948-9 was formed during the first cease-fire of the war. It consisted of two tank companies, one equipped with ten ancient French H-35s and the other with two British Cromwells and one American Sherman. Besides, the problem of variation of type, there was also a language difficulty. The battalion commander spoke only Polish and Russian, and his men a miscellany of almost every European language. It had first been blooded in an attack on Lod Airport, but its role in Operation *Yoav* was the first proper chance it had to show off its paces. It was ordered to attack a fortified village held by an Egyptian company. Disaster struck from the start. None of the H-35s ever reached the objective, being caught in an anti-tank ditch, while the two Cromwells had no sooner entered the Egyptian position than they were knocked out. It was not an auspicious beginning. The Israelis now switched their attention to the east again in order to draw off further Egyptian forces before the centre was re-tackled. After two days hard fighting in this latter sector the IDF managed to break through and link up with the Negev forces. The operation concluded with the Egyptians, because of the threat of their communications, withdrawing from the northern part of the coastal strip, and being cleared from their positions in the mountains south of Jerusalem. Finally, the Israelis dashed into Beersheba.

The bulk of this operation was completed in six days, and was typical of the Israeli style of fighting. It was, along with similar operations during this last phase, all of which were designed to drive the Arabs out of territory granted to Israel by the UN Resolution, to become the basis of Israeli

222

doctrine. For a start, the Israeli objectives were limited in nature. There was no question of attempting to destroy the Arab armies *per se*. The maximum possible use was made of surprise, and preliminary operations were all designed to put the enemy off-balance, by threatening him from several directions, and dislocating his command and communication systems. Indeed, it was the strategy of the 'indirect approach', and General Yadin, the Chief of Staff recognised that it was, when, after the United Nations had organised a series of armistices between Israel and her Arab neighbours during the early part of 1949, the Israelis settled down to analyse the lessons of the war. Thus in September 1949 he wrote:

> 'There is no doubt that the strategy of the indirect approach is the only sound strategy . . . To exploit the principles of war for our purpose and base ourselves upon strategic indirect approach, so as to determine the issue of the fighting even before the fighting has begun, it is necessary to achieve the three following aims:
> (a) to cut the enemy's lines of communications, thus paralysing his physical build-up;
> (b) to seal him off from his lines of retreat, thus undermining the enemy's will and destroying his morale;
> (c) to hit his centres of administration and disrupt his communications, thus severing the link between his brain and his limbs.' [1]

Recognising these three aims of the method of achieving victory and combining them with Wingate's legacy of surprise and mobility, the Israelis found that they had developed a blitzkrieg form of warfare. Significantly, Liddell Hart had had contacts with the Jewish leaders as early as 1938. Also, Yadin himself had used Liddell Hart's writings, in particular his *Strategy of the Indirect Approach* as texts for courses of instruction which he conducted in the *Haganah* during the years 1940-43. Nevertheless, the Israelis continued to be more influenced by Wingate, although Liddell Hart ran him a close second. Interestingly enough, during the final part of Operation *Yoav* they captured a copy of *The Strategy of The Indirect Approach* in its enlarged 1946 edition from an Egyptian fortress commander. As Yadin wrote: ' . . . fortunately for us they did not grasp the essence of the book, and were therefore completely surprised by our strategical plan based on the principles of this book.' [2]

The Israelis were to use this doctrine as a basis for their planning from 1949 onwards. But there were other factors than the doctrine of a highly esteemed military thinker which caused them to pursue it. Because only an armistice rather than permanent peace had been achieved in 1949, it was quite clear to Israel that she would continue to be faced by simultaneous threats from several directions. She did not have the men or equipment to hold Maginot-style defences on her long frontiers. Indeed both these commodities would always remain at a premium, and she would only be able to afford the minimum losses of each. But mitigating against these factors was the likelihood that any war would always be short. After the cessation of hostilities in 1949 a United Nations Truce Supervision Organisation (UNTSO) had been set up with observers patrolling Israel's borders. Consequently any further outbreak of fighting would be speedily reported to the UN, who recognising the area as a continual threat to world peace, would do its utmost to bring the fighting to an early end. Later, it would not be so much the UN as the major world powers, the USA and USSR, which would provide the necessary pressure to end the fighting. But, if the Israelis realised this, then the Arabs were bound to as well, and there was always a danger that they would launch a surprise attack and present whatever Israeli territory they had seized as a *fait accompli* to the intervening powers. Thus the Israelis concluded that they must be in a position to forestall this and, even better, seize a bargaining counter themselves. Out of this reasoning arose the Israeli doctrine of the pre-emptive attack or, as they called it themselves, the 'anticipatory counter-attack'. This was defined by General Allon, who was later to become Chief of Staff and then a cabinet minister, as:

'Israeli operational initiative taken against concentrations of enemy forces, and the occupation on enemy territory of targets having a vital security significance, at a time when the enemy is mustering his forces for an attack but before he has had time to actually start his offensive.' [3]

In this context any Israeli pre-emptive attack had to be launched quickly and achieve its objective speedily before either the enemy or the intervening powers had time to prevent it happening. Thus the attack must be a lightning stroke, employing the blitzkrieg technique. Having evolved a workable strategy, the Israelis now had to fashion tools suitable for this type of war.

The IAF had been used in a variety of roles in 1948-9. Armed with a miscellany of old World War 2 aircraft it had been used in tactical, strategic and logistical operations. It had realised very early on the importance of air supremacy over the land battle, as Operation *Yoav* had demonstrated. The same operation had seen it being used to move troops about the theatre of operations. It had also attempted strategic bombing, albeit one small bombing raid only, on Cairo. In effect, the IAF had initially found itself operating as a balanced air force, not because it wished it so, but because its potential was dictated by the types of aircraft which it had been able to procure. It soon became clear during the years immediately after the 1948-9 War that Israel would not have the resources to maintain an effective balanced force, because she would never have both sufficient strategic and tactical aircraft to make the IAF powerful enough in either role. In addition, the concept of strategic bombing was not relevant to Israeli defence doctrine. The evidence from World War 2 had shown that the quick Douhet style of bombing attack on the enemy's civil population did little to bring him to his knees. A strategic bombing offensive needed to be waged for some time before its effects were significantly felt. Thus such an offensive would hardly have time enough to get properly under way in the type of war which the Israelis envisaged fighting. To use it against the enemy's industrial war effort again did not apply to the Middle East, for

224

there was no war industry to speak of, and both Arab and Israeli relied almost entirely on imports to maintain their respective war machines. Finally, Guernica had shown how such a campaign could influence world opinion, and Israel, if she was to survive, must maintain the support and sympathy of her friends in Europe and America. Thus it was decided that the IAF should be a strictly tactical force, but it was not until 1953 that its roles were spelt out by the new chief of the IAF, Dan Tolkowsky. He laid down that the tasks of the IAF would be firstly the gaining of and maintenance of air supremacy over the land battle, and then tactical strike and reconnaissance in support of the ground forces. For this he decreed that the IAF should arm itself with one basic type of aircraft, a multi-purpose fighter. There was some debate as to how air superiority should be achieved, whether in the air or by destroying enemy aircraft on the ground, but the success of the latter method in 1948, together with the greater element of surprise achieved by it caused it to be quickly adopted. Besides the multi-purpose fighter, the IAF continued to use transports, particularly for use in airborne operations. An airborne force was formed early on, for the Israelis saw this as a major means of dislocating the enemy's communications.

The evolution of the right weapon mix for the IDF was not so straightforward, and in many ways resembled the debate between the supporters of infantry and armour in Britain in the years between the wars. The Laskov Group, which was responsible for synthesising the experience of 1948-9, realised the importance of combined arms. They also concluded that the task of armour should be to cut deep into the enemy's rear, harrying his flanks and rear, but avoiding towns and fortified positions. Thus the armour should be used for independent operations in support of the main force. This faithfully mirrored the view of the British conservative reformers of the 1920s and 1930s. However, the majority view in the IDF was that mechanised infantry rather than tanks were to be the *arme blanche*. The tank disaster during Operation *Yoav* had not impressed the General Staff, and they believed that the tank should be restricted to the role of infantry support only. They argued that battlefield mobility, which Laskov had concluded as the most important characteristic of mechanised forces, should be considered in terms of vehicle speed, and in this respect a half-track APC was faster and more manoeuvrable than a Sherman tank, which represented the main equipment of the Armoured Corps in the early 1950s. The tank was thus better employed as a fire support weapon to enable the mechanised infantry to push on. The main proponents of this school were General Yadin, the Chief of Staff in the years immediately after the first Arab-Israeli War, and Moshe Dayan, who would occupy that position for the 1956 campaign.

Although the Yadin-Dayan school initially had its way, there were two other schools of thought. One supported the Laskov conclusion that armour should operate away from the main axis and content itself with raids in the traditional cavalry role. The third was led by a Lt Col Uri Ben Ari. He, unlike the majority of his compatriots, had made a close study of the Wehrmacht operations in 1939-45. As a result he became convinced that

225

the tank must be the dominant weapon on the Israeli battlefield. But, because so few Israelis had had experience of tank warfare, his thesis at first fell on stony ground. In 1951 Uri Ben Ari was appointed deputy commander of 'S' Brigade, which consisted of two mechanised infantry battalions, a tank battalion and reconnaissance, mortar and engineering companies. The next year gave him the chance to demonstrate his ideas. During the 1952 IDF manoeuvres, he made an 80 mile non-stop penetration deep behind the opposing forces, which looked as though it might bring the exercise to an early end. The only way in which the directing staff could realistically continue was to order him to halt where he was, and a circle was drawn round his position on the map out of which he was not allowed to trespass. After the exercise 'S' Brigade came in for harsh criticism from the Chief of Staff, General Yadin. The following year Uri Ben Ari repeated this manoeuvre, but this time Ben Gurion, the Prime Minister, was watching, and so impressed was he that he ordered an expansion of the Armoured Corps. But, by now the schools of thought on armour had further synthesised their views. While the majority school now accepted that armour could be used independently away from the main axis, besides giving support to the mechanised infantry on the main axis, Ben Ari believed that the IDF should be formed into a number of armoured brigades, consisting of tanks, mechanised infantry and artillery. These would break through the enemy defences, cutting them up into pockets, which would be reduced by the following up motorised infantry while the armour raced on to the main objective. It was an exact copy of Guderian's method of operating.

During the years 1949-56 there were constant minor clashes between Israel and her Arab neighbours. Using the principle of aggressive defence, the IDF launched a series of retaliatory raids into Arab territory. At first these were in company strength only, but later increased to battalion group strength, and during 1955 and early 1956 three brigade group size raids were mounted. At this time the IDF organisation was based on the brigade rather than the division, and a number of brigades made up a Command. Thus by 1956, the IDF had had the opportunity to try out its command and control structure, and give many of its younger conscript soldiers battle experience, which would stand the Force in good stead for the second of its campaigns.

In 1952 a group of young Egyptian Army officers overthrew the Egyptian monarchy, bent on reforming the whole of Egyptian, Arab and, eventually, the whole of the Islamic society. By 1954, one Major Gamal Abdel Nasser had become the undisputed Egyptian leader. His first aim was to rid Egypt of the continuing British presence on the Suez Canal. A year later, the Russians, bent on expanding their sphere of influence in the Middle East, signed an agreement with Nasser whereby, in exchange for cotton, they undertook to re-equip the Egyptian Armed Forces with Czechoslovak armaments. The Western powers made no effort to step up arms deliveries to Israel, and consequently it became clear to her that unless she acted quickly, she would become engulfed. In July 1956 Nasser nationalised the Suez Canal, and the British and French agreed to act together to retrieve it from Nasser's hands. The Israelis got wind of what was afoot, and concluded that the time was now ripe for the first of their 'anticipatory counter-attacks', relying on Anglo-French military intervention to ensure further the success of their own attack.

Dayan's operational directive for the October 1956 campaign laid down three objectives. The first two were the capture of the Straits of Tiran, which the Egyptians had closed to Israeli shipping, hence blockading the Israeli port of Eilat, at the head of the Gulf of Aqaba, and the seizure of vital ground threatening the Suez Canal. The third aim was to ' . . . confound the organisation of the Egyptian forces in Sinai and bring about their collapse.' [4] This was significant. The Israelis realised that they could not hope to destroy the Egyptian forces in Sinai, for this was likely to cost them more casualties than they could afford, while it was believed that it would not take long for the Egyptians to rebuild their forces. But the dislocation of the Egyptian forces would better enable the two territorial objectives to be achieved. This then was an indication of how much they had grasped and understood of the strategy of the indirect approach, something which Hitler, although he used the correct tools for it, lost sight of. In essence, the Israeli plan called for four separate drives across Sinai preceded by para-troop drops deep into Egyptian territory in order to cause maximum confusion. In contrast, to the usual method of ensuring careful co-ordination between the drives by laying down intermediary objectives and phase lines, the IDF commanders were merely given an axis and a final objective. The Israeli view was that 'plans are merely the basis for change', and hence they considered it a waste of time to plan in too much detail. Also, it was felt that too rigid a plan would prevent subordinate commanders from using their initiative. Besides, prime emphasis was placed on speed, and commanders should not have to pause to await further orders from above merely because operations had not gone according to the laid down plan.

The IAF was to be employed in the roles laid down for it by Tolkowsky. Indeed he was insistent that the Egyptian airfields should be struck from the outset. Dayan supported him, writing in his diary on October 3rd: ' . . . if we do not succeed at the very outset in surprising the Egyptians and knocking out their planes while they are still on the ground, our plan will fail.' [5] However, Ben Gurion forbade this, insisting that the Anglo-French air forces would take care of this problem. Consequently, the IAF was dedicated to close support of the ground forces from the start. However, part of its strength had to be diverted to protect Israeli air space. It also engaged in interdiction tasks behind the immediate battle area.

In accordance with the Yadin-Dayan doctrine, the backbone for the offensive was to be provided by the mechanised infantry. Even at this stage the proportion of mechanised infantry to tank battalions was in a ratio of 22:5, and hence even if Dayan had wished it so, there was not enough armour to make it dominant. Nevertheless, Dayan was not prepared initially to make much use of his armour at all. Ben Ari had been given command of an armoured brigade, the 7th, consisting of one battalion of French AMX-13s, a light tank mounting a 75mm, one battalion of Sherman

Fireflies, and a mechanised infantry battalion. In the initial plan this brigade was given the minor task of making a feint attack on the Jordanian front in order to take Egyptian eyes off the IDFs main effort in Sinai. It was only through representations by Laskov, now commanding the Armoured Corps and Ben Ari himself that the brigade was allotted a role in the main offensive. But, even then, Dayan laid down that it was to follow an infantry brigade using its tank transporters, and would be let loose only after the main Egyptian defences had been breached. This was not what Ben Ari had in mind. He felt that the armoured brigade must lead, leaving the infantry to mop up pockets, while his tanks dashed for the Canal. It was identical to the argument which Guderian had over how his tanks should be used in the initial stages of Barbarossa in June 1941.

The Israelis launched their attack on October 29th, 1956 and by November 2nd, they had established control over almost the whole of Sinai. Three days later they had control of the entrance to the Gulf of Aqaba. Meanwhile on October 31st the Anglo-French air forces had started attacking military targets inside Egypt, and on November 2nd Anglo-French landings took place in the Port Said area. The Israeli success had been devastating. The Egyptians, like the French and British in May 1940, had been trained to fight a set-piece methodical battle. They relied on static defence, which played into the hands of the marauding Israeli columns. Significantly the most dazzling success was achieved by Ben Aris's 7th Brigade. Flagrantly disobeying orders, he contrived to arrive in front of the main Egyptian defences at the same time as the infantry, which he was supposed to follow. Leaving them to reduce the Egyptian defences, he dashed westwards, avoiding Egyptian strongpoints, and arrived within sight of the Suez Canal well before the other thrusts. It was this disobedience which would have a radical effect on Israeli armoured doctrine.

As anticipated by Israel, the UN quickly intervened. The Anglo-French forces were withdrawn and replaced by UN troops, and the IDF ordered back to within Israeli territory, but not before Israel had received guarantees that the Straits of Tiran would remain open to her. For the cost of 150 killed, Israel had forestalled any possible Arab invasion. She had also captured vast quantities of equipment, which would more than replace the losses which she had suffered.

The experience of 1956 was added to that of 1948, and further synthesis took place. The strategy of the pre-emptive attack had been proved correct for Israel, and from now on it was assumed that:

' . . . the major battles would take place on enemy soil, and that the Israeli armies should therefore advance as far as was needed to ensure the defeat of the enemy's armed forces, to establish a new strategic posture to meet further possible attacks, and to hold enemy territory until peace was achieved and permanent strategic boundaries fixed.' [6]

Although the IAF had not been given the chance to carry out its own pre-emptive attack, its commanders continued to believe that the priority of roles as laid down by Tolkowsky were correct. Whereas in 1956 Vampires

228

and Meteors had formed the backbone of the Force, these were replaced shortly afterwards by the more modern French Mystère IVA fighters and Ouragan fighter-bombers. Later Mirages were also added to the IAF armoury. With the IDF the situation was not so clearcut. Although the 1956 plan had worked well, the dazzling performance of Ben Ari's brigade cast doubts among the believers in the power of mechanised infantry, and soon there was a steady trickle of officers transferring to the Armoured Corps from other arms.

The Armoured Corps, first under Ben Ari himself, and then under Bar-Lev and Elazar, set out to develop the beliefs of Ben Ari. During the late 1950s the doctrine was developed whereby the Armoured Corps would by-pass all enemy opposition and make for his rear. Once there, they believed that the enemy must realise he was beaten, such was the threat which it offered to his forces and logistical system. However, the increasing Russian influence in Egypt made her adopt more and more Russian tactics, which called for defensive positions between natural obstacles. Thus the open spaces through which the armour had been able to move in 1956, were unlikely to be still in existence by the time the next round came. In effect, there would have to be a break-in operation before the armour could be let loose. The argument that Ben Ari had had just before the 1956 attack had raised its head again. The General Staff only gave away by degrees in their belief that the break-in was still an infantry responsibility, to be done if possible by night.

In 1964 General Israel Tal took over as commander of the Armoured Corps. He had joined immediately after the 1956 campaign and soon became convinced that the tank was the 'Queen of the Battlefield'. For a start, he dismissed the accepted idea that battlefield mobility was directly proportional to vehicle speed. Instead he argued that it was the ability to advance under hostile fire which counted. To replace the old Shermans, the Armoured Corps started to receive in the early 1960s American Pattons (weight 44tons, top speed 35mph, mounting a 90mm gun) and the British Centurion (weight 50tons, top speed 22mph with a 105mm gun). Although the Patton was some 10mph faster than the Sherman Firefly, the Centurion was slower, but its thicker armour and more powerful gun gave it better battlefield mobility in Tal's eyes. Tal also proved that armour was capable of break-in operations, demonstrating this against Russian-style defences in the 1964-5 manoeuvres. The result was that the General Staff were now more prepared to accept armour as the decisive arm. It would soon have the opportunity to prove its worth.

During the early 1960s the situation gradually worsened in the Middle East. In the north, the IDF became increasingly involved in skirmishes with the Syrians on the Golan Heights, who were disrupting life in the Israeli frontier settlements. This was coupled with the emergence of the El Fatah terrorist organisation, bent on restoring Israel to the Palestinians. In the south, life had remained at a more peaceful level, with Nasser still involved in his intervention in the Yemen, which had been brought about by overthrow of the reactionary Iman of Yemen in 1962, and Egyptian attempts to fill the resultant vacuum, which for over five years met little success. On no less than three occasions in 1966 did complaints of aggression between Syrian, Jordan and Israel come before the UN Security Council. During the early part of 1967 there were persistent reports of force build-ups and concentrations by Israel, Syria and Jordan. The climax came in mid-May when the Egyptians demanded the removal of the United Nations Emergency Force (UNEF) from her frontier with Israel and from around the Gulf of Aqaba. The UN Secretary-General acquiesced, and this was followed on May 22nd by the Egyptian closure of the Strait of Tiran to Israeli shipping, thus once again sealing off the Israeli port of Eilat. To Israelis it seemed as though the Arabs were preparing for a repeat of 1948.

Israel was faced with the possibility of war on three fronts — northern against the Syrians, eastern versus Jordan, and to the south against the Egyptians in Sinai. She only had the resources to carry out a pre-emptive attack in one direction, but such an attack had to be carried out. She could not afford to wait for the Arabs to attack. However, from the start the Israeli defence planners had always been clear that Egypt provided the main threat. Indeed her military strength was more than twice that of Jordan and Syria combined. Thus initially the attack must be made on Egypt, while the IDF stood on the defensive in the north and east.

The key to any pre-emptive strike, as had been preached by Dan Tolkowsky, was that the opposing air force must be destroyed on the ground at the outset. The plans for such a strike had been in existence for some years, and the IAF concentrated its training, particularly between the years 1956-67 on quick turn-round times between sorties. They calculated that they did not possess the strength to attack all Arab airfields within range simultaneously, and hence each aircraft would have to make more than one sortie. The longer the interval between sorties, the more time the enemy had to recover, and the less the element of surprise, which played such a major part in ensuring the success of such an operation. The problem in late May 1967 was that the Arabs, because of the closure of the Strait of Tiran must have been expecting an Israeli counter-move. As Yigal Allon wrote:

> 'The possibility of a strategic surprise had been sacrificed, for the opposing armies were already fully on the alert. The only form of surprise still possible was on the operational and tactical levels — in the field, in the theatre of war.' [7]

For the IAF this meant that the Arabs could be expecting some form of air attack. Hence only tactical surprise was possible. This could only be achieved in timing and direction.

On June 5th at 0745 hours the IAF first wave of the pre-emptive strike went in against ten Egyptian airfields west of the Suez Canal. A large part of the Egyptian Air Force was caught on the ground. The necessary tactical surprise had been gained in two ways. The direction of the attack was unexpected. Instead of approaching the targets by the most direct route, which would have meant over-flying part of Sinai and the Suez Canal,

230

thereby alerting Egyptian defences where they would be most on guard, the IAF came in low over the Mediterranean, approaching their targets from the north-west. So great was the surprise, that the Egyptians thought initially that they had been attacked by aircraft operating from the US Sixth Fleet, at that time in the Eastern Mediterranean. The choice of timing was also significant. To have attacked at first light would have been the expected course, and the Egyptians were known to have had several MiG-21s on alert at this time. By postponing H-Hour by three hours, the Egyptians were caught with most of their units stood down, and 0745 hours was at the very time when most Egyptian senior officers were travelling to work. Indeed the only aircraft which the Egyptians had in the air at the time of the attack were four unarmed trainers. With the pounding of the first targets completed, attacks were then concentrated in Sinai, apart from the airfield of El Arish, whose runways were left untouched so that the Israelis could use it to resupply their ground forces. Not until midday did the Jordanian and Syrian air forces make retaliatory attacks, and then, with the attacks on Egyptian airfields completed for the time being, the IAF was able to attack the main Jordanian and Syrian airfields. Late on the same day further attacks were made on Egyptian airfields and these continued during the night. By the end of the second day, the IAF claimed to have knocked out more than 400 Arab aircraft, of whom the main sufferer was Egypt with a loss of 300 of her 450 aircraft. Israeli air supremacy had been achieved at a cost of some 30 aircraft only, enabling the operations of the ground forces to proceed unhindered from the air. The doctrine of Tolkowsky had been proved right, and in such a way as to overshadow the Luftwaffe at the height of its powers.

As in the air, the IDF's main ground stroke was to be against the Egyptians. The Egyptian defences in Sinai were constructed on the contemporary Russian model. They were based on a series of infantry strongpoints, which included dug-in T-34 and JS-3 tanks. Behind these lay a 'mass of manoeuvre' consisting of some 450 modern Russian T-54s and T-55s organised into two armoured divisions. Since these infantry positions were mutually supporting, and designed for all-round defence, the Israelis had appreciated that the gaps, which existed in the 1956 defences would no longer be there. They were facing an estimated force of 100 000 men, equipped with almost 1 000 tanks. Indeed, as General Tal put it, the Egyptians were:

' . . . blocking all the main lines of advance through the desert with massive troop concentrations and strongly fortified positions, some of which had been prepared over the last 20 years. The only line of advance westwards from Israel's southern border that was not blocked was the one taken by General Yoffe and his armoured brigade across the dunes — the Egyptians evidently believed them to be impassible.' [8]

Faced with this problem, General Rabin, Chief of Staff of the IDF, and his planners devised a three phase plan. It was clear that, whether they liked it or not, the first phase would have to be a break-in operation. Two points were selected, one at Rafa in the Gaza Strip, and the other to the south directed on Abu Agheila. With this operation successfully completed, an armoured force would drive hell-bent for the mountains to the east of Suez, and hold the passes through them, thus cutting off the Egyptian retreat. Finally, the now surrounded Egyptian Army in Sinai would be destroyed. The watchwords of the operation would be speed, concentration, surprise and maintenance of momentum.

By 1967, thanks to Tal and others, the Armoured Corps was regarded as the decisive arm in IDF eyes. The majority of its 800 tanks (a mixture of Centurions, Pattons AMX-13 and Shermans with a 105mm gun) were now organised into armoured brigades, with only a relatively small proportion told off for infantry support. Tal himself, nurtured on studies of Guderian, now believed that the tank, with its ability of flexibility and shock action, could produce the necessary dislocation of the enemy's forces on its own. Appointed to command the northern break-in operation at Rafa, he was allocated a third of the IDF tank strength, but rather than use his infantry to carry out the break-in, he proposed to use his tanks as a 'mailed fist' to make the penetration, relying on their high battlefield mobility as defined by him. The mechanised infantry would follow, widening the breach, and providing an insurance against possible counter-attacks, while motorised infantry then occupied themselves with the reduction of those defences which had been bypassed. The system was designed to work like a conveyor belt, with no part of the force having to wait for that behind it to catch up. This was the ideal to which the Germans aimed without success, but the main difference between them and the Israelis lay in the fact that all of the IDF was mechanised or motorised in some way, while this was only true of a small proportion of the Wehrmacht.

The Egyptian positions around Rafa, were strongly fortified and covered by extensive minefields, apart from the extreme north, where the Egyptians felt that the sand dunes precluded the use of armour. Tal therefore resolved to make a two pronged attack, using the sand dunes. These prongs would penetrate well beyond the main Egyptian defences with their first objective the supporting Egyptian artillery (shades of Plan 1919). With the Egyptian artillery silenced they would then turn south and north respectively, reducing the main positions from the rear. Simultaneously the major part of the armour would dash westwards for El Arish, with the airfield there as the main objective. Half an hour after the first IAF airstrikes had gone in Tal attacked. In the north, as soon as the frontier was crossed the Israelis were met with artillery fire:

'But it was not this that delayed the Pattons. The main roads and paths, except for those which were covered by anti-tank guns and troops armed with anti-tank weapons, were heavily obstructed. Anti-tank ditches yawned half-way across these roads, from the left-and right-hand sides alternately, so that vehicles were obliged to move in low gear only, and to zigzag from side to side. Heavy vehicles such as tanks had to manoeuvre back and forth several times to get through, making an easy target . . . Egyptian tanks lurked along tree-lined avenues and behind cactus bushes. The attacking Pattons, in trying to avoid the heavily defended routes, sought alternative bypaths, but here they ran into further difficulties. The paths led them into the narrow streets and alleys of villages . . . Where the valleys were blocked, the Pattons took to the cultivated fields, but these too were difficult to traverse because the small farmed patches were fenced in by stone walls and high soil ramps on top of which grew cactus bushes planted as a protection against erosion and wind; these sometimes proved worse obstacles than those created by the Egyptian Army.' [9]

Nevertheless, the tanks succeeded in breaking their way through. The sheer determination of the crews, who realised that the result of initial battle would dictate the course of the campaign, caused them to push on without regard to casualties or to what was happening on their flanks and rear. The defenders, faced by this 'mailed fist' broke once they were in danger of being cut off, and attempted to withdraw westwards. The story was the same with the southern thrust, but by nightfall Tal's tanks were racing towards El Arish.

To the south, Yoffe advanced through the sand dunes, the one area which the Egyptians had not bothered to defend physically. Although halted every so often by minefields, the heading brigade arrived at Bir Lahfran, ten miles south-east of El Arish, by 1800 hours, having covered 60 miles in nine hours, and went into blocking positions to prevent any reinforcements reaching El Arish from the south. By midnight Tal's tanks were fighting in El Arish, while Yoffe had beaten off one determined Egyptian attempt at reinforcement. However, Tal did have trouble from the bypassed strongpoint at Giradeh, some five miles short of El Arish, from which Egyptian counter-attacks prevented more than one tank battalion getting through to El Arish for a time. He was forced to deploy most of his reserve brigade, which had been directed on El Arish on the southern route, leaving the lead brigade to mop up the Egyptian defences, to reduce this strongpoint, which cost a number of casualties. But, in spite of all, by dawn on the second day of the war El Arish was in Israeli hands. The Israelis stated afterwards that they had suffered more at the hands of the Egyptian anti-tank guns rather than tanks, because their positions were so difficult to pinpoint. As Tal said: 'It was impossible to see where they were and few were destroyed by tank fire. We just advanced on the flashes with our tanks and crushed them.' [10] Undoubtedly Israeli dash and determination had won the day, aided to a considerable extent by the presence of the IAF, which had been available in the close support role three hours after the opening of hostilities.

The defences at Abu Agheila were a much tougher proposition than those at Rafa. Because they covered all approaches through the central part of Sinai, the Israelis could not afford to bypass them. In addition, they were held in over brigade strength, and included several tanks and much artillery. So strong were they, that Sharon, in command of the IDF in this sector did not countenance the idea of a frontal assault by tanks. He had to resort to a night attack by infantry, together with a heliborne operation, and the use of armour to establish a blocking position to the rear, before the defences could be reduced. It was a complicated operation, more so than the Israelis were accustomed to, and it took 24 hours of tough fighting before the battle was won. Only then was Sharon able to let loose his armour to link up with a subsidiary thrust which he had made well to the south. Yet, in a little over 24 hours, the Israelis had broken through some exceedingly tough defences, and their armour was now well behind the main body of the Egyptian forces in Sinai, and pressing onwards to cut them off in the passes guarding the way back to the Suez Canal.

The next phase was simply a question of getting to the Khatmia, Gidi and Mitla passes before the retreating Egyptian columns. The most important of these was the last named, whose seizure fell to the responsibility of Yoffe. By 1800 hours on the third day his forces were there, although during the last part of the advance many of his tanks ran out of fuel and had to be towed into position. At the same time, Tal, having sent part of his force direct to the Canal at Quantara, blocked the approaches to the other two passes by taking up a position centered on Bir Gifgafa. But, as yet the bulk of the Egyptian tank force had not been drawn into battle. It was Sharon's task to drive this 'mass of manoeuvre' into the trap created by Tal and Yoffe. Sharon's advance from Abu Agheila to Nakhl, where he was to meet up with his southern advance, was over difficult country and took him over twenty four hours to achieve a link-up. Nevertheless, he came across a complete JS-3 brigade, whose crews had abandoned their tanks, such was the dislocation caused by the Israelis. By the fourth day the Egyptian armour had been forced to withdraw westwards, and fierce fighting broke out as it attempted to force its way through the passes. At the same time, the IAF was adding to the Egyptian confusion by 'strafing' the Egyptians on their way back. The latter fought desperately to get through the passes, and the pressure on the Israelis holding them was almost too much. However, it was at this stage that the tactical air power of the IAF came into its own. By continuous napalm, bomb and rocket attacks on the Egyptian columns trying to force their way through the Mitla Pass, the IAF succeeded in sealing it at its western end. Even then, Yoffe was forced to relieve the brigade holding this pass because it was out of ammunition and exhausted.

At midday on the fourth day of the war, the Israelis felt that they could now turn their attention to the Suez Canal. By 0200 hours on the next day they had reached the Canal, having launched night attacks against Egyptian positions blocking their way. Nevertheless, they suffered casualties, particularly at the hands of skilfully laid tank ambushes. By this time the UN had once again intervened, and a ceasefire was arranged. In the space of 96 hours the IDF had routed a force twice its size, having broken through defences, which have been compared to those of the Russians at Kursk in 1943, and cleared the whole of the Sinai peninsular of the Egyptian presence. All this had been done without the benefit of strategic surprise.

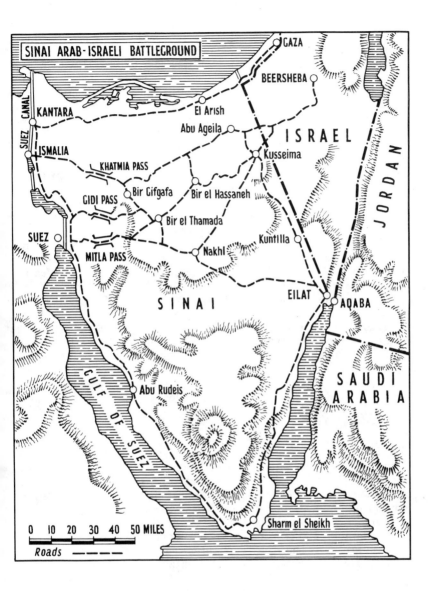

SINAI ARAB-ISRAELI BATTLEGROUND

GAZA
BEERSHEBA
KANTARA
SUEZ CANAL
ISMALIA
El Arish
Abu Ageila
ISRAEL
Kusseima
KHATMIA PASS
JORDAN
Bir Gifgafa
Bir el Hassaneh
GIDI PASS
Bir el Thamada
SUEZ
Kuntilla
Nakhl
MITLA PASS
SINAI
EILAT
AQABA
SAUDI
ARABIA
GULF OF SUEZ
Abu Rudeis
0  10  20  30  40  50 MILES
Roads  — — — —
Sharm el Sheikh

Once again the tank and aircraft acting in concert had been shown to be a formidable combination.

The success of the operation is attributable to several reasons. The Israelis, although they realised that the potential for strategic surprise did not exist, made the most of any opportunity to gain tactical surprise. They appreciated that surprise led to the dislocation of the enemy, which in turn would bring about his defeat at minimum cost. We have seen how this was achieved in the air. On the ground, the realisation that they had to commence operations by breaking through strong defences did not blunt the rapier like tactics of their forces. By making the Egyptian artillery their first objective, they penetrated deeply enough behind the main defences to cause the maximum confusion. But the most significant factor was the IDF belief in maintenance of momentum. Once they had thrown the Egyptians into confusion it was important to keep them off balance. This meant that the Israeli thrusts could not afford to slow down or halt. They had to keep going. Although the Russians have always been believers in night fighting, this was one facet of war, which they did not appear to have successfully handed on to the Egyptians. On the other hand, the Israelis regarded this as part of the Wingate legacy. Indeed Yoffe himself, taking part in a symposium in the honour and memory of Wingate in 1962, said:

'Theoretically, every army in the world claims that full use should be made of the night. Wingate is the man who had planted this feeling, this idea, into us: thus night is not an enemy but a friend; that night is not only a protector of the weak; that night-time does not mean only concealment. On the contrary: night opens up extraordinary opportunities for developing fighting in all its forms and it enables one to act in many situations and solve all sorts of problems cheaply, quickly, and efficiently.' [11]

The Israeli ability to fight effectively by night enabled them to maintain momentum, and also to overcome positions, which had proved too strong for a daylight attack. In addition, night operations saved them many casualties. This nocturnal ability, was something which the Germans did not practise to any great extent, and in this respect the Israelis could be said to have developed the blitzkrieg a stage further.

If momentum is to be maintained, there is one aspect which is vital — an efficient logistic system. During World War 2 both the Germans and the Allies 'ran out of steam' because their logistics could not keep up with the rapid rate of advance. The Israelis attempted to solve this problem by adopting the principle that supplies would be produced for the fighting units as soon as they were available rather than holding them back until the fighting units demanded them. Thus, initially every formation carried three days' supply of food, ammunition and fuel with it, and this was supported by airdrops and the use of captured Egyptian dumps. The supplies were normally carried on requisitioned civilian transport which stayed close behind the armoured columns. Even so, as we have seen, the Israelis did run dry

236

from time to time, mainly because they lost supplies to ambushes mounted from bypassed Egyptian positions. In addition, the foresight (an essential element in logistical planning) to leave El Arish airfield intact, and make it a key objective meant that they were able to establish a main forward supply base deep into Sinai within 36 hours, and significantly cut down the turn-round times for their transport. The logistics factor was also another reason for fighting a short war. For, the longer the fighting went on the greater the strain on the supply system.

Fierce fighting took place on both the eastern and northern fronts. Although the Israelis showed as much guile and ingenuity as in Sinai, the ruggedness of the country and the more limited objectives of the Israeli forces gave no chance to develop the blitzkreig as used in Sinai. Nonetheless, half Jordan was overrun, with the Israelis closed up to the River Jordan by the end of the fighting. In the north, the dominating Golan Heights were wrested from the Syrians.

Immediately after the cessation of hostilities the Israelis themselves paid tribute to those who had developed the doctrine, which had been used to such success in Sinai. Thus, one commentator:

'In accordance with the best tradition of armour operations, as theoretically formulated by the Englishmen Fuller and Liddell Hart, and actually applied by the Germans Guderian and Rommel, the Armoured Corps dashed forward without paying much attention to its flanks and rear, knowing that sooner or later the fate of flanks and rear will be decided by the deep penetration into the rear of the enemy's dispositions, leading to the collapse of the enemy's resisting power.' [12]

Indeed, Liddell Hart himself wrote that: ' . . . the plan was a superb application of the strategy of indirect approach, and its corollary of choosing 'the line of least expectation' to throw an opponent off balance.' [13] The Sinai campaign can be regarded as the high-water mark of the blitzkrieg technique, representing all the essential elements that go to make up its successful conduct.

**Notes**
1 Liddell Hart, *Strategy* p 397.
2 Ibid, p 406n.
3 Allon, *Curtain of Sand* pp 61-2.
4 Dayan, *Diary of the Sinai Campaign* p 212.
5 Ibid, p 34.
6 Allon, *The Making of Israel's Army* pp 64-5.
7 Ibid, p 83.
8 Churchill, Randolph S., Winston S., *The Six Day War* p 103.
9 Teveth, *The Tanks of Tammuz* p 134.
10 The Churchills, op cit p 114.
11 *JRUSI* May 1968.
12 Wallach Col Dr J L, *Voice of Israel* Broadcast 15 Jul 67.
13 *Encounter* Feb 1968.

# 9
# Blitzkrieg — the Future?

The blitzkrieg doctrine arose from determination not to repeat the stagnant and bloody deadlock of trench warfare. It was a successful attempt to restore mobility to a battlefield, where weapon technology had outpaced tactical doctrine. The opportunity for it had arisen because of the introduction of the internal combustion engine on and over the battlefield, which radically increased the mobile potential of the fighting man. It did not find favour among the Western democracies between the two world wars because it was regarded as an aggressive means of waging war, not in keeping with the belief at the time that World War 1, with its appalling casualties, had been 'the war to end wars'. Only in the strident Third Reich, which was set upon restoring Germany to her 'rightful place' in the world order, was it eagerly grasped and put into practice. Russia had been attracted by it, as a means of spreading the creed of communism by force, but Stalin forsook it, when its main proponents seemed to become a threat to his personal position. The years 1939-1942, showed at first that Germany had forged a weapon which seemed invincible against the more pedestrian tactics of her neighbours. Yet, Hitler and many of his staff, half fearful and half over-confident of its success, blunted it in the vastness of the Russian steppes. The Allies, learning from their early disasters, picked up the weapon, but again did not fully comprehend its limitations. The Israelis, in 1956 and 1967, applied the technique correctly, and showed how devastating it could be against an attainable objective.

Blitzkrieg must be regarded as a rapier rather than a bludgeon. Armies brought up on the Clausewitzian idea that the aim of war is to defeat the enemy by destroying his means of defence — the armed forces, naturally gravitated towards the bludgeon. For to ensure defeat of the opposing army it was necessary to bring to bear superiority in strength, which meant men and material, at the critical point. Douhet, Liddell Hart and others, rightly identified that victory could be achieved in another more economic way, namely by destroying the enemy's will to fight. The object of blitzkrieg is just that, achieved through psychological dislocation, which in turn means aiming at the enemy's brain and nerve centres rather than trying to put his limbs out of action by employing brute strength to break them.

For a successful blitzkreig operation the aim must be attainable. This means not merely having enough equipment, but being able to support the operation logistically. One of the major reasons why the blitzkrieg failed in Russia was because Hitler's aim was beyond the limitations of the German

238

armed forces as they were equipped and structured in 1941. It failed for the Allies in North-West Europe in 1944, because they were unable to support it logistically. Israel, on the other hand, selected attainable objectives in both 1956 and 1967. Once the operation is launched the momentum of it must be maintained at all costs. The enemy must never be allowed to regain his balance because a pause is necessitated through exhaustion, lack of supplies or unexpected developments which appear to require a change of plan In other words, the original aim must be rigidly and ruthlessly adhered to throughout the operation at all levels of command. Although, in order to maintain momentum, enemy opposition must be bypassed by the leading troops, those strongpoints which can influence operations on the axis of the thrust must be either quickly reduced or sealed off. If not, a similar situation will occur to that which confronted von Manteuffel at Bastogne or, to lesser extent, Tal over the Egyptian strongpoint at Giradeh. The Germans were always faced with the dilemma that their mechanised forces had a much higher mobility than their follow-up forces. Consequently they were often forced to pause in front of significant strongpoints, until the infantry divisions had caught up and could deal with them. The Israelis being entirely mechanised or motorised, as are all modern armies, did not face this problem and were able to adopt the 'conveyor belt' system, which ensured maintenance of momentum.

An essential element of a successful blitzkrieg is the gaining of air supremacy at the outset. The Luftwaffe and IAF method of destroying the opposing air force on the ground is obviously the most economical way of doing this. It also means that the bulk of the air force is available to support the ground battle at an early opportunity. Its main task in this role is that of interdiction. By attacks on the enemy lines of communication, his command and control centres and reserves, the enemy's psychological dislocation is heightened. Close support of the ground forces in the shape of attacks on enemy positions within the immediate battle area is a secondary role, but it can contribute significantly to the battlefield mobility of the attacker.

This represented the synthesis of the technique at the end of the 1967 Arab-Israeli War. However, on October 6th, 1973 the Syrians and the Egyptians launched attacks across the Golan Heights and Suez Canal respectively. For once the Israeli intelligence services failed, and the Israelis were taken by surprise. Indeed, in the first days' fighting it seemed that Israel was about to suffer a disaster. And, although she recovered from her early setbacks and succeeded in regaining the initiative by the end of the twenty days fighting, the apparent lessons which have come out of the War of Yom Kippur have caused many commentators to question the validity of the blitzkrieg concept in modern war.

The end of the 1967 war had seen the Israelis possessing, for the first time in the short existence of their country, some good natural frontiers. In the north they now held the Golan Heights, which so dominate both sides of the frontier with Syria. In the east, they were firm on the West Bank of the River Jordan, while they now held the whole of Sinai, and the Suez Canal

239

was the new border with Egypt. Apparently secure behind these newly acquired obstacles, the Israelis could afford to adopt a slightly less active defence strategy than previously. The pre-emptive attack now seemed less attractive for two reasons. Firstly, such an attack was now politically unacceptable, as it would not be seen other than aimed at the heart of Israel's neighbours and to the world at large would appear to be naked aggression. Secondly, the Israelis had no further need to acquire extra territory. The occupied areas gave them a sufficient buffer in which to forestall any Arab attack before it reached Israel proper, and their natural frontiers, if sufficiently reinforced with artificial obstacles, would ensure that the Arabs had a very much more difficult task if they chose to mount an invasion, than in the past. Indeed, rather than continue to argue on the lines of the 'anticipatory counter-attack', they fell back on more of a 'Maginot' attitude. Thus Yigal Allon, writing in 1970, made the proposition that:

' . . . the greater the improvement in the enemy's mobility and offensive capacity, the greater the need . . . for the strengthening of the defensive system to make it impenetrable by a mechanised army . . . ' [1]

Thus the Israel defensive system on the east bank of the Suez Canal was designed to act as a 'cover', which would hold up any Egyptian crossing of the Canal long enough for the armoured reserves to be deployed in Sinai to defeat it.

The Israeli Armoured Corps was riding on the crest of the wave at the end of the 1967 War. The spectacular drives by Tal, Yoffe and Sharon across Sinai seemed to confirm Tal's belief in the omnipotence of the tank. Hence, infantry and artillery found themselves taking a 'back seat', while the tanks were concentrated in brigades, with little integral infantry and artillery support. This new attitude came dangerously close to the 'all tank' doctrine which had so permeated the Royal Tank Corps in the 1930s. The few critics of this new approach argued that Tal and the others might not have been so successful in 1967 had they been up against a more determined enemy, but they were brushed aside at what was to be the cost of the Armoured Corps.

The Egyptians succeeded in getting across the Canal on October 6th, 1973 for three reasons. Firstly they achieved complete surprise, and had selected D-Day well in that it was one of the holiest days in the Jewish calendar, the Day of Atonement. The attack had been carefully planned and rehearsed for months. Thus every soldier know his role intimately and this gave him a new confidence. Finally, the Egyptians had been instilled with a new determination, which had been lacking in their earlier brushes with the Israelis. They were assisted as well by a very much more sophisticated air defence system than they had in 1967. Thus the IAF started active operations without the necessary electronic counter-measures and tactics to combat the new generation of Russian built SAMs. In their attempts to take out the Egyptian bridges across the Canal they suffered severely —

240

almost to the same extent as the RAF Fairey Battles in their attempts to knock out the German bridges over the Meuse in May 1940. The IAF also failed to destroy the Egyptian Air Force on the ground, because the Egyptians, having learnt from 1967, had constructed bomb-proof shelters for their aircraft. They also held them back, relying on their air defences to achieve the necessary attrition of the IAF.

It was once the Egyptians were through the Bar-Lev Line, however, that the Israelis learnt their most salutory lesson of the war. During the first two days they attempted to counter-attack by throwing tanks companies piecemeal at the Egyptians without supporting artillery or infantry. These found themselves in for a rude shock:

'We were advancing and in the distance I saw specks dotted on the sand dunes. I couldn't make out what they were. As we got closer, I thought they looked like tree stumps. They were motionless and scattered across the terrain ahead of us. I got on the intercom and asked the tanks ahead what they made of it. One of by tank commanders radioed back: 'My God, they're not tree stumps. They're men!' For a moment I couldn't understand. What were men doing standing out there — quite still — when we were advancing in our tanks towards them? Suddenly all hell broke loose. A barrage of missiles was being fired at us, many of our tanks were hit. We had never come up against anything like this before . . . [2]

On October 8th, a reserve armoured division was moved into Sinai, and one of its brigades, the 190th, was launched in an attempt to reach some of the Egyptian bridges across the Canal. The lesson was driven home even more forcibly when this brigade was cut to pieces. The Israelis realised that tanks on their own were no match for a resolute anti-tank defence, equipped with the latest anti-tank guided weapons. These were the Russian Sagger, which could be carried by one man in a container like a suitcase, and the RPG-7, a handheld rocket launcher. Whereas, in the past the Israelis had been able to overcome anti-tank weapons by charging them in their tanks, which caused many anti-tank crews to run, they now found themselves facing a new type of resolute Egyptian soldier. Again, the IAF was not able to give the ground forces the close support, which they had become used to in the past. The Egyptians took with them across the Canal a large quantity of air defence weapons, including multiple rapid fire 23mm cannons, which were radar controlled, and SAM-7s, which could be carried and operated by one man. During the early part of the war these successfully kept the IAF at arm's length.

Thus it seemed that the Israeli war machine had met its match, and it was the same on the northern front, where the Israelis faced some 1 100 Syrian tanks with only 130 on their own. Luckily, the Syrians, partly because the nature of the country forced them to do so, and partly through over-confidence launched their tanks piecemeal, as the Israelis had done against the Egyptians. This enabled the Israelis to hold on, and defeat the

241

Syrian attacks in detail but not before the Golan Heights had been overrun Here too the IAF suffered severely at the hands of the Syrian air defence system, which used the same equipment and was organised in a similar way to the Egyptians.

The Israelis were quick to learn from their mistakes. They realised that they were fighting a different enemy from that of 1967. Against this enemy the tank on its own was not enough, and hence they went back to the all-arms combat team. They also received the electronic counter measures from the Americans to help defeat the new SAM threat, as well as working out new tactics. Luckily they were helped in this by Egyptian strategy. Having successfully got across the Canal and established themselves the other side, the Egyptians paused instead of pressing home their success. They were not prepared to move until they had deployed their heavier SAM systems on the east bank of the Canal. It is also apparent that they were themselves surprised by their initial success, and had not really developed their plans beyond this initial phase. Unlike the Israelis, the Egyptians were believers in methodical planning and careful preparation. This acted against them in Sinai, for it was not until October 14th that they struck again, by which time the Israelis had had time to rethink their tactics.

The Israelis now adopted a more passive defence, as opposed to mounting immediate counter-attacks. They kept their tanks hull-down behind sand dunes, and as the Egyptians advanced they engaged them, using a number of alternative fire positions in order to give the enemy little time in which to spot targets. This made life difficult for the Sagger teams in particular, for the anti-tank guided missile has a relatively long time of flight and has to be manually guided onto the target. In order to deal with the Sagger teams which accompanied the Egyptian all-arms columns on foot, each Israeli tank battalion had a mechanised infantry company attached to it. When a Sagger missile was seen in flight, the infantry engaged the general area of the controller with fire, thus putting him off his aim. Once the Egyptian columns had been halted, the Israelis then launched their counter-attack. They now used artillery, as well as close air support, and each tank had an infantry APC accompanying it. In this way the Egyptian attacks were blocked, but although they lost heavily in AFVs and men they were not broken.

Meanwhile in the north, the Israelis, having stopped the Syrians in their tracks after two days tough fighting, went into the counter-attack. They recaptured the Golan Heights and penetrated beyond the ceasefire line. However, there was no chance for the blitzkrieg to get under way. The Syrians, aided by Iraqi and Jordanian contingents, fought bravely, only giving ground when they had to, and launching several counter-attacks, all of which slowed the Israeli advance down.

By October 15th the Israelis, thanks to their rapid rethinking, had at least got themselves on level terms with the Arabs. Notwithstanding this, they were fighting the very type of war which they had always sought to avoid, a battle of attrition. They might be pushing the Syrians back in the north, but in front of the Suez Canal there seemed to be no way to expel the

242

Egyptians from the east bank other than by costly frontal attacks. Indeed, what they had always feared had happened. It was the Egyptians who had gained the bargaining counter.

It was at this juncture that General Arik Sharon stepped onto the stage. Trained originally as a parachutist, he had commanded one of the three Sinai thrusts in 1967. Having gained a considerable reputation for dash and initiative, he was now presented with the opportunity to use both to the full. With three armoured and two parachute brigades under his command, he succeeded on October 15th in discovering a gap between the Egyptian II and III Corps to the east of the Great Bitter Lake. He immediately determined to take maximum advantage of this Egyptian weakness. Launching one of his armoured brigades at dusk in a feint attack against the Egyptians of II Corps in front of Ismailia, he sent a second brigade in a southward loop to outflank them, with its objective a likely crossing place over the Canal just north of the Great Bitter Lake. By midnight this had been achieved, and his remaining brigades, with bridging equipment, had linked up with the brigade which had secured the crossing place. An hour later Sharon was across the Canal with some 200 men and some tanks, which had crossed by pontoon ferry. However, he was not able to get his bridges built by first light. Additionally, he had not been able to secure the approaches to the Canal from the Israeli main positions. Nevertheless, Sharon sent what men and tanks he had across on the west bank on a number of raids to shoot up Egyptian installations, particularly SAM sites.

In Egyptian eyes, Sharon had taken the least expected course. They had expected the Israelis to try and push back their troops from the east bank, or to try and encircle and destroy them, but not to brush aside these troops in order to gain a lodgement on the Egyptian side of the Canal. In other words, Sharon had achieved what the Israelis had so far failed to do — he had found the 'Indirect Approach'. A measure of the Egyptian surprise was that they had no plan for this contingency, and it took them 24 hours to mount a counter-attack. When it came, launched simultaneously by II and III Corps against the neck of the Israeli penetration just to the north-east of the Great Bitter Lake, in what became known as the 'Battle of Chinese Farm', the Israelis had sufficient troops to hold open the neck, but only just. Throughout the whole of the night of October 16/17th the battle raged with heavy casualties to both sides. It was not until the middle of the 17th that the Israelis succeeded in getting their bridge built, and further armour was passed through to the other side of the Canal.

The time had now come for the Super Powers to step in. A first ceasefire was established on the evening of October 22nd, but at this stage the Israelis did not think that their bridgehead was a bargaining counter of sufficient size. Hence they broke the ceasefire, and in 24 hours had extended the bridgehead southwards to the head of the Gulf of Suez, at the same time cutting off the Egyptian III Corps from its lines of communication on the west bank. Only then were the Israelis prepared to recognise a ceasefire.

The attitude of some commentators to Sharon's exploit was that he was lucky to get away with it, and that he took an unjustifiable risk, which very nearly led him to disaster. Sharon did take a gamble; yet it was one which showed an understanding of his enemy in that he was able to identify the 'Indirect Approach'. Unless something like this had been attempted, Israel, suffering as she already was from insupportable rate of casualties to men and equipment, would probably have had to concede to the Egyptian position, which would have been regarded as solely a victory for the Egyptians. As it was, both sides were able to claim a victory with some justification.

Although Sharon had shown that, in spite of the reverses of the early days of the war, the Israelis were still capable of mounting lightning thrusts, many commentators have chosen to ignore this phase of the war. They have dwelt more on the lessons of the first days, particularly with the failure of the Israeli armoured tactics in the face of ATGW. Indeed, some, echoing the fallacious 1930s arguments on the superiority of the anti-tank gun over the tank, have propagated the thesis that, the days of the tank are numbered in the face of ATGW. This has been developed into the argument that defence is once more the stronger form of war. Thus, A. J. Barker, writing in the Journal of the Royal United Service Institute, says:

'If the freedom of action of both aircraft and tanks is curtailed (on the latter by the new anti-tank missiles) it looks as if the next war is unlikely to be one of movement unless some novel means of restoring mobility is evolved. The tactical pendulum has swung back in favour of defence, which — as Clausewitz pointed out more than 100 years ago — is 'by nature' the stronger form of war.' [3]

Not all would agree with him, especially the Israelis. A strictly defensive war in their eyes has undertones of attrition — the very type of war, which they cannot afford to fight. Indeed, Jac Weller, who made a visit to the Middle East shortly after the war, came away with the impression that there would be no fundamental change in Israeli tactics. He quotes Tal, who was Director of Operations in 1973, as stating that:

'In our area at least we feel that the tank is still queen of battle. A committee of officers is presently reappraising our Yom Kippur war experience in order to make changes in our combat doctrine, but we will probably continue to fight on the ground predominantly with our tanks.' [4]

A clue to the conclusions which this committee might have reached is summed up by a young Israeli armoured commander speaking to Weller:

'Our main early mistake was that we threw small armoured units into battle too soon and without proper co-ordination. We should have waited, collecting our armour into a strong force, and then hit the enemy hard with our tanks *with full support from other arms.*' [5]

244                                              *Author's Italics.

Seen against the backcloth of the blitzkreig story, the Yom Kippur War did not produce lessons which will significantly change the art of war. The 'all tank' idea had been considered and discarded in the 1930s, and the Germans never attempted to use it during World War 2. It only came about because of the frustration of some of the British apostles of mechanisation of their inability of carry the older arms along with them. The Flesquieres Ridge incident on November 20th, 1917 had shown that infantry and tanks must co-operate closely together in the face of anti-tank and anti-personnel weapons, but the radical reformers forgot this lesson in their desperation to inject some life into the stagnant pond of British military doctrine between the wars. The Israelis only forgot because they mistakenly believed that the use of the tank had so demoralised the Arabs in 1956 and 1967 that they were unlikely ever to recover. The heady fumes of success are very intoxicating, but the first week of Yom Kippur soon sobered the Israelis and they realised the error of their ways. ATGW may have increased the power of anti-tank defence, but this was exaggerated in the first few days of October 1973 because the Israelis had forgotten an elementary lesson in the employment of tanks. Their reverses merely laid further emphasis on an old lesson.

In the employment of air power the Yom Kippur war has shown that with modern weapons, it is now more difficult to achieve air superiority by destroying the enemy air force on the ground. Most modern air forces now keep their aircraft in bomb-proof shelters, and air defence systems are very efficient, requiring more and more complex electronic means to neutralise them. Runways may still be put out of action, but against a determined enemy this will only temporarily inconvenience him, and the cost of keeping them out of action may well become prohibitive to the attacker. Thus, air supremacy will have to be fought for in the air, which will take longer to achieve. Indeed, with two air forces equal to one another, it may never be achieved, and all that could be hoped for would be temporary neutralisation over vital parts of the area of operations. But for the rapier-like action of blitzkrieg, this may well be quite sufficient.

The Yom Kippur war may have deflated Israeli confidence in its early days, but Sharon showed that the 'Indirect Approach' was still possible, and if the Israelis had decided not to observe the second ceasefire a blitzkrieg may well have developed on the west bank of the Canal. Likewise, if the Israelis had been able to deploy greater strength on the northern front, the counter-attack into Syria may well have increased in momentum. Modern technology has not killed the blitzkrieg technique, just as the English bowmen at Crecy did not kill the concept of shock action inherent in the horseman. The horseman merely adapted himself to the changing conditions, in the same way that the Israelis quickly changed their tactics in the air and on the ground to better face the threat of the guided weapon.

This book has attempted to portray the development of a concept of war which is still with us today. The restoration of mobile warfare through the introduction of blitzkrieg was as a phoenix arising from the stagnant ashes of trench warfare. It brought back the art in generalship, and has

245

demonstrated that victory does not necessarily belong to the 'big battalions'. As long as war is not reduced to the suicidal destruction inherent in the Douhetism of strategic nuclear warfare, wars for limited objectives will still be fought, and, as the Israelis, and earlier the Germans have shown, quick and cheap victories will still be the order of the day. Weapons may change, but blitzkrieg will maintain its attraction, and its essence, the psychological dislocation of the enemy through the use of the shock action on land and in the air along the line of least expectation, will survive, as something for which military commanders will continue to strive.

**Notes**
1  *The Making of Israel's Army* op cit pp 99-100.
2  Sunday Times, *Insight on the Middle East War* pp 39-40.
3  *JRUSI* June 1974.
4  *British Army Review* Dec 1974.
5  *JRUSI* Dec 1974.

# Bibliography

HMSO — Her Majesty's Stationery Office.

OCMH — Office of the Chief of Military History OUP — Oxford University Press.

Addington, Larry H. *The Blitzkreig Era and the German General Staff 1865-1941* (Rutgers University Press 1971).

Air Ministry Pamphlet No. 248. *The Rise and Fall of the German Air Force (1933-1945)* (Air Ministry ACAS (13) 1948).

Allehaut, General. *Etre Prêt* (Paris 1935).

Allen, W Cdr H. R. *The Legacy of Lord Trenchard* (Cassell 1972).

Allon, Y. *Curtain of Sand* (Kibbutz Hammenchad 1960). *The Making of Israel's Army* (Valentine, Mitchell 1970).

Ambrose, Stephen E. *The Supreme Commander: The War Years of General Dwight Eisenhower* (Doubleday NY 1970).

Bankwitz, Philip C. F. *Maxime Weygand and Civil Military Relations in Modern France* (Harvard 1967).

Barres, Phillipe. *Charles de Gaulle* (Doubleday, Doran & Co. Inc. Garden City NY 1941).

Beaufre, General Andre. *1940: The Fall of France* (Cassell 1967).

Becker, Cajus. *The Luftwaffe War Diaries* (Corgi Edition 1972).

Bender, R. J. *Air Organisations of the Third Reich Vol. 1.* (R. James Bender Publishing Cal USA 1967).

Berchin, Michael & Ben-Horin, Ellaher. *The Red Army* (Norton NY 1942).

Bidwell, Shelford. *Gunners at War* (Arms & Armour Press 1970).

Binding, Rudolf. *A Fatalist at War* (George Allen & Unwin 1929).

Bishop, Geoffrey S. C. *The Battle: A Tank Officer Remembers* (published privately).

Blumenson, Martin. *Breakout and Pursuit: US Army in World War II* (OCMH Washington DC 1961).

Blumenson, Martin. *The Patton Papers 1885-1940* (Houghton Mifflin Boston 1972).

Bond, Brian. *Chief of Staff: The Diaries of Lieutenant-General Sir Henry Pownall Vol. I 1933-1940* (Leo Cooper 1972).

Bryant, Arthur. *The Turn of the Tide* (Collins 1957).

Bullock, Alan. *Hitler: A Study in Tyranny* (Odham's 1952).

Carell, Paul. *Hitler's War on Russia* 2 vols. (Corgi Edition 1971).

Carr, E. H. *German-Soviet Relations Between the two World Wars 1919-1939* (John Hopkins Press, Baltimore 1951).

Carsten, F. L. *The Reichswehr and Politics* 1918-1933 (OUP 1966).

Cattell, David T. *Communism and the Spanish Civil War* (Univ. of California Press 1955).

Challener, Richard D. *The French Theory of the Nation in Arms 1866-1939* (Columbia Univ. Press NY 1955).

Chapman, Guy. *Why France Collapsed* (Cassell 1968).

Chauvineau, General. *Une Invasion est-elle encore possible?* (Paris 1939).

Churchill, Randolph S. and Winston S. *The Six Day War* (Heineman 1967).

Churchill, W. S. *While England Slept* (Putnam NY 1938).

Cole, Christopher ed. *Royal Air Force 1918.* (Kimber 1968).

Collier, Basil. *A History of Air Power* (Military Book Society Edition 1974).

Collins, R. J. *Lord Wavell* (Hodder & Stoughton 1947).

Colville, J. R. *Man of Valour: Field-Marshal Lord Gort VC* (Collins 1972).

Conquest, Robert. *The Great Terror: Stalin's Purge of the Thirties* (Macmillan 1968).

Crawley, Aidan. *De Gaulle* (Collins 1969).
Crankshaw, Edward ed. *Kruschev Remembers* (Book Club Associates Edition 1971).
Dayan, Moshe. *Diary of the Sinai Campaign* (Wiedenfeld & Nicholson 1966).
De Gaulle, Charles. *The Army of the Future* (Lippincott NY 1941). *War Memoirs*: The Call to Honour 1940-1942 (Viking Press NY 1955).
De La Gorce, Paul-Marie. *The French Army: A Military-Political Study* (Braziller NY 1963).
Dennis, Peter. *Decision by Default: Peacetime Conscription and British Defence 1919-1939* (Routledge & Kegan Paul 1972).
Divine, David. *The Blunted Sword* (Hutchinson 1964).
Divine, David. *The Broken Wing* (Hutchinson 1966).
Douhet, Guilio. *The Command of the Air* (Faber & Faber 1943).
Earle, E. M. ed. *Makers of Modern Strategy* (Princeton Univ. Press 1944).
Eliot, George Fielding. *The Ramparts we Watch* (Reynal & Hitchcock NY 1935).
Ellis, Maj. J. F. *The War in France and Flanders 1939-40* (HMSO 1953).
Emme, Eugene M. *The Impact of Air Power* (Van Nostrand, Princeton NJ 1959).
Erickson, John. *The Soviet High Command* (St. Martin's Press 1962).
Essame, H. *Patton The Commander* (Batsford 1974).
Eyck, Erick. *A History of the Weimar Republic Vol 1* (Atheneum NY 1970).
Flower, Desmond & Reeves, James ed. *The War 1939-1945* (Cassell 1960).
Foertsch, Colonel Herman. *The Art of Modern Warfare* (Oskar Piert NY 1940).
Forester, C. S. *The General* (Mermaid Books Edition 1953).
Frankland, Noble. *Bomber Offensive: The Devastation of Europe* (Macdonald 1970).
Frye, William. *Marshall: Citizen Soldier* (Bobbs-Merill NY 1947).
Fuller, J. F. C. *Armoured Warfare (Lectures on FSR III)* (Military Service Publishing Company Penn 1943). *The Reformation of War* (Dutton & Co. NY 1923). *On Future Warfare* (Sifton Praed 1928).
Fuller, J. F. C. *Memoirs of an Unconventional Soldier* (Nicholson & Watson 1936).
*Tanks in the Great War 1914-1918* (Murray 1920).
*The Conduct of War 1789-1961* (Eyre & Spottiswoode 1961).
*A Military History of the Western World Vol. 3* (Minerva Press NY Paperback edition 1967).
Galland, Adolf. *The First and the Last* (Methuen 1955).
Ganoe, William A. *The History of the United States Army* (D. Appleton-Century NY 1942).
Garder, Michael. *A History of the Soviet Army* (Praeger NY 1966).
Gartoff, Raymond L. *Soviet Military Doctrine* (The Fore Press, Glencoe Illinois 1953).
Gatzke, Hans. *Streseman and the Rearmament of Germany* (John Hopkins, Baltimore 1954).
Germains, V. W. *The Mechanisation of War* (Sifton Praed 1927).
Gillie, Mildred Hanson. *Forging the Thunderbolt* (Military Service Publishing Co. Penn 1947).
Goerlitz, Walter. *History of the German General Staff 1657-1945* (Praeger NY 1953).
Golovine, Lt. Gen. A. A. *Air Strategy* (Gale & Polden 1936).
Gordon, Harold J. Jnr. *The Reichswehr and the German Republic 1919-1926* (Princeton Univ Press NJ 1957).
Gould Lee, Arthur. *No Parachute* (Jarrolds 1968).
Green, Constance, Thomson, Harry & Roots, Peter. *US Army in World War II: The Technical Services The Ordnance Department: Planning Munitions for War* (OCMH Washington DC 1955).
Greenfield, K. R. ed. *Command Decisions* (Methuen 1960).
Greenfield, K. R., Palmer, R. R., and Wiley, B. I. *The Organisation of Ground Combat Troops: United States Army in World War II: The Army Ground Forces* (Washington: Government Printing Office 1947).
Gritzbach, Erich. *Herman Goering: The Man and His Work* (Hurst and Blackett 1939).
Guderian, Heinz. *Panzer Leader* (Michael Joseph 1952).
Guillaume, Gui Augustin. *Soviet Arms and Soviet Power* (Infantry Journal Press, Washington 1949).
Guingand, Maj-Gen Sir Francis. *Operation Victory* (Hodder and Stoughton 1947).
Halder, Franz. *Diaries* (Infantry Journal Inc USA 1950).
Hammond, Paul Y. *Organising for Defence: The American Military Establishment in the Twentieth Century* (Princeton Univ Press NY 1961).

Harmon, Maj Gen E. N. *Combat Commander* (Prentice-Hall NJ 1970).

Higham, Robert. *Air Power: A Concise History* (Military Book Society Edition 1972).

*Armed Forces in Peacetime* (Archon Books, Conn USA 1962).

*The Military Intellectuals in Britain: 1918-1939* (Rutgers University Press NJ 1966).

Hitler, Adolf. *Mein Kampf* (Hutchinson 1972).

Hoffman, Edward. *The Hilt of the Sword: The career of Peyton C. March* (Univ Wisconsin Press 1966).

Holley, I. B. Jnr. *Ideas and Weapons* (Yale University Press 1953).

Howard, Michael. *The Continental Commitment* (Temple Smith 1972).

Howard, Michael ed. *The Theory and Practice of War* (Cassell 1965).

*Soldiers and Governments* (Eyre & Spottiswoode 1957).

Horne, Alistair. *To Lose a Battle: France 1940* (Little, Brown & Co. Boston 1969).

Irving, David. *The Rise and Fall of the Luftwaffe — The Life of Erhard Milch* (Wiedenfeld & Nicholson 1973).

Ismay, General Lord. *Memoirs* (Viking Press NY 1960).

Jackson, Robert. *The Red Falcons: The Soviet Air Force in Action 1919-1969* (Clifton Books 1970).

Johnson, Franklyn Arthur. *Defence by Committee: The British Committee of Imperial Defence 1885-1959* (OUP 1960).

Jones, Ralph E., Rarey, George H., Icks, Robert J. *The Fighting Tanks Since 1916* (National Service Publishing Company Washington DC 1933).

Jukes, Geoffrey. *The Defence of Moscow* (MacDonald 1970).

Junger, Ernst. *The Storm of Steel* (Chatto & Windus 1929).

Keegan, John. *Barbarossa: Invasion of Russia 1941* (MacDonald 1970).

Kemp, Peter. *Mine Were of Trouble* (Cassell 1957).

Kennedy, Maj-Gen Sir John. *The Business of War* (Hutchinson 1957).

Kennedy, John F. *Why England Slept* (Funk NY 1940).

Kesselring, Albert. *Kesselring: A Soldier's Record* (Morrow NY 1954).

Killen, John. *The Luftwaffe: A History* (Muller 1967).

Killigrew, John W. *The Impact of the Great Depression on the Army 1929-36* (unpublished thesis submitted to Graduate School Faculty Indiana University 1960).

Kilmarx, Robert A. *A History of Soviet Air Power* (Praeger NY 1962).

Klotz, Helmuth. *Lecons Militaires de la Guerre d'Espagne* (Paris 1938).

Kournakoff, Sergei N. *Russia's Fighting Forces* (Duell, Sloan and Pearce NY 1942).

Leach, Barry A. *German Strategy Against Russia 1939-41* (Clarendon, Oxford 1973).

Lee, Asher. *Goering: Air Leader* (Duckworth 1946).

*The Soviet Air Force* (Harper Bros NY 1950).

*The German Air Force* (Duckworth 1946).

Leeb, Field Marshal General Ritter von. *Defense* (Military Service Publishing Co., Harisburg, Penn. 1943).

Lehmann-Russbueldt, D. H. O. *Germany's Air Force* (George Allen & Unwin 1935).

Liddell Hart, B. H. *The British Way in Warfare* (Macmillan NY 1933).

*Foch: Man of New Orleans 2 vols* (Penguin Edition 1937).

*The German Generals Talk* (William Morrow & Co NY 1948).

*Memoirs* 2 vols (Cassell 1965).

*The Remaking of Modern Armies* (Little, Brown & Co, Boston 1928).

*The Red Army* (Harcourt, Brace & Co NY 1956).

*The Tanks: The History of the Royal Tank Regiment 1914-1945* 2 vols (Cassell 1959).

*Dynamic Defence* (Faber & Faber 1940).

*The Future of Infantry* (Military Science Publishing Co, Harrisberg, Penn 1936).

*The Rommel Papers* (Collins 1953).

*History of the Second World War* (Cassell 1970).

*Strategy* (Praeger NY 1967).

Lucas, James and Cooper, Mathew. *Hitler's Elite: Liebstandarte SS* (Macdonald & Janes 1975).

Ludendorff von. *Der totale Krieg* (Berlin 1935).

Luttwark, Edward, Horowitz, Dan. *The Israeli Army* (Allen Lane 1975).

Luvaas, Jay. *The Education of an Army: British Military Thought 1815-1940* (University of Chicago 1964).

Mackintosh, Malcolm. *Juggernaut: A History of the Soviet Armed Forces* (Secker & Warburg 1967).

Macksey, Kenneth. *Panzer Division: The Mailed Fist* (Ballantine 1968).

*Armoured Crusader: Major General Sir Percy Hobart* (Hutchinson 1967).

*To the Green Fields Beyond* (Privately by Regimental Headquarters, Royal Tank Regiment 1965).

*Tank Warfare: A History of Tanks in Battle* (Stein & Day NY 1972).

*Tank Force Allied Armor in World War II* (Ballantine NY1970).

Macksey, Kenneth & Batchelor, John H. *Tank: A History of the Armoured Fighting Vehicle* (Macdonald 1970).

MacLeod, Col. R. and Kelly, Denis ed. *The Ironside Diaries 1937-1940* (Constable 1962).

Manchester, William. *The Arms of Krupp 1587-1968* (Michael Joseph 1964).

Manstein, Field Marshal Erich von. *Lost Victories* (Methuen 1958).

Martel, Lt Gen Sir Giffard. *An Outspoken Soldier: His Views and Memoirs* (Sifton Praed 1949).

*In the Wake of the Tank* (Sifton Praed 1931).

Mason, David. *Breakout: Drive to the Seine* (MacDonald 1969).

Maurois, Andre. *Tragedy in France* (Harper Bros NY 1940).

Mellenthin, Maj Gen F. W. von. *Panzer Battles* (University of Oklahoma 1956).

Messenger, Charles. *Trench Fighting 1914-1918* (Ballantine NY 1972).

Metzsch, General von. *Wie weirde ein neuer Krieg aussehen?* (Interparliamentary Mission, Zurich 1932).

Miksche, F. O. *Attack: A Study of Blitzkreig Tactics* (Random House NY 1942).

*Is Bombing Decisive?* (Allen & Unwin 1943).

Millis, Walter. *Arms and Men: A Study in American Military History* (Putnam NY 1956).

*American Military Thought* (Bobbs-Merrill NY 1966).

Minney, R. J. *The Private Papers of Hore-Belisha* (Doubleday NY 1961).

Mitchell, William. *Winged Defense: The Development and Possibilities of Modern Airpower — Economic and Military* (Putnam NY 1925).

*Skyways — A Book on Modern Aeronautics* (Lippincott NY 1930).

Montgomery, Field Marshal Viscount. *A Concise History of Warfare* (Collins 1972).

*Memoirs* (Collins 1958).

Muller, Albert. *Germany's War Machine* (Dent 1936).

Nachin, Lucien. *Charles de Gaulle: General de France* (Paris 1944).

Nickerson, Hoffman. *The Armed Horde 1793-1939 — A Study in the Rise, Survival and Decline of the Mass Army* (Putnam NY 1940).

*Arms and Policy 1939-1944* (Putnam NY 1945).

Nielsen, Generalleutnant Andreas. *USAF Historical Studies: No 173 The German Air Force General Staff* (Arco Press NY 1968).

Nobecourt, Jacques. *Hitler's Last Gamble: The Battle of the Bulge* (Schorken NY Paperback edition 1967).

O'Ballance, Edgar. *The Red Army* (Praeger NY 1964).

Ogorkiewicz, R. M. *Armoured Forces* (Arco Publishing Co NY 1960).

O'Neill, Robert J. *The German Army and the Nazi Party, 1933-39* (Cassell 1966).

Orgill, Douglas. *The Tank: Studies in the Development and Use of a Weapon* (Heineman 1970).

*T34: Russian Armour* (Ballantine NY 1971).

Parkinson, Roger. *Peace for Our Time* (McKay NY 1972).

Payne, Stanley G. *Politics and the Military in Modern Spain* (Stanford Univ Press USA 1967).

Pile, General Sir Frederick. *Ack-Ack* (Harrap 1949).

Pogue, Forrest C. *George C. Marshall: Education of a General 1880-1939* (Viking NY 1963).

Poston, M. M., Hay, D., Scott, J. D. *History of the Second World War: Design and Development of Weapons* (HMSO 1964).

Raborg, Maj Paul C. *Mechanised Might* (McGraw-Hill NY 1942).

Reinhardt, George C. and Krimer, William R. *The Haphazard Years* (Doubleday NY 1960).

Renn, Ludwig. *Warfare: The Relation of War to Society* (OUP 1939).

Reynaud, Paul. *Venu de ma Montagne* (Paris 1960).

Richards, Dennis. *The Royal Air Force 1939-1945 Vol I: The Fight at Odds* (HMSO 1953).
Robertson, E. M. *Hitler's Pre-War Policy and Military Plans 1933-39* (Longmans 1963).
Ropp, Theodore. *War in the Modern World* (Duke University Press Durham NC 1959).
Rosinski, Herbert. *The German Army* (Harcourt, Brace NY 1940).
Roskill, Stephen. *Hankey: Man of Secrets Vol II 1919-1931* (Collins 1972).
Rowe, Vivian. *The Great Wall of France: The Triumph of the Maginot Line* (Putnam NY 1961).
Ryan, Stephen. *Pétain the Soldier* (Thomas Yoscloff 1969).
Saundby, Air Marshal Sir Robert. *Air Bombardment: The Story of its Development* (Harper NY 1961).
Schliephake, Heinrich. *The Birth of the Luftwaffe* (Ian Allan 1971).
Scott, J. D. *Vickers: A History* (Wiedenfeld and Nicholson 1962).
Seaton, Albert. *The Russo-German War 1941-45* (Praeger NY 1971).
Seeckt, General von. *Thoughts of a Soldier* (Ernst Benn 1930).
Sheppard, Major E. W. *Tanks in the Next War* (Geoffrey Bles 1938).
Shirer, William L. *The Collapse of the Third Republic* (Simon & Schuster NY 1969).
   *The Rise and Fall of the Third Reich* (Secker & Warberg 1959).
Slessor, Sir John. *The Central Blue* (Praeger NY 1957).
Slessor, W. Cdr J. C. *Air Power and Armies* (OUP 1936).
Smith, Dale O. *US Military Doctrine: A Study and Appraisal* (Duell, Sloane & Pearce NY 1955).
Smith, Peter C. *Stuka at War* (Ian Allan 1971).
Sokolovsky, Marshal V. D. ed. *Military Strategy: Soviet Doctrines and Concepts* (Praeger NY 1963).
Spaight, J. M. *Air Power and War Rights* (Longman, Green & Co 1933).
Spaulding, Oliver Lyman. *The United States Army in War and Peace* (Putnam NY 1937).
Sternberg, Fritz. *Germany and a Lightning War* (Faber & Faber 1938).
Strawson, John. *The Battle of the Ardennes* (Batsford 1972).
   *Hitler as Military Commander* (Batsford 1971).
Strong, Maj-Gen Sir Kenneth. *Men of Intelligence* (Cassell 1970).
Stubbs and Connor. *Armor Lineage Series, Armor-Cavalry Part I* (OCMH 1969).
Sunday Times Insight Team. *Insight on the Middle East War* (Andre Deutsch 1974).
Swinton, E. D. *Eyewitness* (Hodder & Stoughton 1932).
Taylor, John W. R. *A History of Aerial Warfare* (Hamlyn 1974).
Taylor, Telford. *The March of Conquest* (Simon & Schuster NY 1958).
   *Sword and Swastika* (Simon & Schuster NY 1952).
Teveth, Shabtai. *The Tanks of Tammuz* (Wiedenfeld and Nicholson 1968).
Thomas, Hugh. *The Spanish Civil War* (Harper & Row NY 1961).
Trevor-Roper, H. R. *Hitler's War Directives 1939-1945* (Sidgwick and Jackson 1964).
Tournoux, J-R. *Pétain and de Gaulle.* (Heinemann 1966).
Vanderveen, Bart H. *The Observer's Fighting Vehicles Directory World War II* (Frederick Warne 1969).
Van Haute, Andre. *Pictorial History of the French Air Force Vol. I 1909-1940* (Ian Allan 1974).
Voroshilov, K. et al. *The Red Army Today: Speeches Delivered at the Eighteenth Congress of the CPSU (B) Mar 10-21, 1939* (Foreign Languages Publishing House, Moscow 1939).
Waldrop, Frank C. ed. *MacArthur on War* (Duell, Sloan & Pearce NY 1942).
Watson, Mark Skinner. *US Army in World War II: The War Department Chief of Staff: Pre-War Plans and Preparations* (Historical Division Dept of Army Washington DC 1950).
Webster, Sir Charles & Frankland, Noble. *The Strategic Air Offensive Against Germany 1939-1945 Vol. I: Preparation* (HMSO 1961).
Weigley, Russell. *The American Way of War: A History of United States Military Strategy and Policy* (Macmillan NY 1963).
   *History of the United States Army* (Macmillan NY 1967).
Werner, Max. *The Military Strength of the Powers* (Gollancz 1939).
Werth, Alexander. *Russia at War 1941-1945* (Dutton, NY 1964).
Westphal, Lt Gen Siegfried. Edited by Freidin and Richardson. *Fatal Decisions* (Michael Joseph 1956).
Wheeler-Bennett, John W. *The Nemesis of Power: The German Army in Politics 1918-1945* (Macmillan 1964).

Wheldon, John. *Machine Age Armies* (Abelard-Schuman, 1968).

White, B. T. *German Tanks & Armoured Vehicles 1914-1945* (Arco NY 1968).

White, D. Fedoroff. *The Growth of the Red Army* (Princeton NJ 1944).

Whitehouse, Arch. *Tank* (Doubleday NY 1960).

Williams, John. *France Summer 1940* (MacDonald 1969).

Willoughby, Charles Andrew. *Manoeuvre in Modern War* (Military Science Publishing Co Penn 1935).

Wollenburg, Erich. *The Red Army* (Secker & Warburg 1938).

Wright, Robert. *Dowding and the Battle of Britain* (Military Book Society 1969).

Yale, Col W., White, Gen I. D., Manteuffel, General Hasso E. von. *Alternative to Armageddon* (Rutgers University Press 1970).

Zhukov, Marshal G. K. *Memoirs* (Delacorte NY 1971).

British Periodicals
*Army Quarterly, Journal of the Royal United Service Institute (JRUSI), British Army Review, Royal Artillery Journal, Royal Tank Corps Journal, Encounter, RAC Tank Museum Guides.*
USA Periodicals
*Military Affairs, Armor, Infantry Journal, Cavalry Journal, Field Artillery Journal.*
French Periodicals
*Revue Militaire Génerale, La Revue d'Infanterie, Revue des Deux Mondes, Crapouillot, Revue de Paris, Revue Militaire Francaise.*
German Periodicals
*Militar-Wochenblatt, Militarwessen Schlaftliche Rundschau.*

# Index

253